NOTHING TO HIDE

A Civil Servant Reveals

Attention Authors

'We Convert Fighters into Writers'. That has been the motto of Manas Publications, since more than four decades. Our message to the world is that India can win the battle, not only by the bullet but also by the pen. There is no dearth of intellectuals in our country, but their knowledge is confined to them only. No sincere effort has been made by any other publisher to channelise their knowledge in national interest. That is why the talent of a large number of intellectuals, remains latent. An author transforms his knowledge, into a manuscript, and it is our job to spread his/her knowledge by converting it into a beautiful book.

For over four decades, Manas has been motivating the intellectuals by publishing their manuscripts and would like to publish your manuscript too. If you or your colleagues have any manuscript, ready for publication or are working on it, kindly contact us with detailed synopsis and the list of contents. We would transform your work, into a valuable publication. If you wish, we can also suggest you, the suitable subjects for writing books, related to your area of expertise. Manas is known for its publishing quality and commitments. We take utmost care in production and give wide publicity to the book, as well as its author, through our national and international distribution network.

NOTHING TO HIDE
A Civil Servant Reveals

Surain Singh Dhanoa
IAS (Retd.)
Former Secretary to Government of India

Manas Publications
(We Convert Fighters into Writers)
New Delhi-110002 (INDIA)

MANAS PUBLICATIONS
(We Convert Fighters into Writers)
(Publishers, Distributors, Importers & Exporters)
4402/5-A, Ansari Road (Opp. HDFC Bank)
Darya Ganj, New Delhi-110 002 (India)
Off. 23260783, 23265523, Res. 23842660
Fax: 011-23272766
E-mail: manaspublications@gmail.com
manaspub6@gmail.com
Website: www.manaspublications.in

ISBN 978-81-7049-519-2
₹ 895/-

Designed at Innovative Processors

Printed in India at
R.K. Print Service, Delhi and
Published by Mrs Suman Lata for
Manas Publications, 4402/5-A, Ansari Road (Opp. HDFC Bank),
Darya Ganj, New Delhi-110 002 (INDIA)

Truth is the highest of human virtues but higher still is the truthful living.

–Guru Nanak

***

Dedicated to

Brave Fighter Pilots of the Indian Air Force who brave death while flying and fighting for our country. 16 Fighter Pilots have died in flying accidents in the last 10 years.

Contents

Preface 9

1. The Early Years and Schooling 21
2. The College Days 34
3. Partition of India 45
4. Chasing Uncertain Objectives 53
5. The Aligarh Muslim University 57
6. The IAS Exam and Marriage 62
7. The IAS Training 68
8. As Sub-Division Officer, Deoghar 82
9. As Deputy Commissioner, Dhanbad 92
10. At Ranchi 100
11. Handling Law and Order 124
12. The Training of Civil Service Officers 151
13. As General Manager, Super Bazar Delhi 169

14. To Bihar Again 191

15. Imposition of Emergency 212

16. Agricultural Research 227

17. Last Innings of Bihar 248

18. As Chief Secretary, Punjab 265

19. Secretary, Government of India 319

20. As Election Commissioner 340

21. Conclusion 354

Index 359

Preface

Nothing to Hide is saga of a poor village boy from Punjab who rose to the top in the Civil Service. My narration that is more or less my experience would indicate as to how every opening in life was exploited to succeed and control various vicissitudes and crises that came before me.

I owe it to my father Captain Sant Singh who supported me regardless of my performance in studies or my ideas and beliefs till I joined the IAS (Indian Administrative Services) at the age of 24. He fostered in me a secular and national outlook.

The most important person in my life is my late wife Sukhdev. I met her when she was a school student and I was studying for my MA and LLB at the Aligarh Muslim University in 1952. It was a love at first sight. She wanted me to be a government officer. I was never a studious student. No one took me seriously when I said that I am going to appear for the IAS examination. Everyone was surprised to see me successful for the IAS. There is no doubt that Sukhdev had brought good luck for me. It is not coincidence that even after retirement from the IAS in 1988, I remained on one assignment or the other till 2000, when she left us suddenly. She was a source of strength during all my assignments and vicissitudes. She stood by me even when I took a rash decision to resign from the service in 1965, which was not accepted by the government. Despite her being a matriculate she got recognized as a leader among the wives of other officers. She controlled all the family matters on her own, never permitted me to worry about the family.

My son Air Marshal Birender Singh Dhanoa made me proud by opting to join Indian Air Force as a fighter pilot. Out of 35 Pilot Officers selected among 70 officers in his batch trained as fighter pilots, seven died in air crashes and five ejected during the first ten years of service. I started my service with the belief that servicemen were the best human beings and the politicians were the worst. I would like to endorse the statement of George Bernard Shaw, "*politics* is the *last* resort for the *scoundrel*". I was disabused of this notion during the first five years of my service. It becomes a shock that civil servants, as they go through their careers, get smaller and smaller as human beings while successful politicians acquire empathy and appreciation from all who work with them.

As an IAS officer I served for more than 34 years. I had the opportunity to serve the country during very crucial days after the partition such as during the crisis with Pakistan, days of Emergency, frequent changes of governments, Operation Blue Star, etc. I had no patron or godfather and I did not seek or expect support from my bosses in my decisions. I never hesitated to act if the matter or issue was of public interest. My actions came for scrutiny before four judicial commissions of enquiry and one official committee of enquiry. It is a matter of satisfaction that in all these commissions my decisions stood vindicated. One commission found my action commendable. Nothing happened to me when I explained that all that I did was in the public interest. My experiences in public life, good or bad, may be found a source of inspiration for young generation of bureaucrats.

I am thankful to my numerous friends and colleagues who helped me in various assignments. I must thank Raj Singh Chouhan who helped in arranging all my writings and also coordinated with editors. I am thankful to G Adityakiran and Mrs Sangeetha Adityakiran who edited the first draft of the book and the team of Manas Publications who gave the final shape to the book.

Surain Singh Dhanoa
(Retd IAS)

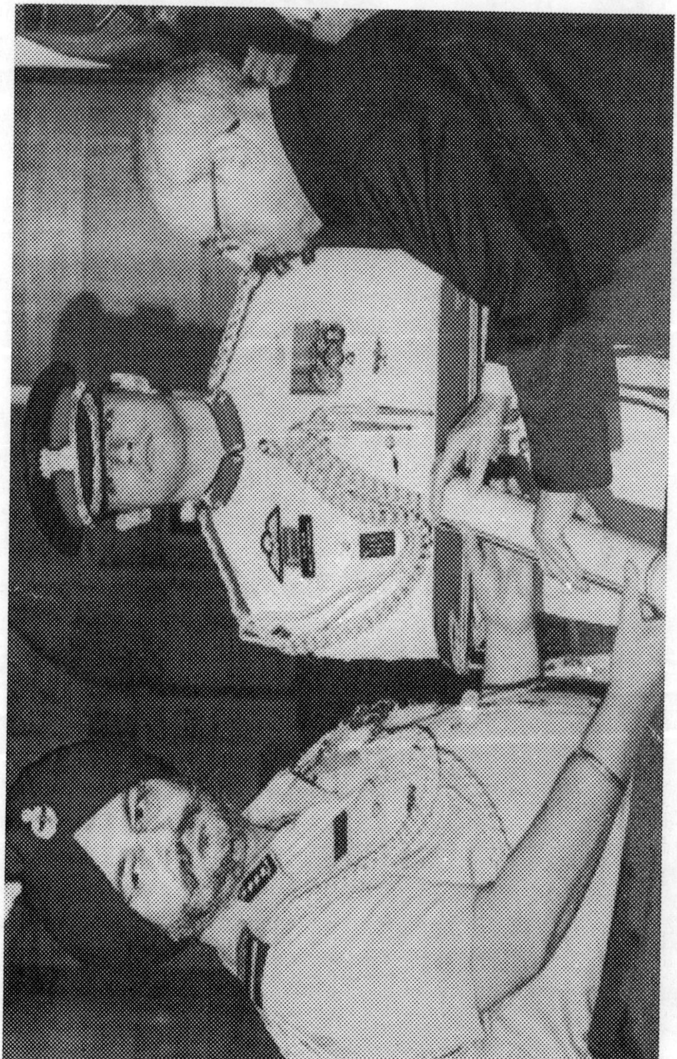

Air Marshal BS Dhanoa, PVSM, AVSM, YSM, VM, ADC (Son of Author) was awarded PVSM by President Sh. Pranab Mukherjee on 26th January 2016

With Suygeon – General of the USA

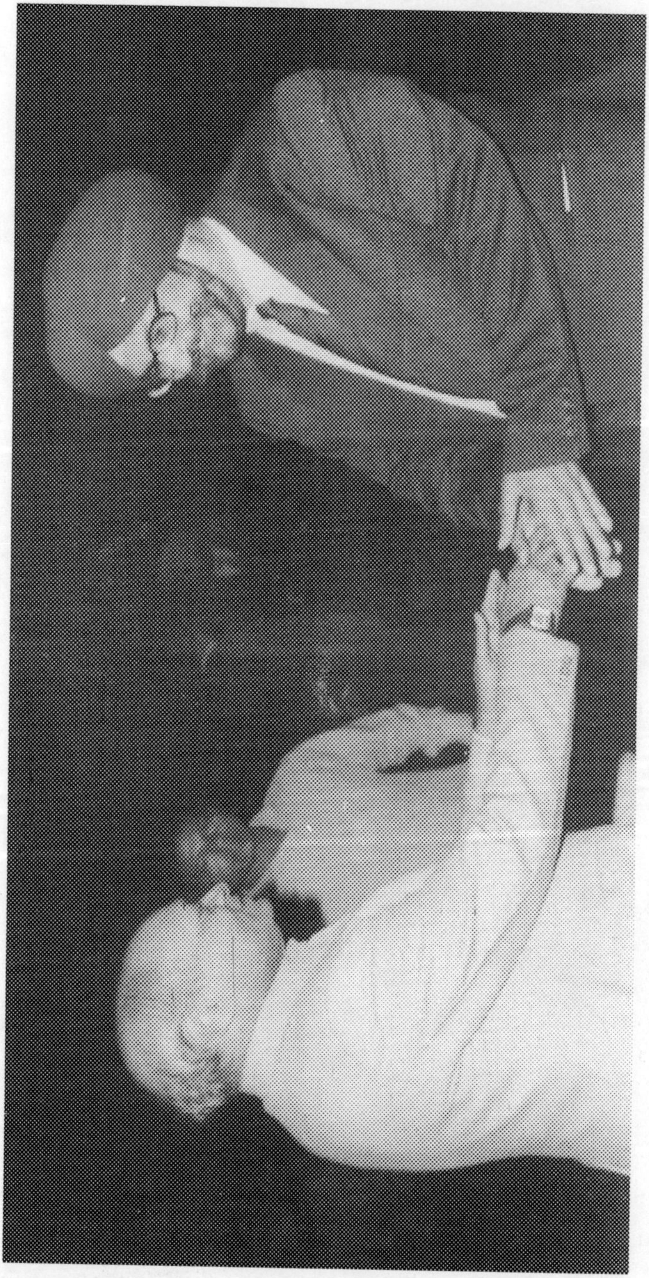

Author with PV Narasimha Rao

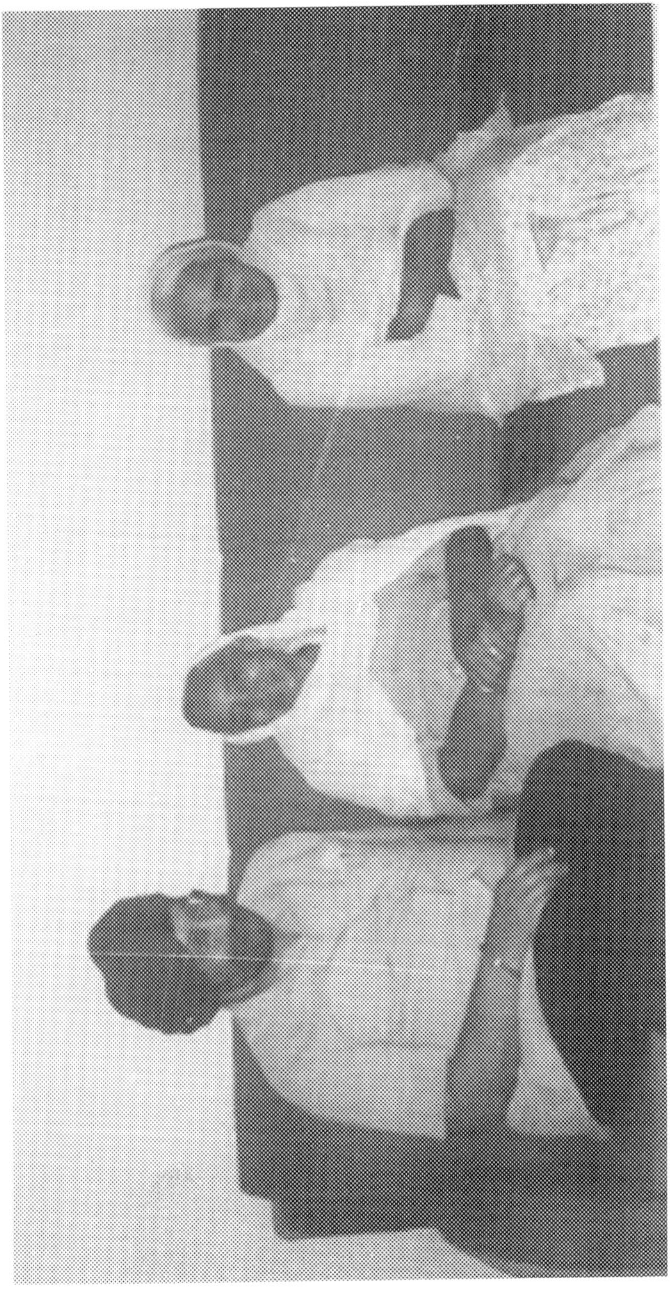

Author with his mother and sister-in-law

With Chief Minister of Bihar, Sh. K.B. Sahay

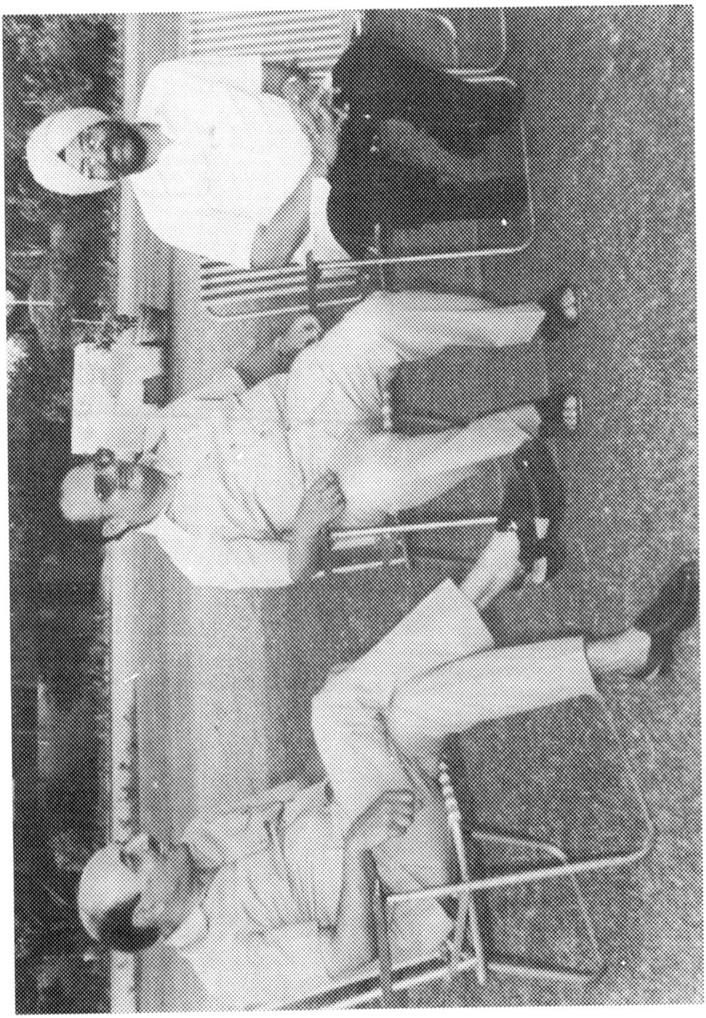

With Governor of Punjab Sh. Arjun Singh

Receiving Prime Minister Morarji Desai at IAS Academy, Mussoorie

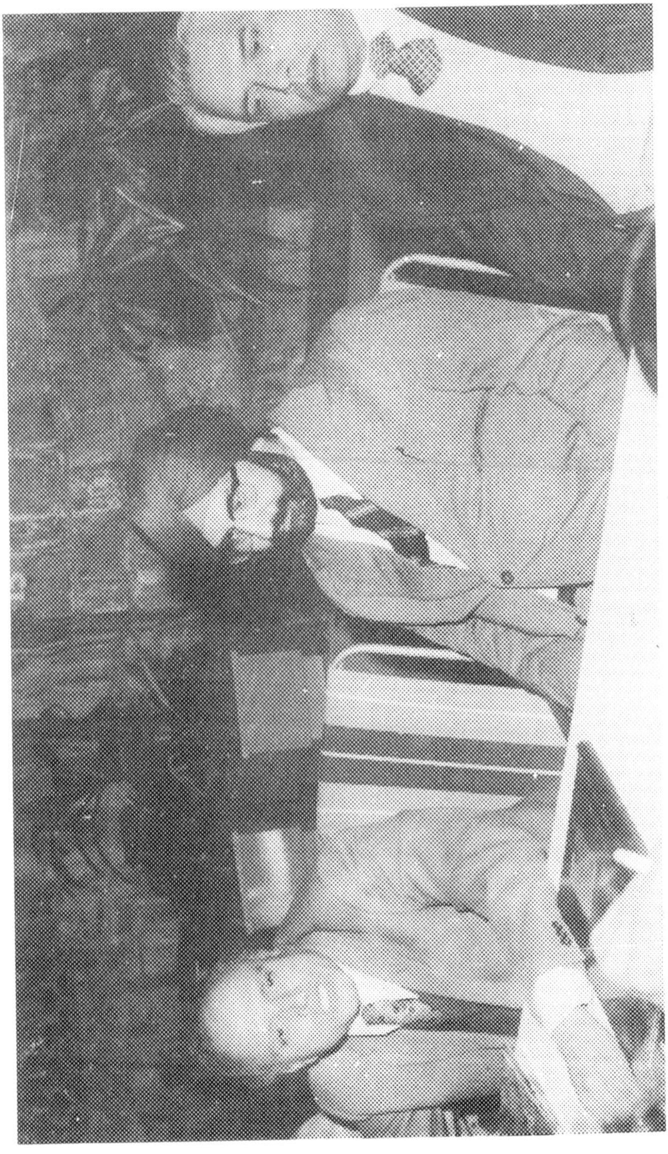

With Dr. M. Swaminathan & Dr O.P. Gautam, 1978

With President Giani Zail Singh

With Prime Minister Mrs. Indira Gandhi

With Minister of Health Sh. Uma Shankar Dikshit, Delhi

1

The Early Years and Schooling

I belong to village Gharuan situated on the Chandigarh-Ludhiana highway, about 20 kilometers from Chandigarh. The village owes its name to the legendary Ghatotkach, the son of the *Mahabarat* Pandava hero Bhim. However, our ancestors moved to the village allegedly on being chased by the authorities for some transgression. This could have happened during the 18th century turmoil when Bari Doab Sikhs or Majha Sikhs were evicted by the Mughals as also due to the expansion and occupation of central and eastern Punjab by the Sikhs into areas where they found the local authority to be weak and the locals found the '*Rakhi* System' to be fairer and more attractive than the Mughal suzerainty.

The founder of our family was Saffa Singh who had one son Dalel Singh. Dalel Singh had four sons namely Attar Singh, Bhagwan Singh, Mall Singh and Narain Singh. All except the eldest joined the armed forces under the British. The youngest, Narain Singh, was the most illustrious. He rose to the rank of a Viceroy's Commissioned Officer.

My father, Sant Singh was born in 1903. He had an elder sister, Sant Kaur and younger brother Pal Singh. My father had been put to study in a school in Basi Pathana, about 20 kilometers away. He stayed in a hostel there. Pal Singh looked after the buffaloes and other household errands. These were the times of the First World War; Mall Singh was offered the job of a Quarter-Master Havildar in a labour company, which he accepted. Soon he was dispatched to Salunica in Greece. He left some money with my father, which kept him in the school for about three months. There was a communication breakdown thereafter between them. My father gave up his studies and joined as a boy recruit in one of the Pioneers regiments of the British Indian Army. He found himself in the Bombay Sappers and Miners where he was given training in the printer's trade. He passed the trade test in the first grade and got posted to Baghdad in Iraq, He spent about three years in Iraq from 1917 to 1920. One important contribution made by him during his stay in Baghdad was that he along with other Sikh soldiers were able to locate the place where Guru Nanak had stayed as a guest of the Peer Bahlol Dastigir during his visit to Baghdad on his return from Mecca-Madina. This was the time when the Sikhs in Punjab were quite upset about the management of the Sikh Gurdwaras by hereditary '*mahants*' who started treating the Gurdwaras as their private property and some of them were accused of grossly abusing their position. The *mahants* enjoyed protection from the British rulers as the Government would not permit a change in *status quo* through intimidation or violence.

The British found nothing in the Sikh tenets or tradition, which could be subversive to their rule. The most important shrines of the Sikhs were the Golden Temple and the Akal Takht at Amritsar from where edicts could be issued concerning various Sikh affairs. These shrines were under a caretaker who was appointed by the British Deputy Commissioner of Amritsar. They had, perhaps for that reason, not imposed any restriction on the literature circulating among the Sikh troops till their authority got challenged by the Akalis in the Gurdwara Reform Movement (1921–1925).

My father and other recruits under his influence numbering about 20 were ordered against wearing black turbans. When the boys did not listen to their officers they were shipped back to India and disbanded in Bombay. My father told me that one British Colonel, Leslie Smith, addressed them and told them that he had nothing against them and if they gave an undertaking that they would observe the discipline of the Army, they were welcome to continue with their jobs. My father said that since they had come under the influence of Master Mota Singh, they refused to budge from their decision. When the Commanding Officer found them to be adamant, he got them dismissed from the

Army. He put them on a train from Bombay with tickets up to Ambala Cantonment from where they could go wherever they liked. They did not go back to their homes; instead they travelled to Amritsar to report for duty in the Gurdwara Reform Movement.

Wherever the Sikhs were, they had to come together at a common place where they would sing hymns or verses written by the Gurus. These places were called '*dharamsalas*' and later on came to be known as *gurdwaras*. A caretaker was generally appointed for the upkeep and maintenance of the gurdwaras. The positions of caretakers later became hereditary. When the Sikhs became a dominant force in Punjab, generally liberal land grants were made to the gurdwaras for organising various services in the gurdwaras. Due to hereditary succession and affluence many abuses crept among the caretakers called '*mahants*'. Mainly because of intensive reading of *Gurbani* by the Sikhs who were in the army, an awareness was generated among the Sikhs that the '*mahants*' were mismanaging the gurdwaras which resulted in a powerful movement among the Sikhs for reform in the management of the Gurdwaras. Initially the British supported the '*mahants*'. Gandhi and the Congress too joined the fray. They extended support to those who were agitating for reform. A large number of Sikh soldiers who were demobilised after the war formed the backbone of the movement. They adopted Gandhi's technique of non-violence. *Mahants* started abandoning Gurdwaras for fear of the Akalis. The agitators formed a committee for the management of the Gurdwaras called the *Shiromani Gurdwara Parbandhak Committee* or the SGPC in 1920. The *Shiromani Akali Dal* which was an organisation for mobilising volunteers for the agitation later became the political party furthering what were perceived as the Sikh interests came in to being in the same year.

My father had remained unheard in the village during all this period. Since the First World War was over, Mall Singh returned to the village. He was very upset about my father, till one day he heard that someone from the village had seen him in Amritsar. He left post haste for Amritsar. This is where destiny seemed to have intervened in our family. My father, after deliberating, decided to accompany Mall Singh to the village and resume his studies. He came back and joined the Khalsa High School at Kharar. My father was slightly older than the boys in his class. He passed his matriculation exam in 1st division in 1925. Those were the days when family *purohits* (Brahmins) or barbers used to get marriages fixed. Female infanticide was common among the Jats. My father was lucky as one retired Subedar Naranjan Singh of a British Indian Army Mule Battery himself came to the village to select a bridegroom for his daughter. He insisted that his would be son-in-law should at least be a matriculate. My father was the only matriculate in the village. Our family had very little land. Subedar Saheb had a tough time explaining to his family that education was more important than landholding.

My grandfather, Subedar Naranjan Singh, meanwhile arranged for my father to join as a soldier clerk in the 14th Punjab Regiment. The regiment was posted for guard duty to the Viceroy in 1930. This was a good posting for my father. He took his newly married wife with him to Delhi.

This enabled my father to redeem the family land from mortgage and also to construct a separate room in the house for his uncles. When I was about to be born my mother returned to her parents in village Dhamot in Ludhiana district as the custom was that the first born had to be at her parent's house. I was born on 12 August 1930. A newly born child was named Surain Singh after a ceremony that was observed either on the advice of the '*kul purohit*' or the Brahmin priest of the family or as per convenience of the family.

The first five years of my life were happy. The times were peaceful. My father's 5/14 Panjab Regiment saw good postings like Delhi Cantt. and Poona Cantt. For a part of the time in Delhi and Poona, we enjoyed family accommodation when my mother and I lived with him. He could also come home on long leaves to our village. My father seemed to be popular with his British officers. He was entrusted with the duties of an officers' mess clerk with some additional pay and perks.

We returned to the village in 1936. My mother told me that time had come for me to go to a school but I had to wait, as I could not tie the knot of my pajama. One day I told my mother that I could tie the knot of my pajama string. She made me demonstrate it. The next day she asked my grandfather to take me to the village lower middle school and get me admitted. The headmaster saw me and told my grandfather that I was a year younger for admission to the school. He was told to write my date of birth as permissible for the school admission and left me there. There was a boy, Harnek Singh, in the neighbourhood, a bit senior to me, who also used to go to school. My mother called him and gave a piece of jaggery and asked him to catch me physically and escort me to the school and further see to it that I did not bunk. That did the trick. I found that I could do well in my studies and thereafter I never looked back. Although Harnek Singh did not go beyond the primary level. Another happy development was that my mother started spending my three months of summer vacation with her parents in village Dhamot in Ludhiana district. Two of my *mamas* (maternal uncles) were also students but senior to me. The elder *mama* took to coaching me so that when I returned to school after the vacation I found myself at the top of the class.

The British had adopted a practice of posting their Indian Army units along the Durand Line on the border with Afghanistan. These postings were designed to toughen up the troops and for their battle inoculation in an area populated by wild tribesmen occupying hill features giving them an advantage over their adversaries. The Lee Enfield .303 rifles with which the British Indian soldiers were equipped were a prize attraction for the Pathan tribesmen. The 5/14 Panjab Regiment had their share of postings in these areas, in places like Razmak, Bannu and Wana, etc. My father took such postings in his stride but the posting of the regiment overseas was taken more seriously. He had promised a school friend of his that if after marriage he had a son and his friend a daughter, they would convert their friendship into a relationship for the next generation. Since this contingency had come about so he thought it appropriate to arrange for my engagement ceremony before he went away with his regiment. I found that one evening there was a lot of commotion in our house. There was dancing and singing by the girls during which I had gone to sleep. Some time later I was woken up and dragged to sit on a wooden *chauki* (a sort of stool).The family *purohit* (priest) read many mantras, applied some *tilak* on my forehead and made the father of the girl to put some pieces of jaggery in my lap and give me a few rupee coins as a token of the engagement ceremony. I was hardly five years old at that time. My stars ultimately did not permit this marriage to take place as the girl to whom I was engaged died when I was still studying in the school. However, this additional relationship with a family from a nearby village proved to be of help to my mother during the long absence of my father during the Second World War.

The 5/14 Punjab Regiment returned to India in 1938. My father came on leave to the village where he came to know that his regiment was posted back to Poona Cantt. My sister Surjit was born in Gharuan in 1937. I was studying in the third standard in the village lower middle school. My father, on reaching Poona, assessed the situation and felt that the regiment would stay there for at least one more year. He was a *Havildar* with three stripes.

He got family accommodation allotted and asked my mother to come over to Poona again. He sent a written application for a school transfer certificate for me that I handed over to my teacher. We took the train from Morinda for Sirhind from where we took the Bombay Express that ran between Bombay to Peshawar. Our journey lasted more than 48 hours. We passed through important railway stations like Delhi, Agra, Gwalior, Jhansi, Baroda and Kalyan, from where we took a turn towards Poona. My father and his friends were there to receive us at Poona.

Poona was one of the best British cantonments in India. During the ascendancy of the Peshwas it was the capital of India. It has continued to be the cultural capital of Maharashtra dominated by the Chitpavan Brahmins who are fair and often have blue eyes. The best part of the city was the cantonment. People all over seemed to be friendly and polite. The family quarters of the 5/14 Punjab Regiment was almost opposite to the city cinema hall near the Queen's Gardens.

Our school was a small primary school having only Muslim students except for the few Sikh students from Punjab. The other students were generally friendly and so were the teachers. The headmaster was a gray bearded well-built gentleman who looked like a Maulana, a Muslim scholar. He carried a long bamboo cane in his hand. Students feared him and in every way he looked a forbidding person, always with a grim look.

My father was considered to be a well-read man. He would read history of the world, dramas of Shakespeare and other literary works. The British Indian Army had optional examinations for the Indian soldiers called second class or first class, more or less of the standard of a middle level or high school level examination. They adopted the practice of teaching Hindustani an amalgam of Hindi and Urdu written in roman script to the soldiers. Almost of the graduate level was the Army Special Course, which my father had passed with distinction; he was also a teacher of map reading for the unit. My father subscribed to the main English daily of the area. I think that it was the '*Times of India*' in Poona, which is now spelt as Pune. My father one day said that my mother and I should get ready to go back to the village as the 5/14 Punjab Regiment would have to move to some theatre of war. Soon the orders came for the regiment to move to Malaya. My father gave an emotional speech in the Gurdwara which made the people cry as he had said that while all of them would be going after having been together in the regiment for so long but he was not sure about whom God had decided that he would return and meet his near and dear ones and who were destined not to return. My father got a fortnight off for escorting the family to our village home.

The first problem that I had on return was that I had only two months to prepare for my third standard final examination and a new compulsory subject had been introduced in which one had to qualify to be promoted to the next class. It was Punjabi in Gurmukhi script. My mother took on herself to teach Punjabi and the best teacher of the school was employed for my extra coaching at a tuition fee of three rupees per month. I was surprised to find that I could master Gurmukhi script and did the entire coursebook only in one week and in the annual examination I stood first in the class. My position thereafter remained unchallenged.

I had stood first in the third standard with only two months of study at the school. There was summer vacation soon after promotion to the fourth standard. My second sister was bom soon after our return from Poona. She was named Mohinder Kaur by nıy grandmother. Mohinder is a male name but among the Sikhs the practice is that mostly male names are used for all. Middle name 'Singh' is used for boys and 'Kaur' for girls. I think that 'Kaur' in the name of the females started being used with the Sikh awareness that got generated through the Sikh soldiers demobilized after the First World War. The Singh Sabhas that came into being after 1873 produced slightly doctored literature to emphasize the separate identity of the Sikhs.

We followed our routine of the summer vacation visit to my mother's village where my maternal uncle would get me to complete the entire course of study of the fourth standard during the two and half months that we stayed there. The village of my mother, Dhamot, was a village of the same size as Gharuan but it was more prosperous. My *Nana's* (mother's father) big house was situated almost in the middle of the village. Dhamot people had the same customs as in other villages of Punjab. The family would get together in the evening on the roof of the house around sunset. My *Nana*, a retired Viceroy's Commissioned Officer called *Subedar*, would take his position as the head of the family. With the darkness setting, we would either listen to stories told by my *Nani* or the reminiscences of the First World War from our *Nana*. The earliest experience of warfare for my Nana was when his unit accompanied Col. Sir Younghusband on his expedition to Tibet. My *Nana* had got a silver medal for his participation in that expedition. His other stories often described as to how the Sikh soldiers could often frighten the enemy by loud shouts of '*Bole So Nihal*' with all joining in the refrain in answer with '*Sat Sri Akal*' meaning that he who shouts that God is the truth or reality, he shall be blessed with happiness. My *Nana* was illiterate. He had joined as a soldier in a mountain battery regiment that carried guns on mules. It was called 41 Mountain Battery some time in the 1890s. His regiment saw action against Turkey immediately after World War I.

Our school was a lower middle school with eight teachers. Our village was a part of the princely state of Patiala. The ruler was a Sikh. The state had the Sikhs in majority but Hindus and Muslims were almost touching 45 per cent. Our headmaster was a Brahmin who was a scholar of Sanskrit. There was a special scholarship examination after the fourth class. The headmaster nominated me for competing in that scholarship examination which was not liked by the parents of another boy who wielded considerable influence in the lower echelons of the state administration. They asked the headmaster to nominate their son too for the scholarship examination. The headmaster refused to oblige them. The family pulled some strings and soon the headmaster got transferred.

We had quite a commotion in the village in 1940–41. I found that one well-to-do family in the village suddenly changed their way of living. They discarded wearing mill made clothes and changed to wearing coarse homespun cotton clothes. The head of the family was a retired engineer, Chanan Singh, who had served in Baghdad. It was his son Bachan Singh, who started moving about in the village with a tricolour flag shouting 'death to the British' and urging others to join him in the national struggle of attaining freedom for India. Our village was in the princely state of Patiala, which came under the British paramountcy. The rulers of the states did not like the movement one bit. As soon as the word reached Patiala, Bachan Singh was called to the police station and put under arrest. The police told him that it was in his interest to desist from such activities, but he remained adamant. A police officer came to the village to caution his father about the activities of his son. Meanwhile, the police brought Bachan Singh to the house so that his father could admonish him. Bachan Singh was a headstrong and temperamental person. The police official was physically pushed out of the chair and slapped throwing his turban on the ground, which was like adding insult to the injury. The police officer could save himself from further harm by running out of the house to the police camp in the village. He came back to the house with full force and demanded surrender of all male members before him. The family locked themselves in their three storied brick and mortar house and from the roof top they threw missiles on the policemen below. The police then opened fire sending the entire village into hiding in panic. It seems that the communication system of the *Parja Mandal* was quite efficient as before the police could move the arrested family out of the village their leaders like Brish Bhan and Giani Zail Singh, who later on became the President of India, reached our village and succeeded in getting the arrested women of the family released on bail. The case against the men went on for some time till the family decided to apologize and make up. Thereafter, the *Parja Mandal* or the Indian National Congress was not heard of till the Independence.

I cleared my lower middle schooling in 1942. My mother was anxious that I should not get spoilt in the company of other boys going to the high schools in the nearby towns. She chose for me the high school that was farthest from our village being about six kilometers away because the Punjabi teacher of the school was our neighbour and his son Gurdev was my class fellow. Every day he preferred to walk down to the school with two of us in tow. My school was known as the Khalsa High School, Kharar. Sardar Baldev Singh, the Akali leader who later became a minister in the Unionist Party government in Punjab, had established the Khalsa High School through a handsome financial endowment along with two or three other schools in the area that was the part of his constituency for elections to the Punjab Assembly. He later moved in 1946 as the Sikh representative in the Interim Government of Jawaharlal Nehru.

1942 in India was a tumultuous year. Mr. Gandhi called upon the British to quit India. The most pleasant surprise for us in 1942 was the return of my father from Malaya. He got two months' home leave during which he straight came to the village. He took me around to visit places. He decided on a visit to Ludhiana, which was the last outpost of the British Empire so long as the Sikhs ruled Punjab beyond the river Satluj up to Jamrod on the Khyber Pass bordering Afghanistan. The first Christian mission and a charitable hospital were set up there. The hospital has since expanded a lot and a well-known Christian Medical College has been established to which the old Miss Brown Hospital stands attached. It was winter. We left on foot for Morinda from where we took a *tonga* for Sirhind. It started raining and our *tonga* could move very slowly because of the mud and slush and near the town of Bassi Pathana, the steel rim of one of the *tonga* wheels came off making traveling in the *tonga* very hazardous. We decided to cover the rest of distance up to Bassi Pathana on foot. We were drenched in rain and shivering when we entered the first teashop at the *tonga* stand. We sat close to their oven and ordered for hot tea. We had a peg each by the time we reached the railway station and from where we caught the train to Sirhind. We had a second-class ticket and we were entitled to occupy the railway waiting room till the train came in the early morning to take us to Ludhiana. We had a room booked for us in a comfortable hotel in the city. The daily room tariff was ten rupees per room with bed and breakfast. I bought a few toys and two packs of fancy playing cards from Ludhiana and we saw a Hindi movie. We returned from Ludhiana after a visit to Dhamot.

The 5/14 Punjab Regiment in Malaya got divided into companies where my father was found to be too senior for their offices. He was to head the records office at the Regimental Headquarters located at Ferozepur. His return from Malaya was not expected, so the regiment had given acting promotion to one of his juniors. He had to revert back to his substantive position to make room for my father. This was not to the liking of my father. The Commanding Officer at Ferozepur mentioned that a new Corps in the Indian Army called the Indian Army Education Corps was being raised and they would be happy to have someone like my father in the rank of a Viceroy's Commissioned Officer. This proved to be a good way out.

After a training course, my father got posted to Secunderabad in South India. Meanwhile, the Japanese attacked Singapore followed by an attack on Malaya in which they achieved a complete surprise. The Japanese *hara-kiri* bombers sank the famous *Prince of Wales* and *Repulse* on the very first day. These ships were known as floating fortresses. The Japanese overran Malaya during the next few days. The whole of the 5/14 Punjab Regiment were taken as prisoners of war. A large number of officers and soldiers taken as prisoners of war of the 5/14 Regiment, died. The Japanese had moved the POWs to Indonesia by ship and when their position there became untenable they decided to again move them away but on their way the Japanese ship was sunk by the Allied bombers with everyone perishing at sea.

My father found that Secunderabad was a good station. He was allotted a good house. The climate was good and his work there was light. He wrote to my mother to join him. My father, at Secunderabad, was selected for being appointed a Lieutenant. He was posted to join the 8th Indian Army in North Africa. It was wartime. The officers were required to attend a briefing in Cairo while the ship with their baggage sailed ahead. During this briefing, my father's posting got changed. He got posted as an Army Education Officer for the Palestine and Egypt area. He stayed at Cairo for some time and then moved to Jerusalem. He discarded his Sikh appearance and got himself clean-shaven about which he wrote to me after quite some time sending a photograph of himself with a helmet riding a motorcycle. I remember that there was no reaction of the news on my mother but quite a few of our relatives came to express their grief over it. Villagers saying that my father must have fallen in love with some white woman teased me. They said that, therefore, he was going to abandon his Indian wife and family. The Allies had won the war in Europe and the Indian troops were returning fast mostly for being demobilized. My father was put on to the task of organizing training courses for the troops earmarked for demobilzation and promoted to the rank of a Captain. He continued writing long letters to me. He asked me to read *History of The World* by H.G. Wells and a few other books.

I started going on a bicycle when I was in class 9, which proved to be faster and gave me more time to play in the village. I spent a part of my vacation in Chinarthal village where my father's sister was married.

Gharuan has been considerate to those who devoted their lives to spiritual pursuits. The village community had given land grants to the village Brahmins for their services. The other groups to whom land grants were given were *Udasis* who are followers of Baba Siri Chand, the elder son of Guru Nanak, and then there were *Bairagis, Gosains, Nirmlas* and others. One saintly person from a nearby village was given a land grant of about 20 acres. He was called Baba Jagga. His *samadhi* or cremation site is still preserved. Newly married couples come to the *samadhi* for blessings. There was a Sikh minstrel accompanied by his three associates who had a considerable impact on the village. He was addressed as '*sant*' or a saint. He had a melodious voice to which the villagers felt attracted.

When I reached class 10, my father asked my mother to put me in the school hostel. The hostel was a premises built round a small temple which belonged to a Sikh landlord. Along with the temple he had made an arrangement to have a priest, '*poojari*', living on the premises with his family so that the daily worship of the deity went uninterrupted. The school had taken the whole building on rent for the students. My going to the hostel was decided during the mid-session when the hostel was full. However, two of my class friends were sharing a biggish room. They offered a seat in their room for me. I was happy to join them. I did not do too well in the final examination. I came third in my class and I was placed in the second division. I was happy that I had passed the examination, which was sufficient for me to join a college.

It seems that my father, sitting in Palestine, was more concerned about my going to college. I had grown up to be a handsome young man though still without any hair on my face.

My mother gave birth to a son some 13 years after me on 1st September 1943. He was named Maan Singh. Later in the day we distributed sweets in the village announcing the happy event in our family. My father was informed about the birth of another son to him. Maan Singh was to see his father after he was more than three years old. My mother was quite sought after in her village Dhamot, where a number of her cousins and their wives requested her to find suitable matches for their daughters in Gharuan as the old system of the family barber locating a groom for the daughters of the village had broken down. She could arrange marriages of four girls from Dhamot in Gharuan including that of her younger sister to a boy who had just cleared his matriculation examination. She had to attend all these marriages and she got the VIP treatment in all marriages because of her having been a go-between.

As the war ended the British started releasing the Congress leaders who were in jail due to the 'Quit India' agitation launched by Gandhi in 1942. Britain was engaged in a life and death struggle against the Fascists and Nazis and the trend of war in 1942 was going against them. Muslim League in India created their base among the Indian Muslims due to the vacuum created by the Congress leaders having gone to jail precisely during this interval. The 1935 Government of India Act transferring limited powers to Indians had come into force in 1937. The Congress had rejected the formula for participating in the Central Government but at the provincial level the Congress had fought the elections and won in most of the states. The Muslim League was nowhere in these elections. Punjab had rejected both the Congress and the Muslim League. A party of landholders called the Unionist Party had won in the elections and they were ruling Punjab when fresh elections were announced in 1946. The Akalis had enjoyed power in alliance with the Unionist Party in Punjab. After the Congress leaders had been jailed in 1942, a Muslim League ministry was sworn in the North West Frontier Province. One Akali minister had joined the Muslim League ministry. Somehow, the Akalis seemed to be confused in 1946. They had an understanding with the Congress on some seats where either of the parties did not put up a candidate against the candidate of the other party and for others they put up a friendly fight. Our area was one where both the parties had a friendly fight The Akalis had put up Sardar Baldev Singh as their candidate whereas the Congress had put up an advocate of Ambala, Sardar Gurbakhsh Singh whose mother was from Gharuan. Baldev Singh was also the patron of our school, so we had campaigned for him wholeheartedly. We were happy when it was declared that Baldev Singh had won by a few hundred votes. The Unionist Party was almost wiped out as the Muslim League had won almost all the Muslim seats (73 out of 85) and they emerged as the biggest group in the Punjab Legislative Assembly of 175 members.

2

The College Days

My father, in his letters, started preparing me for the next stage in my life after joining college. He was of the view that I should join the best college in Punjab which he thought was the Forman Christian College of Lahore. He was aware that I had studied in the village schools. He wanted me to go to Lahore on a visit to see for myself how people there lived and conducted themselves. My mother gave about one hundred rupees for my visit to Lahore. I took the train from Sirhind for Lahore about 150 miles away. My style of turban and dress was a giveaway for anyone that I had come straight from some village, far away from Lahore. Anyhow taking carefully measured steps I could walk to a nearby hotel where I booked a room for myself for three days. The next day as I stepped out of the hotel a boy who claimed to be dentist accosted me. He said that I was a handsome boy and if I permitted him to put gold or a brass cover on my front tooth I would look much more handsome. I then proceeded to visit Anarkali Bazaar, the well-known shopping market of Lahore and spent the day in window shopping. I decided to watch a movie in the evening. I came back to my hotel. Next day I decided to visit the F.C. College. My father had given me a letter for the principal, which I had carried with me. I hired a hackney carriage to take me to the college. I found the college closed for vacations after the annual exams.

A peon of the college told us that the principal of the college lived nearby and I could see him at his house. I found that the principal lived in a huge house with beautiful grass lawns around it. I went around the house but did not see anyone. After waiting there for someone to come out I decided to quit without seeing the principal.

We were told in our village that students in the college have to go in pant and coat to attend the college. I was given five hundred rupees to get two suits stitched from Ludhiana. My cousin who had come from the INA accompanied me. I came back happy to the village with three suits packed in a bag. My father had sent me by parcel post a suit piece of woolen cloth. We had a tailor in our village, Tulsi Ram, who offered to stitch a suit for me.

Our college admissions were to take place in June 1946. I reached Sirhind to take a train for Lahore. I bought a second-class ticket for travel. When the train reached the platform I found that I had a companion dressed like a villager standing next to me. I greeted him and came to know that he was Sohan Singh Josh a well-known communist leader of Punjab. I introduced myself to Mr. Josh and I shared with him my fear of going to Lahore. He also felt that I might not feel quite at home among the better off and sharper Lahore boys of the F.C. College. His advice to me was to join the Khalsa College in Amritsar where most of the students would be like me from the villages. I accepted his advice. The Khalsa College too was a product of the *Singh Sabha*. It was established as the central Sikh institution of learning in 1892. It had an Englishman Mr. Wathen as its first principal. I cut short my journey to get down at Amritsar thanking Sohan Singh Josh profusely for his advice. I did not know anyone at Amritsar, so I proceeded to the Golden Temple Complex. I reported at the Guru Ramdas Sarai to ask for a room to sleep. Next day I put on one of the new suits and went to the Khalsa College. I filled up the admission form and went to deposit the same with the principal Dr. Jodh Singh. He was a venerable old gentleman. He looked at me and smiled. He took my form and asked me to come the next day and he smilingly told me that it was not necessary for me to wear a suit. I walked as fast as possible to the college gate from where I took a *tonga* to reach the Golden Temple. I took off my suit and came out of the *sarai*. When I reached *Manji Saheb* I found that there was a big gathering of the Akalis to discuss the current political developments in the country. I took my seat on a small raised platform and started listening to the speeches being made. I was feeling somewhat sleepy and as I dozed and leaned to my left side I touched the body of the person sitting next to me. I looked at him to say that I was sorry. He also turned to look at me and both of us recognized each other with a start. He was a boy from Chinarthal village two years senior to me who was studying in the third year at the Khalsa College Amritsar. The speeches that were being delivered were against accepting the proposals made by the British Cabinet Mission for the transfer of power to the Indians. My friend Sukhdev Singh took me with him to his room in the Patiala hostel. He showed me round the vast campus of the college. Next day I went to the college with Sukhdev Singh in ordinary shirt and pyjamas. The principal granted admission to me in FSc (medical). My subjects were English, Physics, Chemistry, Biology with Divinity as an optional subject. I was allotted a room in the Nabha hostel, which was meant for all the first year students. The college was proud in having been champions in most of the sports in the Punjab University. We got ourselves registered in our new classes and met our teachers. There were to be summer vacations after a fortnight or so. No serious teaching was started in any of the subjects. We were told about the books that we could read during the summer vacation.

Nothing much happened during the summer vacation except that during the rains when our big village pond was full of water I started going there for a swim from one end to the other end.

Our college opened after the summer vacation. Our combined merit for the hostel room came second, so we could get the room of our choice on the first floor. Each wing of the hostel had a senior student as student warden who on and off visited to see if all of us were present and everything was alright in the rooms under his charge. I often went to the swimming pool for my bath. The college had a gurdwara in the campus close to the swimming pool. Some of us returned to the hostel after sitting with the congregation in the gurdwara for some time. We had our breakfast either in the college tuck shop or in a shop at the college gate. Lunch and dinner we had in our hostel kitchen. The hostel organized a competition for selecting a 'kitchen athlete' every year. It consisted of a competition in eating the maximum number of *chapattis* in one sitting on a day when meat curry was served. All of us competed for the kitchen athlete trophy. The champion and the runner-up, who was a boy with a huge body went up to 56 *chapattis* each. The other boy who was thin and lean but he ate one *chapatti* more and got declared as the kitchen athlete of the year.

I started liking the college and its atmosphere. A majority of the students were from villages. The teachers were helpful and polite. We had Dr. Ganda Singh who later distinguished himself by becoming a historian of the Sikhs, and Professor Saheb Singh, the author of grammar of the *Granth Saheb* and a translation of the *Granth Saheb* based on grammar, as our teachers of Divinity. The chemistry teacher was Professor Joginder Singh, famous for his textbook of chemistry. I had one problem in attending classes in the college. None of the teachers could hold my attention as my mind would jump ahead of them and I would give myself to mind wandering and daydreaming. Another reason for my complacence was that I got convinced that whatever was being taught in one hour in the college, the same I could master on my own from a book in less than ten minutes.

My interest in the current events attracted the attention of a senior student Shamsher Singh of Kakron village near Gharuan who was an admirer of the late M.N. Roy who was the Secretary General of the Comintern founded by Lenin but he could not pull on with Stalin. On returning to India, he founded a party called the Radical Democratic Party. He took me with him to a study circle of the leftists. I found Marxist ideas gripping. The dirt cheap Marxist literature published by the USSR came in handy for me.

I found the Communist manifesto to be a moving document. I thought that I had got something that made me see everything in a new and true light. I joined the Communist led Students Federation and put my heart and soul into it. There was a very good response from the students of the Khalsa College of Amritsar for our federation. A number of college teachers sympathized with us. Marxism said that religion was something invented by the exploiting classes to exploit the poor. I started questioning my own beliefs and conduct. My preoccupation with the Communist movement among the students provided me an excuse to neglect my regular college classes.

I had deliberately neglected my college studies and I had friends who were no good in studies. I devoted myself to the Communist literature when I happened to be alone. I, along with my friends utilized my time in exploring the historic city of Amritsar founded by the fourth Guru of the Sikhs who was a Sodhi Khatri, who had married Bibi Bhani, the most beloved daughter of Guru Amar Das, the third Guru. The fifth Guru compiled the Sikh scripture, the *Guru Granth Saheb* in Amritsar and the same was installed in the Golden Temple in 1604. The Sikh ruler of Punjab, Maharaja Ranjit Singh patronized Amritsar. He had put gold sheets on *Darbar Saheb*, and the place started being called the Golden Temple. He laid outside the city some beautiful palaces and gardens called the Ram Bagh gardens. It was a very busy place in the evenings, always full of .people in their best dresses.

The most pleasant happening in January 1947 was the return of my father from the Middle East. He came to Bombay in a ship. He had been given a leave of two months before he took up his next assignment. He decided to visit me first in Amritsar before going home to Gharuan. I found a smart army soldier coming and saluting me in my hostel. He gave me a letter from my father in which he wrote that he was staying in a hotel called Amritsar Hotel in Amritsar Cantonment and wanted me to accompany the soldier to meet him there. I rushed to Amritsar Hotel with the soldier. We were both overwhelmed seeing each other after more than four years. My joy on seeing him knew no bounds. I was seeing him as a clean-shaven smart army officer for the first time. He really looked handsome. Lunch was announced while I was with him. He invited me to join in lunch with him in the hotel dining room. When food was served, in about five courses he continued guiding me while commenting on how I was succeeding in mastering the Western table manners. The whole of the afternoon we exchanged notes about everyone in the family and how life had been with my father. He told me that he had a serious motorcycle accident around Gaza in 1944 that resulted in his hospitalization for some time. He found that caring for his beard and hair had become a problem for him, so he called a barber and got himself clean-shaven. He started liking his clean-shaven appearance and according to him every one in the officers' mess also congratulated him on what he had done. Of course there were no Sikh army officers in his mess. I went to see my father again on the next Sunday. My father told me that he had taken a fancy for a horse-drawn carriage called Victoria. The carriage that he had selected looked stately and beautiful. The mare that came with it was milk white in color the like of which I had not seen before. The deal was struck at rupees two thousand and three hundred. The carriage was meant for self-driving. We took possession of our carriage, thanked our broker and left for our hotel. My father left for Gharuan early next day. I was asked to visit Gharuan as soon as I had two or three holidays.

The political events in India were moving fast with the Labour Government coming to power in the United Kingdom. The Labour Government was committed to transfer of power to Indians. The two principal political parties in India, involved in negotiating an agreed framework for the transfer of power, had reached a deadlock. The Muslim League had swept the polls in all Muslim Provinces except the North West Frontier Province under Mr. M.A. Jinnah. They insisted that after the British left, the Muslim majority Provinces must be grouped together to form an independent sovereign state to be called Pakistan but the Indian National Congress and the Akali Dal were deadly opposed to it. The British government sent a Cabinet Mission to break the deadlock. The Cabinet Mission had on its staff an ex-Sikh Regiment officer called Major Short who had successfully persuaded the Akalis to disassociate from the Congress for 'Quit India' agitation in 1942. He was hopeful that some via media could be worked out for the Sikhs but the two major political parties had for once come to accept the formula proposed by the Cabinet Mission though reluctantly and with some reservations. The Muslim League immediately went back on their commitment and came back to their demand for Pakistan. They decided to pressurize the British as well as the Congress by declaring a Direct Action Day in August 1946. The Direct Action was marked by an outbreak of communal riots in Calcutta (now Kolkata) followed by riots in Noakhali and other places in the interiors in East Bengal, now Bangladesh. The Sikhs in Calcutta joined the Hindus in those riots.

The position soon changed in favour of the Hindus in Calcutta but the massacre in East Bengal went unabated. Gandhi took upon himself to get the rioting in Calcutta stopped. He went on a fast to death, which brought about a qualitative change in the situation and the rioting stopped in Calcutta, but the situation in East Bengal became worse. Gandhi formed a one-man peace brigade and he decided to personally visit the riot-affected villages. He remained in East Bengal till India became independent. The riots came to a stop in East Bengal too. It seemed surprising that when all the rioting was taking place in Bengal there was not even a ripple of it felt in Punjab. However, the Premier Mr. Khizar Hayat Khan Tiwana, who had the support of only ten or so Muslim legislators, submitted the resignation of his coalition government on the 2nd of March 1947. It was likely that the Governor of Punjab, Sir Evan Jenkins, would call upon the Muslim League, to try and form the government. Master Tara Singh took the lead in opposing any such eventuality as the Akalis under him were firmly of the view that the Sikh community could not live in a state ruled by the Muslim League. The Hindus and the Sikhs of Lahore joined together under the leadership of Master Tara Singh and took out a procession on the 3rd March consisting mostly of students to the Punjab Assembly.

We had the annual sports matches of the Punjab University in February 1947. Our college had reached the finals in Hockey and Football. Almost all the students would go to Lahore that was only 33 miles away to see the final matches and to buck up our teams. Our final match in hockey was against the Government College, Lahore. After some very interesting exchanges the final match in hockey was won by the Khalsa College, Amritsar. The next final match after a few days was of football against the Islamia College, Lahore. The Islamia boys and the Khalsa boys were quite vociferous in shouting for their respective teams but there was no communal tension in the air even after the victory of the Khalsa College team. The Khalsa College that year, which became the last year of the united Punjab University, was declared the university champions in athletics.

The Akalis again proved that they would talk big but they would do nothing to translate even a fraction of their big talk in to action. The Sikhs lived in a Muslim majority Province. They had participated in a Muslim League government in the NWFP. Democracy had become the order of the day after the Second World War. It had become clear that the British would leave India after handing over to the Indians as either one country or two countries if the Indians failed to agree between themselves. The Akali refrain remained that they would not tolerate Muslim rule over them come what may. The rigid anti-Muslim stance of the Akalis was contrary to the Sikh tradition and heritage. The boycott of the Muslims at the social level though slightly relaxed in the times of Guru Nanak due to the influence of the Bhakti movement and Muslim Sufis, was a fact of life.

The doors for understanding with the Muslim League got almost shut after the March riots. The Sikhs were a miniscule minority in the West Punjab bordering the NWFP. It was in the area that the Muslim League had decided to strike. There was arson and looting of Sikh houses accompanied by massacre of men and mass rape of women. This gave the repeat of Medieval Rajput *Johar* ceremony among the Sikhs where all women of Thoa Khalsa village, on being attacked by the Muslims, read a mass prayer and jumped into the well of the *gurdwara*. Every Sikh was seething with feelings of revenge against the Muslims. There was curfew in the city. We were confined to the hostels not knowing what to do. We put up volunteers to guard the college campus at night. All the Sikh boys were smarting under the humiliation that had been brought on the community.

The college was closed for a week due to the riots. I went to the village during this interval. I carried the fear of Muslims from Amritsar. I would not move out from the village unless I had some weapon in my hand. I went to see my sister Surjit in Jaspalon School. I returned from Jaspalon via Dhamot, my mother's village. There were a number of Muslim villages on the way. I was shivering with fear inside but no one took notice of me or of the sword that I was carrying. The life in the villages was absolutely normal. It was while passing through a Sikh village that an old man noticed the sword in my hand. He stopped me and shook my hand saying that as a Sikh he was very impressed by my carrying the sword when I was so young. I learnt on my return that my father had been posted as a Captain to the 3rd Armoured Brigade located at Risalpur near Peshawar in the NWFP. The armoured regiments were considered the cream of the Indian Army. Earlier they were called as the cavalry regiments where officers who came from the well-off landlord families were generally posted. India at that time had only one Armoured Division consisting of three Brigades. Indian Army had started recruiting Indian officers as Kings Commissioned Officers who had their training at Sandhurst in Great Britain. The armoured regiments generally had only the British officers as was the case with the 3rd Armoured Brigade. My father was the only Indian officer at the Brigade Headquarters when he joined there.

I returned to Amritsar after spending about ten days in Gharuan with my parents. There was a sort of invisible tension in the air. We visited the city during the day when there was no curfew. All of us at the Khalsa College felt that a second round of violence would breakout after the Sikhs had prepared themselves for taking revenge on the Muslims on a massive scale. One ex-Army Lieutenant in our class undertook to train us on the use of a rifle. We attended the classes taken by him regularly. I saw my father on the train that was passing through Amritsar on way to Nowshehra in the NWFP. My father decided to take the family with him expecting an undisturbed stay for a year or two at Risalpur. Nowshehra apart from being the railhead also happened to be the Regimental Center Headquarters of the famous Sikh Regiment, one of the most decorated regiments for bravery in the Indian Army. Our annual examinations for the first year in the college were announced to be held in April. The college, as against the second year examinations that were conducted by the university, conducted these annual examinations internally.

I found that there were a large number of students to whom the examination appeared to be a nightmare. We decided to go on strike with a demand that all of us must be promoted to the next class without any examination, as we could not fully prepare for our examinations due to the communal riots, curfew and closure of the college. We remained on strike till riots broke out a second time in Amritsar. The college authorities after about ten days of strike conceded our demand and promoted us to our next class. It was the second year F.Sc. for me. We had to move to a new hostel after promotion.

A large number of Sikhs from West Punjab, especially women and children, had moved to Amritsar. They had virtually taken over the *sarai* called 'Guru Ram Das Ki Sarai' meant for the visiting pilgrims. They would eat in the common kitchen where there was abundance of wheat flour and pulses, the staple diet of the Punjabis. The Akali leaders were all the time indulging in saber rattling and gnashing their teeth. Still no one talked of a dialogue with the Muslim League. After the initial success of the Muslim League cadres against the Sikhs, a feeling had grown among the Muslims that the Sikhs had lost their elan. They no longer posed a threat to their design of wresting Pakistan from the British.

The Akali preparations, started after they got a bloody nose in March 1947 riots, were mostly in Central Punjab as the objective was to attack the Muslims in areas where the Sikhs were in a strong position. This preparation came in handy after the Radcliffe Award on the boundary between the East and the West Punjab was announced. However, the most pressing need was for preparedness in North and West Punjab where the Sikhs were in real danger but nothing was done in those areas. I did not hear nor have I since come across any condemnation of this satanic theory of hostages in which it was justified that for the atrocities suffered by the Hindus and the Sikhs in West Punjab, it was just and appropriate to inflict similar imagined punishment on the innocent Muslims of East Punjab. I spent about a month in Amritsar after our promotion without any examination. The summer vacation was declared a bit early because of the chaotic conditions prevailing in Punjab especially in the urban centers. I came to Gharuan for the vacation while my father and mother were in Risalpur.

My having joined the college in Amritsar had made me a somewhat distinguished person in the eyes of my friends, most of whom did not make the grade to pass the matriculation examination. Every other day one friend or the other invited me to meals in their houses. I fully enjoyed my new status during my stay in Gharuan. My father was very anxious that I should join him in Risalpur during my summer vacation, which were to last till September 1947. I left for Risalpur by an express train that I took from Sirhind. I got down at Nowshehra Railway Station. There was tension in the air but in the NWFP, where the Congress was ruling, there were no riots. It was a journey of about seven kilometers through a beautiful countryside. I was dropped inside a spacious house with a huge compound and a long driveway. My father was there to receive me. My sisters and my younger brother, who was about four years old, were delighted to have me with them. I found that a stay of two months with my father had completely changed them from a rustic village family to a middle class urban family at least in their appearance and lifestyle.

My father, I found was the only Indian officer at the Brigade Headquarters. He was responsible for the education of the soldiers posted in the various units of the brigade, which took him to visit places like Bannu, Kohat and Mardan, etc. Peshawar was the Area Headquarters of the Army. Sometimes he would take me along in his jeep. I thoroughly enjoyed those visits. It was July–August 1947 when everywhere in Punjab there was communal tension particularly in urban centers but not a whiff of that tension could be perceived in the Frontier Province because it was the Indian National Congress led by Khan Abdul Ghaffar Khan and his brother who ruled the Frontier Province. The Congress leaders ditched the Khan brothers when they accepted the Partition of India with the Frontier Province going to Pakistan. The stratagem adopted to give the Province to Pakistan was through a referendum on the issue, which was boycotted by the Khan brothers because only a year ago the people of the NWFP had voted against the idea of Pakistan by rejecting the Muslim League.

The Risalpur Cantonment, where we lived, was a beautiful small cantonment with a lot of greenery because of irrigation being available from a nearby canal. The cantonment had an officer's club with a swimming pool. It was quite hot otherwise, so I made it a routine to spend some time in the swimming pool daily. The British army officers were in the process of being repatriated, being replaced by Indian officers on quick promotions. The available Indian officers who were often given additional charge were managing the shortage of officers on the fast exit of the British officers. My father got the additional charge of the post of the Station Staff Officer, which meant that he had to look after the administration of the station, which made him someone in Risalpur who was much sought after.

3

Partition of India

The events were inexorably moving towards the division of India and in its place the coming into being of two independent countries. Lord Mountbatten had taken over as the Viceroy of India who was in a hurry to leave India. He advanced the calendar for the transfer of power from 1948 to 14th and 15th August 1947 despite all the killings and mayhem that was going on in the name of religion. His success lay in the fact that he was able to carry with him all the political leaders of India who mattered. A Boundary Commission was appointed under Sir Cyril Radcliffe to decide about the areas that would go into the new divided provinces. Similarly, Bengal agreed to be divided. The presence of Gandhi in Bengal saved the province from further bloodbath. I did not find any change in the climate as August 1947 approached. The 3rd Armed Brigade changed in complexion as many Muslim army officers came over to relieve the British officers. The All India Radio gave news about sporadic riots in Punjab. We heard that in West Punjab even the Sikh army officers were not safe while traveling in railway trains but we were in the dark about the events in East Punjab and the mass exodus of the Hindus and the Sikhs from West Punjab. The NWFP was still a haven of peace. We heard speeches of Nehru, Jinnah and Baldev Singh on the eve of the Indian Independence. The Peshawar Radio Station could not broadcast the speech for some technical fault. The new Pakistan government dismissed the government of Khan Saheb and in its place the Muslim League Government was installed. My father could sense that our staying at Risalpur could spell danger for us. The Indian Army also got divided. My father's regiment the 5/14 Punjab Regiment got allotted to Pakistan. The 3rd Armoured Brigade too was given to Pakistan. One of its constituent regiment called the Poona Horse was allotted to India. The regiment was ordered to move to India by train. My father got a compartment in the train for us. We took the special train along with the troops. Our compartment got very crowded as everyone who wanted to leave for India was accommodated in the train. It was on the 2nd of September 1947 that the train left Risalpur for India.

The train moved out of the Frontier Province. When it crossed the Attock Bridge, we got a taste of the danger that lay ahead despite our being in a train that was carrying troops when we got fired on by snipers hiding in the hills that dominated the railway line near the bridge. The troops in our train opened up with machine guns, which silenced the guns of the snipers. I found that the army personnel became extra alert after that. A number of Sikh men and women came to our train begging us to take them on the train but we pleaded our helplessness as only the train commander could take such a decision. It is there that I got an inkling about the disaster that the Partition of India had brought on the Punjab.

Our train moved from Rawalpindi at a very slow speed. Sometimes we had to stop on wayside stations for hours that became a torture for me, as I had to sit behind a closed window in the sultry September heat. We crossed Lahore on the 4th night. The army soldiers were good enough to pass on food for us from their kitchen. We crossed the new border and reached Attari in the morning of the 5th. As the train stopped there we were surrounded by Sikh volunteers from the villages with hot '*chapattis*' and pickles. All of us including the army soldiers really enjoyed the first good meal after we had left Risalpur. It was at Amritsar Railway Station that I came to realize that the Sikhs had no place in Pakistan as the station was teeming with mostly Sikh refugees occupying all the available space on the railway platforms and even beyond. All had their tales of woes to tell. It was Gandhi alone, among the leaders who wept for the great tragedy that the freedom of the country had brought. I understand that Mr. Jinnah, when he was taken on an aerial survey of the column of poor Muslim refugees fleeing from India had spontaneously remarked, "Oh God! What have I brought on these people?". All the political leaders of India, the British Viceroy and the British government stand condemned in history for the holocaust, the British even more so as to the manner in which they had transferred power to the Muslim League resulting in Pakistan losing its democratic character soon after the Partition.

Our train moved slowly from Amritsar. We learnt on the way that sometimes the trains carrying Muslim soldiers in the opposite direction would open fire on the Hindu and Sikh refugees occupying the railway platforms. The Baluch Regiment was said to be notorious for such shootings. We were virtually cooped up in our compartment because of which it became impossible to stretch ones legs for almost three days. I learnt later that the troops in our train had come to know at Ludhiana that a detachment of the Baluch Regiment in a train, while passing a railway station, had fired on the refugees occupying the railway platform. It was that particular train that had crossed our train near Rajpura Railway Station. The troops in our train had opened fire on the train that was carrying the troops to Pakistan while both the trains were in slow motion. When the train reached Ambala Cantonment, I pleaded with the train commander to permit me to take our luggage from the brake van. We got carried to Saharanpur, where we got off-loaded from the train. Incidentally, the incident of firing by the soldiers of the Poona Horse during their transit from Risalpur to India finds a mention in their regimental record but with a grain of untruth as the firing is purported to have taken place in Pakistan and not in India as it actually happened. Saharanpur is an important rail junction on way to Delhi and Calcutta. Here everything seemed to be normal. I went to the ticket window and bought first class rail tickets for Sirhind. It was only when we moved to the railway platform that we learnt that no trains were going to Punjab. It was a relief to know after some time that a mixed passenger and goods train would be leaving for Punjab. When the train came we rushed to occupy our seats. It had only third class compartments. We managed to get our luggage loaded in the train and we had a place to sit.

It became dark by the time we crossed Ambala Cantonment Railway Station. When the train reached Sirhind, it was pitch dark. There were no lights at the railway station. Somehow there was lights in the railway signals. I was familiar with the Sirhind Railway Station surroundings, as I had passed through the railway station so often. I asked my mother to get down from the train. We had seven or eight trunks as luggage. I found one wheelbarrow of the porters lying on the platform. This came in handy for me and my mother to cart our luggage to the passenger hall outside. A strange sight met us in the passenger hall. The whole place was full of armed Sikh groups. Some of them were wearing turbans like *Nihangs*. All of them were armed with swords and spears. We put our luggage in a comer that was empty. I went to sleep immediately as I was tired. The band of armed Sikhs left after daybreak. I went to see if any of the railway staff was available to tell us about the branch line train that could take us to Morinda, the railhead for Gharuan. I was told that there were no trains moving on the branch line for the last fortnight. We found ourselves stranded at Sirhind, notorious for the killing of the two sons, aged seven and nine, of Guru Gobind Singh on the orders of the Mughal Governor after a mock trial. My mother remembered that there was a distant nephew of hers from Dhamot, Pritam Singh who did business as a commission agent in Sirhind. She went to him and met him. He was happy to see her. He brought a bullock cart to take our luggage and us to his house. Seeing all the disturbances around we decided that there was no point in our going to Gharuan where we could expect at best Pal Singh to be there. We knew that he would be of no help to us. We decided that we should try to reach Dhamot where my mother had her three brothers and her parents. All means of communication stood paralyzed. Our host told us that all over the area the Sikh *Jathas* (bands) had some system of communication through which he would get a message sent to Dhamot about our arrival in Sirhind. We got a message a day after that my *mama* Balwant Singh would be coming to pick us up. We were warmly welcomed when we reached Dhamot.

I started feeling out of place in Dhamot. I longed to go to Gharuan but there was no transport that could take me to Gharuan. Around 15th of September I met an old man who told me that he would be going to Gharuan to see his daughter who was married there. He planned to travel on foot and cover the distance in two days. I fell in with his plan and left Dhamot on foot. Both of us had three feet long swords in our hands. We reached village Malikpur near Khanna by the time it was dark. The old man with me knew someone in Malikpur. We enquired about him and reached his home. He was surprised to see us. He gave us food and a place to sleep at night. We left early next morning via a shortcut through the villages. We reached Morinda in the afternoon where I met some of my school classmates. They were very happy to see me and accompanied me to Gharuan. They told me that my uncle Pal Singh had acquired a wife whom I met when I reached home. My school friends when they heard about my arrival came to see me. When I reached Gharuan the Muslims outwardly appeared to have become Sikhs sporting beards and long hair. It was obvious to both the Sikhs and the newly converted Muslims that there had been no change of heart among the converts but both the sides kept up pretence as it suited them both. The Muslims wanted to save their lives and the Sikhs did not want the odium of having to kill their erstwhile friends and neighbours.

One of the family members got elected as a Municipal Councilor there. Dr. Gyanendra Pandey in the course of writing his book. "*Remembering Partition*" had visited Gharuan. His book partially covers what I have described in my account. The local administration after remaining dormant for more than four months decided to reassert their authority. Gharuan being a big village, notorious for disturbances even otherwise, was selected by the police for a special treatment that could serve as a lesson for others. They came in a lorry to camp in the village. They were followed by a contingent of the mounted armed police. The police action succeeded in its purpose that was to show the villagers that the days of lawlessness were over. The village reverted to the normal placid life as if nothing had happened.

My father returned to India sometime in mid-October 1947. We had no news about him after we left Risalpur. He told us that by the end of September the exchange of troops between India and Pakistan was completed. The communal situation in the Frontier Province became worse after the Muslim League replaced the Congress ministry. The Governor of the Frontier Province, Sir Rob Lockhart, passed an order that all Hindus or Sikhs in isolated posts in the formations allocated to Pakistan must leave the Frontier Province. My father was made the Commanding Officer of all such Hindu/Sikh remnants numbering about two hundred and fifty. The group was asked to escort about one thousand Hindu/Sikh refugees. They were asked to move by road. A convoy of about one hundred trucks left Risalpur under the command of my father. The Pakistan Army assured my father that they would provide security to the convoy. Still not believing in their word he arranged that after every two trucks carrying refugees there should be one truck of soldiers. What was feared came to pass as the convoy came under fire after they crossed Nowshehra. The convoy was moving with a fixed distance of thirty yards between two trucks but the firing made the convoy go bumper to bumper. They moved to the Attock Bridge in that position and found that the gate of the bridge was locked. The sentry on duty said that since the convoy would be crossing over to Punjab, they must have a count of the vehicles and passengers who were leaving the Province. My father asked the sentry to take him to his Commanding Officer who was an Inspector of Police. He saluted my father but refused to open the lock. My father had to shoot the inspector as the whole convoy standing bumper to bumper on the bridge stood in the danger of being wiped out. The escorting Pakistan Army contingent was nowhere to be seen. The convoy after shooting down the inspector rushed from the Attock Bridge to Rawalpindi. A message had reached Rawalpindi about the shooting down of the police inspector. The Pakistan Army took my father to their army mess and told him that he was under arrest. The rest of the convoy was taken to a separate camp. Next day the Pakistan Army Headquarters ruled that since my father was an officer of the Indian Army, he could be court-martialled only by the Indian Army. He was asked again as the Commanding Officer, to take all his men and refugees to India by train for which a special train was placed at his disposal. The special train got taken to Sialkote and stopped.

The Pakistani authorities relented after a while and allowed the train to proceed to Lahore on way to India. The travel adventure of my father took more than fifteen days instead of the one-day that was required. My father got relieved of the train at Jalandhar and headed straight for Gharuan.

My father had been allocated to the Madras Regiment as the 14th Punjab Regiment had gone over to Pakistan. Pakistan had already attacked Jammu and Kashmir through raiders from the tribal areas of the Frontier Province and irregular troops. The Indian Army had officially moved to defend Jammu and Kashmir. My father got posted as an Intelligence Officer in 161 Brigade then posted at Uri on the Srinagar-Baramula road. My college also reopened at about the same time. My mother was left alone in Gharuan as Pal Singh also decided to proceed on his usual tours.

One significant event towards the end of our vacation was the assassination of Mahatma Gandhi by a Hindu fanatic. Gandhi considered himself to be a devout Hindu. His Hinduism was a reconstruct of his own. He had taken a lot in it from Christianity particularly from Quakers and Tolstoy. He swore by truth and absolute non-violence. He was on top of the world till the onset of the Second World War. He advised nonviolence against Hitler and started demanding immediate declaration of Independence for India. When Britain and allies were engaged in a life and death struggle against the Nazis and Fascists he gave a call for Britain to Quit India in 1942. All the Congress ministries in different Provinces resigned. The Congress leaders including Gandhi were arrested and put behind the bars. The Muslim League took full advantage of this political vacuum. Despite the fact that he fully backed the Indian Muslims and wholeheartedly supported the Khilafat agitation at the end of the First World War, the Muslims at the collective level opted for the Muslim League except for certain pockets and the NWFP. The British left India literally burning with Muslims killing Hindus and the Hindus and Sikhs killing Muslims. The Muslim League's call for Direct Action could not be met at the political level by the Congress. He had to resort to fasting to get the internecine killings stopped in Calcutta and later in Delhi. The country so dear to him stood divided. The influx of a large number of Hindu and Sikh refugees into Delhi led to further inflammation of communal feelings and violent riots in which the Sikhs were in the vanguard along with the Hindu RSS cadres. Gandhi had to come and camp in Delhi. He lashed out against the Sikhs and the Hindus for violence in Delhi. He angered the Hindus and the Sikhs all the more when he openly rebuked the Government of India for reneging on their commitment to pass on the allocated share of cash balances from the Reserve Bank of India to Pakistan. Although in one of his statements he justified the Indian police action against the Pakistani raiders in Kashmir. The anger against him first led to a bomb explosion in one of his evening prayer meeting. Later, Nathuram Vinayak Godse, a Hindu fanatic shot him dead on 30th January 1948. It was obvious that he no longer had his finger on the pulse of the people when he died. No doubt that he was a great man, perhaps the greatest Indian born in the 19th and 20th centuries. He lived by certain moral values that he applied to his private and public life and he kept his life as an open book.

Most of my class fellows came to the college after the Partition of Punjab. A number of Hindu and Sikh students who were in Lahore colleges also joined our college. The Punjab University examinations could not be held that year. The government decided that those who were to appear in the University examination could get their degrees without the examination by doing social service in the refugee camps. I was to appear in the University examination only in March 1948. Our summer vacation had got prolonged because of the disturbances. The scheduled March examinations got postponed to June 1948. I resumed my contacts with the Marxists and the radical humanist cadres. I soon became an activist of the All India Students Federation, a body affiliated to the Communist Party of India. The Communist Party of India under B.T. Randive adopted a line hostile to the Congress under the influence of the Communist Party of the Soviet Union. The Government of India had to ban the Communist Party of India. The line adopted by the CPI did not affect my loyalty to the communist ideology and I continued to be a member of the AISF. I again neglected my studies. I got very nervous when the final examinations approached in May. I got sick with nervous diarrhoea due to my lack of preparation for the examination. I allocated, according to the schedule fixed for the examination, two to three days for the study of each subject. It came as a surprise to me that with only two to three days of study I passed the examination with fairly good marks.

4

Chasing Uncertain Objectives

My father had another adventure in his posting in Jammu and Kashmir. The Brigade had asked for a young army officer to serve as an Intelligence Officer. The Army Headquarters posted my father for the job who was near his retirement from the Army. Anyhow, my father took his job seriously. He developed some pain in his leg due to the effect of the extreme cold in the winter. He walked out of his tent for a meal in the mess after perhaps a drink or two. He stumbled and fell in a depression just outside his tent. He did not get up from the fall. Either because of the fall or drunken stupor, he became unconscious. He got fully covered by snow during the night. No one missed him for the dinner. There was further snowfall during the night and the next day. His absence was noticed the next day. The army got seriously concerned about the missing intelligence officer. They feared the worst for him at the hands of the raiders. While looking for his trace of footsteps etc. they noticed a mound of freshly fallen snow outside my father's tent. Someone on a hunch they started digging snow with a shovel. They soon discovered that there was a human body buried under the snow. A little more digging showed that it was of my father. Fearing the worst they brought him out of the snow. They were amazed to find that he was breathing softly as perhaps an air pocket got formed in the snow, which enabled him to breathe. He was quickly covered with woolen blankets and given some brandy as first aid. He was taken to the field hospital where he soon recovered and declared fit. He was posted out of Jammu and Kashmir to Jalandhar Cantt, which was quite near Amritsar and not very far from Gharuan. When my father told his saga in snow, we took the story with a pinch of salt. I had to regret for our hasty judgment as the whole story as described by my father finds mention in the book written by L.P. Sen the then Brigade Commander of the 161 Brigade titled "*Slender was the Thread*". Our whole family moved from Gharuan to Jalandhar Cantt. There was an acute shortage of accommodation in Jalandhar for army officers. We could only get a two bedroom apartment that was earlier occupied by a Sergeant of a British Army unit near the Lal Kurti Bazaar. I joined the family in June 1948 after my Intermediate examination. I had started visiting Jalandhar on every weekend after my father had moved there. A class fellow of mine, Saran Gurdev Singh, whose father was posted as the Civil Surgeon at Jalandhar, would also visit his parents on weekends like me. I had to bid good-bye to the Khalsa College, Amritsar after the Intermediate examination.

I took admission in the DAV College, Jalandhar. It was left to me to choose my subjects. I decided to study English, Chemistry and Botany with Punjabi as my optional language. Since my father was posted in the Cantonment, I decided to become a day-scholar commuting daily to the college on a bicycle. There were two to three other boys from the cantonment who were commuting like me. I became quite popular with them when I narrated some of the smutty folk stories that had been narrated to me by Pal Singh. I continued my interest in the AISF but the students in the DAV College mostly Hindus were more serious-minded. Most of them made it plain that they were not interested in Marxism. The cadres of the Communist Party of India had gone underground after the failed Railway Strike in 1949. I was a communist sympathizer but not an activist. Another thing that I did was to study about sex. I read Van De Velde's book '*Ideal Marriage*'. I found in the college library Havelock Ellis's book '*The Studies in the Psychology of Sex*' on the shelf . I would read the tome in two volumes in the night when everyone in the house had gone to sleep. My mother, if she got up during the night, found me studying. She was very impressed by my studying hard. She told my father and my friends that I was studying really hard for my examination.

My attendance in college remained poor. Normally, I should have been detained in my class due to poor attendance. A sympathetic assistant clerk who held custody of the College Attendance Register helped me with this. Meanwhile, the relations between the Communist Party of India and the Government of India started improving. The Communist Party softened their policy a bit, which made the Government relent on the activities of the party as being legitimate political activities. Sohan Singh Josh, the top CPI leader of Punjab called a press conference at the hotel '*Rain Basera*' in Jalandhar City. Officially, he was still underground. He was not sure if he would be allowed to address the press conference. The party was not sure as to where to keep him when he came to Jalandhar. I was living with my father in the cantonment. The civil police generally did not look with suspicion on persons living in the cantonment. I offered to take him as my guest in our house. I told my parents that I had a friend coming to stay with me for the night. It was a grave risk that I was taking so far as the service of my father in the army was concerned. This was a streak in my character that would appear many a times but somehow Waheguru protected me from any serious harm. It happened when some banned posters and literature of the Communist Party had to be distributed. The literature consisting of pamphlets and posters was brought to my room in the hostel.

We got up around mid-night and completed our task of pasting Communist Party posters all over. I was a believing Marxist. I questioned myself as to why I was sporting a Sikh appearance with long hair and a beard. I decided to do away with it. I got a haircut and a close shave from a barber. It must have been in October 1949. I went on the weekend to look up my parents in the cantonment. My father who himself was clean-shaven said nothing. My mother reacted rather violently on seeing me. She said that she would not stay at Jalandhar if I remained clean-shaven and immediately left for Dhamot. I returned to my hostel. My father advised me to come back after some time but for the time being he asked me to not to visit them. He would off and on come to the college to see me. Two things happened while I was clean-shaven. There was a cold wave in December with almost arctic winds blowing in Punjab. I felt almost frozen on the ears. I had to go back to my turban to protect myself. The second incident happened when I sat in a *tonga* or 'hackney carriage'. There was a Sikh passenger too in the *tonga*. The driver, in order to balance the weight for the horse, asked the Sikh passenger to move forward from the backseat by addressing him respectfully as Sardar ji and to me he just addressed 'O Babu'. I felt slighted by his address. I therefore decided to re-grow my beard and hair. It was necessitated also by the fact that I had to go home to my mother after the examination where I anticipated some trouble if I remained clean-shaven.

The army in India was neglected after the British left. The salaries of the Commissioned Officers were revised downwards twice. It was the Pakistani aggression in Kashmir that saved the day for the army to some extent. The eyes of the people in India really opened only after the Chinese Army defeated the Indian Army ignominiously in 1962. Nehru was carried away by his rhetoric of peace and neutrality, so much so that he considered the expenditure on the army as superfluous. He promoted Generals who got the army to do other jobs like construction of housing, etc., to keep them usefully occupied during peacetime. My father could not afford to support me for another five to six years when my sisters and brother were growing up, demanding equal care for them. The problem of schooling of my brother got somewhat solved after my father got an English medium school started in the cantonment in his capacity as the Sub-Area Station Staff Officer and the Area Education Officer at Jalandhar. The school was mainly for the children of the army personnel but it also admitted others. The school soon flourished and it still exists.

There was a tragedy in our family around this time. My sister Surjit was taken ill. We took her to the Military Hospital where the doctors said that she had contacted tuberculosis. My mother took Surjit to our village where a doctor tried to treat her with traditional and *Ayurvedic* medicines. I rushed to Gharuan as soon as I was free. She apparently was waiting only to see me before she breathed her last. There came up a vacancy of a civilian teacher in the Army Hospital at Yol Camp near Dharamsala in the hills. I decided to try my hand on the job. I moved to Yol Camp that was a prisoners of war camp for the Italian prisoners of war during the Second World War. It was a beautiful small town. I was three months there. The army offered to take me on the rolls of the regular army. I got a strong urge to go for further studies. My father agreed to support me for a postgraduate degree. He made me promise that if Maan Singh went for higher education after his retirement from service I would support him. I resigned from my job of a civilian teacher in the army. My father developed some angina trouble in his heart.

5

The Aligarh Muslim University

He was sent to the Base General Hospital at Delhi Cantonment for his treatment. The postgraduate studies of the East Punjab University had not yet stabilized after Partition. I decided to try my luck for admission in some university in U.P. I filled up the admission form in Agra from where I came to Aligarh Muslim University. I met Dale Jagjit Singh from Jalandhar, who had taken admission in that University. I was impressed by his description of the university teaching and general atmosphere. I decided to apply for admission in the University for a double course of graduation in law and post-graduation in political science.

Sir Syed Ahmed Khan founded the Aligarh Muslim University for imparting modem education to Muslims who had suffered badly after the advent of the British.

The university although located in an area that could never be a part of Pakistan that was demanded by the Muslim League, became the brain trust for the Pakistan ideology. It were the bands of Aligarh students moving from village to village in Punjab that got the Muslim population lined up behind the Muslim League in 1946 assembly elections. Pakistan became a reality in 1947. Aligarh did not know how to adapt themselves with their sympathies for Pakistan and their location physically in India. The Government was aware of the dilemma that the Muslim students faced in Aligarh. They appointed an outstanding nationalist Muslim educationist Dr. Zakir Hussain as the Vice Chancellor of the university. The Communist Party of India thought that they had made a niche in the hearts of the Muslims as they had supported the demand of the Muslim League for Pakistan. They realized that after Pakistan coming into being there was a vacuum in the Muslim minds, which they planned to fill. We were asked to be more active in student politics. Some of their handpicked Muslim student activists and ideologues joined the Aligarh University. A number of left leaning professors were there from before as most of the pro-Pakistan dons had gone over to Pakistan.

I found the Aligarh University very different from the Punjab colleges. The Punjab University after the partition functioned only as a university. The new campus of the university at Chandigarh came into being much later. Islam is known for equality and brotherhood among the believers. These values seemed to have become a part of Muslim culture.

The first noticeable change from Punjab was an environment of courtesy and some sophistication in the daily lives of the people that we came across. I was told that Sir Syed Ahmed Khan had chosen the Oxford University as a model for the Aligarh University. There was a very good central library with an open shelf stacking system for books. There were adequate places to sit and browse books in the library. The system helped me a lot in organizing my studies. In addition every department had a seminar library that remained open till midnight.

The university had good facilities for sports. I took advantage of those facilities by joining tennis and horse riding. The university tried especially to recruit sportsmen from Punjab. Their captain of Hockey was from Punjab Sardar Gurdev Singh who happened to be posted as the Deputy Commissioner of Amritsar when Bhindranwale, the Sikh extremist leader had taken his abode in Akal Takhat building in the Golden Temple Complex in 1984. Soon after joining we had elections for the Student's Union. The nationalist minded students, the Hindu communalist students and the leftists combined to give a fight to the Muslim League sympathizers who had been getting elected to the Student's Union throughout. The canvassing for the elections was done in a very impressive manner. The candidates for the various posts circulated their bio-data listing their distinctions and achievements. The campaigning was extremely orderly in my two years in the university. Later, the atmosphere for the Union elections got somewhat disorderly . 1951 happened to be the first year when the Muslim League sympathizers were defeated. The ceremony that followed the declaration of results was very dignified. The winning candidate with his supporters went to the losing candidate's camp. There the losing candidate who handed over to him a list of his principal supporters congratulated him.

The group would come back to the winning candidate's camp. Whenever the students gathered in the Union Hall it would be the President of the Student's Union who would preside over the meeting even if the vice chancellor happened to be present.

We found that after some time we ceased to relish the hostel food. We had often to supplement our hostel meals from various small cafes located on the campus. I did not give up my habit of not attending classes but I devoted a lot of time in studying in the History and Political Science seminar room and in the main university library. I had casually come across a write-up about the Indian Administrative Service, the successor service to the Indian Civil Service, reputed to be the steel frame of the British colonial rule in India. I requested the Union Public Service Commission, responsible for recruitment to the IAS, to send me the syllabus for the competitive examination held for the selection of candidates for the IAS. I tried to cover the subjects that were prescribed for the IAS for my study in my M. A. class. Some of my friends knowing my habit of not attending many classes and sleeping till late in the mornings laughed when they came to know about my ambition. The important development that took place while I was studying for my M. A. classes was the death of Joseph Stalin the Soviet dictator followed by disclosure of the excesses and atrocities that were committed in Soviet Russia. This was the time when some of the former communists like Arthur Koestler, Ignazio Silone and Louis Fischer, etc., brought out the book "The God that Failed". The revelations and the contents of the book were shocking for me for whom the Soviet Union was the ideal. I could not swallow the idea that truth was a value that did not matter to the Communists. This was the time when I came across the book '*Karma Yoga*' by Swami Vivekananda. My father had hosted a tea in Jalandhar City on my passing the B.Sc. examination. He had gifted to me a small compilation of verses from the Granth Saheb with a commentary and explanatory notes. I started reading passages from it that I liked. I would hum some of those verses in the morning. As a communist I had turned to Marxism to explain all that was going on in the world around me. Suddenly I was face to face with a vacuum in its place. I started replacing Marxist views with the religious and spiritual worldview derived from Hindu and Sikh sources. Gandhi's autobiography *'My Experiments with Truth'* left a deep and abiding impression on me.

I visited Bassi Pathana on one of my vacation visits from Aligarh. It was mainly to meet my *mama*, mother's brother, Tara Singh, who had joined there as a *sepoy* clerk in the police. I met visiting my *mami*, a beautiful young girl from the neighbourhood. I just got bowled over on seeing her. My *mami* told me that she was studying in a school. Her father was a practicing lawyer from village Lassoi in Sangrur district. I told my *mami* that I liked the looks and the personality of the girl. My *mami* wrote to me in Aligarh that she talked to the girl who was a friend of hers. She said that the response of the girl towards me was also positive but it was the parents who decided such matters in our society. She said that she would talk to my mother about it. I came back to Aligarh to concentrate on my studies. I did extraordinarily well in my M.A. final examination. We had a *viva voce* examination of one hundred marks conducted by an external examiner. We were a class of about seventy students and the well-known Professor of Political Science Dr. V.K.N. Menon was the examiner. He would examine about 10 to 15 students in a day. I had gone to the Political Science Department just to watch what was going on when the Head of the Department saw me and said that the student who was to come for the test had not turned up so I could appear for the test. I hesitated a bit as my turn for the test was on the next day. He just insisted that I must appear as the examiner was sitting idle. I therefore went inside the examination room. Professor Menon started asking questions about the United Nations Organisation. I was fully prepared on the subject and I answered all the questions satisfactorily. Professor M. Habib, the famous historian, who was sitting with him, took over from him to test me if I really deserved a first class. I answered his questions well too. I was given 74 marks out of one hundred, which was a record. The Head of the Department escorted me outside and congratulated me on my excellent performance, which I attributed to the grace of God towards whom I had turned after a long time. This success further led to strengthening of my belief and faith in the Sikh Gurus and the *Granth Saheb*. The university gave about three weeks of time to prepare for the Law examination. Almost all of us studied Law only during those three weeks. I returned to Jalandhar towards the end of April.

6

The IAS Examination and Marriage

I started seriously considering marriage with the girl that I had met in Bassi Pathana. I sought the help of one of my uncles. He had married the younger sister of my mother. Convincing my parents about the suitability of the girl and the girl herself was not much of a problem. The father of the girl being a practicing lawyer was seen as an advantage as I could look forward to some help if I went into practicing law instead of service of the government.

The parents of the girl, whose name was Sukhdev Kaur, were reluctant in accepting the proposal for her marriage as they said that she was too young for marriage and secondly, their priority was to fix the marriage of their elder daughter who was of a marriageable age. The access of my *mami* to the family proved to be helpful. She was able to get all the ladies approve the match between Sukhdev and me. It took some more time to get the men agree to this proposal. Around August 1953, the father of Sukhdev, Sardar Kartar Singh advocate, accompanied by two of his friends and a cousin came to Jalandhar to formally propose the marriage of their daughter Sukhdev with me. They said that since their daughter was very young the formal marriage could take place after a year or so. Through my *mami* I came to know that Sukhdev was happy about our engagement. I made bold to write a letter to her, which I enclosed with my forwarding letter addressed to her father Sardar Kartar Singh seeking his permission to write to his daughter. He was good enough to break tradition and pass on my letter to Sukhdev. I was optimistic when I had written my letter to Sukhdev. I was delighted and on the ninth heaven when I got a loving reply from her. Thereafter, we started writing to each other regularly.

Sukhdev encouraged me to go all out for the IAS, etc., competitive examination. I went to Bassi Pathana and spent a happy day with the family of my wife to be. It became late in the evening while talking and meeting the family. I did not require much persuasion to stay for the night with them. I returned to Jalandhar the next morning, extremely happy with myself.

I went to appear in the Civil Services Competitive Examination in September-October 1953 at Simla, which was an Examination Center in Punjab that I had opted for. This was my first visit to Simla, the summer capital of India and Punjab. The center for my examination was in Saint Edwards High School. I enquired from a co-passenger in the taxi about the nearest hotel from the Examination Center. I lodged myself in that hotel a day before the examination was to begin. I went for a walk on the Mall Road in the evening.

I walked up to the popular place called the Ridge and returned to my hotel a bit early as I had to prepare myself for my examination.The examination, I found was in two spells with a gap of about a month. I had to come to Simla twice. I felt somewhat restive on my return to Jalandhar. My younger sister was about to complete her schooling and my younger brother was fast growing up. I felt confident about my success in the competitive examination for two reasons. First, I thought that Sukhdev, with whom I was exchanging love letters would prove to be lucky for me and second, my faith in the grace of the Waheguru had deepened and strengthened. I would daily pray for my success and visit *gurdwara* as often as I could, in the evenings mostly as I continued to be a late riser in the mornings. My prayers and wishes of Sukhdev brought success to me in the written examination. My interview date was 7th January 1954. I went to Delhi and booked myself in a hotel in the Chandni Chowk area of Delhi because there was a historic *gurdwara* located nearby.

It is the *Gurdwara* that marks the place where the ninth Guru of the Sikhs, Guru Tegh Bahadur was beheaded under the orders of the Mughal Emperor Aurangzeb in 1675. I visited the *Gurdwara* early in the morning to seek blessings of the Guru for my success in the interview. Meanwhile, we got an invitation from our university to come for the University Convocation to receive our degrees. I remember that it was the 28th of February 1954 when we had gone to receive our degrees to the convocation hall. As we were returning to our hostel, I met a group of my friends congratulating me on my success in the IAS examination. While we were in the convocation hall the morning newspaper had just reached Aligarh carrying my name as one of the successful candidates. However, there was a catch in it. The newspaper said that there were forty vacancies in the IAS and IFS. The result showed that my name was the 46th in order of merit. I would therefore have to go for the Indian Police Service or some other Allied Central Service. I did not like the prospect of joining the IPS although somewhat unthinkingly I had given IPS as my next choice after the IAS. On my return from Aligarh I had stopped at Delhi for the night. I had gone to the *Gurdwara* in Chandni Chowk for thanksgiving.

Everyone was happy over my success in the IAS examination. I also felt that Waheguru had blessed me in getting me selected for the IAS. There were only two *Jat* Sikhs who made it to the IAS in 1954. However, the situation, as it prevailed immediately after the declaration of result was that I might have to join the IPS. The parents of Sukhdev approached my father for an early marriage. I had nothing to do till September as the call for the IPS was expected to come only by September. I hinted to my father that we could agree to their proposal. Sardar Mohinder Singh Zaildar, the elder brother of Sardar Kartar Singh had come to Jalandhar with the proposal for marriage.

Zaildar Saheb took out his pocket diary and said that the marriage should take place on a Sunday for the sake of convenience of the relatives who worked in the government. He read out two three dates for Sundays out of which my father picked up Sunday, the ninth May 1954 for my marriage. It was decided that the marriage would take place from Gharuan, from where the groom's party would travel to Lassoi, a distance of about 50 kilometres. My father could get about a week's leave for my marriage. My mother and I moved to Gharuan to make all the arrangements that were required for the marriage. We had to hire a bus for the marriage party of about forty persons. My fiancee Sukhdev was a vegetarian and she did not like drinking alcohol. I decided to become a vegetarian and a teetotaler before my marriage. I also decided to go for the *Amrit* ceremony or baptism with a double-edged sword on *Baisakhi* that was on the 13th April at Akal Takhat, Amritsar. *Baisakhi* or the New Year according to the Indian calendar was the day in 1699 when Guru Gobind Singh had baptized the first five Sikhs into the *Khalsa* order. A few days before the marriage our friends and relatives started arriving at our house in Gharuan. My uncle Pal Singh also joined us for this occasion. We left Gharuan on the 8th of May for Lassoi by a bus and a car. I, as the bridegroom, sat in the car along with my close friends. We were to pass through Dhamot on way to Lassoi.

My *nana* insisted that we must have a short stopover at Dhamot. We were served tea and refreshment at Dhamot from where my *mamas* joined the party. Everyone was very impressed by the turnout of Pal Singh. We reached Lassoi towards the evening. Sukhdev's father and the elders of the village came out to receive us as we entered the village.

We were accommodated for the night at the village guesthouse called '*dharamshala*'. The bride's side had got professional caterers and cooks from Green Hotel, Patiala who served an excellent non-vegetarian meal but there was hardly anything for the vegetarians. I shared my table with the priest (*granthi*) who was also a vegetarian and we had to be satisfied with salad, curd and a sweet dish. The most auspicious hour for the Sikhs for anything is the early morning, just before dawn. I got up very early in the morning for the marriage ceremony. I had an early bath in the morning and I got dressed up for the occasion and sat waiting for being called for the marriage ceremony. I recited all the *Gurbani* verses prescribed for daily recitation of the devout Sikhs. It was only around nine o'clock that we were formally invited for the marriage ceremony. There was singing of *Asa-di-var* going on, as is the custom, in the morning in all the *gurdwaras*. The musicians appeared to be a makeshift group who lacked coordination. One or two from our side joined in the chorus singing of the *Asa-di-var*. (*Asa-di-var* is a composition of 24 cantos of Guru Nanak. It is sung daily in all Sikh congregations as the verses in *Asa-di-var* clear away various superstitions of the Hindus and the Muslims. The Sikh worldview is described very simply and directly.) I was asked to come and sit facing the *Granth Saheb*. After we had sat down, as we were required to sit, the priest asked us to stand up along with our parents to join in a prayer before *Waheguru* seeking His blessings for our marriage. After the marriage ceremony was over, Jia Lal Singh, my friend read a self-composed poem called '*Sehra*' which is a poem in praise of the bridegroom and his family. Normally, a poem is read for the bride too called '*sikhia*' or a lesson for the married life. Thereafter, when it was past ten o'clock the priest who had especially come to give a sermon on the sanctity of the Sikh marriage got up and started speaking. Everyone by that time was tired and hungry as the breakfast was to be served after the marriage ceremony.

This ended the ordeal for the marriage party. Thereafter, the guests from both the sides touched the heads of both the bride and the bridegroom with currency notes, which they then placed on our laps. These notes were collected by volunteers on both the sides and passed on to each of us. We found that the money thus received by us was sufficient for a week's honeymoon in a hotel in Simla. We returned with the bride in the evening. Women who were our guests or neighbours singing marriage folk songs received us. The women along with the barber woman and the family Brahmin woman performed various other ceremonies to welcome the bride while the '*mirasan*' sang. Everyone remained occupied till about midnight.

We had a short honeymoon in Simla. We stayed in the same room in which I had stayed earlier for my IAS examination. We returned to Jalandhar. We loved and liked each other. Our friends invited us for meals.

I tried to remain a vegetarian and abstained from taking alcohol for some time but somehow the rational part of my mind refused to accept such restrictions about eating and drinking as I could see that in Abrahamic religions there was no ban on meat eating and the Christians had no taboo against alcohol. One could not say that there were no persons of spiritual attainment among the followers of those religions. It was obvious to me that the religious attainment was linked to ones thinking and mind. The more a mind was kept clear of one's self or ego the more capable it became of grasping the truth or Reality in the words of John Hick. The religion is only a transformation of human mind from self-centeredness to Reality-centeredness or Guru-centeredness. Gurbani recognizes only two categories of human beings. They are either man-mukhs (guided by their minds) or gur-mukhs (guided by the Guru). By mind is meant a human organ responsible for a cumulative approach to the world around us acquired through personal experience and knowledge with one's self at the center. The aim is to become an instrument for the will of God while living the life of a householder in a station and society where God may choose one to place. Life is to be lived like the lotus flower in water remaining unaffected by water or like the crane in water swimming against the current without allowing water to wet its feathers. The SGGS verse at page 522 '*Nanak satguru bhetiyai poori hovai jugat, hasandian khelandyan painandian khavandian vichey hovai mukat*' meaning "by meeting the True Guru, one comes to know the perfect way. One gets one's salvation while laughing, playing, dressing and eating" further confirmed my faith in having a relaxed style in my day-to-day living. I literally adopted the popular saying about Guru Nanak's mission as my ideal which is in Punjabi, '*sach bolna te kamai karni dharma di, baba berha banne lavega*' (one should speak the truth and have an honest earning to sustain one self in the society and leave the crossing of the ocean of worldly existence to Baba Nanak who will take the ship across safely.) I as an officer of the IAS assumed as my mission to fight against injustice and ensure delivery of justice in all issues that came before me always working without favour or fear.

I got a letter in a thick envelope from the Government of India. I presumed that the letter was an offer of appointment in the IPS. When I opened the envelope after a week I was surprised to know that the letter was an offer of appointment for the IAS and I was asked to report for joining the IAS training school at the Metcalf House Delhi immediately after appearing in a medical test. I went to Amritsar for my medical examination. I was found medically fit. I could have reported for training at Delhi immediately but I decided to wait for a formal call from the Ministry of Home Affairs. I learnt that the Government of India was considering an increase in the IAS recruitment so that the annual intake could be raised to sixty from the existing current intake of 35 to 40. This was to come into effect in 1955. Some bright person in the Home Ministry proposed in the government file that since already it had been decided to increase the intake to sixty from the next year, the Government could take additional five or six who had qualified in 1954. This proposal was readily approved at all the levels, which brought me entry into the IAS.

7

The IAS Training

I reported for joining the Indian Administrative Service in the morning of 21st June 1954 at the IAS Training School located in Metcalfe House in Delhi. All the IAS and the four Indian Foreign Service trainee officers had gone to Jammu and Kashmir for a three-week attachment with the Army. There was only an administrative officer Mr. Mirchandani who was holding the fort. I was used to meeting army officers who wore their ranks on their uniforms. I thought that Mr. Mirchandani was a senior officer so I remained standing in his presence. He was visibly embarrassed by my deference. He would again and again ask me to sit down. I was asked to sign a Joining Report. I was told that in about a week the other trainee officers would be back. I was allotted a room in an Annexe. I used the week in roaming about in Delhi. The other trainee officers came back by the 25th, and I introduced myself to them. I was struck with a sense of inferiority on meeting my other fellow IAS officers as most of them came from public school backgrounds and they were more fluent in English. I generally moved about with the trainee officers who had a rural background like mine. The trainee officers were called IAS probationers as our appointment was on probation for one year, which meant that if our conduct during one year after joining the service was not found to be satisfactory, we could be sacked. Anyhow such a contingency rarely arose.

We were left to ourselves mostly so far as training was concerned. We were given a list of books to read and a syllabus covering the Constitution of India, Law of Crimes, Procedure and Evidence. We had to study Public Administration. I found that I did not have to study hard for anything as I had a good grasp of all the subjects due to my study for the Master's Degree in Political Science and Bachelor of Law. We had only a part-time Principal and a part-time Vice-Principal. Both of them, when they came to the IAS training school, tried to share their varied experiences in handling men and matters in the course of their service careers. They belonged to the Indian Civil Service. I found the environment to be ideal for me as a continuation of my student days. I attended only a few classes that I considered to be of interest to me. Our mess was adjacent to the classrooms. I would often be sipping tea in the mess lounge when classes would be going on in the adjacent rooms. I even did not refrain from having a dig at our Vice-Principal in answering one of his question papers. The Vice-Principal who joined towards the end of our training was one Mr. Vaghaiwalla, ICS, a Parsi gentleman. He would begin his class with what he called a thought for the day. It would often be a quotation from the Gita or other Hindu religious literature. There was a paper set by him. I knew that he would evaluate it. I therefore plagiarized a poem to begin my paper. It was titled as a 'Thought for the Day'. It said, "Do not search for the flaws as you go through it. If you really find them; it is wise and kind to be somewhat blind and look for virtue behind them." I was not present in the class when the VP returned those papers after marking. He called out my name but I was having tea in the lounge. He then told the probationers about my being cheeky even in an examination paper. He said that he was seriously considering recommending my name to the Government of India for termination of my probation in the IAS. He read out the poem that I had written. Everyone who heard liked it as relevant to the occasion. They immediately told me about the black mood of the VP as soon as the class was over. I allowed him some time to cool down before I went to him. He still seemed to be angry and asked me as to why I tried to make fun of him. I told him that during the short time that he had been with us he had completely identified himself with us more as a friend than as a boss. I had written the thought for the day hoping that he would like it. He let me off the hook telling me that I should realize that I was a student no more. I walked out of his room somewhat sobered by his advice.

We had every week formal dinners in the mess where we wore formal dress of closed-neck or Jodhpuri coat and trousers. A number of senior officers would be called to join us for such dinners for the purpose of exposing us to the service environment and the experience of those who had done well in service. We also had some outstanding personalities coming for delivering lectures to us on various topics considered as important or relevant for our training. We had with us Nirad C. Choudhury who had written the book that made him famous from being a retired low-level civil servant called the "Autobiography of An Unknown Indian". We enjoyed his lectures.

We also had K.M. Pannikar, who had been our ambassador to the communist China. He spoke more like China's ambassador to India than an Indian Ambassador to China. Very soon the Chinese taught us a lesson in 1962 and Pakistan has continued to be their closest ally in this region. The subsequent events proved that Nehru and his cohorts were living in a fool's paradise. We also had Mr. Banerjee, the UPSC Chairman, who had presided over the interviews for our selection to the IAS. We were curious to know as to how marks were awarded for the oral interview. He had brought with him the record sheets of our interview. He read out the assessment as was recorded on hearing that most of us had to agree that the assessments made were fair and objective. We were taken around on train visiting places of historical or cultural importance in the country. We saw Ajanta and Ellora Caves, Bombay, the commercial capital of India, Chittaur, Udaipur and Jaipur in Rajasthan. A funny incident of Bombay I find to be worth, our reserved first class railway compartments got parked at the Bombay Central Railway Station, which was the last railhead on the railway line. We had got tired of bathing cooped up in the railway toilet. We decided to go for a good bath in the railway first class waiting room presuming that the train would stay on the siding till our next move. We returned to the railway platform having towels around our waists. We were shocked to find that our train was nowhere to be found. We were quite a sight running about in the station in that awkward dress trying to find out as to where our train was. It was after some time that we learnt that our train had been taken to the siding for washing trains. We thanked our stars when we reached back to our compartments. We reached Udaipur, the capital of Rajputs who had defied the Mughals. We were introduced to a decrepit old man who was the erstwhile Maharana of Udaipur. The Maharana gave a broad smile of understanding of our position. We were lodged in the personal guesthouse of the Maharana where a few years earlier Lady and Lord Mountbatten had stayed. A lavish dinner was hosted in our honour in the evening. We were served choice drinks from the Maharana's cellar. We got one Mr. Radhakrisnan, ICS, as our whole-time principal about three months before the completion of our training. He was a Tamil Brahmin and like all Tamil Brahmins he was convinced that when the God Almighty distributed intelligence among humanity, he gave 95% of it to the Tamil Brahmins and the balance 5% was all that the rest of humanity got. I did not impress him. He wrote in his final assessment that I appeared to him to be a sub-standard material for the IAS whose performance was required to be watched. It was I who had the last laugh. My career profile came out to be the best among the 1954 Bihar cadre IAS officers that included two Tamil Brahmins.

We reported for our training in the State at Patna. We were attached to the Secretariat as Supernumerary Officers for four weeks; we called on the Chief Secretary Mr. L.P. Singh, ICS, a legendary character who had become Chief Secretary of the State when he had put in just 12 years of service because the Chief Minister was allergic to the presence of British ICS officers in Bihar. I found the climate and the official environment at Patna to be relaxed and friendly. We were daily invited to dinners to the houses of the senior ICS or IAS officers. Everyone talked of his prowess vis-a-vis the politicians. One Mr. C.K. Raman became our hero, as there were so many stories about him describing his incisive wit in making a fool of the political masters. One such story was of a cabinet meeting in which he was explaining some point when a minister said that he did not understand the point that Mr. Raman was making. Mr. Raman's repartee was that he could only provide the minister all the reasons for his point of view but he was unable to provide him understanding. Mr. C.K. Raman had a somewhat spoilt son. His teacher in the college did not sponsor his name for appearing in the University final examination. He came to know about it on the last day before the examination. He tried to throw his weight about on the Vice-chancellor of the University to over-rule the teacher but the VC refused to oblige. We had an ICS officer Mr. Narasimhan as the Chief Justice of the Patna High Court. Mr. Raman approached him to intervene late in the night.

The ICS Chief Justice convened the bench of the High Court to meet at his house late in the night and issued a writ to the Patna University to permit Mr. Raman's son to appear in the University examination to be held the next morning. The VC did not give up. He went in appeal against the High Court order to the Supreme Court of India. The Supreme Court reprimanded the Chief Justice and Mr. Raman in no uncertain words and reversed the order of the High Court. Mr. Raman became a laughing stock in Bihar as the judgment of the Supreme Court was reported in all the newspapers. Mr. Narasimhan, who was aspiring to be a judge of the Supreme Court had to quietly retire and go into oblivion. One of my batchmates categorized the ICS officers as either SOA or SOB. SOA was for stuffed old ass. I generally agreed with his assessment except that we had an outstanding officer in Mr. B.D. Pande, ICS, who later became the Cabinet Secretary in the Government of India and was appointed Governor of Punjab after retirement from service. The ICS had seen service when they were accountable only to their British masters who were themselves mostly career bureaucrats. The British allowed the Indian politicians very grudgingly particularly in the Congress dominated provinces to have some share in running the government. The power in the Central Government remained firmly in the British hands till the swearing-in of the Interim Government in 1946. A partial autonomy was given to the Provinces under the Government of India Act, 1935, with law and order remaining the responsibility of the British appointed Governor. The Congress had decided to give a try to the 1935 scheme of Provincial autonomy. Dr. S.K. Sinha became the first Chief Minister of Bihar in 1937. He had a brilliant Parliamentary Secretary in K.B. Sahay. One bright ICS officer Mr. Brett was the Chief Secretary. He came across a case where a minister on tour issued an oral order to a field officer, which he had hesitated to carry out. Mr. Brett dashed off a circular to all field officers in Bihar clarifying the statutory position that the oral orders of the minister could not be construed to be the government orders. The minister's orders became government orders only after the orders were formally conveyed to the officials through a written order signed by an officer not below the rank of an Undersecretary to the government. K.B. Sahay brought this order to the notice of the Chief Minister. Malafide was imputed to Mr. Brett in the issue of that circular which was legally correct but it was contended that the matter should have been brought to the notice of the Chief Minister before such a circular was issued. The Congress government threatened to resign on that issue. The British were keen that such a contingency should not arise as they wanted their scheme of Provincial autonomy to work. The Governor persuaded Mr. Brett to withdraw his circular so that a political crisis on the issue could be averted. Mr. Brett issued a letter withdrawing his circular but simultaneously he put in his resignation from the ICS and left for his home in the United Kingdom.

The Bihar Civil Service tradition was to keep a distance from the politicians. Yet, the system could not work unless the politicians and civil servants worked in tandem. Every successful civil servant evolved his own *modus vivendi* in achieving his objectives while working with the political masters. However, he would not share his experience with his colleagues. The IAS has by now existed for more than fifty years and this pretence can no longer be kept yet there is no consensus where the line or '*lachhman rekha*' between the politicians and the civil servants should be. The balance by now has clearly shifted in favour of the politicians. The conditions in provinces like Punjab were slightly better as the ruling party that emerged in Punjab was the Unionist Party consisting of landlords mostly, who were close to the British. The relationship of civil servants and politicians in provinces like Punjab was more even and relaxed.

I decided to adopt a principle or a talisman for me that I should not be associated in any action that I might not be able to own up in writing and I should not evade accountability for all actions performed under my explicit or tacit orders. Secondly, that I should be ready to do for a politician all that I could do for a friend or a relative. Thirdly, that I should master the laws and procedures of work in the government, so that it should be my writ that should run in the area of my responsibility and not the writ of the clerks who had the custody of papers and the precedents?

I had been sent to Darbhanga for my district training. I was received at the railway station of Laheria Sarai, the civil station for Darbhanga, by the district *Nazir,* who had come with a liveried peon to receive me. I was very respectful to him as I thought that he was a big official of the district.

I later learnt that *Nazir* meant that he was a clerk assigned for protocol duties of the district. The District Magistrate was a former Professor of Economics, Mr. Sachin Dutt. He almost made me a member of his family. He would encourage me to sit with him when he inspected an office, or met a political leader, or dictated an important report to the government. I found that with politicians his attitude was to get around them through his sharp intellect and to accommodate them, by bending the rules slightly in their favour, sometimes at the cost of the public exchequer like, when he would recommend grants for flood relief for an area that had not suffered from floods in the district. There was a bye-election for an assembly seat in the district. It was for Benipatti in Madhubani subdivision. He sent me there to act as a presiding officer for the conduct of poll. I saw at firsthand how the local politicians tried to bully government officials to keep their eyes closed when they brought bogus voters for polling. In one incident, the politicians were able to collect a crowd of protesters over one of my orders, which brought the District Magistrate to my polling station. I told him about the attempt to get a minor to vote was the reason for the protest. He listened to me but he did not want to buy any trouble with the local politicians. He overruled my order and bought peace.

I went through my attachments with the various departments of the district office learning the nitty-gritty of the administration at the district level. Meanwhile, my wife also joined me. Her uncle who was a *Zaildar* of the village escorted her to Laheria Sarai. He understood the working of the administration at the lower levels very well and he gave me valuable advice as to how to control lower subordinates who were corrupt and greedy. We had a problem with him as the Circuit House where we were staying had only European style flush toilets. He saw the same and he refused to go in. We had to arrange for a jeep vehicle every day to take him to the fields outside the town for his morning ablutions. He had moved out of Punjab for the first time in his life. He was fascinated by his journey by motorboat for crossing the Ganges River, as there was no bridge on the Ganges throughout its length in Bihar. He also observed that the grinding poverty that he had seen in Bihar was nowhere to be seen in Punjab.

Bihar has about 15% Muslims in population. There were communal riots in Bihar in retaliation of the East Bengal riots perpetrated by the Muslim League in 1946. The most sensitive issue in the situation was the slaughter of cows by the Muslims at the time of *Id-ul-Zuha* or *Bakr-Id*. Darbhanga was considered a sensitive district from the Hindu-Muslim communal angle. There were more than fifty places in the district where it was feared that riots might break out during *Bakr-Id*. The District Magistrate deputed a Magistrate with a section of armed police in all these places as a precautionary measure. I was deputed to a village in the interior of Darbhanga called Bharwara. I went to that village with another Magistrate in a jeep vehicle. The police parties had already reached there. There were three to four villages that I was to look after. As per government instructions, I called the opinion leaders of both Hindus and Muslims to explain to them the government policy. There was no ban against slaughtering cows or calves but in order to keep the situation under control the government had ordered that cow-slaughter would be permitted only if it was customary in a particular place to slaughter a cow or a calf at the time of *Bakr-Id*. The Muslims insisted in the meeting that they had been slaughtering a cow on the occasion of *Bakr-Id* and they said that they could prove it. The Hindus in the meeting contested the claim of the Muslims. After the meeting dispersed I told the police officer that to me it appeared that the local Muslims were going to sacrifice a cow. I told him that we should stop it by passing a formal legal order banning cow-slaughter in the village. The Sub-Inspector of police who was in charge of the armed police force was very reluctant to enforce the legal prohibitory order. I got my force ready early in the morning and got them paraded in the three villages considered as sensitive. It was all quiet and peaceful everywhere. I returned to my camp by around ten o'clock. Just when my meal was brought to my table, a villager came running. He said that the Muslims of Maheshpatti, a village adjacent to Bharwara had sacrificed a cow. I asked my police force to get ready for going there. They were still cooking in the kitchen in their underwear. Meanwhile, the village watchman also came running to tell me that the Hindus of Bharwara had come to know about the killing of the cow and an armed mob of Hindus had collected for attacking Maheshpatti. I did not wait for my police constables to get ready. I proceeded for Maheshpatti following the village watchman through a footpath that was a short cut. I saw a Hindu mob armed with sticks and other lethal weapons preparing to attack Maheshpatti. I asked them to disperse immediately. They just gaped at me. I had a small baton in my hand. I rushed with my baton on the man nearest from me and hit him squarely on his head. He shouted a cry and ran away. On seeing him running the entire mob that had collected started running. I chased them for a short distance. I then advanced towards Maheshpatti. I saw that at some distance from me a Muslim mob similarly armed had collected too. They started running as soon as they saw me turning towards them. They too disappeared into the village bye-lanes. I saw some thick smoke coming out of a nearby hut. I turned towards that and saw that nearby another police officer with a loaded revolver in his hand was standing with three rifle bearing police-men surrounding him. His hand holding the revolver was trembling and he was perspiring profusely. I asked him as to what he was doing. He mumbled that he was afraid for his life from the Muslim mob. I asked him about the thick smoke. He said that the cow was sacrificed was in hut. I got slightly afraid as the entire village consisted of only thatched huts that could catch fire from the one fire that was smoldering. I rushed towards the hut that was smoldering and saw a young calf with its neck half cut lying inside. I immediately caught hold of one or two men nearest to me and asked them to take water from a nearby pond and start extinguishing the fire. I found that somehow they did not have their heart in extinguishing that fire. I could see some Hindus peeping at us from the other side of the village. I waved to them and they came running. Meanwhile my police party too joined us. We had no buckets to bring water from the pond after the earlier Muslim volunteers had run away which gave me an impression that the fire to the hut was the handiwork of the Muslims to make a counter case against what they had done. The policemen with the Hindu volunteers got the fire under control within no time. My priority was to save the village from fire. The villagers brought out a chair and a small stool for me. I sat down and drafted an order under section 144 of the Criminal Procedure Code banning cow slaughter in the area and prohibiting a gathering of five or more persons. I handed over the piece of paper with my signature on it to the Sub-Inspector of the police. He looked at it and asked me as to what he should do with it. I told him that it was the first order that I had passed in my capacity as a Magistrate of the First Class and I did not know as to what was to be done with it. He also said that this was the first case for him also as he was not from the regular police force. He was from the home guards. He walked four kilometres to a place where a regular police officer was located and returned with the information that the promulgation of the order passed by me had to be done through a beat of drum in the village. I started enquiring about the incident, as I had to send a report to the District Magistrate. I found that the village had a history of communal tension. Some years back there was a case of rioting also for which there were cases going on in the courts. The Muslims sacrificed cows in every *Bakr-Id* but the police refused to record it as being customary for the Muslims. The police while prosecuting Hindus and Muslims discriminated against the Muslims in booking them for severer offences and in booking all the Muslims considered respectable as against booking only the menials and servants from the Hindu side. My factual report to the District Magistrate resulted in both sides getting treated similarly and equally for the first time that opened the eyes of both the communities. They worked out a compromise and as I learnt later, the village remained free from communal tension thereafter. The incident taught me that the police, as an instrument of the government, was undependable in maintaining public peace as it suffered from a bias in favour of what they considered to be the rulers or for their own interests and beliefs.

I had to spend a week in Bharwara, meanwhile Sukhdev stayed as a guest in the house of Mr. Sachin Dutt, the District Magistrate. There was heavy rainfall during this period. This was a new experience for me. The whole of North Bihar is like a huge saucer placed North of the Ganges below the Himalayan foothills. There are rivers like Kosi, Baghmati, Kamla Balan,and Gandak that drain out water from the North but during the Monsoon rains water fills-up the saucer that is North Bihar. This being an annual phenomenon, the people of the area remain prepared for it. They moved to higher grounds that often happened to be the raised embankments of the railway lines. They ate crushed rice called '*choorha*' with milk curd and waited for the floodwaters to recede. The receding floodwaters left their fields richer and more fertile as a layer of silt got deposited on the fields that contributed to an increased yield the next year. The villagers had very little possessions in their houses since they were used to leaving their houses at a very short notice. When clearance came for me to leave Bharwara, the whole area was flooded and there was no sign of any roads. I had to hire a boat to take me to Laheria Sarai and the journey took one whole day. The introduction of vote for political power made the political leaders vie with one another in seeking material and monetary relief for the flood victims from the Central Government. The teams of officials sent by the Central Government, were often moved by the plight of the people living on railway embankments. They recommended liberal relief for the sufferers and an idea got floated for raising Kosi embankments on both the sides to control floods and to channelise the excess water into a canal. The implementation of these ideas has caused more harm than good to North Bihar. The rich silt from the foothills no longer is available for farming. The Kosi canal while benefiting farmers in Purnea district has led to waterlogging and desertification in a larger area of North Bihar. The sturdy peasantry has acquired the habit of begging for their needs and of looking to the government for a redress of their real and sometimes imagined hardships. The contractors and middlemen have corrupted the administrative system. If a balance sheet is drawn for all that has been done since Independence, it would surely turn out to be a negative balance sheet clearly in the red.

I completed my six months district level training at Laheria Sarai and received orders to move to Purnea for our land survey and settlement training. It was Todar Mal, the Revenue Minister of the Mughal Emperor Akbar who had started the system of land surveys through simple instruments in order to have an accurate record of ownerships of landholdings. The British made it a bit more sophisticated and added to it a comprehensive record of rights based on the tenancy laws of the area. We in Punjab mostly had peasant proprietors who collectively owned all the land of the village. The revenue authorities always kept the land records up-to-date. The British had gone for the *Zamindari* system in Bengal and Bihar.

This meant that the Government gave large tracts of land to a few persons through bidding or otherwise. They were accountable to the Government for payment of land revenue by a fixed date every year, failing which, under the Sun Set Law, their lands would stand confiscated to the Government. It was the responsibility of these *zamindars* or landlords to get their lands cultivated by tenants. Most of the *zamindars* had intermediaries called tenure holders or sub-tenure holders through whom tenants were settled on the land. The Bihar Tenancy Act, 1885 was promulgated to protect tenants from eviction at the whims of the tenure-holders or the *zamindars*. The tenants often had subtenants or share-croppers doing the actual cultivation. The Government prepared an authoritative record of rights once in about 35 years. The position was made more complicated by the social structure and customs prevailing in rural Bihar.

The Bihar Government, without giving adequate thought to the complications involved, passed the Bihar Land Reforms Act in 1946, giving the right to ownership of land to the tiller. The law was hailed as the most progressive land reforms law in India. It was our duty during the survey and settlement operation to prepare the Record of Rights in accordance with the new law. The survey and settlement operation involved five stages of work. A map was prepared field by field in the first stage. A Record of Rights field by field was prepared in the next stage. The records prepared were attested in the third stage after hearing and disposing off objections in the presence of the village community. A Judicial Officer heard appeals against the attested records in the fourth stage. The fifth stage was the final publication of the land records that carried a presumption everywhere of being authentic until proved otherwise in a court of law. We had gone for our training when attestation of records was going on. I had my headquarters in an *ex-zamindari* building located at Kajha Katcheri. I lived in a tent and toured about on a bi-cycle. I had to attest the records of about twenty villages that included Parora, a stronghold of *Bhumihar* landowners. I found that the records prepared in the earlier stage reflected more the wishes of the landowners than the actual position. It would come out in hearings in the presence of the village community that the person in whose name the land was recorded did not cultivate that land. Sometimes the tenants were so afraid of the landowner that they preferred to forgo their rights than incur the wrath of the landowner. Many a times having satisfied ourselves about the actual cultivator of the land, we would record the land in his favour. Little did I know that all our efforts were going to be of no avail as the state power was firmly in the hands of the bureaucracy, mostly belonging to the upper four castes and the Chief Minister was a *Bhumihar* whose caste men were notorious land grabbers in rural Bihar. So, the so-called most progressive land reforms law became a dead letter. Neighbouring West Bengal brought their land reforms much later after the Marxists came to power but their implementation of the law was much more effective as the Marxist Party cadres joined the cultivators to ensure that the lower revenue functionaries did not come in the way of the land going to the tiller although the Chief Minister came from the exploiting '*Bhadra Lok*' or the upper caste. There is no doubt that communism had changed the Communist Party workers in their thinking and their deeds. The Congress leaders pretended to follow Gandhi but they would not go beyond lip service. They continued to be guided by caste considerations and they would flout all laws to remain in possession of their illegally grabbed lands. The land reforms or social reforms stood no chance of success in such an environment. One could, in the beginning, come across a few genuine followers of Gandhi but with the passage of time such believers in Gandhi got thrown overboard. The only visible sign that remained was the *Khadi* Gandhi cap. The other problem was the rampant corruption among the lower functionaries involved in the operation. We would hold open courts under a tree or some other place located conveniently in the village. We would encourage them to tell us if any of our staff had made any demand for illegal gratification. If we received any complaint we would hold an enquiry on the spot and if any of our staff was found guilty, we would punish him right in presence of the villagers often removing him from service there and then. Once a farmer came to me for a small correction in the village map as a corner of his field was shown as a part of his neighbour's field. The map was prepared during the first stage of the survey operation and the same '*amin*' or the draftsman had prepared the record in the second stage called '*khanapuri*'. The villager told me that he had requested the '*amin*' to make the necessary correction in the map but he refused to oblige him. When the villager told him that he would seek redress of his complaint from his superior officer, the '*amin*' told him that the officer had to supervise the work of one hundred '*amins*' and he may take a month to come to his village. The '*amin*' said that by the time the officer came to the village he would get his whole plot of land to disappear from the map. Therefore, he said that he got reconciled to the loss of one corner of his field rather than forgo the whole of it as was threatened by the '*amin*'. He felt encouraged to seek redress from me because of my open dealings and open invitation to the villagers to complain if they had any grievance.

We were posted-out as soon as the working season of the survey and settlement operations was over. It was expected that I would go back to Darbangha but the Bihar Government changed their mind about my posting. I was sent to Sarath block in Deoghar sub-division of Santhal Parganas district to familiarize myself with the community development work, which was a new programme, launched to transform the lives of the villagers in India who constituted more than 80% of its population. The villagers required being motivated to go for what they considered good for themselves. They instead got something that the self-appointed experts considered good for them.

They were not asked to contribute 50% for the facilities being provided which surely they had neither asked for nor did they intend to make any use of those. It was a sheer waste of effort and resources contributing to inflation that hit the fixed salaried workers adversely and cost the country dear. We were helpless and on the defensive as the entire bureaucracy had become a suspect for far as amelioration of the condition of poor was concerned. I had not yet develped enough confidence to take on the personalities like S.K. Dey to enjoy the backing of no lesser person like Jawaharlal Nehru, the Prime Minister. Our vice-principal Mr Vagaiwallla had tried his best to brainwash us completely during our training. It was clear that his posting as vice-principal by the Governement was done on purpose. I think that the ICS steel frame got their first blow when they permitted such wooly-headed policies being executed with all the fan-fare.

8

As Sub-Division Officer, Deoghar

I was posted as Sub Divisional Officer, Deoghar in June 1956. Deoghar is also known as *Baidyanath Dham*. It is one of the 68 holy places of the Hindus. The sub-division is now a district. It had a population of about a million out of which the urban population accounted for about a hundred thousand, distributed over three towns namely Deoghar 60,000, Madhupur 30,000 and Jasidih about 10,000. Deoghar was one of the six sub-divisions of the district of Santhal Parganas with headquarters at Dumka. The tribal population in Deoghar was less than 20 percent. It consisted mainly of *Santhals* with only a sprinkling of *Mai Paharias* on the border. The administration was run on paternalistic lines. The Sub Divisional Officer enjoyed powers under the Criminal Procedure Code, the Civil Procedure Code and the Santhal Parganas Tenancy Act. Criminal and civil cases were heard at Deoghar but revenue cases were heard in camps in the interiors where appearance of professional lawyers was barred. The Sub Divisional Officer was also the custodian of the Currency Chest on behalf of the Reserve Bank of India, which meant that the banks in the subdivision, if they ran out of cash, would draw currency notes from the Currency Chest to meet their commitments and the Reserve Bank would include the amount drawn in the total for the currency in circulation. The police had a Deputy Superintendent of Police as their Chief who was accountable to the Sub Divisional Officer. The Sub Divisional Officer had a set of six to seven State Civil Officers to assist him.

Deoghar was comparatively a peaceful sub-division. The center of attraction in Deoghar was the *Baidyanath Shiva temple* that was managed by hereditary priests. They shared the offerings from the devotees in proportion to the hereditary rights of the various priest families called '*pandas*'. They had a vested interest in keeping egress and ingress to the temple dark and narrow so that devotees could go inside to offer prayers only with the assistance of the pandas. The pandas had opposed tooth and nail the proposal to install electric lights inside the temple.

The '*lingam*' of Shiva that is worshipped as a symbol in the temple in Deoghar is somewhat unique, as it does not protrude out and it is embedded in stone around. The legend is that Ravana, the demon in the epic *Ramayana* had pleased Shiva with his worship and austerities. Shiva granted him a boon that he would go with him to Lanka, his kingdom but he laid a condition that he should be taken to Lanka in one go without a stop on the way. He said that if he stopped on the way, he would go no farther. The Hindu gods who were upset over Lord Shiva going to Lanka as it would make Ravana invincible, conspired to make Ravana stop for a pee. He could not pee holding Shiva's *lingam* in his hand. He handed it over to a Brahmin nearby who was a god in disguise. He shouted to Ravana while he was peeing who could not hear him because of the pressure in his bladder. He, thereafter, placed the *lingam* on the ground. When Ravana tried to pick it up, it would not move. Ravana, out of frustration and anger, pressed the *lingam* down, stamping it down with his foot with full force and the *lingam* got [1] embedded in stone. It is the only Shiva *lingam* that is worshipped in this manner. I was pleasantly surprised to know from an *Udasi sadhu* that Guru Nanak had visited *Baidyanath Dham* during his journey to the Eastern part of India. A small room with a copy of the *Guru Granth Saheb* commemorates the visit of Guru Nanak.

My wife joined me in Deoghar after spending somewhat unhappy six months with my mother. My father had retired from service in 1956 and he had taken a house on rent in the newly upcoming capital town of Punjab called Chandigarh, Chandigarh was the first city designed by the famous French architect Le Carbusier. We were young and we occupied the centre of the stage in Deoghar. We lived in an old house built in the early nineteenth century with a huge compound, most of it being a forest. The grave of the British Sub Divisional Magistrate killed in the Santhal Uprising in 1856-57 was also located in this compound. We put up a badminton court with electric lights in our compound where a number of our friends would join us for a game of badminton. The posting at Deoghar did not have problems except for the frequent visits of the VIPs for worship at the temple.

The most important work done during my tenure as the Sub Divisional Officer was the conduct of the 1957 General Elections. I was appointed as the Returning Officer, for the constituency covering the entire Sub Division. I found that the work of the conduct of elections was in a mess. The Constitution of India made every citizen, who was above 21 years old (now 18 years) a voter. We had to group about 1000 voters for a polling station so that there was an orderly poll everywhere. Sometimes we had to join together voters of 5 to 6 villages to establish a polling station at a place, which was central and convenient for all the voters. I, undertook to visit every polling station personally. This lasted for more than two weeks. A fortuneteller, came to our house and on seeing my wife, he predicted that she was going to have a son and, after that, I was to be transferred. It was a normal routine for IAS officers that after doing a sub division for one or one and a half years, they were transferred for doing a stint at the State Secretariat as Undersecretaries but this fortune teller was categorical that I should be going South on my posting whereas Patna the state capital was in the North. Both the predictions came out to be true.

I enjoyed the work of a Sub Divisional Officer. I had about 25 clerks, who kept records of the criminal, civil and revenue cases. I came to know that a fixed sum of money was paid to the clerks for getting copies of records or for getting bills passed in the Government Treasury. This petty corruption, had been the bane of the Indian administration from the earliest times to date. It could not be stopped so far.

The limited success that I had was, to ensure that the clerks who sat on desks did their work efficiently without causing any harassment to the public because if I received any complaint, about delay in their department, I would simply transfer them to a department, where there was no money under the table. It was a contingency that they dreaded. I could, therefore, work without fear or favour. I found that my impartiality and my independence in decision-making earned a lot of goodwill from the people. I made it my objective in my administration, that I shall ensure efficient and effective delivery of services and the redress of all grievances with full protection to the subordinate officials, who did their work honestly and faithfully. I found that my official work and the style of my working, made me popular among the general public which in turn, brought me the appreciation of the political leaders of the area.

I took a break after the General Elections to visit Punjab. During the break I met a fortune teller. He cautioned me to be a bit careful particularly during the last week of April. It was a casual meeting when the observation was made. On my return from Punjab, towards the end of April 1957, I suffered a serious accident while driving a jeep during the very week, about which I had been cautioned. My wife and my father reached Deoghar the next day. The Bihar Government flew in two top doctors from Patna for my treatment. They examined me and advised my shifting to Patna for treatment. I was moved to Patna Medical College Hospital by train accompanied with one doctor, my wife and my father. This was the time when Sukhdev must have been quick with her child in the womb and my son Birender born on the 7th September 1957. I returned to Deoghar after a fortnight in the Patna hospital.

My father, though retired from the army, was physically quite fit. Somehow he found the life of a retired army officer living with his son somewhat hanging heavy on him. When my transfer orders came for me to move to Ranchi as an Assistant Development Commissioner to Ranchi in December 1957, he decided to move to our village Gharuan along with my mother. He was elected *Sarpanch* or the headman of the village council called *Panchayat*. He remained a *Sarpanch* of the village so long as he lived till January 1979.

I moved to Ranchi where my job was to oversee development in some eighty-community blocks. The work involved a lot of touring in the Chota Nagpur Division. Chota Nagpur was the most beautiful and picturesque area of Bihar with a network of excellent roads. The road network came because during the Second World War the

British had selected this area for training the army that was to fight the Japanese. The most important work that I did was to expose a fraud being committed by a set of officers and a few contractors in the name of the community development work in Mahuadanr block of Palamau district. The schemes prepared centrally. The local people, mostly tribal were very poor and they had not expressed any desire for the works that had been devised for them. Officials and contractors combined to show false execution of works and to draw the sanctioned funds against such execution. The money drawn was distributed among the officials involved. A visit to the actual location of the works exposed the conspiracy and the fraud. The whole set of officers and contractors were prosecuted for conspiracy and fraud. I had a short stint at Chaibassa, the headquarters of Singhbhum district, as a Charge Officer in the Survey and Settlement operation. Nine officers of the 1957 batch of the IAS were placed with me for training. Our six-month association on this assignment made us lifelong friends as close as batch-mates. The Settlement Officer was one promoted officer Mr. J.P. Singh, gave a gem of an advice for success in the civil service. He said in Hindi that an officer must be '*baat cheet men chust aur kaam men sust magar kagaz rakhe drust*'. Our daughter Rosy, later named Prabhsaran Kaur was born in Chaibassa on 1 September 1959. The delivery took place at our residence.

I got my posting as a District Magistrate in 1960 when I was posted as Collector of Shahabad. The district officer is called Collector in what were known as the regulated areas and Deputy Commissioner in areas that were the non-regulated areas. The whole of Punjab fell in the non-regulated area. The whole of Bihar except for Chota Nagpur and Santhal Parganas fell in the regulated area. Shahabad was a huge area with about three and a half million population extending from the Ganges River in the North to the Kaimur Plateau in the South. The boundary in the East was up to the Son river and in the West was the river Karamnasa and the Ganges. It was an area more or less like Punjab. A part of the district was covered by the Son Canal, making it agriculturally the most productive district of Bihar. The district had been selected in consultation with the Ford Foundation of USA as a model district where a modem package of agricultural practices were to be introduced to ensure the maximum agricultural production. One district with the maximum potential was selected in each state to serve as a model. Ludhiana in Punjab had been similarly selected. Ludhiana became a model district for the entire country but Shahabad showed only a slight improvement for the reasons narrated and for the lack of infrastructure support in Bihar.

I also noticed that the Bihar environment required a tight control if public peace was to be maintained. Any slackening of the tight leash would result in everyone for one's own self and devil take the hindmost due to the weakness of the social fabric. I came across a report of looting of a local trader by a notorious gang of robbers. The gang collected a booty of a million rupees but the leader of the gang got only a sum of fifteen hundred rupees as his share. I advised the district police chief to use his intelligence to set up an encounter with the robbers during their operation of robbery. Bihar police was not used to such measures and our first and last attempt in setting up an encounter led to a disaster resulting in our police decoy getting killed in the crossfire, leaving us all red faced. We had succeeded in nabbing the leader of the gang, one Lallan Singh. I was surprised to find that among others arrested in that operation, there were two regular college going students.

One faceoff against recalcitrant farmers who were instigated to not to pay canal revenue was interesting. My predecessor in office had avoided taking any action in the matter as according to him if the administration pressed for forcible collection of canal revenue, the farmers would resist with full force and the police might have to open fire in which some farmers might get killed. He wanted the Government to give him in writing that the Government would stand by him if there were such an eventuality. No reply came from the Government, so no action was taken. As the District Magistrate, it was my duty to collect canal revenue and the law gave me powers to get the revenue collected by force if the farmers did not pay it willingly. I decided to visit the village. I had taken with me the canal officials and other staff so that if the villagers had any grievances the same could be redressed on the spot. We had a long meeting. An old farmer at that stage got up to address me. He said that their village had stopped paying canal revenue on the call given by the socialist leader Ram Manohar Lohia and they had resisted paying canal revenue for the last ten years. He said that if I wanted to really collect revenue from them then I should do something that I would show that they were men of some courage and standing and the Collector was a he man and a hero. I ordered a company of the Bihar Mounted Police to join the police force in the village and start operation against the worst dodger.

The farmer called himself '*kaljugi hanuman*' that is the modem day monkey God. He jumped to the roof of his house, where he was nabbed. This demoralized the other villagers and they started paying the arrears of their canal revenue. A problem that had festered for ten years got resolved once and for all.

I had set about my work in Shahabad with a great commitment and devotion. I tried to master the nitty-gritty of the district administration. I inspected almost all the subordinate offices. During my inspections I tried to see that all offices maintained their records properly and they delivered the services that were expected from them efficiently and smoothly. I inspected even the departments that were not directly under me like the Police and Excise. We thoroughly enjoyed our stay and *shikar* on the Rohtas hills while creating a sort of record by being the first District Magistrate to visit and inspect the block and the police station after Independence. It was interesting that the boundary of the district in the North was the mid-stream of the Ganges. The Ganges after entering Shahabad at Buxar got split into a number of streams spread over a vast stretch of land that was called '*Diara*'. Every year, after the end of the Monsoon rains, joint inspection teams of the Collector of Ballia in Uttar Pradesh and the Collector of Shahabad in Bihar would set off in boats, taking measurements of the depth of water in each stream. The stream that was found to be the deepest was declared to be the boundary between Uttar Pradesh and Bihar. Ganges had been moving a bit northwards for some years, adding additional area to Bihar. The Bihar farmers stood to benefit every year. The Collector of Ballia would avoid constituting a joint team every year. I succeeded in persuading him to constitute such a team. When he discovered that the deepest stream would deprive farmers of Uttar Pradesh of a considerable parcel of land, he would try to help them by providing them with a backing of the Police. I wrote to him that his action was illegal and that the Bihar Police had been given orders to protect the area that had come to Bihar. He had to withdraw the police force. The Uttar Pradesh Government appealed to the Central Government. The Central

Government appointed a one-member tribunal under Sir Chandu Lai Trivedi, ICS, to arbitrate in the matter. We had a number of meetings, alternately in Uttar Pradesh and Bihar.This problem ended once and for all when the arbitrator decided that there should be a permanent boundary between Uttar Pradesh and Bihar.

Chief Minister Shri S.K. Sinha, I discovered acted like the erstwhile British Governors. He occupied the whole of the Circuit House which served as the official guesthouse. No one had access to him except the Collector and the district police chief. Congress leaders had to seek an appointment from the Collector to see the Chief Minister. When he addressed them he sat on a chair while all his partymen sat on the ground. He would call the police chief with his first name. He was a stickler for propriety.

He was a Diabetic. A doctor accompanied him wherever he went for food, to give an insulin injection.

The district police chief, who met me frequently, once said that Sahu Jains of Dalmianagar also called Dehri-on–Son, were very arrogant but they were too powerful for the district administration as they had direct access to the Chief Minister. He told me that there was a violent incident involving an ex-employee and the top officials of the Sahu Jains. The police had booked the accused persons from both the sides but on the intervention of top officials from Patna the cases had been withdrawn. The police chief said that the local police at Dalmianagar had received two complaints against some top officials of Sahu Jain, he had, therefore, directed the local police to ask for a bond from both the parties to keep the peace. I almost exulted on receiving this information and rushed to inform the Commissioner Mr S.V. Sohoni, ICS. The Commissioner, who knew more about it, just smiled. I told the police chief that I would see how the Government in Patna came to the rescue of the Sahu Jain officials. The Commissioner asked me to take a personal interest in the case instead of leaving the same to the Sub Divisional Magistrate, who was a newly recruited officer, on his first posting. I called for copies of all the papers concerned with the case to be given to me for my study. Meanwhile, what the police was doing was that they would get all the nine or ten top officials to the court at Sasaram at 10 a.m. when the court opened and make them wait under a nearby tree for the whole day and announce at the end of the day that the case had been adjourned to the next day. When I went through the papers, it became obvious to me that the entire case against the Sahu Jains was a trumped up case. On enquiries I also learnt that a politician, close to the Chief Minister and friendly with the district police chief, was trying to extort money from Sahu Jains. The Sahu Jains in the normal course contributed to the Congress Party but the demands made by this politician were so heavy that they preferred to face the harassment being inflicted on them rather than pay the money demanded. I felt very bad over my unwittingly becoming an instrument for such illegal extortion. I wrote a mild letter to the Government with a copy to the Commissioner that a mistake got committed in launching prosecution against the Sahu Jains and that such an action by the police had brought a bad name to the Government in the eyes of the general public. The Commissioner wrote to the Government that he did not agree with my views and according to him the law should take its course, which in other words meant that the harassment to the Sahu Jains should continue. He sent a copy, of his letter to the Government, to me. It pushed me with my back to the wall. I sat down and marshalled all material that supported my views in the matter. I also consulted the District Public Prosecutor. He fully endorsed my stand and recommended withdrawal of the prosecution of Sahu Jains. I told my wife, on the day that I signed my letter recommending withdrawal of the prosecution of Sahu Jains, that she should start packing as I expected to be transferred out of the district soon. She never complained nor did she ask me to be cautious or accommodative for the wishes of the powers that be. The Chief Secretary called me to Patna to tell me that I had incurred the anger of the Chief Minister for what he thought as having made a foolish recommendation to withdraw a case that was sub-judice. I explained to the Chief Secretary as to how I had been taken for a ride in endorsing a false prosecution. He saw the papers and said that what I had written could have serious implications. It seems that after meeting me the Chief Secretary got worried about facing the Chief Minister. He called the Home Secretary while I was sitting with him and asked him as to what he should do. The Home Secretary told him that they should ask the police intelligence chief to give them a report in the matter. The Chief Secretary gave a sigh of relief in endorsing his advice and dismissed me from his presence. My transfer orders came soon thereafter. Most of my senior and wise colleagues thought that I was rash in getting involved in a police matter where it was not necessary for me to intervene. I got posted as a Deputy Secretary in the Finance Department. I felt bad about it because the premature transfer from the district implied a failure on my part to successfully run a district, which is considered as a basic qualifying test in the career of an IAS officer. What was more hurting was that having been branded a failure, even my senior colleagues started cold-shouldering me.

I was, however, not disheartened as my faith in *Gurbani* provided me the necessary solace in adversity and also the confidence that truth shall prevail. The Chief Minister fell ill while he was on a visit to Calcutta after about a month of my transfer. As luck would have it, for his treatment in Calcutta he had to stay as a guest of Shanti Prasad Jain, the head of Sahu Jains. Dr. S.K. Sinha was shifted to Patna almost half-dead. He died in the next two weeks. There was a revolt in the Congress Party against the small coterie who was really ruling the state in the name of Dr. S.K. Sinha. The leader of that coterie was a corrupt politician whose ill-gotten wealth his family is enjoying through siphoning that money to a shipping company. This politician got defeated when he made a bid for leadership after the death of Dr. S.K. Sinha. Binodanand Jha from Deoghar got elected as the leader of the Congress Legislative Party. Binodanand Jha, after he was sworn in as the Chief Minister, called for the file in which orders had been passed for my transfer and also the file about the prosecution of Sahu Jains. He recorded a note in the file praising me observing sadly that in the whole episode in which many senior IAS and IPS officers were involved, the only upright person that he found was me. He ordered that I should be transferred back to Shahabad. This gave jitters to the Chief Secretary. He enquired from me to know if I had met the Chief Minister and asked for going back to Shahabad. He was relieved when I told him that I had not met the Chief Minister nor was I interested in going back to Shahabad but I would like a district posting in order to prove the point that I was capable of running a district. He said that he would be happy to give me a posting of my choice. It was some satisfaction that Sahu Jains had taken the matter to the Patna High Court. The Judges of the High Court completely vindicated my stand and passed severe strictures against the Sasaram Police, who had been handling that case.

9

As Deputy Commissioner, Dhanbad

I was posted as Deputy Commissioner of Dhanbad. It was a district small in size but most important because of the coal mines, cement, power and fertilizer industries and technical education institutions. The famous Dhanbad School of Mines was located at Dhanbad. The district had a first rate network of communication. All police stations were linked with telephone and wireless with the district headquarters. This was a district after my heart as one had a full grip over everything that was happening in the district.

Most of the coal mines in the district were owned by foreign companies, mostly British with their head offices in Calcutta. The top officials of these companies were also mostly British. There were clubs in the district that had only the Whites as members. The deputy commissioner was given the privilege of membership in all these clubs. Dhanbad Club was the most prestigious club. The Chief Inspector of Mines and the Deputy Commissioner were the only Indian members of the club.

The district had only one block that was rural while the rest of the district was urban in character. The labour mostly came from Eastern Uttar Pradesh. The four hundred and odd mines employed more than 1,00,000 labour. One Kanti Mehta, a socialist, had got the labour organized by forming trade unions. One Mr. B.P. Sinha, a teacher of English, split from Kanti Mehta and led his followers to form a trade union affiliated to the Indian National Trade Union Congress which was the labour wing of the Congress party. Mr. Kanti Mehta got marginalized as most of the mine owners wanted to remain on the right side of the Congress party. B.P. Sinha got his muscle men planted in all the coal mines. When it came to marshalling his forces during any confrontation against rival unions or recalcitrant mine owners, he could have a mighty force of rowdies who could overawe any opposition. A Central Government functionary oversaw the affairs of the coal mines' labour unions. We met every month to review the activities on the labour front, so as to be ready for action if there was any threat to public peace. There was some turmoil on the labour front ever since Mr. Jha took over as the Chief Minister because B.P. Sinha was politically aligned with the group led by one K.B. Sahay who was an aspirant for the position of the Chief Minister. Mr. Sinha started cornering trade unionists who he feared were not loyal to him. I called him to warn him against spreading lawlessness. He said that for him it was a battle for survival and if he felt threatened by the rival rowdies, he had no alternative but to marshal his forces to defend himself. I told him that we could not permit private wars to be fought in the district and promised him that whenever he perceived any threat from his rivals, he should inform us before he mobilized his men. I briefed the district police chief about my meeting with Mr. Sinha. Mr. Sinha remained true to his word. We became friends in the process. The Chief Minister set up a Minister against Sinha who had some support among the labour. We started having frequent tension in the district. The followers of B.P. Sinha disrupted one meeting of the Minister. We had to arrest some of his supporters. I expressed my helplessness in helping his men who were accused of committing violent acts. I told him that incidents like the one that had taken place would erode his support base and after some time even the managers of the coal mines would abandon him. He told me that he would like to make up with the Chief Minister and he wanted me to help him in that. I declined to get involved in the matter, as it was purely a political and group matter of the Congress party. I however told him that I could convey to the Chief Minister his desire to meet him, which I did. As could be expected Mr. Sinha and his supporters professed their loyalty to the Chief Minister presenting a purse of fifty thousand rupees in a public meeting on his next visit to Dhanbad. I heaved a sigh of relief on this development as I was saved from frequent tensions and turmoil in the district.

My wife was pregnant when we came to Dhanbad. Our daughter Noni, later named Niripjit Kaur, was born on 22nd of November, which happened to be the day when the Sikh community of the coalfield, hosted a dinner to celebrate the birth anniversary of Guru Nanak. It was a coincidence that at that particular time most of the top officials at Dhanbad happened to be Sikhs. The Sikhs of Dhanbad hosted the Annual Sikh Educational Conference. The Sikh Educational Conference had been started by the Chief Khalsa Dewan, which was a group of moderate Sikhs generally sympathetic to the Government. The aim was to promote modern education among the Sikhs. Some new institution came up at the place where the annual conference was held. The Dhanbad Sikhs started a Khalsa High School adjacent to the *Dhanbad Gurdwara*. Dhanbad had a sizeable population of Sikh from Gujrat district of West Punjab in Pakistan. Their residential locality was called Nanakpura. They had invited one Sant Nischal Singh of Jagadhri to give discourses on the Sikh religion. They set up a new *Gurdwara* in their locality. I laid the foundation stone of the *Gurdwara* with the blessing of Sant Nischal Singh. Whether one liked it or not, being a Sikh with a distinctive appearance gave one a certain amount of salience in public, making one the focus of attention wherever one went. The result was that as compared to our Sikh colleagues in Punjab, we had to be more particular about the prescribed code of conduct for the Sikhs. None of us among the few Sikh officers in Bihar resorted to trimming of beard or cutting of hair.

The debacle of India against China in 1962 took place while I was at Dhanbad. Militarily the operation was most ineptly handled but it unleashed a lot of patriotic fervour under which the politicians in power and the army brass could successfully cover their failure. A National Defence Fund was launched in which money, gold and materials, for various amenities and entertainment for the soldiers fighting on the front, were collected. My wife joined in this campaign, mobilizing the ladies. Dhanbad topped in the state on this front. I got hailed as the most dynamic and successful District Magistrate in the state. My excellence in achievement extended to all fields of administration and public life. The state government asked me to organize a conclave for other districts to galvanize the administrative process in the state. I met Mr. K.B. Sahay at a function hosted by a coal mine manager who was an Englishman. I accosted him and said that I was happy to meet a Congressman who was not a hypocrite. I said that it was well known that many among the Congress drank liquor but they did it on the sly. He had a hearty laugh on my remark and shook my hand declaring that he considered me to be a friend.

Mr. Binodanand Jha found himself on top of the world and looked forward to enjoy his position for the next few years. He had subdued all his rivals and he became the undisputed master of the destiny of Bihar. Jawaharlal Nehru, who was feeling somewhat shaky after the Chinese episode, brought in what came to be known as the Kamraj Plan named after K. Kamraj, the Tamil president of the Congress. He eased out some party men, who were proving to be the thorns under his flesh, in the name of strengthening the Congress party.

Morarji Desai got eased out from the Central Government and Mr Binodanand Jha had to make way for a new Chief Minister. Mr. K.B. Sahay was elected as the leader of the Congress Legislative Party. He decided to visit his home at Hazaribagh and Dhanbad to thank his friends who had stood by him. He was the Chief Minister designate but not the Chief Minister. I conveyed to our mutual friend Mr. B.P. Sinha that I should be excused for not going to the airport to receive him as he was not the Chief Minister yet. As a Deputy Commissioner, I was supposed to receive only the Governor or the Chief Minister at the airport. When Mr. K.B. Sahay landed at Dhanbad he announced that he counted me as a friend and that he would go calling on me after having met his other friends and well-wishers. He came to our house where he spent an hour, drinking coffee and joking with our family. The visit caused quite a sensation in the district and the state capital. One lady of not a very good repute once called him for some function to which he agreed to come. I thought that I should caution him, as in my view his association with the lady somewhat compromised his position. I took him aside and told him that the lady concerned did not enjoy a good reputation among the general public. He enquired if there was anything else against the lady. I replied in the negative. His retort thereafter was, that in public life in India, we did not have *satis* or *savitris* (chaste ladies) and it should not bother me. He thanked me for my concern and said that he had told all his followers that they should consult me before they fixed any program for him in the district. He confessed that he had been in political wilderness for long and he knew as to who stood with him and those who were only fair weather friends. He did not mind if his position slightly got compromised in accepting invitation from someone who stood with him through thick and thin. He said that after considering all that he had said if at any time I still felt that it was inappropriate for him to accept any particular invitation, he would definitely go by my advice. I found in all these matters that he was a man of his word throughout.

I found that K.B. Sahay was a very competent person. He would get up at about three in the morning and dispose off all his files. He held a First Class First Master's Degree in English Literature. He would tolerate no nonsense. One had to be thorough and precise with him. He would often correct the language or spellings of officers in their notes in the files. He always gave clear and bold orders in all matters that were placed before him. He could show all patience in going through a fifty page noting on the file, he had no patience if anyone was slow in placing his point before him orally. Most of the officials were afraid to face him and most of the public went away unhappy after meeting him as he would abruptly cut them short while they were trying to place their point before him. He had really the making of a bureaucrat. He would repay manifold a small favour done to him when he was in the political wilderness but woe befell the person who tried to pay him money and link the same to some official *quid pro quo*. He was always in a hurry. One fine morning he announced that he had decided to constitute a fund called Bihar Nirmata Kosh to commemorate the memory of the three leaders whom he considered to be the makers of modem Bihar. They were Babu Rajendra Prasad, the first President of India, Dr. S.K. Sinha the first Chief Minister of Bihar and Dr. Anugraha Narain Sinha who was the Finance Minister with Dr. S.K. Sinha. Incidentally, the three represented the three important castes that had dominated Bihar socially and politically. Dr. Rajendra Prasad was a Kaistha, and Dr. S.K. Sinha was a Bhumihar Brahmin while Dr. Anugraha Narain Sinha was a Rajput or a Thakur. He personally rang me up requesting me to help him collect about five lakh rupees from Dhanbad. I told him that I would do what I can provided he got the Chief Secretary to issue a general relaxation permitting IAS officers to associate themselves in the collection of the particular fund. The required circular was issued the very next day. K.B. Sahay expected me to raise the money by the time he came. I convened a meeting of the Committee that had been collecting money for the National Defence Fund. A sum of about two lakh got promised in the meeting and for the rest it was decided to make a temporary advance from the funds available with the committee. The advance was to be recouped within three months. K.B. Sahay went happy. I was able to get the amount advanced recouped from the Calcutta based English coal mining companies within the stipulated three months. Later, the politicians opposed to K.B. Sahay charged him that he became a party to the temporary misappropriation of the National Defence Fund for which he had to face a Commission of Enquiry headed by one Justice Aiyer. K.B. Sahay had no hand in the transfer of funds from the National Defence Fund yet he assumed full responsibility for it in his statement before the Commission of Enquiry. When I reminded him that it was not he but I who was the culprit, he floored me with his reply that as a politician, such charges did not matter for him but he would not have liked a civil servant like me to suffer in his career for something done on his bidding.

My wife was opposed to having any more children after Rosy was born but somehow I could not make up my mind and we got a son Dipender in January 1964. With his coming I realized that we could not go on having more children. I consoled myself that it was also not right to impose my will on my wife, so we had no child after Dipender. Birender my elder son joined the De Nobili Convent School. My younger brother, Maan Singh, had been staying with us for his studies. We tried for his admission in the Dhanbad School of Mines. He got the admission there but he could make it to Petroleum which was a new subject introduced in that institution. He would have preferred to be a coal mine manager. He appeared for the test that was held for the selection of pilots for the Indian Air Force. Our family and I were very happy that he got selected for the Indian Air Force and he became a transport pilot. My father felt happy that with his joining the armed forces our family tradition of serving the armed forces continued. My father in the meanwhile arranged for the marriage of my sister Mohinder. She later immigrated to the United Kingdom with her husband, who was a school teacher. She got selected for the British Revenue Service. She worked as a Customs Officer at the Heathrow Airport, London for a long time.

Jawaharlal Nehru died in May 1964. He had actually died when the Chinese aggression exposed his policies as hollow and the country appeared to be in so bad a shape in 1962. Like the novel *Gone With the Wind,* it could be said that after 1962, Nehru was a person living after the mainspring in his life had got busted. It was a living only in appearance. He willed that his ashes, after cremation, be scattered all over the country. Every Chief Minister was handed over an urn containing his ashes. K.B. Sahay ordered all district officers to come to Patna along with one politician nominated by him and collect the urn of ashes, marked for their particular district, that were later to be ceremoniously consigned to some stream of water flowing in the district. Everywhere the ashes were taken in a train going to the particular district railhead. From Patna we brought the urn containing Nehru's ashes in a small Cessna plane owned by Mr. Pran Prashad, the Chairman of the English owned Bird and Company. A big crowd of people, who formed a procession to carry the special urn to the town hall, received us at the aerodrome. The urn was kept there for more than 24 hours and prayers from all religions were said. The urn was taken to a small stream that was flowing close to Jharia and Nehru's ashes were consigned to the flowing waters with recitation of '*mantras*' by a set of Brahmin priests. Nehru was not a believer in religion for all the appearances, but it seems that in his last days he came to believe in the traditional Hindu religion of his forefathers.

One hazard of the assignments of public salience, like the district officer, is that it attracts the public gaze and attention of the media. One tends to have a life of a goldfish in a glass bowl. It came to my notice that there were a number of local journals or newspapers that functioned either to make money on selling the subsidized printing paper in the black market as it was mostly imported paper, otherwise in short supply. Second purpose was to extract money from officers and departments that were known to be corrupt. Third was to blackmail officers in order to get various errands done on priority. Fourth was to get their importance registered among the general public. There was one dismissed clerk of the Deputy Commissioner's office who had made quite a nuisance of himself in this regard named Kaushal Kumar Srivastava. I had cautioned him several times but he did not mend. The Deputy Commissioner, representing all the departments of the state government, had to meet the press once a month. It was one such press conference when I objected to his way of reporting. I said that despite my warning the gentleman did not mend his ways. I, therefore, announced that henceforth he would not be called to any official press conference. There was one All India body representing small newspapers that happened to be having their annual conference in Patna. He succeeded in mobilizing that organization in his favour. The parties in opposition to the Congress took up his cause. A series of questions and motions in the Bihar Legislative Assembly were moved, accusing me of high handedness but the Chief Minister stoutly defended my action. The State Government further streamlined the policy with regard to the release of government advertisements so that the yellow sheets like the one involved in this case got deprived of the government patronage. The owner and editor, Mr. Srivastava, had to lie low so long as I was the Deputy Commissioner of Dhanbad, but he kept a running battle against me for the next five years or so.

10

At Ranchi

Everything seemed to be hunky-dory for Mr. B.P. Sinha with K.B. Sahay firmly ensconced as the Chief Minister. He continued to be friendly and grateful to me. He came one day and asked me if I wanted anything done for me by the Chief Minister. I told him that if he wielded that much influence with the Chief Minister, he should get me transferred from Dhanbad. He was shocked to hear such a request from me. I explained that I had come to Dhanbad when the powers that be in Bihar wanted to destabilize his position through illegitimate exercise of authority. I said that with K.B. Sahay as the Chief Minister, Mr. Sinha would like to settle scores with his rivals who would seek help from me which I could not deny to them because of my duty. He saw the logic of my argument and conveyed the same to the Chief Minister. I had almost completed my tenure of three years at Dhanbad. The Chief Minister got me posted as the Deputy Secretary in the State Mines Department of which he was the Minister-in-Charge. B.P. Sinha would repeatedly ask me if there was anything that he could do for me. I thanked him for his concern and told him that as a principle I did not ask for any particular posting at any time. One reason for it was my firm faith in *Waheguru* and the belief that whatever posting came my way would be good for me. It was not necessary that what I might have craved for would turn out to be right for me. He overheard my wife talking to a friend in one of our numerous farewell parties that from a palatial Deputy Commissioner's house, she would have to shift to a room in the Circuit House in Patna and manage that way for a year or so till we got a proper house allotted to us at Patna. B.P. Sinha went *post haste* to Patna, asking for a change in my posting. Meanwhile, serious communal riots broke out in Ranchi. The Deputy Commissioner of Ranchi was found to be remiss in handling those riots. The Chief Minister decided to kill two birds with one stone. I was ordered to proceed to Ranchi to take over as the Deputy Commissioner there instead of going to Patna. I moved to Ranchi in July 1964.

Ranchi had experienced serious communal violence, particularly in the new township of the Heavy Engineering Corporation. I do not know whether by design or by coincidence a giant size statue of Birsa Munda, a tribal freedom fighter against the British, in handcuff chains greets everyone at the gate of the complex. This precisely has remained the position of the giant plant. A rumour spread in the area that some Muslims had put poison in the drinking water coming from the water tower that supplied water to the entire township. The rumour got generated because two persons in order to have a view of the township from a height had climbed up the water tower. They had started running away as they came down when the company watchman challenged them.

One of them was found to be a Muslim when caught. It was surprising that the effect of the rumour was so much that a dozen persons from the township got admitted to the local hospital with symptoms of vomiting and purging as if they had been really poisoned. The Deputy Commissioner and the district police chief had to go in front of the angry crowd that had collected, to demonstrate by drinking water from a public hydrant that no poisoning of the water had really taken place. Meanwhile, mobs ransacked Muslim shops and Muslim houses, committing arson, looting and mayhem. The worst happened on the border of the district adjoining Orissa (now Odisha). Tribal mobs from that side converged on Muslim villages on the border. The mob numbering more than ten thousand set fire to the houses at Bano, which was the block headquarters, and proceeded to surround village Girda. In panic, all the Muslim families took shelter in the village mosque. The Block Development Officer rushed to the Sub Divisional Headquarters for more armed force. The

Sub Divisional Officer who was an IAS officer had just gone to sleep after a harrowing day. His P.A. took the decision that he should not be disturbed. A half sick Magistrate with a section of police force was sent to relieve Girda of the siege. The party stopped on seeing the mob that had swelled even more during the night. A German priest, Father Ruskett, came on a bicycle and told the party that he would try to pacify the mob. He pleaded with the leaders of the mob who went on insisting that as per wishes of Nehru they were on a mission to rid the area of the Muslims and they would disperse only after they had completed their mission. When Father Ruskett persisted someone from the mob shouted that the Father was a Muslim. The mob fell on the father and lynched him, killing him in no time. Then the mob killed everyone in the mosque and burnt the dead bodies with the firewood lying in stock in the village. The Magistrate and the police entered the village after the dead bodies had been set on fire. The police in their record later noted that the entire village population was missing. K.B. Sahay came to Bano to see for himself as to what was happening. It was on that visit that he suspended two Magistrates and transferred the Deputy Commissioner, holding them responsible for the failure in maintaining law and order in the district. I found that some thirty persons from Girda had escaped from the holocaust by escaping into the standing crops during the night. I arranged their accommodation in tents and sanctioned liberal relief for their upkeep. I was surprised when the Intelligence Chief of Bihar reported that there was some resentment among the Hindus because I was pampering the Muslims. I wrote back to the Bihar Government exposing how the police had firstly failed to protect the Muslims and secondly, how the police had tried to cover up the mass murder by showing the entire village as missing. The Intelligence Chief got a rocket from the Government. Ranchi town had been listed as one of the communally sensitive towns of Bihar. Muslims who were paid protection money by the Hindu traders and businessmen dominated the underworld of Ranchi. Communal polarization in Ranchi started appearing in Ranchi during the late thirties when some Hindu traders started celebrating the birthday of Lord Ram by taking out *Ramnaumi* processions, carrying bamboo sticks and buntings as a counter to the Muslim celebration of *Muharram*, the death anniversary of Hasan and Hussain, grandsons of the Prophet.

Some Hindu musclemen were brought from the up-country to strengthen the Hindus. The local administration, as a precautionary measure, had banned carrying of sticks or swords in the *Ramnaumi* processions, causing a lot of resentment among the Hindus. Ranchi town, when I reached, was tense but under control. I found that even the Sikhs, though small in numbers, were seething with resentment, as they could not hold elections of the Managing Committee of their local *gurdwara*.

Ranchi was the Summer Capital of Bihar. It had a temperate climate all the year round. The army, which had fought against the Japanese, was trained around Ranchi. Ranchi was the Headquarters of the Army Eastern Command for some time. The debacle of the Indian Army against the Chinese resulted in various activities for improving the defence capability of the country. A new Mountain Division, under the dynamic and most decorated General P.S. Bhagat, was being raised in Ranchi. Public Sector giants like Hindustan Steel, National Coal Development Corporation and many others were located in Ranchi. General Bhagat was a very innovative and popular general. My wife Sukhdev associated herself with a lot of welfare activities that Mrs. Bhagat was spearheading. General Bhagat was a very unorthodox army officer. We were preparing ourselves to deal with the *Ramnaumi* procession in the next year. He got an army officer to liaise with us in our planning so that in the event of breakout of violence, the army did not waste any time in coming to the aid of the civil authority. A day before the *Ramnaumi* day, he ordered a routine army route march through the town. The result of all these preparations was that *Ramnaumi* procession passed off peacefully in the town. I noted that the Indian Army had not revised their pamphlet, covering military aid to the civil in the light of the Constitution of India. I anticipated a lot of difficulties in the conduct of a coordinated operation with the army if really there was a breakdown of public order. I wrote to the state government to take up the issues raised by me with the Government of India. I found that General Bhagat was very quick on the uptake. He found that with the raising of the new Division, his officers had problems in finding married accommodation. I told him that there were a large number of houses of Bengalis who lived in Calcutta. They came to Ranchi only during the Puja holidays in October. He immediately asked his officers to make a survey of such houses and file a requisition with me for acquiring those houses under the Defence of India Rules. Thus, he got his problem solved within a week. When war broke out with Pakistan on the Western front, he proposed that his half equipped units could move to the Eastern border as a precautionary measure. The Army Headquarters gave him permission as well as orders for fast supply of equipment that was lacking provided he could move to the Eastern border within a week. He asked for the civil assistance in requisitioning private transport for moving the army. There was no problem in finding adequate civilian trucks as the area was crawling with trucks engaged in the transport of coal. He ensured that the truck owners and drivers were paid generous compensation for the requisitioned trucks.

Civil and Army Interactions

There was a bizarre episode involving the army and the civil administration during the Indo-Pak War. I got a message from the Railway Control Room that one of their Stationmasters on the border of Orissa had reported to them that he had seen some paratroopers dropping near the railway station. I asked the reporter to recheck his facts and report back. He reconfirmed the message. I immediately contacted the District Superintendent of Police, Mr. G. Narain, a very competent police officer, who suggested that we should personally proceed to the spot. I contacted the local army commander who placed a company of an artillery regiment that was being raised in Ranchi and the South Eastern Railway arranged a special train to take us along with the troops to the affected railway station. The train was to start from Ranchi Railway Station at about 7 p.m. the same evening. When we got onto the car to catch the train Mr. Narain got somewhat emotional. He said that he would have to take the command of the force that would confront the paratroopers who were expected to be trained army commandos. He said that he would ensure that no harm was caused to me but he feared that he would not survive the operation. He said that he had confidence that Mrs. Dhanoa would take care of his family after him and therefore, he did not feel afraid. However, he said that he had not savored the *Chivas Regal* Scotch whisky so far and for that he would carry a regret to the next world. I asked the driver to turn back, as in our house we had a bottle of the Scotch whisky for which he had so strong a yearning. We had a few drinks and headed for the railway station again. The train was on the platform waiting for us with the troops already on board. I presumed that by the time we were leaving, the paratroopers would have taken over the railway station. I decided to check the position on the railway telephone. When the contact was established I enquired if everything was alright at the station. When the reply came that all of them at the station were OK, we started wondering about the mission of the paratroopers. We had alerted all our field officers about the paratroopers. A full patrolling of all vulnerable points was taken up in the district. Many of those patrols met our train at various points as the train proceeded reporting all clear everywhere. When we reached the railway station that had reported seeing the paratroopers dropping, we found that the whole thing was a false alarm due to hallucination of the concerned stationmaster. I ordered the arrest of the stationmaster for spreading panic and asked the guard of the train to take the train back to Ranchi. Everyone at Ranchi had a good laugh at our misadventure that became a talk of the town for some time.

The soldiers of the army and officers had moved to the Eastern front on a very short notice and their families were left behind. The Chief Minister decided that the civil officers should take a lead in mobilizing support for the families of the army personnel. Sukhdev took a lead in setting up a welfare committee consisting of the civilians and army wives headed by Mrs. Bhagat. The Chief Minister personally came to inaugurate the welfare initiatives. Bihar is comparatively a conservative society. When K.B. Sahay saw so many pretty ladies, he almost fell down with a sort of shock. He rushed to me to ask as to what he was expected to do. I told him that such functions were quite a routine in the army. He was only to cut a cake and give his blessings to the ladies who had undertaken the welfare effort. Thereafter, I found that he was in his element and while leaving he asked me to organize more such meetings.

The Indo-Pak War was soon over and General Bhagat along with his troops of the 9 Mountain Division, now fully equipped, returned back to Ranchi. General Bhagat was soon promoted as a Lieutenant General and went away to take the Command of the 11th Corps at Jalandhar in Punjab. He was succeeded by one George Bharat Singh, who was a dyed-in-wool soldier, having generally a contempt for the civilians. Our interaction with the army became infrequent. He did not even bother to pay a return call after I called on him. He did not bother to come for the Independence Day Parade in which the Chief Minister, Bihar had come to take the salute. I thought that it was a bit too much. I formally reported the matter to the Bihar Government, who sent my report to the Government of India. Soon the poor General was sent home on retirement.

Most of Bihar was covered by the army through Dinapur (now Danapur) sub-area. Dinapur was the Regimental Centre of the Bihar Regiment. The Biharis were well-represented in the Bengal Army through whom the British had conquered Punjab but after 1857 the British had restricted recruitment to the Indian Army to what were called the 'martial races' leaning heavily on Punjab. It was because of Mr. Jaipal Singh, the Olympic hockey player and a leader of the tribal people of Bihar from Ranchi, the British approved raising of the Bihar Regiment with one third of the contingent coming from the Bihar tribes. Jaipal Singh was known among the tribals as '*marang gomke*' meaning the big leader. The Dinapur sub-area had requested the Bihar Government to nominate one officer to participate in a civil-military liaison conference hosted by them. I had attended that conference as a nominee of the Bihar government. I discovered in that conference that the army had still continued with their manual on 'military aid to the civil authority' that was there during the colonial period. The manual talked about 'martial law' for which under the Constitution of India there was no place and the reading of the instructions by the army officers gave me an impression that the army officers assumed that once the civil authority invited them to restore order, they came to acquire some control over the civil authority. I pointed out during the conference that the prevailing understanding about the role of the army was untenable and that there would be problems galore if ever the army got called out to restore public order. I apprised the Bihar Government too about my misgivings in this regard. What I had anticipated came to pass in 1967 in Ranchi. My correspondence on the subject got noticed by the Ragubar Dayal Commission of Enquiry on Ranchi riots. The State Government got a rap on their knuckles for ignoring my letters. The Government of India revised their manual on 'military aid to civil authority' in the light of the observations which were made by me. The revised brochure is titled '*Instructions On Aid to the Civil Authorities by the Armed Forces, 1970*'. There are areas which are still confusing as everywhere the civil authorities who have to call the armed forces for assistance would confirm. It is not clear as to how the armed forces got involved in Punjab in 1984. The then neither Governor of Punjab Mr. B.D. Pande nor the Deputy Commissioner of Amritsar had asked for such aid. No one in Punjab considered that calling the army would solve their problems. The core group on Punjab seemed to have opted for the army. B.D. Pande was asked only on the 2nd of June to formally provide a cover for the army operation that was already under way. It is evident that all decisions about handling the Punjab affairs were taken by the Central Government. It can be said that army is not suited to restoring civil order in a democracy except in situations of widespread insurgency supported by foreign powers. If anything, the ten years of turmoil in Punjab has shown that the most effective and lasting instrument for restoring public order in any disturbed area is the civil police force.

The Indo-Pak War of 1965 was launched by Pakistan in order to grab Jammu and Kashmir by force before India acquired an edge over Pakistan in military balance between the two countries in wake of the all-out preparedness of the Indian armed forces after their debacle against the Chinese in 1962. Pakistan had launched a very clever operation from Chhamb Jaurian side to outflank and cut off Kashmir at Akhnoor from India without violating the international boundary. India had Lal Bahadur Shastri as the Prime Minister. He surprised the world by permitting the Indian Army to respond through an all-out offensive against Pakistan across the International border. Fortunately for India, we had two brave Generals who could take the risks that were required to face the Pakistani offensive. General Harbakhsh Singh defied his chief by not withdrawing beyond Beas River in the face of the Pakistani armoured force attack by Paton tanks, considered invincible at that time. The grapevine that we heard was that the US Ambassador to Pakistan rang up his counterpart in New Delhi to tell him that the Pakistani Armoured Division had moved from Kharian and that he should tell the Indian Prime Minister to receive them in Delhi after 48 hours. India found the answer to the challenge in General J.S. Dhillon, who got the famous Paton tanks bogged down in the freshly irrigated agricultural fields while hiding his deadly guns in the tall sugarcane crops. When he opened up on the Pakistani tanks, Khem Karan became a graveyard of Paton tanks and the decisive battle of the war was lost by Pakistan. Both the countries did not have the capacity to fight beyond a three week war. The Soviet Union offered their good offices for restoring peace. Overnight, the little man from India became a hero when he flew to Tashkent to sign the Peace Accord. He was not destined to return as he got a massive heart attack during the night and passed away. His enemy General Ayub Khan became his pall bearer at Tashkent. Lal Bahadur Shastri was a very honest and transparent person. He came to Ranchi after the ceasefire. There was a massive crowd at the airport and in his public meeting. The Chief Minister of Bihar was escorting him. Immediately after the ceasefire the Prime Minister had urged the nation to prepare themselves for sacrifices and economise in all spheres of government activities avoiding ostentation. K.B. Sahay had arranged a lavish dinner in his honour at Jamshedpur with festoons and buntings all over. When Lal Bahadur Shastri reached the Circuit House he saw all the lavishness of the host. He enquired as to what it was about. When he was told that all the show was in his honour, he told the Chief Minister in his simple quiet manner that he would like to have his dinner alone in his room. It came as a bombshell to K.B. Sahay. All the officials had to run to telephone the already invited guests to tell and apologize that the dinner in honour of the Prime Minister stood cancelled.

Gulzari Lal Nanda was a Gandhian from Gujarat with a Punjabi-Hindu origin. He remained a Minister for Labour in the Central Government. He was known to be a true Gandhian with simple living habits wearing khadi. (hand spun cotton clothes). He was known to be an honest person. He was an obscurantist Hindu in his beliefs with tremendous faith in astrology. There was a refugee Hindu astrologer, Mr. Haveli Ram, who had come to Delhi from Lahore after the partition. Sardar Baldev Singh, who became the first Defence Minister of India, was a great devotee of Haveli Ram, so much so, that when he went for medical treatment to the USA, he went there only after Haveli Ram's clearance. He returned to India before he was cleared for his return by the US doctors because he did not want to stay in the USA after the date that was given by Haveli Ram for his return. This was told to me by his personal physician Dr. Chhokar of Jamshedpur. Dr.

Chhokar was of the view that Haveli Ram was an agent of the Indian Intelligence Bureau. It is known that the Sikh leaders were quite upset over the dispensation that the Sikhs received on the Independence of India. There was a secret meeting of the Sikh leaders at Chail hosted by the Maharaja of Patiala, late Yadvindra Singh, where Baldev Singh had gone incognito in a friend's car. The fact was known to Haveli Ram. Baldev Singh was shocked when the very next day after the meeting, Sardar Patel, the Home Minister enquired from Baldev Singh about the secret meeting of the Sikh leaders. Haveli Ram had surrounded Nanda like an octopus. Nanda would consult him every day, the first thing in the morning, even enquiring from him as to which side of the Prime Minister he should sit in the Cabinet meeting fixed for that day. The Chief Inspector of Mines under the Ministry of Labour had made wearing of safety boots compulsory for all the workers in mines. Haveli Ram got Nanda to issue orders that the only boots according to the safety norms prescribed were those that were produced by a company in which Haveli Ram had an interest. The simple order must have made the company richer by two crores or 20 million rupees. This is the sort of risk that all officials exercising executive authority have to bear in mind and remain vigilant because one can never know as to whom among one's acquaintances or relatives would try to cash on his access to the official concerned. Mr. L.P. Singh, ICS, the then Chief Secretary of Bihar, used to caution us that we should remember that each new acquaintance of ours was a potential threat to our integrity in public service.

Gulzari Lai Nanda was sworn in as the Prime Minister on the sudden demise of Lal Bahadur Shastri. We had a perennial kind of minister in the Central Government, Mr. Satya Narain Sinha from Bihar who was the Communication Minister in the Shastri Cabinet. When he heard about the sudden death of Shastri in Tashkent, his first worry was about his future. He could not even go to receive the dead body of Shastri. He asked an industrial house to fly his astrologer in a chartered flight from Patna, which they did.

The astrologer poured over the birth chart and other papers as relevant for him and pronounced that though the Prime Minister would change but his chair was going to be safe. It was only after hearing the good omen that Mr. Sinha dressed up and went to 10 Janpath, the residence of Mr. Shastri to pay his homage to the dead leader, whose body had been lying in State for quite some time. He fell flat on the ground in front of the dead body and got up only after he was physically lifted by the security men. He told Mrs. Shastri that at his residence too he had fallen unconscious as he could not bear to hear the sad news. He came late as it took a long time for him to recover from the shock.

The Congress stalwarts could not agree among themselves as to who should be the next Prime Minister. They agreed on Indira Gandhi, the daughter of Jawaharlal Nehru, as she seemed to be suited to be a Prime Minister, as a stop gap leader till the real one emerged. She displayed all traits of a leader, though not sure of herself. She could hardly handle the Parliament. Ram Manohar Lohia, a socialist and an inveterate critic of the Nehrus called her a '*Goongi Gudiya*' or a dumb doll. However, slowly she started acquiring confidence and mildly asserting herself on some issues. This made the stalwarts in control of the Congress party to join their heads in developing an appropriate leash for Mrs. Gandhi. The AICC fixed a conclave at Ranchi to work out their strategy. We had K. Kamraj, the Congress President, Biju Patnaik, the strongman of Orissa, Atulya Ghosh, the strongman of West Bengal, Gulzari Lal Nanda, the Home Minister and others with K.B. Sahay hosting the meet in Ranchi. I had to go to the airport to receive Nanda as he was the Home Minister of India as per protocol of the Government. I found that he was holding in his hand a paperback book, '*Autobiography of a Yogi*', which was supposed to be an autobiography of a Hindu ascetic who had done his yoga in the Himalayas, acquiring a mastery over age. The yogi had established an *ashram* (monastry) at Ranchi. I had read the book. I mentioned to Nanda that a Christian missionary had written a book in response to the claims made in the yogi's book called '*In Search of a Yogi*'. I gave him my copy of the book to read on his specific request. It seems that he suspected my motives in suggesting to him the book to read. When I went to see him off at the airport the next day I found that he was carrying with him the book that I had given him and as he was leaving to take the plane he enquired loudly as to who had given him the book. I identified myself as the culprit. He handed back the book to me with the remark that was heard by everyone who had gone to say goodbye to him that he found the book to have been very superficial.

Actually, his fixation with the Hindu religion, as understood by him, proved to be his undoing. The obscurant Hindu sections with whom Nanda sympathised wanted cow slaughter in India to be banned by law. The Congress party under Nehru had identified itself as a secular political party who would not take up a measure to please a particular religious community even though it was the majority community. When a Hindu delegation met Nanda demanding a ban on cow slaughter, Nanda told them that he sympathized with them but to enable him to do what the delegation was demanding, they should do something concrete in order to create a climate in the country favoring a ban on cow slaughter. The hint was taken and the All India Sadhu Samaj, patronised by Nanda, called for a massive rally in Delhi to demand a ban on cow slaughter. The rally almost stormed the Parliament which was in session, but it turned unruly and violent on the way. It also turned anti-Congress. The house of Mr. Kamraj, the Congress President, was attacked from where he had to escape through a backdoor, wearing only his *loongi*. This proved to be the end of the career of Mr. Gulzari Lal Nanda, who had aspired to be the Prime Minister of India.

Mr. Kamraj, the Congress President, came in the Bihar Government plane escorted by K.B. Sahay, the Chief Minister. I had to go to the airport to receive the Chief Minister. I received a telephone call from the chief of the Bihar police intelligence, Mr. R.A.P. Sinha, IPS, just as I was to step into my car for receiving the Chief Minister. What he told me stunned me. He said that the Congress conclave being held at Ranchi was meant to strengthen one group in the Congress with which K.B. Sahay was aligned. He said that the group opposed to him would like to embarrass him. He said that they had planned to stop the cavalcade of Mr. Kamraj at a particular point enroute to garland him as a sign of welcome to Ranchi and at the same time they had kept a garland of shoes with them to put the same around the neck of K.B. Sahay. It seemed to me that it was mischievous on his part to pass on such information virtually after the 11th hour, as nothing could be done to stop what had been planned. I immediately stopped in my tracks and asked the district police chief to take charge of the situation. Mr. G. Narain called the veteran inspector of the Kotwali Police Station, one Mr. Rajinder Singh, and gave him specific instructions to ensure that what the detractors of K.B. Sahay had planned does not take place. He drafted about 100 hefty policemen in *mufti* and placed them at the point where Mr. Kamraj was to be garlanded with the direction that except for the person who was to garland Kamraj, none should be allowed to be anywhere near the two leaders. The inspector saved the day for us. The mob became quite unruly after the two leaders passed out of their cordon. They beat up some of the junior leaders in the cavalcade, making them shout, on peril of physical harm, that 'K.B. Sahay was a thief'. The leader of the Congress dissident group was one S.K. Sinha who was once the Private Secretary of Mr. C.P.N. Singh, when he was our Ambassador to Nepal. It was rumoured that during the turmoil in the Nepalese capital, when King of Nepal had taken shelter for some time in the Indian Embassy, Mr. Sinha was able to filch some gold and jewellery from the King and started his political career in Ranchi. I had directly asked him to confirm or deny the story. He frankly told me that it was not in his interest to deny the story because he found that a number of his followers believed in the story and were with him in the hope of sharing his wealth. He came and sat in front of the office of the Deputy Commissioner on a hunger strike in protest against the alleged excesses committed by the police. The Bihar Government desired me to take him into custody, but I did not accept their direction because I did not want that he should present himself as a hero fighting for the cause of the people. I put a security cordon of the police around him ostensibly for his protection. I had told the police that no food item should reach him. He was on his knees by midnight and begged me to save him from the situation in which he found himself. I conveyed a message to Mrs Jaipal Singh, who was his patron to come and save his face by persuading him to break his hunger strike. Both of them took part in the drama arranged and went away happy thanking me. The Chief Minister of Bihar personally thanked me for handling all these matters in a manner that brought credit to him. He asked the General Secretary of the BPCC to personally convey his appreciation to me. The General Secretary came to call on me with his team of office-bearers. As they sat down to have a cup of tea with me, the Chief Secretary, Mr. T.P. Singh (Junior), ICS, who was also camping in Ranchi, dropped in to say hello to me. He was not very happy to see all the politicians in my house and carried a suspicion about my impartiality and integrity which brought on me some serious trouble later on.

The Chief Minister left Ranchi the next day. He could not restrain himself in explaining to me that the Congress conclave was meant to give a message to Indira Gandhi that she was the Prime Minister because the leaders controlling the party, who later on came to be known as the 'syndicate', were permitting her to continue as the Prime Minister. She may better be beware. It is now history as to how Indira Gandhi proved to be a master politician and got the veteran politicians of the Congress to eat dust. The leaders who had collected together in Ranchi thought that they were the arbiters of India's destiny, forgetting the fact that in a democracy the power to decide stood vested in the people. The Congress leaders who had gathered together at Ranchi were successful party managers who had feet of clay that could topple them any time when the issue got joined.

K.B. Sahay belonged to Hazaribagh near Ranchi. He almost made it a practice to visit Ranchi every week. He would usually get up around 3 a.m. and start working on his files. He had a good command of the English language and he could not restrain himself if in any of the official notings he found a mistake of spelling or grammar. He would make corrections in official notes like a teacher of the English language. He had all the patience to go through reams of papers, but he had no patience with a person in flesh and blood if such a person did not know as to make a gist of what he wanted to say. Any diversion from the main issue or any attempt at some explanation would bring the meeting to a close with some rude remark from K.B. Sahay. Despite his intelligence, he could never become a popular leader. Another blind spot that he shared with all politicians of Bihar was that he had no vision about the future of Bihar. He equated his prompt disposal of all the papers that came to him with speeding up of the development of Bihar. His greatest achievement touted was the Bihar Land Reforms Legislation where he had taken the lead in India, to pass a law giving land to the tiller, which was the first Land Reforms Law passed in Independent India. However, the law remained more on paper than on the ground. He came to acquire more and more confidence in me as a person, as a friend, as he often called me, and as a competent official in handling complex human situations whose example he would off and on cite. He often joined me for a drink which was a privilege that hardly anyone enjoyed with him. I knew of only three other persons of Bihar in whose company he could take a drink. He had generally a drink as a night cap but always alone. He had specially distilled liquor for himself that was provided by the owner of the Ranchi distillery, Mr. Lakshmi Narain Jaiswal. I came to discover that despite his forbidding exterior he had a heart of gold, that was simple, almost childlike. My closeness to the Chief Minister created a sense of jealousy among the civil servants in higher echelons of the civil service. However, often some juniors would approach me to help them to get out of the various peccadilloes in which they got involved. One such person was a rash South Indian IAS officer Mr. Srinivas Ramanujam. He was the Sub Divisional Magistrate posted at Sahebganj, through which the main line of the Eastern Railway passed. He got detained for some time on the level crossing as more than one train was to pass the level crossing at the same time. He ordered the operator to open the railway gates to enable him to cross the rail lines. The gateman refused to oblige him. Mr. Ramanujam got so infuriated on his refusal that he got him arrested on the spot leaving the railway gate unmanned. The railway authorities sent a report on the incident to the Bihar government. The Chief Secretary had recommended a warning to the erring official for his irresponsible and illegal conduct but the Chief Minister ordered that the official concerned should be suspended and chargesheeted for ordering an illegal arrest. This order made a delegation of junior IAS officers run to me. Luckily, I was to meet the Chief Minister the same evening. I suggested to him that young officers were prone to commit mistakes and the governments were generally tolerant about such mistakes. It would be enough for Mr. Ramanajum if he was let off with the punishment proposed by the Chief Secretary. I told him that I had been approached on his behalf by a group of young IAS officers and assured him that not only Mr. Ramanujam but a whole lot of IAS officers of Bihar have learnt a lesson from his orders and none of them would dare to repeat such irresponsible act in the future. I also said that his gesture in letting off the young officer would be well received in the civil service circles. He somehow got convinced by my argument and graciously recalled his order.

It was in this background that another set of five officers of Bihar approached me to help them in a situation where they were facing a Commission of Enquiry presided over by a retired judge of the Patna High Court. The senior most among them was an IPS officer, Mr. Pande, and the next was an IAS officer, Mr. S.K. Srivastav. Mr. Pandey was promoted as the district police chief. A farewell party was arranged for him at the Rajmahal PWD Inspection Bungalow. All five of them were traveling in a Fiat car driven by Mr. Pandey. They were travelling on a single-lane road that connected Bihar with Calcutta. They found that a loaded truck was travelling slowly on the road, blocking their way. They blew their car horn for the truck to give them the way. Nothing happened. They had to follow the truck for more than five kilometers and they happened to be the top officers of the area wielding authority. This made them angry. They overtook the truck by taking their car on the muddy side of the road. They signaled the truck driver to stop. The truck driver happened to be a hefty Punjabi, Charan Singh. He had his hair and beard cut but he supported a well-groomed moustache. He took some time to get down from his seat. When he came down, the officers found him twirling his moustache. The officers wore no uniforms and Charan Singh presumed them to be some local businessmen. He asked them nonchalantly as to why they had blocked his way. One among the officials rudely asked him as to why he did not give them a pass. He said that his truck was loaded because of which he could not take the risk of taking one wheel on the muddy side of the road and said that he would have given them a pass as soon as he would have found some space. The officers were already late for the party, so they hastily went ahead. About half a mile ahead was a police station. The group of officers stopped there and told the police officer-in-charge to get the truck blocked and seized as the driver of the truck had to be taught a lesson and they proceeded for their party in the inspection bungalow.

The police officer soon appeared in the inspection bungalow along with the truck driver and his helper who was a Sikh while the party was still going on. He asked his boss the police chief as to what he was expected to do. The police chief asked him to check all papers of the truck and the driving license of Charan Singh and book him under all the laws that he might have violated. The police officer said that he had already done that exercise and there was nothing wrong with his papers. The police chief was at the point of letting them go when a junior officer who had accompanied them said that Charan

Singh was twirling his moustache a bit too much, so if he wanted to go, he must get his moustaches shaved off otherwise he said the truck should be detained till they had a thorough look at all the papers. The Sikh helper told Charan Singh that as he was not particular about his *Sikhi* or the Sikh code of conduct so he could better do what he was asked to do and proceed ahead rather than spending the night in the mosquito infested police lock-up. Charan Singh went back to the officers to enquire if he could be permitted to trim his moustache slightly and leave. Somehow the officers took it lightly and said that they wanted a clean shaving off of the moustache. Charan Singh did what he was told by going to the barber just outside the inspection bungalow and drove on to Calcutta leaving the officials laughing and cracking jokes. However, the whole episode seems to have hurt his vanity.

Charan Singh talked about what had happened to him to his fellow truck drivers in Calcutta. They had among their advisors one who was known as Dalip Singh Mamlebaaz, who generally drafted various complaints and grievances of the truck drivers and mailed those to the authorities concerned. He drafted a very emotionally worded petition from a Sikh driver who cared for his hair more than his life and alleged that the Bihar officers had got his hands tied behind his back and while Charan Singh was crying and pleading for mercy all the time declaring that he was a Sikh who would prefer his head to be chopped off rather than permitting his hair to be cut. These petitions were sent all over, from the President of India down to the Deputy Commissioner of the District along with copies to the Shiromani Akali Dal and the Chief Minister of Punjab. This happened to be a time when the Akalis were restive but they did not have an issue for attacking the Government of India who were allegedly persecuting the Sikhs. The issue of alleged forcible shaving of the Sikh truck driver came very handy for the Akalis. The issue was raised in various religious congregations of the Sikhs all over India. A committee headed by my friend J.S. Grewal was formed in Bihar to take up the issue with the Government. He knew senior Bihar officials well, particularly the Commissioner of Bhagalpur, who was the senior most field officer required to look into the matter. The Commissioner heard Mr. Grewal but decided to believe in the officials who had combined in the meanwhile to say that nothing of the sort, as alleged, had happened. The committee thereafter got hold of the barber who had shaved off the moustache of Charan Singh and paid him five thousand rupees to say that all that was alleged in the petition of Charan Singh was true. His statement was tape recorded and copies of the same were made for wide circulation. The Bihar Government was confronted with the statement of the barber and the fact that the Commissioner had never visited the spot where the driver's shaving was alleged to have taken place. The Akalis were trying to put the Government of India on the dock. The GOI wrote a stiff letter to the Chief Minister to get at the root of the problem. K.B. Sahay asked the Chief Secretary Mr. S.J. Mazumdar, ICS, to enquire into the matter. Mr. Mazumdar decided to act as a sleuth personally. He let his beard grow for a week and went to Rajmahal, incognito in his personal car. He spent the night in the Inspection Bungalow. He called for the same barber, who was involved, to give him a shave. He enquired from the barber, while he was giving him a shave, about the truth of the allegations being made on behalf of the Sikh driver. The barber made a sign that he should not speak about it as he was scared to death to talk about it because of the fear of the local police but he said that what was alleged was true. The Chief Secretary went back to Patna and ordered the transfer of all the officers suspected to have been involved and at the same time reported to the Chief Minister that in his assessment the alleged incident did take place. The Government of India was breathing down the neck of the Bihar Chief Minister for some action in the matter. The Chief Minister appointed a Commission of Enquiry to be presided over by a retired judge of the Patna High Court. The accused officers were in high spirits till they were transferred. Their morale went down when they found that the Bihar Government refused to assist them in their defence as what was alleged against them could not be called as an official act by them. The Government fixed the headquarters of the Commission at Dumka in Bihar, which was the district headquarters and a very difficult place to reach. Still the officers put up a brave face when the sittings of the Commission started. They got totally demoralized when the barber appeared against them and stuck to the version that was tutored to him by their opposite party. The opposite party too had their problems. Charan Singh the truck driver on whose complaint all the action had got initiated had just disappeared.

The Sikh committee pursuing the case could locate him with some difficulty somewhere in Amritsar district of Punjab and found that he had no interest in pursuing the case. He was found to be an opium addict and a smoker. The committee could persuade him to come for the case on payment of some remuneration that could take care of his upkeep, opium and smoking. The officers finding themselves at the end of their tether unwisely took a decision to withdraw themselves from the hearings of the Commission that made the Commission to order *ex-parte* hearings. The Sikh committee side found themselves on the ninth cloud and started smelling a cakewalk to victory. They had no problem of funds or lawyers. They had five lawyers appearing for them at Dumka, whereas the officers involved could not afford even one lawyer from their resources.

V.K. Krishna Menon had offered the Committee to appear before the Commission at the hearing stage without charging any fees. It was at this stage that the accused officers approached me for help.

I told the officers that perhaps it was a bit late in the day to do anything in the matter. I promised them that I would give it a try. The Chief Secretary of Bihar had come on a visit to Ranchi. I discussed the matter with him but his response was negative as he thought that the incident was a blot on the secular credentials of the administration of our country and for that objective if we have to sacrifice the careers of some officers, according to him it was not a high price for the Civil Services to pay. Fortunately, the same evening I met the Chief Minister at a dinner at the BNR Hotel in Ranchi. I broached the subject with him. At first he made a sarcastic remark, telling me that the Civil Servants considered themselves to be very clever. He said that he knew from day one that there could be no smoke without a fire somewhere, whereas the Civil Services took the position that nothing had happened. He said that the Chief Secretary got scared on the statement of the barber putting his seal of authenticity on the whole episode. He said that these *babus* who respected clerks, would now face the music and sing before the High Court judge. I told him that he was being unfair to the Civil Servants as they were not being defended by the Government, whereas on the other side resources of the community had got mobilized to prove them guilty. He expressed his helplessness in the matter because of the pressure from the Central Government but made an observation that if in some manner the

Sikh community's feelings could be assuaged, he would not go for his pound of flesh from the accused officers.

This remark encouraged me to think that the ticklish matter could be resolved. Knowing Sikh tradition, I enquired from the accused officers if they would be prepared to offer an apology before a Sikh congregation at the historic Patna *Gurdwara* which is also recognized as a *Takhat* for resolving secular matters like the one we had concerning Charan Singh. The officers concerned assured me that they did not know that Charan Singh was a Sikh nor they had ordered him, as alleged, to get all his hair shaved off, but they would all the same be prepared to render an unqualified apology for what had happened. After getting this assurance, I contacted my Dhanbad friend, Mr. J.S. Grewal, to know as to what should be done. He invited me to Dhanbad to meet all the members of the Committee who were pursuing the follow-up of the Commission of Enquiry. I went there the same evening. The members of the Committee were in high spirits as they thought that they had already won. I cautioned them that they should not take the judge for granted and remember that so far the Sikh's have lost all the cases where a judge of the High Court had held an enquiry. Moreover, they should not forget that the judge was a Bihari Hindu and so were the five accused officers. I also told them that even if they won, they would be committing a moral wrong. They were taken aback on my words. I explained to them that they knew that the story that they were trying to prove was false. They retorted that everything was fair in war and they were at war. I said that I did not agree with them because a Sikh has to stand for the truth, and left for the Circuit House to sleep. I got a phone call from the Committee asking me to get all the officers in the Patna *Gurdwara* after two days, for tendering an apology. I consented for what was asked and the Committee made a formal request to the Commission of Enquiry for an adjournment to enable them to make an out-of-court-settlement. The Commission readily agreed for it and the scene of action shifted to Patna.

A rumor had already reached the Sikhs of Patna that for the first time in its history five officers of the Bihar Government were coming to tender an apology for their conduct. The *gurdwara* hall was full. We gathered together in the room of the manager to decide about the modalities of the ceremony that was to be observed. Some radical

Sikh youth also joined us. They insisted that the apology from the officers should be in writing and they should clearly admit all that was alleged against them as according to them copies of the apology would have to be sent to all the Sikh *Sangats* in India from where money had been collected for fighting the case in various fora.

The officers were agreeable to admit in writing what really they had done but not what was being alleged in the version of Dalip Singh Mamlebaz. There was a stalemate on this issue. The congregation who were awaiting our appearance was asked to disperse for the next day. I took the floor the next day in the Committee room and asked them a question that in Sikh history this was not the first time when someone who had wronged the Sikhs and had come for tendering an apology and never such apology was taken in writing. The reason was that an apology had to come from the heart when one was face-to-face with the Divine, so let it be. This argument carried the day as particularly the *Bihari* Sikhs supported my contention fully. We next moved to the *Takhat Harimandir Saheb* congregation hall. Jathedar Maan Singh, a Bihari Sikh presided over the function. The spokesman for the officers was Mr. Pandey, an IPS officer, who was to later become the Director General of Police, Bihar. He stood up and said "That to err was human and every day we apologize before our Gods for the transgressions committed by us". He said that they had come before the Sikh congregation in that house of God in Patna to beg apology for the transgression that was committed by them. As soon as he completed his piece, we in the congregation shouted *'Bole So Nihal'* which got answered from the congregation as per the Sikh tradition with a collective *'Sat Sri Akal'*. That was the end of the incident because as far as the Sikhs were concerned the Guru's word that came from the *Granth Saheb* at the end of the congregation was apt and to the point for the occasion. It was meant that the worldly affairs in which we have our being have made us blind, so how could we know the path shown by the guru. Mr. J.S. Grewal had insisted that since representatives of all the Sikh social and political organization were present, they should give in writing to me that the Sikh community had no grievances left against the Bihar officers involved in the Sikh driver's shaving episode. The young Sikh radical boys had informed the Patna Press, and they had got the apology recorded on a tape-recorder. Next day, all the newspapers of Bihar made the event as their first page news with my name being prominently splashed in the write-up. I discovered that my presence in Patna was unauthorized, for which I had to apologize to the Commissioner of Ranchi, who was my immediate boss. I called on the Chief Minister early morning the next day, 11th November 1964, and handed over the paper given by the Sikh organizations. He asked me to give him an explanatory note about Sikh traditions so that the Bihar bureaucrats did not stall a final decision in the matter. I gave him a note on the subject as a Sikh citizen of Bihar. Mr. K.B. Sahay was true to his word and without calling for the relevant file he ordered that the Commission of Enquiry be wound up. I thought that it was the end of the matter, as far as I was concerned. After a month, one of the officers involved came running to me saying that the Government of India wanted the case to be reopened. It was because an Akali M.P., Sirdar Kapur Singh, an ex-ICS officer, asked a question in Parliament that it was true that the Sikhs as a community had accepted the apology from the officers but how could the Central Government overlook the misconduct of the officers belonging to the All India Services. I, therefore wrote a letter to Kapur Singh explaining that the Akali Party was bound by the commitment given that the Sikh community had no grievances against the Bihar officers. He was good enough to withdraw the request that he had made to the Home Minister of India. The incident had gained a lot of importance in the Sikh circles, as borne out from the fact that one Sikh scholar, Dr. Gurmit Singh, belonging to the school who believed and who wanted every Sikh to believe that the Sikhs had been given a raw deal by the ungrateful Indian Hindus after Independence, had listed this incident as an important instance of Hindu oppression on the Sikhs in his book "*The Sikh Struggles*".

I believe that the mission of Guru Nanak was to get the humanity recognize that there was one creator of humanity who had his abode in each living being and in every atom of the universe who could be invoked by human beings and the One Reality made itself manifest in various human personalities who have given us various religions. Guru Nanak found that in religious tradition its founders had taught as to how the indwelling Divine, in each human being was to be awakened and recognized. Those whom he considered as having been successful in their endeavour were selected by Guru Nanak in his fifth incarnation for inclusion of their spiritually inspired poetry in the sacred book called the *Granth Sahib* that was compiled by him, regardless of the spiritual tradition to which the writer belonged. Guru Nanak recognizes only two classes of human beings, one being self-centred or '*Manmukh*', the other being Guru-centred or '*Gurmukh*'. The fifth *Nanak* in *Raag Ramkali,* addressing both Hindus and Muslims, clearly says that one says "*Ram*" while the other calls the same as "*Khuda*" and sums up his argument with the saying that the secret of the Almighty gets known only to a human being who can perceive the Divine order prevailing all over.

It was Indira Gandhi, who had succeeded Lal Bahadur Shastri when Sardar Manjit Singh, a Sikh IFS officer posted in the Indian High Commission in London, discovered that the family of Lord Dalhousie, the Governor General who had annexed the Sikh kingdom, had some weapons in their possession which had belonged to the tenth Sikh Guru Gobind Singh.

He negotiated with the family to return the weapons to India. Indira Gandhi decided to hand over those weapons to the SGPC for custody and display.

Indira Gandhi had also decided that before the weapons were taken over by the SGPC, the same should be displayed all over India at state level functions. The weapons came to Ranchi from Orissa where K.B. Sahay received the weapons on 25th December 1966, at a small public function. The *Jathedar* of *Keshgarh Saheb,* one Giani Sharam Singh, was accompanying the weapons that were taken to the local *gurdwara* after a display to the public. Meanwhile, Sant Fateh Singh had resumed his fast to death, declaring that if his demands were not conceded by a particular deadline, then he would immolate himself in a special tub installed at the *Akal Takhat* at a date and hour that was announced by him beforehand. I had, by now, come to realize that the demand for the Punjabi speaking state was only a facade for achieving a Sikh majority state where the Akalis could wield political power. I asked Giani Sharam Singh, if the action announced by the supreme leader of the Sikh community, was justifiable under the Sikh tenets as *Gurbani* was clear on the point that one could die only as per will of the Almighty and not by one's own volition. Giani Sharam Singh tried to get around my question by saying that we should judge such acts from the results that such actions brought. I told him that I had raised a moral issue and I expected an answer on the same plane from someone like him, whom people expected to be an authority on the Sikh tenets. He evaded the answer saying that as a *Jathedar,* he expected himself to be on the panel that might be officially asked to give a verdict on the issue, therefore, he would not like to commit himself in any manner at that time. Anyhow, for me he had given the answer that it was expediency alone that was behind the decisions that were taken at all the levels and in all the bodies that claimed to be representing the *Khalsa Panth.* I followed up my question with a letter addressed to Sant Fateh Singh in Punjabi, so that he could understand it directly. Unlike the earlier time, there was no reply this time to my letter.

Seeing as to how the Sikh community was being taken for a ride by the self-seeking leaders, I wrote a long article reviewing the vicissitudes of the Sikhs for the 300th birth anniversary issue of the journal '*Spokesman Weekly*', on the birth of Guru Gobind Singh, in 1966. What surprised me then and later when Bhindranwale came on to the scene, was the near silence of the Sikh intelligentsia in the face of total blatant blasphemy.

11

Handling Law and Order

Professionally too, I continued to be cited as the best district officer of Bihar. The *Indian Journal of Public Administration* had requested the Bihar Government to nominate one district officer from Bihar for writing an article for their special issue on "*Collector During the Sixties*". The choice of the Bihar Government fell on me. I made all the prescribed inspections of all the government units in Ranchi which included units like the excise vends, which earlier no district officer had ever inspected. I worked on the assumption that problems required to be tackled before any of the issues took the shape of a problem. The district had a sizeable tribal population mainly consisting of *Mundas*, *Oraons*, *Santhals* and others like *Birhors*, who survived on eating monkeys. We had a group of tribal called *Tana Bhagats,* who were influenced by Mahatma Gandhi. They wore handspun cotton clothes and they had joined the Non-Cooperation Movement against the British rule. Whenever they had a problem, genuine or merely perceived, they flocked to the office of the Deputy Commissioner and made a nuisance of themselves in every sense till they were pacified. The work in courts and other offices came to a standstill so long as the *Tana Bhagats* were there. No one could think of using force, against the freedom fighters. So, everyone suffered the nuisance. I knew that basically they were well meaning poor people. I simply ordered the police to round them up and take them away about twenty miles on a forest route and release them on the road from where they had to walk to their homes on foot. This action ended the menace of the work in courts and district offices for all time to come. The politics of creating a constituency started having its impact on the tribal population, who had their seats reserved in the State Legislature and in the Parliament. One Mr. Kartic Oraon, who was a serving Chief Engineer in the Heavy Engineering Corporation, thought of having a tribal following by whipping up hatred against the non-tribal population called *'dikkus'*, or trouble makers. We started getting reports about non-tribal teachers getting beaten up in schools in the interior, on his instigation, to serve the larger purpose of driving the non-tribals out of the tribal areas. I called him and told him that I suspected his hand behind all such incidents and if there was any such happenings hence forth, I would see to it that he was behind the bars. Again it seemed that I had hit the bull's eye, as such incidents ceased, so long as I was in Ranchi. The tribals, if they became a mob, could be tackled with great difficulty. We had an instance where a tribal woman was declared a witch by a tribal village and they fixed her punishment according to their tribal customs. They had their secret code to spread the message among others of their tribe by moving around a sapling of the *'Sal'* tree in the village weekly markets which are social and economic institutions in the tribal areas.

By the time the Government agencies came to know about it, it was too late to stop. A police force was provided to the family, from which an old woman had been declared a witch, but in front of thousands of tribals who had collected for what they called *'Bithlaha'* or dispensation of tribal justice, the police could do nothing. The house of the woman was stormed and razed to the ground. The police opened fire to save the woman, killing something like 17 persons. Wave after wave of tribals descended on the house which they not only destroyed but in vengeance they even eased themselves in the debris of the house. However, if one was informed on time the tribal mobs could have been easily tackled by isolating them from the places where they had started and overwhelming them with a superior force. I often used this technique when some tribal leader tried to instigate the tribal villagers to blackmail the HEC Management into granting them one benefit or the other. However, the technique for dealing with communal tension has to be a bit different. It had to be firm and hard-hitting but it should appear fair and just for all the communities. On the outskirts of Ranchi town the Bihar Government had acquired land covering fields and dwellings of some twenty villages, to set-up the HEC Complex. One of the villages, called Jagnathpur, had a hut in which Muslims of the village used to gather for their '*namaz*' or prayer. The revenue authority deposited the compensation for the hut in the Government Treasury as no one claimed ownership of the hut. The Heavy Machine Tools plant was to come up for which the entire ground of the village had been levelled. My predecessor, sought instructions from the State Government who advised that we should persuade the Muslim Opinion-Leaders to agree to the demolition of the Mosque. I called a group of Muslim Opinion-Leaders and their leading *Mullahs* who had brought with them some religious tomes from which they read out that if there was a mosque in a building, the building would remain a mosque till the Day of Judgment. This was not very helpful particularly because the official program of the Prime Minister of Czechoslovakia, who was to inaugurate the Plant, had got announced. The construction work was already going on around the disputed hut and it was a prohibited area for the public. I asked the police not to permit anyone, to come into the prohibited area. Somehow, Pakistan seemed to be worried about the completion of the HEC Complex. We had arrested a Pakistani spy who had confessed before a Magistrate that his masters had instructed him and others to do everything that was possible to delay the commissioning of the various plants of the HEC. After visitors were barred from the area, a group of Muslims tried to force their way in but they were stopped by the police. One of the hardliners happened to shout '*Long Live Pakistan*' which provided the police enough excuse to round them up and send all of them to jail. Next day, the leaders of the Muslim community came to me to protest against what they called the high-handedness of the police. I apprised them about the anti-national conduct of the group after which the leaders had no face to protest. They begged me to be a bit lenient as they said that they had got misguided. I officially asked the contractor to go ahead with his construction, as there was no mosque existing on the site. I also informed the State Government about it but heard nothing further from them. The secret, in all cases of civil disturbances, was to show sufficient patience, so that the public at large came to realize that the police had no alternative other than the use of force against the miscreants. The authorities in India had this peculiar problem as India was supposed to have won freedom through non-cooperation and non-violent defiance of the British. The use of force at an earlier stage often became counterproductive.

Ranchi was known for, one of the biggest defalcations under the British Rule in the forty's. It had been committed by a clerk of the little known Namkum Vaccine Research Institute, under the Department of Health. The *modus operandi* was simple, the clerk would prepare a routine bill for various petty expenditures incurred and after the bill was signed by the officer- in-charge, the clerk would write before the amount, in a space deliberately left blank by him, while writing the original bill. Three or four figures were added before the bill amount which enabled him to siphon off a few thousand rupees in each bill. The clerk was soon able to amass something like 40,00,000 rupees. The Accountant General detected that the expenditure being incurred at the small Vaccine Research Institute was far beyond the Government grant. He would write to the officer- in-charge about it, however, all mail in the government offices is generally received by a clerk who opens it and sorts out the important from the trash. The clerk saw to it that the letter of the Accountant General never reached the officer. This is one thing that I never allowed in any of the offices that I presided over, in my career. The Accountant General, after about six months wrote a letter to the Director of the Health Department, who was the controlling officer for that particular Government allocation, to look into what was going on in Ranchi.

The clerk, one Mr. Mitra, received in the office mail a program of the visit of the Director to Ranchi. He knew that his goose was cooked. He had invested his ill-gotten money in two flats in Bombay where he had kept a concubine of his. He got the rest of his money converted into gold and he put all the gold in a bag and scooted for Calcutta. He ran into a classmate of his who was in the police at the Calcutta Railway Station. His friend seeing him hailed him but Mitra because of his guilty conscience started running away. His friend thought that his behaviour was odd, so he chased and nabbed him, and on getting his bag opened, the cat was out of the bag. He was arrested and tried for the defalcation and fraud in Ranchi. He was convicted for life imprisonment and all his property was confiscated. The government revised the Bihar Treasury Code in order to ensure that such a contingency never occurred again. I was amazed when I found that the notorious Fodder Scam associated with Laloo Prasad Yadav, the Chief Minister of Bihar during the nineties, had exactly the same *modus operandi*. The real reason as to why such episodes happened is the system of administration and accounting in India wherein the responsibility for the nitty-gritty is with the lowest functionaries who are clerks. Despite all the instructions, the supervision of the higher officers has been becoming less and less over time. The accountability of the officials, after Independence, is ultimately to the political masters who have no time for the nitty-gritty of the administration. They judge the performance of the bureaucracy differently. Their favourite officers are those who enable them to achieve the ends they had in mind, be it money or unsound projects in their areas or some political mileage for the elections that they have to face. I devised a simple system of inspection of some key points in the form of a questionnaire which should not take more than 15 minutes for a supervising officer to complete. I insisted that all my subordinate officers must fill in the questionnaire before the 5th of every month and then send the same to me. The power of the clerk also comes from his mastery over the precedents as more often a clerk is at the same desk for years. I always went for mastering the rules, especially the purpose that the rules were supposed to serve. I felt that it was a more secure basis for decision making than the precedent and if the precedent went against me, I would reject the precedent. We had a shortage of GI sheets and the government had prescribed that whatever quota was available, the same should be distributed on a first come first served basis equitably. Some persons in connivance the office clerks had made a mockery of the government policy through a flood of applications for a very limited quantity that were available. I ignored the government policy and constituted a Citizen Advisory Committee to advise me on the basis of their personal knowledge so that whatever quantity of GI sheets were available, the same went to the applicants whose needs were genuine. Those interested tried to raise a storm in the State Assembly against my dispensation but when I explained the rationale of my policy, the State Government fully endorsed what I had done. The other fear that prevents officers from over-ruling their clerks is the fear of prosecution if later things went wrong. The officer who signed on the dotted line, was considered to be safe in the company of all those who had signed on the paper before him. The Bihar Government took away all the initiative from the officers because of the witch-hunting that followed the officers, after the various Commissions of Enquiry whereas no officer in the government had ever suffered if he took no decision or did nothing.

The system of the field administration in India has continued to be the same as was left by the British. The basic function of the administration was to maintain public order and to collect revenue for the government under the personal leadership of a District Officer supported and assisted by the district police chief. The overall overseeing authority for field administration was the Board of Revenue or the Financial Commissioner (Revenue). Quite often the Board of Revenue member would be senior to even the Chief Secretary. It was only recently that the position of the Chief Secretary had been made senior to everyone else in the state. We had a state level meeting of the District Officers in which Mr. C.K. Raman, ICS, the Member, Board of Revenue had made a special mention in the meeting that in his inspections of records in various districts he found that the records in Ranchi were in the best condition. Somehow, Mr. Raman suffered from an impression that his word was the last word so far as interpretation of financial and other rules was concerned. The Board of Revenue had an officer of the rank of a District Officer as its Secretary to manage the office of the Board. He got Mr. Raman to issue a circular that the Secretary, Board of Revenue, as the Controlling Officer of the funds allocated, would be inspecting offices of the District Officers. This was an absurd interpretation of a rule in the Bihar Treasury Code. I wrote to the Secretary that he was welcome to meet me but he could not inspect my office and the interpretation of the rule quoted was absurd. Mr. Raman, who was till then all praise for me, suddenly changed and took my views on the subject as a personal insult. He wrote a 60 page note on the issue quoting Goldsmith's poetry and recommended to the Chief Secretary to get me charge-sheeted. The Chief Secretary referred the matter to the Department of Finance as a financial rule's interpretation was involved. The Minister of Finance had a great respect for me. He asked me as to what he should do. Mr. Raman was about to retire. A South

Indian officer, who was close to him, told me that Mr. Raman was not able to sleep because, as he said, no one had defied him in service and got away with it and of all I, whom he had publicly admired was delivering the parting kick to him. I asked the Finance Minister to not to over-rule him and suggested a via media to delete the relevant rule that was at the root of the whole controversy. This did not assuage the feelings of Mr. Raman. I did not want him to carry any personal ill feelings about me over a purely official matter. I, therefore, wrote a personal letter to him, clarifying that my official position on the issue remained as it was, but I had not meant to insult him in any manner and if he felt that way I would tender an unqualified apology. I had clearly written that the apology was personal from a junior to a senior colleague for whom I had all the respect. Mr. Raman wrote to me that my letter did credit to me and closed his file by placing my letter on the file. I had a number of encounters with senior service officers and on most of the occasions I found the seniors to be small and petty. Mr. Sohoni, who was my first Commissioner, never left an opportunity to do me down because I had defied him as a District Officer in 1960. He gave an adverse remark to me in 1966, when he was looking after Civil Supplies, stating that I had failed to send a report to him which on my representation had to be expunged as he could not cite any proof for his observation. Mr. M.S. Rao, the then Chief Secretary when I had a tiff with the Chief Minister, tried to avoid me, even meeting socially, when I needed his support badly and the same Chief Secretary, when Binoda Nand Jha had praised me to the sky, bent over backwards to invite me for a meal before I left Patna. Binoda Nand Jha expected his Chief Secretary to know about his officers and if Mr. Rao chose to remain ignorant, then he had no use of him as his Chief Secretary, and Mr. Rao was shunted off to the Government of India for being posted as the Chief of Personnel in Hindustan Steel Limited with headquarters at Ranchi. When I went to Ranchi as the Deputy Commissioner, he would go out of his way to claim a special relationship with me. Another colleague, Mr. P.P. Naiyar had fallen foul of Mr. Jaya Prakash Narayan, a Bihar leader. He represented the socialist wing in the Congress.

The Bihar Government found Jaya Prakash Narayan too big for them and ordered summarily the transfer of Mr. Naiyar. I found him in Ranchi and took him under my wings. He was a General Manager in the National Coal Development Corporation under the Government of India where his boss, Mr. S.T. Raja, got him transferred from Ranchi as he suspected his loyalty. Mr. Raja had ordered Naiyar to vacate his house the same night.

He and his wife came running to me. I told them not to worry. I asked the city Deputy Superintendent of Police to pay a visit to some of his friends who were working in the NCDC during the office hours to create a sense of fear in the Chairman, Mr. Raja. I asked Naiyar to go and see Mr. Raja and tell him that he could not leave Ranchi until the Government of Bihar recalled him and till then he would like to retain his house as well as the assignment that he had. I had sent the Sub-Divisional Magistrate with him to wait outside unless Mr. Naiyar called for him. I told the SDM that in all probability Mr. Raja would back down but in case he was not inclined then on the complaint of Mr. Naiyar he was to be booked under the law and sent to jail. As anticipated Mr. Raja did back down and Mr. Naiyar, who later had got close to Mrs. Gandhi during the 1975 Emergency, had the satisfaction to see Mr. Raja booted out because of his inability to handle his own subordinate staff. The same Mr. Naiyar, when he became the Chief Secretary of Bihar, went to the extent of getting me charge-sheeted for at worst a technical lapse. I think that after joining the service, as human beings, the civil servants got retarded and stunted in the growth of their personalities. Most of them turn up to be vain, petty and petulant by the time they retired. I found that it was worse in the Foreign Service. The first four or five in every batch generally went to the Foreign Service. The nature of assignments in the Foreign Service was such that their jobs had no challenge or real content. I was shocked when I found two of our brilliant colleagues from the Foreign Service spent two hours discussing if a visiting dignitary should enter the embassy from one gate or the other. The lack of challenge in the job combined with the culture of cocktail parties left many of them good for nothing.

It is necessary to have a look at the corruption in the Civil Services. I joined service from a family which had a tradition of serving in the armed forces. The family tradition and what I understood from the *Granth Saheb* taught me to make both ends meet with the salary that I received. I was unaware about the illegal money floating about at the lower rungs of the Civil Services. Many Field Officers did not find it objectionable if, for meeting their hospitality obligations, money came from the *Nazir* or the like in the office. I also discovered that payment of '*mamul*' or customary incentive or reward at certain levels could not be stopped. I believed in meeting my obligations from my salary and the same was the case with the majority of the directly recruited IAS officers, but some exceptions were there, however, mostly the evil was confined to the officers promoted from the State Civil Services. We lived frugally and everyone would notice if anyone tried to live ostentatiously. I remember an incident while I was a Sub Divisional Officer, one small entrepreneur came to call on us when I had gone out. He brought with him some presents like a *sari* and a gold chain for Sukhdev. She got nervous on seeing the presents and returned the presents in a fit of anger. The guest who had come was also a bit upset and said that he had taken a similar set of gifts to the Deputy Commissioner. Mrs. Deputy Commissioner had gladly accepted the gifts. The IAS Conduct Rules permitted one to accept a gift that was not more than 25 rupees in value. My wife however, was firm and refused to accept the gifts. When she told me about it, I said that I was proud of her. We lived poorly but we were happy.

Corruption can be defined as the use of one's official position or influence for one's personal benefit. There is considerable confusion when one tries to draw the line as to where influence can be considered to be attached to one's official position or purely to the private person. I followed the policy of taking participative decisions in all matters, even if all the statutory authority was vested in me alone. This provided me a useful input in my decision-making and saved me from gossip mongering. I generally recorded the minutes of such meetings that were held at least once a week, if not more often. The second decision that I took was to not to invest in any property because I had often seen fingers being raised on my colleagues who had gone for buying property. Thirdly, I avoided making friends with businessmen and the rich. This helped me to face the crisis that got generated for me. The Chief of the anti-corruption authority for a long time was one Mr. Rajeshwar Lal, IPS, a very ambitious officer, who started lining his own pockets through blackmailing or conniving with the corrupt officials. He asked me to send him records of three revenue cases that had been decided by my Additional Deputy Commissioner, as he suspected some underhand dealing in those cases. I called for the case records and had a look at those records before sending them to Mr. Lal. I found that in all the cases the final orders had been passed by me. I, therefore, did not send the records but wrote to him that the decisions in the three cases were above board. He perhaps did not like my response because after my transfer from Dhanbad, Kaushal Kumar Srivastava, the press reporter who was licking his wounds, leveled some baseless allegations against me relating to my stay at Dhanbad. Some of the allegations were outlandish and frivolous like, I being responsible for some rail wagons carrying wheat not reaching Dhanbad from Vizag docks. The government, in their wisdom, had laid down that if an enquiry had to be made about an IAS officer a prior clearance of the Chief Secretary was a pre-requisite condition.

The Chief Secretary was Mr. T.P. Singh, who had got slightly prejudiced against me on seeing a group of politicians at our house in Ranchi. Neither had he asked nor did I deem it necessary to explain that they had come to thank me on behalf of the Chief Minister of Bihar for having saved him from extreme embarrassment if the plan of his detractors had succeeded. When Rajeshwar Lal put up the Dhanbad newspaper before him, seeking his permission to hold an enquiry against me, he just signed on the file giving his concurrence. The former Commissioner of Ranchi happened to be the Additional Chief Secretary at Patna. He was shocked to see the file and rang me up about it. The implications of the order were that my future career would depend on the mercy of Mr. Lal. I decided to take the bull by the horns. I could use my closeness to the Chief Minister to get the enquiry closed, but such a closure would always carry a question mark and as soon as Mr. K.B. Sahay ceased to be the Chief Minister, it could be restarted with a vengeance. I decided to write a provocative letter to the Chief Secretary, accusing him of a caste bias against me for having earlier defied Dr. S.K. Sinha, who was of the same caste as the Chief Secretary. Simultaneously, I cited chapter and the verse to show the absurdity of the allegations made against me. I also sent in a letter of my unconditional resignation from the IAS accompanied by an application for home leave. I had taken these steps after guidance from the *Guru Granth Saheb*, where again and again the Guru's word was that a gurmukh had to fear nothing. Mr. T.P. Singh, I think, was filled with remorse. He requested me to take my letter back and he promised to get the enquiry closed. I consulted a colleague who advised me to not to take the letter back. I told the Chief Secretary that I would not take the letter back and proceeded on home leave to our village Gharuan in Punjab. Mr. T.P. Singh was good enough to place before the Chief Minister, that a mistake had been committed by him in ordering an enquiry against me, for which there was no basis. The Chief Minister ordered my recall from leave at the cost of the government sanctioning my return journey by air, which was my first air travel in a commercial passenger plane. Somehow, no action was taken against Mr. Rajeshwar Lal, who remained to fight against me yet another day. He started unauthorized checking of my personal mail. I came to know about it from the postmaster. I did not bother about it as I had nothing to hide. I got a letter from my father accusing me of not doing anything for the family as I had declined to buy a plot of land in Chandigarh, the new capital of Punjab. He gave up after he saw the letter in my mail. One of his inspectors started harassing an honest Electrical Engineer known to me. He was a hefty and somewhat short-tempered person. He saw the inspector sitting on a chair, in the compound of his government quarter. He could not restrain himself on seeing him and he got down to give him a physical beating. The inspector rang up Mr. Rajeshwar Lal, who came to Ranchi and got a case registered against the Engineer. I happened to be on tour. When I returned from tour, he rang me up requesting me to take him out of the jam. I came to know that the police had charged him for a simple assault that was a bailable offence. I asked the engineer to go to the police station and surrender himself before the police and to ring me up from there. When the police inspector rang me up, I told him that I would stand surety for the engineer in my personal capacity. This was enough for the police inspector to release the engineer on his personal bond. I then advised the engineer to file a counter-case against the Anti-corruption Department inspector before the Sub Divisional Magistrate, who took cognizance of his complaint and issued a process against the inspector. I, as the District Magistrate, had revisionary jurisdiction in both the cases. I *suo moto* issued a notice in both the cases, calling for records. I received the records but I deliberately did not fix a date for hearing. Mr. Rajshwar Lal, who had been rebuked badly by the Chief Minister for initiating the enquiry against me, did not have the courage to pursue the case further.

The national elections were expected in 1967. Mrs. Gandhi had strengthened her hold on power, but she had to fight for it on two fronts. One was within the Congress party where the party managers tried to obstruct her at every step. They even forced her to endorse their own candidate for the post of the President of India against the one whom she had proposed. She decided to side with the radicals and leftists in the Congress party and go for populist policies and ultimately she had the better of her detractors. The Congress had continued to be the ruling party much to the chagrin of leaders like Ram Manohar Lohia, who was a socialist. He believed that for making the people go against the Congress he should destroy, in the minds of the people, the image of its top leaders particularly Nehru and later Indira Gandhi. He along with his erstwhile mentor Jaya Prakash Narayan had a lot of expectations from the students whom he would try to place in the vanguard of any agitation that he launched. All these parties, vying for political power, started statewide student agitations in Bihar towards the end of 1966. They projected, in Bihar, the issue of corruption of Mr. K.B. Sahay, on the basis of lurid and generally baseless stories planted in the media. K.B. Sahay had come to alienate the powerful Rajput group in the Congress. '*K.B. Sahay chor hai*' or K.B. Sahay is a thief, was the refrain of all the student demonstrations, so much so that one day in his own house K.B. Sahay heard his small grandson shouting '*K.B. Sahay chor hai*', which made him say that the 1967 election would be the last that he would be fighting. Students of Ranchi also announced their programme of demonstrations that we prohibited under the authority that we had under the law. The students decided to take out a massive students' procession from the Ranchi University campus to the city, where other students were expected to join them. We had full presence of the police all over the city and the massive police presence succeeded in most of the students remaining present in their classes. However, a few hundred students of the Ranchi University campus took out an illegal but peaceful procession. They passed on the road adjoining the Deputy Commissioner's house where my son Dipendar was playing in the verandah. Some mischievous youngster threw a small stone inside the compound. All of them were shouting slogans against K.B. Sahay. Dipendar had never witnessed a scene like that. He rushed inside to his mother saying that some Chinese had come who had thrown a stone at the house. He was only about three years old at that time. How he associated the students' behaviour with the Chinese remained an enigma for us. I overtook the procession in my jeep and told the leaders to disperse as what they were engaged in was illegal but they did not listen. I moved a little ahead of them and selected a spot that was somewhat open and asked the police to put a barrier to stop the procession. When the procession came to the spot, their numbers had swelled. When I said that they must disperse, their leaders became a bit rude. One of them shouted an insult at me personally. I lifted the small baton that I had in my hand and said loudly that he was being ill-mannered in abusing the Deputy Commissioner and before I could complete my sentence the police who were already fed up with their behavior starting wielding their sticks. They targeted the leaders, particularly the most abusive ones. I found to my horror that one of the leaders had fallen down and a number of policemen were showering blows on him. I saw blood on him and shouted at the policemen to stop but they stopped only when I physically threw them away. The leader, in sheer terror, begged me to save him. I supported him to get up and found that he had urinated in his pants. I pointed it out. He got so ashamed of himself that he was never heard of again in any student agitation. The students ran away helter-skelter after the *lathi* or 'stick' charge, leaving behind their books, *chappals*, slippers and bicycles. We were preparing ourselves for the regrouping of the students when a whole column of military, on a routine route march, appeared on the scene, demoralizing the agitators completely.

This was a contribution that General Bhagat had made for us, without our having asked him to assist us. We found that some of those who had abandoned their cycles were watching from a little distance away, for an opportunity to recover their cycles. I signaled to them to come and reclaim their cycles. They came running and went away profusely thanking me after they recovered their abandoned belongings. The whole episode ended on a happy note. I went home happy at having tackled a ticklish situation well. I heard in the evening news, on the All India Radio, that there were police firings on the student agitators all over the state, mainly in the towns where headquarters of the universities in Bihar were located.

The first thing that came before me the next day was the intelligence report that said that in the night some opposition politicians had come to the students' hostel and addressed them, saying that the students of Ranchi had let them down by failing to provoke the Ranchi police to open fire on the students, whereas all over the state the students had made them proud by their defiance of the authority that invited police firing. They, therefore, asked the student leaders to observe the next day as a protest day following the same agenda as they had earlier. I called a meeting of the police officers and Magistrates at my residential office to chalk out a strategy for the day. We did not know as to where the trouble would break out. Police officers and Magistrates were spread over all the vulnerable points, with clear instructions that on any sign of unruly behavior, on the part of the students, they must disperse them with force that could go up to opening of fire. I gave only one caution that if in their judgment, at any time, it appeared to them that they had to order opening of fire and they had time, they must inform me before they ordered the police to open fire, as I believe that killing someone for taking part in an agitation was an avoidable act. Mr. G. Narain and I sat down, waiting for the situation to unfold. We came to know that students in various institutions had come out of their classes to demonstrate. It was around 1 p.m. that I got a telephone from a Magistrate posted in the Ranchi main bazaar, that students had entrenched themselves in the post-graduate campus of the university. They had with them a large collection of brickbats with which they had paralyzed all traffic on the main road and a number of policemen had been injured by brickbats. The students would come out in small groups to indulge in brick batting and would run away inside the campus when chased and according to the Magistrate, there was no alternative to opening of fire. I asked the Magistrate to wait for our arrival. I rang up the Dean of the University, who had his office inside the post-graduate campus.

The Dean said that he himself had been locked inside his room from outside and he was helpless. I rang up the Vice Chancellor, Mr. Markham, to do something, but he told me that in a situation like the one prevailing, he thought that there was nothing that he could do. I decided to move out and take charge of the situation. I went to the *Guru Granth Saheb* for blessings and the Guru's word was from *Raag*

Suhi Mahala Panjwan 'santan de karaj aap khloa har kam karawan aaya ram' which meant that for the work undertaken by *sants* or holy persons, the Almighty Himself has joined to get it completed. It was a very reassuring random opening blessing. Just when we were to get into the jeep, which was to take us, my wife, Sukhdev, stopped us, saying that lunch was ready, so we must have lunch before we left. It proved to be a welcome intervention, as we could return back home quite late in the evening. As we were proceeding towards the scene of action, we had to pass the wall of the post-graduate campus from where a small pebble was aimed at me and it hit me on the left temple causing a contusion and slight bleeding. As we proceeded further, we found that the Magistrate and the police had taken shelter behind the wall of the GPO and many of them were injured. I proposed that we should make one determined baton charge against the student hooligans but the Magistrate was not willing for it as he said that it would serve no purpose because the hooligans would regroup as soon as our back was turned to them. I still persisted and snatched a baton from a policeman. I asked the police force to follow me as I hit out on the nearest bystander. The police also joined me and the hooligans started running away. However, as predicted they would regroup after running a short distance. This gave me an idea and I seized a van from the road. I asked a section of the police force to sit in the van while I took the steering of the van. I drove at a breakneck speed towards the group that was reforming and the speed with which the van came on them took the hell out of them who ran as fast as their legs could take them. We arrested the few who were nearest to us and advanced towards the other reforming group. That took the wind out of the sail of the hooligans, who decided that discretion was better than valor and disappeared. The group inside the campus was a problem, so I ordered that the front gate of the campus be broken open and all those who were inside should be taken into custody. The whole action had taken place in the centre of the town. A number of press reporters were covering the entire operation.

The police had used teargas before entering the campus and because of their predicament since the morning, some of them gave vent to their anger by roughing up some of the students who were taken into custody. The situation was tense when some of the press reporters wanted to interview me. I was a little brusque with them and asked them to report what they saw. My offhand attitude to them made their coverage hostile to us. When the Dean came out of his room he had tears in his eyes because of the teargas but the press reporters said that the Dean had weepingly told them that the police had entered the post-graduate campus without taking his permission and without informing him. We learnt on the police wireless that a number of small students' processions were on the way, towards the city centre. We ordered that all such processions must be dispersed by force. One such procession was intercepted by the police, very near the Ranchi courts and just in front of the bar association building, the procession was lathi charged and dispersed, without giving them any warning. The police action was watched by many of the lawyers of Ranchi and somehow it put their hackles up. We had a very hostile coverage of the police action in the press. The Bar Association of Ranchi passed a resolution condemning our action. Even the Vice Chancellor, A.F. Markham, wrote me a letter of protest. I was quite sad that despite our success in avoiding killing of any demonstrator, we stood condemned in the public eye. I called the President of the Bar Association, to explain that our action was legally correct, and on seeing the relevant section of law he was good enough to accept that the Bar Association was wrong in passing that resolution. I wrote a stinging letter to the Vice Chancellor, reminding him and the Dean about my telephonic conversation. Mr. Markham rang me up to say that he was sorry for his letter and he would like to close the chapter by returning to me the letter that I had written to him. I decided to not to pursue the matter further and in return I sent his letter back to him but I retained a copy of the same in my file.

We overlooked another aspect of handling public order. There is always present, in all situations, a sort of climate of public opinion which can be best described as Zeitgeist. An awareness of Zeitgeist is a must for devising the strategy of handling a situation. We should have known that in Bihar the opposition political parties had created a climate that was hostile to the executive authorities of the state. We had to be more than patient in explaining our action to a level where our compulsion for taking the action that we took should have appeared as obvious to all and sundry. We had a sideshow on our hand as the employees of the Civil Hospital, Ranchi went on a lightning strike because I had failed to recognize the head clerk of the hospital standing near me as a sightseer, like so many others, and he was hit by my baton. I pacified them as the incident happened in the heat of the moment. I showed them my own injury. They broke their strike by giving first aid to me. The politicians who had successfully brought the whole thing about were jubilant. We had a super demagogue, Mr. Mahamaya Prasad Sinha, as a leader espousing the cause of the students. He would shed copious tears on public platforms while sympathizing with students who had suffered injuries or death in the police action and called the students as pieces of his heart and liver. He would get so much emotionally charged while speaking that he would tear his white muslin shirt from the front to demonstrate his anger against the police. His Private Secretary, generally carried with him half a dozen muslin shirts for him to change in the car while going for the next public meeting. He declared that if he came to power he would ensure that the heartless officials like the Ranchi officials were brought to book. Meanwhile, another opposition leader who was the erstwhile Raja of Ramgarh came to visit the students, arrested by the police, in jail. He carried with him a few baskets of sweets for the students. The Jail Superintendent sought instructions from me if he should permit him to get the sweets distributed. I told him that only a relative could be permitted to give any eatable to a prisoner but not a political leader. The Raja was turned back from jail. He came straight to my house while I was having my siesta. My orderlies at the house could not stop him from entering my private drawing room. Sukhdev woke me up. It took me some time to meet the Raja, who was not used to being kept waiting. We greeted each other and he said that while he was running from pillar to post, I was calmly sleeping in my house. I said that it was a matter of choice for the both of us. He had chosen to become a political leader and therefore he had to run around before the elections, while we could have our share of sleep, and when he came to power, he could make the likes of me run from pillar to post. He laughed at this and asked me as to what he should do with the sweets. I told him that he could take the baskets home. He said that he would go to the press about it. I told him that he would be within his rights in doing so. I found that in such situations there were many who wished to benefit. I had seen one college dropout, Vijay Ranjan, who was looking for opportunities to become a leader. I visited the Kotwali Police Station in the evening and I found that along with some other students, Vijay Ranjan too was in the lock up. I asked the officer-in-charge as to why he was there. He said that he had gone to the hostel to round-up some students involved in the previous day's hooliganism. When he had got them into his van, Vijay Ranjan laid himself down in front of the van and said that he would not permit his friends to be taken to the police station. He had, therefore, to be arrested. I knew that Vijay Ranjan wanted to appear as a martyr for the cause of the students. I asked the police officer to release him on a personal bond. The police officer came back to me saying that Vijay Ranjan did not want to be released. He wanted to go to the jail along with the others. I told the police officer to fulfil his wish but send him to jail in the sub-divisional town of Simdega which was almost 190 kilometres from Ranchi. As soon as he was told about these orders, he broke down and started begging for mercy. I told him that he could still be released on bail provided he found one surety to guarantee that he would behave in the future, which he did. As long as I was in Ranchi, he did not figure in any trouble, but he did figure as the instigator of the biggest communal riot in Ranchi after I had been transferred from Ranchi.

One of the important functions of an IAS officer in India, though unstated, is to train the political leaders who become ministers, to function within the system of the civil administration, as given in the framework in our Constitutional document. The Congress party was reduced to a minority for the first time in Bihar. A coalition arrangement was hammered out in which all the political parties and some independent candidates, who had won against the Congress in the Assembly elections, joined to form a government with Mahamaya Prasad Sinha as the Chief Minister. The *ex-Raja* of Ramgarh was an important minister in the new Government. I was called by the Chief Secretary to see him at his house. He lived in a palatial house in Patna although he was known to be one of the biggest tax dodgers of India. He made me wait for about ten minutes before I was called to his presence. I greeted him and sat down. He said that he wanted to visit Ranchi. I told him that he was welcome to Ranchi and whatever arrangements he desired, the same could be made. He said that he would like to visit Ranchi jail and he wanted me to escort him during his visit that perforce I had to do as he would be visiting the jail as a Minister. However, nothing untoward happened during the visit except that in his mind he thought that he had settled the score with me for my refusing to permit him to visit the jail a month or so earlier. We had earlier Mr. K.B. Sahay appointing Mr. S.K. Bage, a tribal leader a Cabinet rank Minister. He did not like that I did not go to receive him at the airport when he came to visit Ranchi, his home town. I did not go because the protocol required me to receive only the Governor or the Chief Minister of Bihar. He did not say anything to me but he told in a public meeting of the tribals in the interior, where the Sub Divisional Officer, Mr. B.P. Verma, IAS, was present, that by becoming a minister he had become a big man and the Sub Divisional Officer had to remain standing in his presence. He further said that so far as the local Block Development Officer was concerned, he was at his mercy and just to show that he was ordering on the spot to place him under suspension. He later met the local press and told the press reporters that he had ordered the suspension of the BDO, Jaldega, in Simdega Subdivision. It was a press reporter, who informed me about it. I immediately wrote to the Chief Secretary, that in my view the Minister, Mr. S.K. Bage, had gone berserk. I requested the Chief Secretary to give a chance to the BDO, to explain his conduct, before he was placed under suspension, on the orders of Mr. Bage. I did not get any reply from the Chief Secretary but after about a week I received a government order directing me to place the BDO, Jaldega, under suspension and frame a charge sheet against him. I wrote back to the Chief Secretary that I could not implement the Government order as nothing wrong had been committed by the officer concerned. The Minister visited Ranchi, in the meanwhile, and found that the BDO was still working as usual.

The Minister went back to Patna and threatened to resign from the ministry if his order did not get carried out. The Chief Minister was in some spot, politically, so he shouted at the Chief Secretary. The Chief Secretary, knowing my obduracy, ordered B.P. Verma, the SDO, to serve the order on the BDO, failing which the Government would place him under suspension. Mr. Verma asked me for advice. I told him that I was quite clear in my mind that I could go to the extreme to defy the Government on an issue like that but I would not force him to take the same stand on the orders that he had directly received. He decided to accept the orders of the Government. The Chief Minister came to Ranchi on the week end. I told him to relieve me of my responsibility, as having failed in protecting an innocent subordinate officer, I would no longer command respect among my subordinate officers. K.B. Sahay pleaded his helplessness in the matter, where a badly needed cabinet colleague had staked his prestige over the order. May be, there was no fault but he was a prisoner of his compulsions. He said that if I could see the Minister when he visited Ranchi next and tell him that I was satisfied about the conduct of the BDO and that I would recommend recall of the orders of the suspension of the BDO. This face-saving exercise would enable him to recall the orders of suspension of the BDO. I did what was asked from me and within a week we had the BDO back in his seat.

The new Chief Minister made a public pronouncement that appeared in all the Bihar newspapers, saying that he had ordered the police in Bihar that henceforth it would not be permissible for them to use force against students. I asked the Chief Secretary to send us the new instructions. The Chief Secretary said, on telephone, that no such instruction had been issued by the Government and he had put up before the Chief Minister that he should issue a denial of the remarks attributed to him by the newspapers but he was not passing any orders on that proposal. Meanwhile, we observed that there was general defiance of authority in the air. There was a minor clash between some students and taxi drivers over demand of fare which led to violence and smashing of a few taxis. When the police was informed, a Magistrate with police, rushed to the spot, where the clash had taken place.

The hooligans, who generally used to run away on seeing the police, this time assembled and adopted a threatening posture. He rang me up as to what he should do. I asked him to run away from the scene. He visibly hesitated on the telephone as he thought perhaps I was not serious. I asked him if he was prepared to open fire against the hooligans, who were students. He replied in the negative. I then asked him if he was prepared to give his life for his duty. He could not answer in the affirmative. I then asked him to run away as fast as he could, which he did, spreading panic in the city. I sent a wireless message to the Chief Secretary that I had decided to withdraw police force from the city, in absence of any instructions from the Government regarding the use of police force against the students, and panic prevailed in the city. A number of public leaders from Ranchi bitterly complained to the Chief Minister and other ministers on the lawlessness that was allowed to prevail. Mr. G. Narain, however, had kept the police in plainclothes on duty, so that the taxi-student clashes did not spread. Next morning, the Chief Minister and four senior ministers flew to Ranchi where they were given a very hostile reception by the citizen of Ranchi. Mr. G. Narain and I met them in the Circuit House. Mr. Narain was emotionally upset over the fact that he had to serve such an irresponsible set of political leaders who had put the life and honour of the citizens at peril because of sheer populist slogan mongering. At one stage, during the discussions, he took off his belt and revolver for handing over to the Chief Minister, who seemed to be more obsessed about his public image than the issue of public order and police morale. This had the desired effect and the Chief Minister promised that he would go back and issue a public statement about the police continuing to enjoy all powers under the law as hither to. I intervened to say that it would not do. If he was serious then he should go to the university campus and address the students, clarifying that lawlessness would not be tolerated. The Chief Minister and his colleagues did as they were asked. The Chief Secretary thanked me for helping him to get the Chief Minister disabuse the public impression that students enjoyed any sort of immunity from the police if they broke the law. The same night a longish wireless message was received by all the District Magistrates and the Superintendents of Police that in all situations the law shall prevail as hitherto.

I was later quite surprised when the officials of Uttar Pradesh Government carried out illegal orders of the state government to not to use force against the *kar-sewaks,* who were gathering together at Ayodhya, to illegally demolish the Babri Masjid and the Government of India kept silently watching when they had all the powers under the Constitution, to dismiss the state government which was clearly failing in its Constitutional obligations.

The new government in Bihar was very upset about me because of the humiliation they suffered at Ranchi. Mr. Rajeshwar Lal was already smarting under the rebuke that was administered to him by K.B. Sahay. They specially went over all my official decisions taken by me as Deputy Commissioner of Ranchi and earlier at Dhanbad. Some portions from my letters that were considered objectionable were leaked to the press. Two actions of mine were included in the charges that were collected against K.B. Sahay for which the Government appointed a retired Supreme Court judge, Justice Venkataramani Aiyer, to hold an enquiry. The public hearing on the charges went on for a long time, exposing the views of the officials on the various issues that came before the Commission and quite often the judge made some personal observations during the hearings, questioning the bona fides or the wisdom of the officials, who had recorded those notes. If there is one single cause for the collapse of the Bihar administration later on, the same can be ascribed to the appointment of the Aiyer Commission. It is the expose before the Commission that made the officials lose all initiative and leadership. Those officers who were known for their negative responses to anything that came before them, were the ones who came for appreciation by the Commission. A judicial commission suffers from two great disadvantages. One is because their conclusions are based on a reconstruct of events through hindsight in absence of all the facts, compulsions and pressures that had played a part in the decision-making. The second blind spot for the judge is his own background of having spent his career in an ivory tower. It is a very costly expediency that the politicians resort to in appointing a Commission of Enquiry over issues which they find awkward to handle or for political mileage which they hope to get out of it. The Commission did not summon officials whose participation in various decisions was the subject matter of any of the charges. Anyhow, the Commission, in my case, threw out one charge as unsubstantiated and the other, according to the Commission, was technically faulty though not mala fide. The technically faulty decision had been taken by me but Mr. K.B. Sahay assumed full responsibility for the same. I went to see him after the report of the Commission. He was no longer in power. He was staying with his son. I told him that for my hasty decision he need not have taken responsibility. He floored me with his reply that all the time he knew that I had taken that decision but he felt that as a civil servant I had my whole carrier before me. Any aspersion that the Commission's report might cast against me, might affect my career adversely, whereas he being a politician would lose nothing if the Commission made any adverse observation against him. I was really touched by his reply. However, nothing came out of the Commission, so far as I was concerned.

The Mahamaya Prasad Sinha Government appointed Commissions of Enquiry in all cases where the police had resorted to firing on the students. Ranchi was an exception where a Commission of Enquiry was appointed even though there was no firing on the students. I was simultaneously transferred as a Joint Secretary in the Department of Cooperatives on the basis of my record of fostering and supporting cooperative movement wherever I was posted. The worst was that we were just abandoned by the state government. No senior officer took any interest in the presentation that we had to make before the Commission of Enquiry except for the Inspector General of Police, Mr. B.P. Akhauri, IPS. He sat with us and went through the draft of our written statement giving his valuable advice here and there. Still worse was the appointment of a lawyer as our counsel, who had moved the resolution in the Ranchi Bar Association, condemning the police action under our orders. I wrote to the Chief Secretary that if I had served an ordinary businessman and in carrying out his wishes something happened because of which I had to face charges in a court of law the businessman concerned would have provided me the best legal assistance available, when I was doing something in the service of the President of India, the Government of Bihar was providing a lawyer of such low standing in the profession and that too when he had gone against us which was on public record. The Bihar Government changed their orders and appointed a senior advocate to represent the officers facing the Commission of Enquiry. I refused to accept him as my counsel but I advised all others to let him handle our brief. The written statement that was prepared basically by me, presented our case in a manner that described all decisions as having been taken on the orders of the Deputy Commissioner or the Superintendent of the Police. I got copies of the written statement circulated to all the officers who had any role to play in handling of the student disturbances so that they could always recall their part in the episode. The new government had another brush with the bureaucracy when they ordered on the spot, to transfer the Deputy Commissioner of Santhal Parganas, Mr. Yashwant Sinha, later Finance Minister of India, because he called a group of unruly students who had gone to receive the Chief Minister as riff raff. I was one of the IAS officers who had gone in a delegation to the Chief Secretary, Mr. B.D. Pande, who later was appointed as the Governor of Punjab, to protest against the arbitrary orders of the Chief Minister. The Chief Secretary advised us to be patient as it was a new government. He later worked out a face saving formula for both the sides, by arranging a berth for Mr. Yashwant Sinha in the Government of India. Before I had left Ranchi I had written a long letter to the Chief Secretary of Bihar, cautioning him that the communal situation in Ranchi was explosive and if there was any relaxation in vigilance, it might lead to a communal conflagration. The new government went ahead with the transfer of all the senior officers and their replacement by inexperienced or incompetent officers. Over and above, the new government hastily decided to give Urdu the status of the second language in the state. Urdu is the cultural language of the Muslims. Vijay Ranjan was able to mobilize the students of Ranchi against Urdu being made the second language in Bihar. A procession of students was taken out and while the procession was passing through a Muslim locality on the main road, a Punjabi refugee shopkeeper was stabbed. He was rushed to the hospital where he died the next day. His funeral sparked off serious communal riots in which there was a terrible backlash against the Muslims. Bihar had an erstwhile constable, who was the orderly of Mr. Akhauri when he was a Superintendent of the Police, as the Minister in-charge of the police. He rushed to Ranchi to take charge of the situation but his presence made the situation worse. Mr. Sohoni, who had never run a district, was made the Chief Secretary. He ordered the police to arrest five hundred bad characters during the night and desired compliance with his orders before he got up in the morning. The police completed their quota of arrests during the night but it was discovered that it were not the bad characters who were arrested but it were mainly Muslims, who were already on the receiving end, who were arrested. There was no stopping of the arson and killing of Muslims in Ranchi. The Deputy Commissioner had served mostly in the State Secretariat, moving files. He acted like a babe in the wood and ran to the Commissioner for guidance. The Commissioner too found himself to be out of depth. They decided to call the Army. The cordiality and personal equation with the Army that was there in our time, no longer existed. The whole day the Commissioner and the Army Station Commander quibbled over the modalities of the Army takeover while the city burnt. It was only the next day that the army got the Commissioner to sign an illegal order handing over the city to the army and placing the civil police under the army. The authorities forgot about the Zeitgeist completely and could not stop the police constabulary from going berserk in victimizing and torturing Muslims who had been rounded up.

It was after about a week that peace got restored. I could have a close look at what was happening as I was commuting between Patna and Ranchi for preparing our defence before the Commission of Enquiry that was to start its public hearings soon. It increased my standing among the public which helped us a lot in our defence. The Congress had been defeated in the general elections in a number of states including Bihar but at the Centre the Congress had a clear majority. There were communal riots after the elections in a number of states. The Central Government, under Mrs. Indira Gandhi, appointed a Commission of Enquiry under a Supreme Court judge, Justice Raghubar Dayal, assisted by two other eminent persons, to go into the causes of the communal riots and their handling.

The day the enquiry was to start against us, the Bihar newspaper '*Indian Nation*' carried on the first page a letter addressed by me to Mr. Pran Parshad, the Chairman of M/s Bird and Co., on behalf of K.B. Sahay, requesting for a liberal contribution for the makers of Bihar Fund '*Bihar Nirmata Kosh*' that had been launched by him under the chairmanship of Jaya Prakash Narayan. I had written that in the mining industry, much more than I was asking for, the fund got spent on faults, frustrations and frayed tempers, so the 2,50,000 rupees that I was asking was not a princely sum in that context. The word 'faults' in my letter referred to the geological faults that one came across in coal scams and not to human faults. Mr. Rajeshwar Lal thought that it was a proof of my threatening Pran Parshad and for that he got the letter splashed in the media to prejudice the Court of Enquiry judge, Justice S.P. Singh, against me. My wife Sukhdev, who was in Patna, got worried on seeing the newspapers and rang me up in Ranchi. I told her to have faith in Waheguru and pray for our vindication, which she did. When I reached the Commission chamber, I found that there was a battery of ten lawyers led by the most notorious lawyer of Ranchi, Mr. Tribeni Sahay, who specialised in humiliating officials of the government in court. He lived in great style, but paid no income tax as no income tax officer had dared to issue a notice to him asking for filing his income tax return. I was told that the one who did so had to rue the day because Tribeni Sahay appeared before him and asked him to record his statement on oath. He said that he earned little but he got friendly with the wife of an income tax officer, who was corrupt and she had been passing his ill-gotten money to him and the income tax officer was none other than the officer recording his statement on oath. This statement made the income tax officer lose his temper and assault Tribeni Sahay in the witness box. Tribeni Sahay immediately filed a complaint against the IT officer slapping all the sections of law that could be brought in. The IT officer had to get the matter closed after tendering an apology. The city police chief, anticipating some dramatics, handed over to me a local newspaper that had carried a story about the crafty and corrupt ways of Tribeni Sahay. I kept the newspaper in my pocket.

Mr. Sahay, without much ceremony flashed the Patna newspaper before me, accusing me of having been a tool of K.B. Sahay. I denied the imputation and I was able to convince the judge that what I did was legitimate. Then I took out the newspaper from my pocket and placed before the judge, with the observation that in a court of law, newspaper stories can be equally cited by the other side. The judge read out the story from which Mr. Sahay learnt that the source of the story was none else than a lawyer, Mr. Gupta, who was the number two lawyer among the battery of lawyers against us. He hit the ceiling on that and right in the court he declared that he was giving up the brief of our opponents. This changed the whole scene in our favour. The father of Mr. G. Narain, IPS, was a leading lawyer of Gaya. He was always with us. I had not officially accepted the lawyer provided to us by the government, therefore, I appointed him as my lawyer so that he could officially participate in the proceedings of the Commission. We could prove our case to the hilt. I argued in the end that it would not be adequate for the judge to merely say that what we did was justifiable and that the learned judge should declare that the whole handling of the situation by us was commendable. Justice S.P. Singh, was good enough to say so in the report. The Chief Secretary passed orders to record a note of commendation in the record of all the officers who had taken part in handling the student disturbances.

In the meanwhile, the Raghubar Dayal Commission announced the date of hearing on the Ranchi communal riots. The Commission issued a public notice that anyone who knew anything about those riots was welcome to file an affidavit before the Commission and if considered relevant or necessary by the Commission such a person could be called to appear personally before the Commission. I knew that the Bihar Government and Administration would try to cover their lapses. The government officials under the rules cannot criticize any action of the government that they served but there was an exception that one could speak the truth if there was government appointed commission of enquiry. Taking advantage of the statutory provision, I filed a written statement before the Commission highlighting mishandling and failures in dealing with the communal riots despite having been alerted and forewarned. My affidavit resulted in my being called for a long sitting with the Commission and the impact of my testimony can be read in the report of the Commission on Ranchi riots of 1967. The Army revised their manual on aid to the civil authority in the light of my testimony before the Commission. I claimed reimbursement of the legal expenses that I was supposed to have incurred in defending my official acts before the Commission of Enquiry. I was not sure if the government would accept my demand and I was pleasantly surprised when the Bihar Government enquired from me the amount that I had incurred as expenses and the person to whom it should be paid. I gave an off-hand figure of 7,500 rupees and named the father of Mr. G. Narain for payment. I was pleasantly surprised and felt vindicated when the Bihar Government sanctioned and paid the amount. This also vindicated my faith in the random word of the *Guru Granth Saheb* after a formal prayer or *ardas*.

Lest it may appear all hunky dory, I may describe the minus side too. I had gone for a meeting at Calcutta along with a few mine owners. They took me for an outing in the evening. It was the house of a dancing girl where there was a lot of singing and drinking. All the time I prayed to *Waheguru* to save me from any untoward happening. I was lucky to have come out without compromising myself and without having invited a police raid on the premises. I had acquired a bad habit on the advice of a doctor to take '*Dexedrine*' pills whenever I was not too well or there was a bit too much of pressure of work. Generally, I started doing my office work in the night after taking one or two pills of *Dexedrine* that would keep me awake during the night but the next day it made me lazy and very irritable. It was in this state that I was rude to many persons who came to see me. One or two were such persons who had done a lot for me. I get up with remorse even now when I recall a few of such unpardonable episodes.

12

The Training of Civil Service Officers

I had opted for a deputation under the Government of India from Ranchi. My liking was to go to a public sector undertaking as I thought that my executive capability, as demonstrated in district administration, would enable me to show results. I served for a short time in the Cooperative Department where I got picked up for the job of Registrar Cooperative Societies in August 1967. The Registrar is the key assignment in the Cooperative Department. Registrar is called the *Brahma*, *Vishnu* and *Mahesh* of the cooperative movement. He is the creator that is *Brahma* of a cooperative society when he registers a society, he is also the one who nurtures, as all assistance and supervision of a cooperative society is through him, and he is the *Mahesh* or the destroyer, as he has the authority to wind up a cooperative society if it went astray or ceased to work. The cooperative structure of Bihar was one of the weakest in the country, mainly because the money or loans advanced were not recovered. Maharashtra and Punjab were the models of success. I visited both the states and geared up the recovery system. I was there only for a short time of about 8 to 9 months in the post but I had set up a record in the recovery of loans. The Minister for the Cooperatives was a professional wrestler who became a Minister for the first time. He had mainly two concerns. One was to find a way to oust the Congress supporters from the control of many important cooperative societies, the other was to foster and register a cooperative society of wrestlers. He prevailed upon me to issue a few uncalled for notices to the office bearers of the cooperative societies under the control of the Congress supporters. I stopped in my tracks when one of the office bearers appeared before me and accused me of acting in a partisan manner. He said that he was shocked to receive the notice from someone like me about whom the whole of Bihar knew that I had stood up against the stalwart Chief Minister like Dr. S.K. Sinha. This ended my short effort to become acceptable to my minister. My testimony before Justice S.P. Singh Commission of Enquiry and its reporting in the press made me a sort of *persona-non-grata* with the government, particularly after my answer to a direct question before the Commission appeared in the media in which I had clearly said that the student disturbances in Ranchi were instigated by the political parties, then in opposition and the Congress dissidents. I got my orders of posting as Deputy Director at the National Academy of Administration at Mussoorie, responsible for the foundational training for all the Civil Services and the professional training of the IAS officers before I could find my way to register a cooperative society of the wrestlers. The minister himself did not last long as one group of dissatisfied legislators joined with the Congress to bring the Government down. A new government got formed before I left Bihar, consisting of the alienated legislators supported by the Congress from outside. I was selected for the position in Mussoorie by Mr. M.G. Pimputkar, ICS, who was the Establishment Officer in the Government of India, designated to be the Director of the National Academy of Administration. He was an officer of his own type. He was scrupulous, honest and totally unsparing in applying the rules prescribed. He was reported to have got his wife booked for violating traffic rules when she drove her car after her driving license had expired and he was the District Magistrate there. He was a great believer in the theory that the position of the District Magistrate in the Indian Administrative set-up was such which brought out the best in an officer. He went over with a tooth comb over the records of all the officers of a particular seniority and earmarked me for the post of the Deputy Director for the training of the IAS officers, preventing me from going to a public sector undertaking.

I reached Mussoorie via Lucknow. Maan Singh was posted at Lucknow in the Air Force, so was my friend Mr. J.M. Shukla, the ex-Superintendent of Police in Dhanbad. Shukla and his wife really looked after us well at Lucknow. They gave us a sumptuous lunch and snacks for the children on the way. I did not need a car at Mussoorie. I had sold my car in Patna. After repaying the government loan I was left with enough money to enable me to clear all my bills with something still left. We found that unlike our training days, the IAS trainees were almost having a regimented routine. The wearing of a jacket and tie was a must. Punctuality was virtually a fad with Mr. Pimputkar. If a lecture was to begin at ten o'clock then the attendant had instructions to close the gate of the lecture-hall at exactly 10 a.m., even if the lecturer had not entered the hall. Those who could not make it to the hall in time had to be on half a day's casual leave. Mr. Pimputkar had microphones fitted in the lecture halls to enable him to know all that was going on in the classes from his office in addition to his private espionage network. He had introduced eleven minutes of five basic exercises for the physical fitness of the trainees adapted from the exercises prescribed for the Canadian Air Force Pilots and every one had to be regular for the physicals. The beauty of the system was that if one was not regular in exercising, one could not pass the test at the level prescribed for the age of the trainee. I found the system useful for my own fitness that had got neglected in Bihar. The 11 minute schedule was so convenient and the five exercises could be done in one's bedroom. There was a comprehensive compilation of rules called the Probationer's Handbook that guided every activity of the trainees.

Mr. Pimputkar was known for applying those rules on himself and other training staff. The life for the family in Mussoorie was good. There were good schools. My daughters, Rosy and Noni, and my small son Dipendar, joined the well-known Waverley Convent and my son Birendar joined St. George School. The Waverley Convent was within a walking distance from the Academy that was located in the old Charleville Hotel campus on the Mall Road. Birendar went to his school by bus. The children had access to all the sports, entertainment and the mess facilities of the probationers. The Director was assisted by a Joint Director and three Deputy Directors. I was to take the position of the Senior Deputy Director and for the time being I was to acquire the traditions, modes and the culture of the training that had been introduced by Mr. Pimputkar. The Joint Director was Mr. T.N. Chaturvedi, a very learned, scholarly type officer but fully worldly wise too. Mr. R.P. Khosla, Mr. Krishnamurthy and Mr. Bagchi, from the Postal Service were the three Deputy Directors. The first contact with all these officers, who sounded so intellectual, gave me an acute sense of inferiority because my reading had stayed where it was when I joined the IAS. It was my wife who proved to be a pillar of strength for me in those days. I was the favourite of the Director.

The Director had nominated me for a course in the University of Pittsburgh, USA, even before I joined the Academy. It was a Fellowship Grant of the Ford Foundation that was placed at the disposal of the Academy. Mr. Chaturvedi had made a bid for that fellowship before I joined but Mr. Pimputkar had turned it down. The problem in a small place, where one has to interact among a small group, is that one started walking on the other's toes and factions got created among even the small group. Mr. Chaturvedi was a natural faction leader, expert in innuendo and intrigue that which probably could be ascribed to his experience of having worked as the Secretary to the Chief Minister of Rajasthan, Mr. Sukhadia. I unconsciously found myself in his faction. Everyone remained in tension because of the environment fostered by Mr. Pimputkar. The Director fell foul with one Mr. T.N. Dhar, the Professor of Economics and he got him sacked by the Government of India. He ordered him to vacate the campus forthwith. The trainee IAS probationers did not know the reason for his sudden departure. He seemed to have been a popular teacher. The IAS probationers decided to host a farewell dinner for him in the Mess. The President of the Mess Committee was one Mr. Karl Reddy, an IAS officer, who stood allotted to Punjab. Mr. Pimputkar hit the ceiling when he came to know that the professor whom he had turned out was being honoured by the IAS trainees. He asked Khosla to tell the President of the Mess Committee that the Director did not approve of the dinner, so the invitation to Profesor Dhar should be withdrawn. Mr. Karl Reddy refused to withdraw his invitation. It created an awkward situation in the Academy. The Director then resorted to the powers vested in him under the Probationer's Handbook and formally ordered Karl Reddy to cancel the dinner. The teaching staff of the Academy had invited Professor Dhar for a meal in a restaurant. When they heard about the Director's order to the Mess Committee, they cancelled their contributory private dinner for fear of inviting the wrath of the Director. Mr. Pimputkar in his vindictiveness could go to any extent. We were having tests for the final examination of the trainees after which they would be confirmed as IAS officers. A word was passed to all examiners that Mr. Karl Reddy was to be disqualified in all tests other than the written tests. I was co-opted as an examiner for horse riding. Karl Reddy was not a good horse rider, but so were many others. When I proposed pass marks for him, the other two examiners tried to persuade me to give marks as per the wishes of the Director. I did not agree, as I thought it would be unjust, on which the other two examiners gave him so low marks that he failed in the test and consequently his probation got extended by six months. In the meanwhile, Mr. Pimputkar got transferred to Delhi. It was suggested to Karl Reddy that the Director be invited to a farewell dinner. He took the position that he could not be trusted with his discretion as to whom to invite and whom not to. The Director might issue him an order that he should invite him for a farewell dinner. He resisted pressure from his colleagues and teachers and did not budge from his position. Mr. Pimputkar himself hosted a tea party on the lawns of the Academy, to say goodbye to all of us. There was a convention that the Director's car was pushed by the probationers when he left the campus for good and the Academy riding squad led the cavalcade up to the turning on the road. There were many probationers who admired Pimputkar for his discipline and strictness. Many of them went on their own to Dehradun Railway Station to say goodbye. The opposite group of probationers held a celebration on the departure of Mr. Pimputkar, celebrating the occasion with a lot of drinking. Their boisterous refrain was that horses went up to the academy gate to see off the Director but the asses went up to Dehradun. I followed up the career of Karl Reddy because I was impressed by his principled tough stand on the issue of hosting a dinner in the Mess. He was posted in Amritsar for his district training. I made it a point to visit Amritsar to see how he was doing. Everything appeared to be okay. He invited me for a dinner that I accepted and remarked that in the context of the dinner for the Director of the Academy, I should consider his invitation to be a privilege. Everyone had a good laugh at it. Somehow, in his subsequent career, Karl Reddy did not do well as he would pick up a quarrel with every boss and towards the end of his career he was just sidelined on positions that did not count for anything. It seems that in the IAS a little accommodative attitude or better still, a spirit of empathy is needed for the persons and parties that one has to interact with along with toughness and firmness.

I got busy with finalizing my itinerary for my first visit abroad. I went to Delhi and did the required paper work for my official passport. I also met the officials of the Ford Foundation. They suggested that along with the eight weeks at the Institute of Management in the University of Pittsburgh, PA, I should visit various training institutes in the USA, UK, Honolulu, Tokyo, Manila and Hong Kong. They on their own authorized me a round-the-world air ticket on Pan American Airways. The Department of Personnel in the Government of India did not object to the modified itinerary. My family remained at Mussoorie while I was abroad. I thoroughly enjoyed my air journey. I remember that the airhostess brought a meal for me but then quickly returned to take it away. She said that she had served the meal by mistake as she knew that Indians did not eat beef. I told her to not to bother as I did not mind eating anything that others can eat. Pittsburgh was another eye-opening experience. I was put in a room in a hostel tower meant for graduate students. It was something like a 20 storeyed tower with a few floors marked for female students. We had our meals in the Cafeteria at the basement. We paid 60 cents for the breakfast, for which we had to buy a coupon. It was breathtaking for an Indian inside. We could drink as much and have as many servings of fruit juice as we could. There were side dishes like, cereals, buns, pastries, muffins and a variety of fresh diced fruits. In India one read in history that in ancient India there were canals of flowing milk. I literally saw that spectacle, which one had read about in the books, daily in the Cafeteria where milk of different varieties was filled in containers from where one could take as much as one could in one's glass. The eggs to order were available along with bread and toast, with butter and a variety of jams. I put on three kilos of weight in one week after which I started cutting on meals. The course was well-designed and I found it very beneficial for my career and self-confidence. Professor Burk Sheeran, who had spent a term as an Expert Advisor in Pakistan took a special interest in me. He often invited me for a meal at his house. They had an adolescent daughter.

What struck me was that no one tried to impose ones views on the other. The girl, who was only a school student, participated in our discussions as a full-grown adult. Her father at one time overruled what she said and that made her walk away from the dining table in protest. Professor Sheeran arranged for me a visit to the Army School of Management and Training at the Rock Island. I was elected as the leader of the group of trainees coming from some ten countries. A girl student in our tower got interested in me as she was a stamp collector. I misunderstood her interest and not knowing the Western culture I proposed to date her. She was simply shocked and she would avoid me if she saw me. I was mortified when I realised that I had made an ass of myself. We were taken to the TVA at Knoxville which we thoroughly enjoyed. There was a local society that looked after foreign visitors. I opted to go to a farmhouse, on their invitation for the weekend. It was a great learning experience. The farmer was a fulltime dragline operator. He managed, with his family, a farm of one hundred acres, a dairy of about fifty cows and a poultry of seven hundred birds, without any hired labour. The farmer, his wife, a school-going son and two grown-up daughters managed the whole show. I visited New York, Washington, Chicago, San Francisco, Tokyo, Hong Kong and Manila, before I returned to Mussoorie. Sukhdev came to receive me at Delhi. She had stayed with a school friend of mine, Jia Lal Singh, who was an assistant in the Army Headquarters and he had a heart of gold, keeping his house always open, even when it was only a two-room apartment.

We had a new Director by the time I returned. He was Mr. K.K. Das, ICS. He was a sophisticated and a smart looking officer, who was every inch a *Saheb*. He had gone as the Secretary in the Ministry of Health in the Government of India. He was the senior most civil servant at that time, next in-line to be the Cabinet Secretary, but he was passed over. The moment he heard that he was not being appointed the Cabinet Secretary, he put in his papers and took retirement to settle down at Lucknow. He had a pretty Punjabi wife, a Christian from Gurdaspur. He did not seem to be much interested in the training of the IAS officers and for all practical purposes Mr. T.N. Chaturvedi was the Director. He felt very happy about it, but I could not help noticing a streak of pettiness in his decisions. The Director had desired a minor change in the timings of the film show, but since the time did not suit his family, he refused to oblige the Director. His children would pick up books of their interest from the book shops and he would pass on the bills for payment to the Academy library. We had a water shortage in the Academy during summer. We had one C.S. Ramchandran, ICS, visiting us. He was a typical South Indian Brahmin, who would spend a long time in his *Pooja*. He got the Academy staff to open the water supply very early in the morning which would have dried up the water in our water tank by the time our trainees and mess came up for their needs. I countermanded his order and he hit the ceiling on that. He frightened Mr. Chaturvedi so much that he called me as his confidant and asked me that for his sake I should go and apologize to him. Mr. Chaturvedi was always very kind to me, so against my better judgment I went to Mr. Ramchandran and silently received a dressing down from him, all the time cursing myself for having fallen in the trap to become a scapegoat. I think that this was the first and the last time that I suffered such direct humiliation at the hands of anyone.

Mr K.K. Das was replaced by Mr. Dinkar D. Sathe, ICS, from Maharashtra Cadre. Mr. Chaturvedi deputed me to escort him from Delhi where he was staying with his elder brother Mr. R.D. Sathe, who later became the Secretary of External Affairs in the Government of India. D.D. Sathe did not take much notice of me nor show much interest in the Academy. He and his pretty wife mostly remained talking to each other. Mr. Sathe came from a well-to-do family of *Chitpavan Brahmins* from Poona. Mrs. Sathe was the scion of the family of Peshwa General, Sadashiv Rao Bhau, who was the Commander-in-Chief of the Maratha Army that had fought against Ahmed Shah Abdali in 1761 at Panipat. Mr. Sathe appeared to be an ease loving person who would get up quite late in the mornings and then laze in the Sun, in the beautiful compound of his house. Mr. Chaturvedi remained happy as he was the *defacto* Director. Suddenly, I found that Mr. Sathe started developing interest in the affairs of the Academy and slowly sidelining Mr. Chaturvedi. I discovered that behind the facade of his ease loving lifestyle he had a very incisive and sharp mind, with innovative ideas that would often surprise me. His mind was at its best when he had about two sundowners. I was the only one among the Directing Staff who could join him in drinks and he seemed to have liked my company. Later, Mr. J.K.

Kohli of the West Bengal cadre and Mr. Mitra from the Income Tax Service joined as Deputy Directors. Mr. Sathe preferred, for his brain-storming sessions, that I remained with him. It would be in such sessions that he would come out with his best ideas. Mrs. Sathe generally took a peg of rum but she kept a watch on the drinks of her husband. Mr. Sathe after about three drinks would not know how to stop. He would start losing control over his legs and arms, and sway from side-to-side, when Mrs. Sathe would take away his drink. The surprise about Sathe was that he would not forget a word of whatever he said and he would surprise me the next morning for specific action that he had desired. I generally forget if I take drink beyond a limit. My wife Sukhdev, saved me in such situations by telling me about the instructions for me from the Director. Sukhdev did not drink nor did she like that I should drink. Apparently, while sitting in our company, having small talk with Mrs. Sathe, she kept one ear attuned to what was going on between me and Mr. D.D. Sathe. Mr. Sathe proved to be the first Director who changed the methodology and the content of training at the Academy. The teaching of management and quantitative techniques in decision-making were introduced in the curriculum. He started taking IAS trainees for hitchhiking in the forests as also on visits to various places in the Himalayas. The training at the Academy was divided in two parts. One part was for theoretical training while the other part was after the exposure to the administration and the people at the grass root level when the trainees would come back and share their experiences with their colleagues in different states. Our assessment procedure was such that other than the Directing Staff no one was involved in it. A Deputy Director could not be expected to assess something like three hundred trainees who came for the Foundation Course. Mr. Sathe introduced the Counselor System, allocating a group of about twenty trainees to each member of the staff. This improved the participation of the academicians in the training process and the interactions in small groups resulted in better assessment of the performance of the trainees. We also for the first time introduced the in-service training for the IAS officers. One course was started for the IAS officers of 5 to 11 years of service and one was for the IAS officers of 15 to 18 years of service. In addition, an induction course was started for the State Civil Service Officers on the select list of the IAS. Mr. Sathe felt that the wives of the Directing Staff could also be a resource which the Academy could benefit from. The upkeep of the Academy lounge and various cultural activities were thus taken care of. The best was the Academy Staff Welfare Association that undertook the education of the children of the lower staff and they provided medical and other assistance for the poor. He got funds raised for the welfare activities by organizing an Annual Fete for which the local businessmen and others were encouraged to give advertisements on generous rates. I visited the Academy on the Golden Jubilee Retreat of the 1954 batch in 2004 and found that the innovations and systems that Mr. Sathe had introduced had continued to be practiced although the buildings and infrastructure at the Academy had expanded a lot since Mr. Sathe's days. Mr. Sathe enjoyed a good equation with the politicians of all hues, particularly if they happened to be from Maharashtra. He was a favourite of Mr. Y.B. Chavan, who had actually brought him to the Central Government when Jawaharlal Nehru had selected him as the Defence Minister in place of V.K. Krishna Menon after India's debacle against China. Mr. Y.B. Chavan paid a visit to the Academy after Mr. Sathe joined. One could easily see the regard and the warm feelings that Chavan had for Sathe. Equally impressed by him was Mr. Moraiji Desai, who hated anyone who drank. We did not drink in Mr. Sathe's house when Moraiji came but the bar in the drawing room remained as it was.

Mr. T.N. Chaturvedi felt ignored in the new environment. He managed to get posted as the Director of the Indian Institute of Public Administration at New Delhi. He was given a farewell from the Academy but before he could take up his new assignment, the academicians in the IIPA, who had good political links in the Government of India, got active to block his joining. It was made out that the IIPA was an independent think-tank for the Government of India and if an IAS officer got posted as its Director, the advice from this think-tank would get tainted. Somehow the argument found a favour with Mrs. Gandhi and Mr. Chaturvedi was asked to await further orders. Mr. T.N. Chaturvedi opted to come back to the Academy. He confided in me that he felt humiliated by the politically aligned academicians. He got two of us to write to all young IAS officers to become members of the IIPA so that the IAS officers came to control the IIPA, safeguarding its misuse against the service. We really went after it seriously, resulting in the change in the complexion of membership of the IIPA. T.N. Chaturvedi got elected to the Executive Council of the IIPA. He later became the editor of its prestigious journal. Mr. Chaturvedi and Mr. B.C. Mathur of the same batch acquired a stranglehold over the IIPA that has continued all along. Mr. Sathe almost ignored his coming back and gave him no work which made him all the more bitter and what shocked me most was that he started hitting Sathe below the belt. His batch-mate and friend was Mr. B.C. Mathur of Orissa cadre who was the Director of Training in the Government of India. He would torpedo many of the proposals of Mr.Sathe. Anonymous petitions against Mr. Sathe started reaching the Government of India. He had recommended the extension in deputation of a section officer in Mussoorie on which an innuendo got spread that Sathe was having some illicit relations with his wife. Sathe had a lady houseguest staying with him when Mrs. Sathe was away on which rumours were spread that Sathe had converted the Academy into a brothel. Stories were spread in Delhi about drinking bouts taking place in the Academy, in the Director's house. There was a group of trainees who had gone for an outing, involving hiking and rock climbing. Mr. Sathe went to meet them on the way at a forest rest house. He asked the mess to arrange for them a barbeque dinner and drinks at the forest bungalow. I had gone there but not Mr. Chaturvedi. I found that in the next anonymous petition against Sathe, lurid details of the dinner had been given. I had by this time no doubt in my mind that Chaturvedi was the brain behind those petitions. Chaturvedi still considered me to be his sympathizer. I decided that he should no longer be in the dark. I told Mr. Chaturvedi to his face that I was not with him in his nefarious games and that I shall stand by the Director as my duty demanded. I apprised Sathe of our exchange. I think that it was neither wise nor necessary for me to expose myself that way. I became a target for Mr. Chaturvedi thereafter. Mr. Sathe said that he was a Maratha, who excelled in guerrilla tactics. He decided to pay back Chaturvedi in the same coin. He got a lower category staff and one Dr. Dubey, the Hindi Professor, to send similar dirtily worded anonymous petitions against Chaturvedi. Anyhow, this resulted in a respite in mutual mudslinging. Because of involvement of B.C. Mathur on the side of Chaturvedi, the complaints against Sathe reached Indira Gandhi. She ordered the Secretary, Department of Personnel, Mr. H. Lal, ICS, of Bihar cadre, to personally enquire into the whole matter and give a report to her. Mr. H. Lal came to Mussoorie and made his enquiries. He saw me also. I told him the truth, including that drinks had been served to the trainees from the Mess. He was satisfied that no mala fide was involved on the part of Mr. Sathe. Mr. Chaturvedi was transferred soon to the Government of India.

There was a serious move to shift the Academy to Delhi. A site had been acquired for it in South Delhi. Mr. Sathe placed Mr. J.K. Kohli in Delhi to oversee the construction of the new campus in Delhi. Sathe was of the rank of a Secretary in the Government of India. I found that if, for getting his work done, Sathe had to go to an Under-secretary in the government, he gladly walk into his office to place his request before him. In 99 out of hundred cases I found that he got what he wanted. The other trait that I noticed in him was that he was quite at home with businessmen and other public men, and that he was a great opportunist. Wherever he found that he could be of help to anyone, he would do so and wherever he could get assistance from anyone, in the job that he had in hand, he willingly went for it and generally got it. He was one Director in Mussoorie who reached out to the people of Mussoorie. He got the project of the new campus completed ahead of schedule. The Academy generally had a vacation during winter. It was decided that the new session of the Academy should be in Delhi. We issued an advertisement in the newspapers inviting quotations from transporters for our moving to Delhi. It was this advertisement that made the people of Mussoorie see red. Mussoorie was established as a hill station by the British in the early 19th century, as a station where the families of Englishmen serving in India could move to during the harsh summers of India. Some ruling princes and *Zamindars* of Uttar Pradesh and smaller princelings of Punjab also got their summer palaces built in Mussoorie. There is still the bandstand at the Library Point where daily the Army band had played in the colonial times. During the British days only the Englishmen and their families could enjoy the band playing. Indian men could at best walk past the bandstand but Indian ladies could stay on, if they felt like that. When the British left India, Mussoorie lost its attraction and businesses started to close down. Mr. G.B. Pant, who was from Garhwal, was the Home Minister. The Mussoorie public leaders met him and succeeded in persuading him to shift the IAS Training Academy to Mussoorie from Delhi in 1958. Again on the alarm caused by the advertisement, the Mussoorie leaders ran to Indira Gandhi for intervention. She too had a soft feeling for the people of Mussoorie and ordered that the Academy stayed put in Mussoorie. The Delhi campus was handed over to the Jawaharlal University as their camp office till their main building came up. Mr. Kohli came back to Mussoorie. My wife Sukhdev and Sudarshna, the wife of Mr. Kohli became great friends. We had a trip together along with a group of trainees to Badrinath and Kedarnath. We also visited, on our return, the *gurdwara* at Hemkunt, associated with Guru Gobind Singh in his previous birth. It was an exciting climb of 16,000 feet. Sudarshna's mother was staying in a house at Haridwar, which was on the way, because Hindus believed that if one died at a place like Banaras or Haridwar, one went straight to heaven. We stayed with her for one night before our return to Mussoorie.

Mr. T.N. Chaturvedi had a lot of contacts with scholars and intellectuals. He would invite them as guest lecturers for the trainees. I found that Mr. Chaturvedi was a walking encyclopedia for all books published in India and generally he would have read those books. He suffered from two handicaps. One was his inability to organize his erudition as to be of use to him and others, and the other was his inability to articulate either in writing or in speech. We continued the practice of inviting guest speakers. We had invited Dr. Manmohan Singh when he was teaching in Delhi University.

He was found to be a very learned person who deliberately kept a low profile. Everyone was very impressed with what he had to say about the Indian Economy. Ever since the Academy had kept him on their guest list. We also had Dr. Jagjit Singh from the Indian Railways, who had mastered the quantitative techniques in decision-making. He shared with the trainees his experience of problem solving. I think his best was his success in solving the problem of the bottleneck in the movement of goods wagons at Mughalsarai. He went about explaining the Queuing Theory or the Monte Carlo Theory, etc. His punch line was that he visited Mughalsarai to see for himself the reason for the bottleneck. He discovered that the delay was caused in the shunting of wagons, as the same engine had to turnaround to pull back the wagons and the delay got solved when another engine was provided. We had Sirdar Kapur Singh, an ex-ICS officer of the Punjab cadre, to deliver a lecture to the IAS trainees.

We had among the trainees, Gurtej Singh of the 1969 batch, who was a great admirer of Kapur Singh. He was a maverick, who seemed to have been suffering from a persecution mania. He was dismissed from service on charges of moral turpitude which of course he bitterly contested. He ascribed his removal from service to the vendetta of the communal Hindus. I found that although he was hailed as a great scholar of the Sikh religion and history but he lacked all the values that go to make one a Sikh. He had no humility and he would lose his temper frequently over the observations of others that did not meet with his approval. No constructive discussion was possible with him unless one became his yes-man. The same streak of bitterness against the world could be seen in his disciple Sardar Gurtej Singh, who was cut up with the Government because he did not get allotted to the Punjab cadre. He was a hardliner in his approach to Sikhism. He questioned the current '*ardas*' of the Sikhs as it started with an invocation to '*Bhagwati*' or *Chandi*, worshipped as a goddess by the Hindus. He ultimately resigned from the IAS and he continues to see the Sikh community as slaves in India. Surprisingly, he has his admirers who are very impressed by his having resigned from the IAS, ostensibly for the sake of the Sikh community. The whole tenor of *Gurbani* is thoroughly optimistic. I cannot bring myself to accept the negative and extreme pessimism of scholars like Sardar Gurtej Singh.

I was also the Course Director for a workshop on improving agricultural production in India co-sponsored by the Ford Foundation in which some selected District Officers from all over India, agricultural experts and specialists on agricultural extension took part. The workshop was presided by B. Sivaraman, ICS, who later became the Cabinet Secretary. Mr. G.S. Kalkat, Joint Director of Agriculture, Punjab participated in the workshop. Everyone was impressed with him and very soon he was picked up by the Government of India for the post of the Commissioner for Agriculture in Government of India. He later went over to the World Bank. B. Sivaraman gave a scheme that appeared to be very innovative. It was to grow '*dhancha*', a plant used for green manuring around the boundaries of the farmers' fields along with the sowing of the paddy.

These plants grew much faster than paddy and when the plants had grown to two to three feet height these plants were to be ploughed into the same fields to serve as the green manure. However, despite the promise and the push from the above, the scheme did not give the results which were expected and it was given a quiet burial after Mr. Sivaraman.

The Academy took the initative to host a seminar on the maintenance of law and order in India in which some participants had come from the National Police Academy at Hyderabad. The police somehow have been resenting the position accorded to the District Magistrate in the Indian Police Act, 1861, according to which the District Superintendent of the police has to function under the overall guidance and control of the District Magistrate. Somehow, the District Magistrates also had been neglecting their responsibilities under the Police Act and the Police Manuals of States. The inspection of a police station by the District Magistrate as provided in the Police Manual, is unheard of these days, whereas I as a District Magistrate had made it a point to inspect about half of the police stations in my districts. District Magistrates in Bihar have been initiating the character rolls of the district police chiefs and the relationship has been like between two brothers with the District Magistrate being the elder brother. It almost led to a storm when I tried to introduce the Bihar system in Punjab where the police chief functioned almost independently. The role of the District Magistrate, in the metropolitan cities, has been taken over by the Police Commissioner which is a step in the right direction. The separation of the Judiciary from the Executive has taken away a valuable input in the maintenance of law and order that used to come from the Executive Magistrates under the District Magistrate. One important consequence of the seminar was that violation of prohibitory orders under section 144 of the Criminal Procedure Code became a cognizable offence as the Home Secretary of the Government of India came to recognize the contradiction that was involved in the current situation where during disturbances the media reported that orders to shoot to kill had been given for those who would violate the curfew orders. The actual position was that violation of the curfew orders was only the violation of orders under section 144 CrPC which was punishable under Section 188 of the Indian Penal Code which was a bailable offence, meaning that for that offence the police could not arrest a violator without a warrant. The Government rectified the situation by amending the law later.

We had toyed with the idea to introduce psychological testing in assessing the performance of the IAS trainees. The armed forces had been making an assessment of the potential of the candidates appearing for selection before the Services Selection Boards for the position of officers in the armed forces. I met the chief of the division concerned with the psychological testing of the candidates. He was one Dr. Sinha. He explained in detail the system that they had followed from the thirties. I enquired if the army had undertaken validation of their selections on the basis of the career profiles of the officers. I got a reply in the negative. We also had with us, for an interaction, a team of Instructors from the Minerva Academy, Chandigarh, who had enabled a large number of boys to get selected as officers in the armed forces. After a lot of discussion and soul searching we advised the Government of India against introducing psychological testing in the IAS at any stage.

The sandwich pattern of training for the IAS was introduced in 1969. I had the responsibility to keep track of what was going on in the states when the IAS trainees were with them for one year for an on-the-job training at the grass root level. The Uttar Pradesh Government decided to send the trainees to the Agricultural University at Pant Nagar for three months. The Vice Chancellor of the University was one Mr. D.P. Singh, known to be a hard taskmaster. He told the trainees that the best way for them to get awareness and a feel for agriculture would be to grow a crop themselves. It was summertime. The trainees were asked to personally do all the operations like ploughing, sowing and weeding of the crop to be grown by them. Most of the trainees came from cities and they folded up in the sultry heat of the farm. They resorted to reporting sick. D.P. Singh told the doctor to be strict with the trainees and reject the sick reports. One day someone from among them shouted that he had seen a snake, on hearing which all of them ran out of their plots of field demanding insurance for them against snake bite. They sent an SOS to the Academy also. When I came to enquire into their complaint I found that they had failed in officer like qualities in order to escape from physical hardship. I made it plain that in case Mr. D.P. Singh chose to report against them they would stand dismissed from the

IAS. Luckily, good sense prevailed and they decided to come to terms with the physical hardship involved in farming.

The Academy was a hunting ground for matchmaking. Various friends and relatives would come visiting Mussoorie requesting us on the directing staff to help them to find a suitable match for their daughters. The value of an officer in an arranged marriage exceeded a million rupees. The result was that most of the brilliant boys selected for the IAS ended up marrying daughters of mostly corrupt engineers, particularly in Bihar. One Mr. Darbari, a senior IPS officer, came to my office to know about eligible Kaistha IAS trainees for his daughter. He suggested that while he was sitting with me. I should call a particular officer to see me so that he could have a look at the boy. I called the boy but as soon as he entered, Mr. Darbari darted out without telling me anything. I made the boy sit and engaged him in pleasantries. Meanwhile, Mr. Darbari returned to my room accompanied by his wife. I released the boy to go back to his class. Mr. Darbari said that he liked the boy as soon as he set his eyes on him but he remembered that his wife always blamed him that he selected boys for their daughter who were dark in complexion. He wanted her to see the boy so that she did not blame him. Mr. J.K. Kohli was married in a family of Ludhiana who had done very well. The brother of Mrs. Sudarshna Kohli, Mr. R.K. Soni, had risen to be an industrial tycoon. Mr. Soni had a younger unmarried sister. He wanted Sudarshna to find a match for her from among the IAS trainees. Sudarshna and my wife Sukhdev together undertook this exercise. They located a handsome Punjabi boy Mr. B.R. Bajaj. Everything was going fine but in the meanwhile the orders of the Ministry of Home Affairs were received in which Bajaj was allocated to West Bengal. Mr. Soni over-ruled the selection of Bajaj on that account. Then the choice fell on Mr. V.K. Duggal, who was an equally handsome officer allotted to the Union Territories cadre. Duggal was an ex-army officer belonging to a lower middleclass family living in Daryaganj. The engagement went through smoothly but Duggal's mother would not agree to a date of marriage. Finally, when pressed, she said that she could not perform the marriage of her son from a slum. Mr. R.K. Soni bought a house in the posh colony of Greater Kailash and handed the same over to Duggal's family. It was after that only that the marriage was solemnised.

Sonal Mansingh visited the Academy as a guest lecturer. She was married to an officer of the Indian Foreign Service. Her brother-in-law was an IAS trainee in the Academy. The Academy had laid out a formal dinner in the Mess. We had a few drinks before the dinner in the Director's house.

Mr. Sathe decided to tell a joke instead of addressing the trainees. The joke was about a gentleman who was asked by his wife to buy and bring for her a bra. She told him about the size that was something like 36B. The salesgirl asked the gentleman about the type of bra that he would like to purchase. The gentleman got foxed on the question and requested the sales girl to be a bit more explicit. The sales girl told him that they had with them three types of bras. One was called 'preacher' as it uplifted the mass, the second was 'dictator' as it suppressed the mass and the third was 'diplomat' that made mountains out of molehills. Addressing Sonal Mansingh, he said that the third was like her dear husband who was a career diplomat. The story of the joke after a few drinks by the Director reached Indira Gandhi who had already been poisoned against Sathe by the coterie of Chaturvedi. Mr. D.D. Sathe was soon transferred. He was replaced by Mr. R. Prasad, IAS, who was for some time the secretary with Lal Bahadur Shastri. He carried a chip on his shoulders of honesty and integrity and his ascetic living. I was invited as a guest lecturer to the Academy to participate in the farewell functions of D.D. Sathe. Mr. R. Prasad ran into me while he was being taken around the Academy. We greeted each other and I casually asked him about his priorities in the Academy. He said that his first priority would be to try to improve the image of the Academy and its Director. I do not know as to what the trainees of his tenure remember about him but one thing about which a lot of stories got circulated was his obsession with the Hindu epic *Ramayana* that he got staged by the trainees in the Academy with his daughter participating as *Sita*. The other lasting contribution of his was to add the name of Lal Bahadur Shastri to the name of the Academy. Mrs. Indira Gandhi did not make Sathe a Secretary in the Government of India. Maharashtra immediately grabbed him and appointed him as their Chief Secretary.

13

As General Manager, Super Bazar Delhi

I could have stayed on in the Academy but meanwhile Mr. Gopalakrishnan of Andhra cadre, who was my batch mate, also had joined as the Senior Deputy Director at the Academy. Since only one of us could be the Joint Director, one had to go out. I opted to try new pastures and opted for a tenure at Delhi. Mr. P.K.J. Menon from Bihar was the Secretary, Department of Personnel, in the Government of India. He asked me if I had any preference for an appointment. I told him that I had four school going children and that I was financially hard up, so I would prefer a post that carried with it some perks. I was therefore posted as the General Manager of the Super Bazar, Delhi. The position provided a free transport, both for official use and private use with a driver, a rent free house and a sumptuary allowance of rupees 350 per month in addition to reimbursement for the official entertainment in hotels and restaurants. I was entitled to stay in 5 star hotels on my official tours.

Super Bazar was a cooperative store wholly financed by the government. It had a nominated Managing Committee and Congress M.P., Mr. Vyas, as the Chairman. All executive power for running the Super Bazar was vested in the General Manager. It was established in 1966 as the pet project of Mrs. Gandhi, who could find some time in her busy schedule for personally looking after Super Bazar. The project was meant to cushion the consumer from high prices due to the profiteering by the middlemen and shortages in essential commodities. Unfortunately, from the first year of working, Super Bazar went into loss which had continued. Mrs. Gandhi, while approving my appointment as the General Manager, had noted that I should be tried for one year and if, in the meanwhile the Super Bazar did not turn the comer, I should be sacked and the Super Bazar closed down.

I went on to call on the officials dealing with the Super Bazar in the Government of India. I met Mr. A. Das, who was the Joint Secretary, who in turn escorted me to the Minister of State, Mr. Paharia. It was there that I was told that the Chairman of the Managing Committee, Mr. Vyas had changed his mind and he had refused to accept me as the General Manager. The Minister who was also from Rajasthan said that I should get my joining time extended as he was trying to persuade Mr. Vyas to honour his earlier commitment. I agreed to wait for a day or two. Mr. Vyas did not relent. I was told that Vyas had known Mr. T.N. Chaturvedi well. He had seen in my character roll some good observations made by Chaturvedi. He thought that he should inform Chaturvedi that he had selected me for the job because of the appreciatory remarks of Chaturvedi. Mr. Chaturvedi told him that he should not go by the remarks on my record and that he would come to a grief if he selected me. The matter went to Mr. Fakhuruddin Ahmed, who was the Cabinet Minister. Mr. Vyas refused to budge. Meanwhile, in this tussle I was going without any salary. I could not afford to remain in that position too long. Sukhdev and Sathe asked me to come back to Mussoorie. I found the idea of going back to Mussoorie to be repulsive. I met the Agriculture Secretary, Mr. T.P. Singh Senior, a Bihar officer. He said that the Minister had referred my case to the Prime Minister for orders, so I could not be given a regular posting in the Ministry but in order to enable me to draw my salary, he could show me against a vacant position in the Ministry. This solved my immediate problem as it also enabled me to get a flat allotted to me. I was allotted a DII flat on Vinay Marg overlooking the Safdarjung airfield. Sukhdev and the children moved there. I did not have a car. My friend from Bihar, Mr. Amaijit Singh Sodhi, IAS, who was working as a Director of Extension in the Agriculture Ministry, came to my rescue as he would provide a ride to me for going to the office and if I needed anywhere to go he would leave the car at my disposal. I saw the Joint Secretary to Indira Gandhi to tell him that I was not fascinated by the prospect of being the General Manager of the Super Bazar. I would be equally happy in any other assignment. It was early 1972. Mr. Bishan Tandon, the Joint Secretary had a look at my file and told me that the Prime Minister had kept the file for him to arrange a meeting with Mr. Vyas. There was some election that was about to take place because of which he had not been able to get a meeting fixed between the two. He assured me that knowing Mrs. Gandhi, as he knew, I should be rest assured that she would stick to her earlier order regardless of the objection of Mr. Vyas. According to him, it was only a question of time. That was precisely what happened after a lapse of about three months. Mr. Vyas threatened to resign. Mrs. Gandhi told him that he was incorrigible, so if he so felt he could resign. Mrs. Savita Behan was appointed the Chairman in his place. Mr. Bishan Tandon rang me up to inform me of the Prime Minister's decision and added that they had appointed a brainless woman as the Chairman. It was for me to carry her along but for the results I alone would be held responsible. I assumed charge as the General Manager, Super Bazar, with the above brief from the highest quarter on the 6th April 1972.

The Super Bazar, when I took over, was in a bad shape. Monthly sales were falling and the fall continued for the next three months. The staff, about 850 in number, stood alienated. Quite often they sat on hunger strike to press for their demands. A number of cases were pending against the management in local courts. There were some 15 managers including two branch managers. Most of the managers were political appointees and some of them flaunted their political connections. The Government was breathing down the neck of the General Manager with their plan for the revival of the Super Bazar. The central part of the Government remedy was retrenchment of about 20 per cent of the staff. The gap between income and expenditure exceeded 4,00,000 rupees every month with cumulative loss touching 16 million rupees. The store functioned on the overdraft provided by the Syndicate Bank and their executives threatened stoppage of the overdraft on the slightest provocation. The number of customers had shrunk to a trickle. The merchandise was spread over five floors.

The store had facility of lifts for all the floors. I found that mostly it were the staff that went up and down the lifts. Every step of the new General Manager was being watched and I wondered, if at all, my coming to Super Bazar was a wise decision. I had great faith in *Waheguru*. I believed that perhaps it was the design of the Almighty that I had been brought in to solve a problem that had been taken note of at the level of the Prime Minister.

I continued the monthly review meetings that were taken by the Secretay, Cooperation, Mr. Qureshi, ICS, from Uttar Pradesh cadre. He was a true and cultured aristocrat, who was polite to a fault. I generally listened to the advice that was doled out to me but I acted only on the advice that did not add to my problems. I went ahead with gusto to restrict trading to two or three floors and rent out the portions vacated to generate non-trading income. Similarly, I permitted advertisers to use the facade of the building to promote various products. I also concentrated on supplying stationery and paper requirements of the Government Departments. I found in my weekly review with the managers that while sales were slipping in some departments but in some the sales were stable or increasing. I sacked the manager of one of the bad departments in the second month of my tenure. This had a sobering effect on the others and the lower sales staff. I visited Punjab where one young officer in the Food and Supply Department told me that they had some stock of old rice in storage that Punjabis did not like to eat and in case I could sell it they could give it to me almost free. I jumped at the offer and acquired all the stock of the old rice. It was found to be excellent for the South Indian *idlis* and *dosas*. It sold like hot cakes, even with a two hundred per cent mark up. We had actually to restrict quantity that could be bought by an individual customer. The queues of customers that came to buy rice went away buying along with it other goods that were on sale. We had our sales jumping up from October onwards. Seeing my success, the Review Committee started showing less and less interest in the Super Bazar, leaving me free to experiment and decide as suited me. I persuaded the Government to permit me to sell custom's confiscated consumer goods seized from smugglers at fixed prices instead of destroying them or letting them rot in the godowns. The craze for foreign goods brought droves of customers to the Super Bazar and made me quite important among the wives of my colleagues who would try to cajole me to tip them off whenever some popular items were received for sale. The shortage of edible oil was something that brought everyone to Super Bazar as the Government would channelise the available supplies through the Super Bazar. The ex-Chief Secretary of Punjab rang me up to say that he was sending someone to me for a tin of vegetable oil. Soon, someone appeared and asked about the tin of oil. I gave it to him when a few moments later his wife personally appeared for the same tin of oil. She said that she could not find her servant so she had come herself. I did not disappoint her but I was wondering as to who could be the trickster who came just before her. It seemed that someone from the telephone exchange had heard the telephonic conversation that I had with her husband and he was smart enough to come and pick up the tin of oil before her. I took two more steps for sales promotion. One was a notice at the reception that our endeavour was to sell goods at the lowest price in Delhi but in case any customer found the price of any item to be higher than any other trader, he should fill in a slip and drop in the box kept there. Some slips were received in the beginning on which the managers concerned were pulled up. Later, we found that the system functioned smoothly for us as well as for our customers. The other was that housewives were price-conscious over some items of grocery but not on all the items. We started selling items like sugar, tea and wheat flour at their cost price. The sales went surging up and there was no looking back. The Super Bazar broke even in the very first year of my stewardship.

There were a number of girls working as sales girls and we had a few girls in other departments including a few managers. This was my first experience of working with so many female employees after Ranchi where there were a few clerks working in my office. There was one who was a bit of a flirt. She caused problems wherever she was posted as she attracted male admirers everywhere who would become a nuisance. I decided to post her in my personal office, as a receptionist. She was happy with the appointment because it gave her some distinction and importance among her colleagues and others. I was happy that apart from solving the problem of her placement, my visitors did not mind waiting for me in the reception because of her company. Stories reached Sukhdev and her friends that I had engaged in my office a smart receptionist. I had at that with me Mr.

N.K. Singh for his district training. He had become a part of our family, as the tradition required. This was also due to his personality and affection he had for us. Sukhdev asked him if they could have a look at the new smart lady receptionist. He got a small chit of paper sent to her through an orderly attendant saying that the Deputy Commissioner wanted her at the house. Luckily, I was at home. She came straight to me and handed over that slip of paper to me. I was simply aghast at seeing the paper. I told N.K. Singh that if the lady had some bad intentions she could have blackmailed me or create a scandal. It was indiscreet on his part to have written that slip of paper. Any how it satisfied the curiosity of my wife and her friends who were playing Majong in our house. I found that Super Bazar was a different cup of tea. I had to visit shop floors where often I found that some sales girls tried to make passes. I ignored such behaviour except in one case where the young sales girl happened to be the girlfriend of the Union President. I did not discourage her. She was happy that she could consider herself close to both the General Manager and the Union President. This gave me the leverage to influence the activities of the Labour Union. The Union kept the Chairman and the Managing Committee in check and even the Government felt shaky in advising me about any retrenchment because the Labour Union was set against it. I had a young spinster, Miss Nishta Kashyap, who had access to the Prime Minister as a manager in one of the departments. My predecessor handled her really with kid gloves because of her connections. I found that the Super Bazar and other public undertakings were used by the politicians and the senior bureaucrats as the dumping ground for their relatives or supporters or simply hangers on where they could enter without any entrance test or qualifications or even a vacancy. The lady was a housekeeper with Mrs. Vijay Laxmi Pandit, the sister of Jawaharlal Nehru.

She approached Indira Gandhi for a job after Mrs. Pandit ceased to hold any public office. Mrs. Gandhi got her staff to get her fixed up as a manager in the Super Bazar. Incidentally, Mrs. Pandit was a regular visitor to the Super Bazar and whenever she came Nishta Kashyap would escort her. Once, she came when Nishta was not there, so her supervisor, Nazeer Ahmed escorted her. She wanted a few small items which Nazeer got for her. He apprised Nishta, when she came, of the visit of Mrs. Pandit and the small purchase that she had made. Nishta rebuked him telling him that Mrs. Pandit was notorious for not paying her bills and his desire to be of help to her had left a bill for her to clear from her own pocket. She felt insecure after I joined. She saw the program of my official visit to Shimla from where I was to introduce in our merchandise some handicrafts that could be sold in Delhi. She said that she would like to accompany me to Shimla to which I had no objection. I casually told her that my wife would be accompanying me to Shimla. I did not know the reason but on the next day she gave some excuse regretting her inability to visit Shimla. I returned from Shimla and made a routine change in the departments. I moved the lady manager to an unimportant position. As I was leaving office, I found her at the gate looking very morose. I stopped to say hello to her and she started crying. I took her in my car to drop her at her house which was close by. She wept bitterly and begged me to restore her department, as according to her, my orders had affected her social standing very adversely. I remained non-committal. Next day, a young IAS officer, who was my ex-trainee, Mr. Navin Chawla, considered to be close to the Prime Minister came to see me. He said that the Prime Minister had received reports that I was victimizing the lady manager and the Prime Minister would not like any action against the lady. I told him that I was on trial for one year as the General Manager and I would have to quit if I could not turn the corner in sales and profit because of which the shakeup that I had ordered was necessary. If no action was to be taken against the manager whose sales had been falling, then I should be absolved of responsibility in this regard. He said that the Prime Minister would not like her removal from the job but she would not like to interfere in my discretion in placements. I assured him that I had no plans to sack the lady manager. A few days later the *Hindustan Times*, the leading daily newspaper of Delhi, carried a main story on its Delhi page that the General Manager of Super Bazar was a sort of a philanderer. All the ladies working there felt unsafe. The General Manager, it was alleged had transferred a lady manager to an unimportant position because she had refused to go with him to Shimla. The story was from a lady journalist who was a friend of Nishta Kashyap, Mrs. Promilla Kalhan. My PRO advised that I should file a defamation suit against the newspaper. I was wiser after my fights with the press in Ranchi and Dhanbad. I sought an appointment with Mr. B.G. Verghese, the editor. He called me to see him the same day. He had anticipated the purpose of my visit. When I met him I introduced myself as a minor functionary of the Government but I said that *Hindustan Times* was a paper of national importance. I said that I was simply surprised to see its focus on a person like me. He said that he saw the newspaper as soon as I had rung up for appointment and he confessed that what had appeared was one-sided and against the policy of *Hindustan Times*. He said that he had ticked off the journalist concerned and such a thing would not happen again. He asked me to write my side of the story which he promised to carry in the *Hindustan Times* equally prominently. I told him that the earlier story was from his correspondent, similarly my side should be also from a correspondent. He agreed to that and thus put an end to the ugly chapter, to the satisfaction of both the parties. The lady manager lingered on for some more time and resigned on her own but after painting me black in the PM's house. I ran into her again in 1980 when I was the Secretary of the Indian Council of Agricultural Research. I had gone to the PM's house for an official function, to get a new variety of rose, named after Jawaharlal Nehru, released. Dr. B.P. Pal, the ex-Director General of the ICAR had developed the new variety. Mrs. Gandhi had just come back to power after the jolt of her defeat in 1977. I found Nishta Kashyap running around on various errands during the *darbar* sort of gathering in the PM's house. She made it a point to recognize me and greet me. She seemed to remember her days spent with me with some happiness. She agreed to meet me for a meal in the India International Centre but at the last minute she regretted her inability to honour the commitment. She later explained that all the staff working with Mrs. Gandhi were discouraged from socializing with outsiders and the intelligence agencies kept a watch on them always. She was afraid that she might lose her job again. I was a bit surprised at her somewhat lame excuse but for all one knew she might have been telling the truth. Whatever I could read about Mrs. Gandhi was that she did keep a close watch on all people who were allowed access by her. Mr. Sathe lost his chance to become a Secretary in the Government of India because he liked his drink and he did not make it a secret. I found that none of the staff close to her could be seen drinking in public. It was during the time of Rajiv Gandhi that some of the staff in the PMO could be spotted enjoying their drink in the presence of others. The other anathema that she had was womanizing officials. There was one of the West Bengal cadre who had this weakness. One or two girlfriends of his I found in the ICAR where he was the Secretary earlier. There was one agricultural scientist who later became the Director General of the ICAR who had gone to Bangkok in a delegation along with the Secretary ICAR. The host who was a Dean of the University gave a dinner in honour of the visiting delegation. After dinner, young girls wearing numbers were paraded before them and they were told to pick up anyone that they liked for their entertainment in their rooms, before drinks were served. None dared, except the Secretary. He used his access to such facilities to curry favour with the circle close to Mrs. Gandhi and got rewarded with the appointment as the Defence Secretary, Government of India. He was reported by a secret agency to have spent a night with a fashionable call girl. He was unceremoniously sacked. I heard the late Giani Zail Singh confessing that as Chief Minister he collected money for the party but he dare not keep any part of it with him as Mrs. Gandhi remained informed about the activities of the Congress Chief Ministers and her Ministers. Not keeping a close watch on relatives and friends by men/women in power led to undoing of many in India. I came across cases where some persons having access to me got advantages for themselves, without my knowing it. Again, I have to accept the wisdom of the caution of Mr. L.P. Singh that every acquaintance should be viewed as a potential threat to one's integrity, if one happened to wield executive power.

I was lucky that the Chairman, Mrs. Savita Behan, in the Management Committee was isolated. We had one member from the Jan Sangh, Mr. Balraj Khanna, whose primary concern was to ensure that the Chairman, who was from the Congress party, did not have the opportunity to use her position in any manner to further the interests of her party. He never permitted any move that weakened the position of the General Manager. Mr. Jag Parvesh Chandra, the veteran Congress leader was another member on the Managing Committee and he too generally supported the General Manager because he wanted his pet scheme of supplies to the students of books and stationery to be backed by the Super Bazar. The business was booming and all the trump cards were with the General Manager. The next year turned out to be a year of profit. We decided to pay bonus to the employees for the first time.

I was visited in Super Bazar by a Manager of the State Trading Corporation that was being presided over by the ex-Levers man, Mr. P.L. Tandon, with the proposal that the Super Bazar should initiate export of consumer goods to Africa and the Middle East. He said that there was a Trade Fair being held at Ndola in Zambia where Super Bazar should participate on their behalf. I said that I could have no objection to the proposal provided all the cost of participation was borne by the State Trading Corporation. He said that he would let me know in due course. I did not take the discussion as anything more than kite flying. I was pleasantly surprised when I received a formal approval of the proposal within the next three days asking me Godspeed for my participation in the Trade Fair. The State Trading Corporation was a public undertaking in the Government. I became curious to know as to how the decision-making could be so fast in a governmental environment. I was told that Mr. Tandon had introduced a new system of management where all responsibility was assigned to the divisional heads. No files moved from desk-to-desk. It was the divisional head who formulated a proposal, in a maximum of one page, which would go before a management committee presided over by Mr. Tandon. Finance or Law or any other division could call for the relevant file but the decision had to be taken in the meeting. The discussions and the decisions were minuted to serve as a record. We finalized a list of items that could be exported and collected samples of those items in my personal baggage. I went to Ndola via Nairobi and Lusaka. It was something of an eye opener, to see Nairobi, which appeared to be better managed and more modern than Bombay or Delhi. Indians, particularly Gujaratis were there everywhere. I was new to the place. The STC representative was not able to meet me at the airport. A Gujarati gentleman, seeing me a bit lost, took me along to reach me to my hotel. He took me home. He told that they had been in Kenya for the last three generations. I joined the family in their meal. They were two brothers and their wives who had prepared the meal. The three of us men sat on the table to eat a simple Gujarati vegetarian meal while the two ladies remained standing and serving the meal to us. The contrast with Punjabis was striking in this regard. The Punjabis everywhere took to the Western ways in the very first generation of immigrants but not so the Gujaratis. Next day I landed at Ndola. It was around Christmas time. The Custom's Officer was in a hurry to go home. He enquired if I had anything to declare. I told him that I had a few sample items for the Trade Fair. He said to me that he was in a hurry to go home, so he had not heard what I said about samples. He put a cross mark on my bag in token of his clearance and he rushed out of the airport before I could say even thank you to him. The actual Trade Fair was a disappointment. Very few developed countries had participated and the whole thing was like a district fair in India. The Deputy High Commissioner of India was however happy with the stall put up by the Super Bazar. I found that there were quite a few Indians in Zambia, particularly those who had an accounting background. The closing function was presided over by the Zambian Trade Minister. The Zambian guests I found did full justice to the drinks that followed the closing function. I went shopping in Nairobi on my return. I did not have the Kenyan currency, so I pulled out my purse for a change in the local currency. The STC officer, Mr. Dasgupta, who was with me stopped me and took me aside. He said that the unofficial conversion rate for the English currency was more than the double of the official rate. He just grabbed the Pound note in my hand and gave me the local currency that was more than the double of what the store would have given. It did not strike me if any malpractice was involved in it. Mrs. Dasgupta told me that they had their earlier posting in Delhi where their son was studying in the convent school near Gurdwara Bangla Saheb. She said that their son had a feeling that the God in the school church was not his God but the God in Bangla Saheb was his God. She said that around Diwali, while playing with crackers, he got severe burns on his face and neck, for which they had to rush him to the hospital. The boy insisted on being taken to Bangla Saheb and while being taken to the *Guru Granth Saheb* he rushed to the small tank sanctified by the touch of Guru Harkrishan the eighth Sikh Guru and sprinkled some water on his burnt face before he could be pulled back. Mrs. Dasgupta said that it was a miracle that wherever the water had touched his body there was no burn scar whereas on the other parts, the scar of the burns could be clearly seen. I returned to Delhi after a week's jaunt at the cost of the STC.

My friend from the Aligarh University, Mr. Abu Hakim, made it to the IAS three years after me. He was allotted to Bihar. I was the District Magistrate when he was posted as the Sub Divisional

Magistrate at Sasaram. Sasaram was famous for the tomb of Sher Shah Suri, the Pathan ruler who had defeated Humayun, the son of Babur, the founder of the Mughal dynasty. Sasaram also had the famous Rohtas Fort. Abu Hakim came to Delhi as a Special Assistant to the Minister for Agriculture, Mr. Ahmed. It seems that Mrs. Gandhi enjoyed a lot of respect among the Arab socialists. Mr. D.P. Dhar, in her cabinet was a great friend of Sadam Hussain, who was the Vice President of Iraq. He had made a request for deputation of teams of agricultural experts to initiate programs for the growth of agriculture in Iraq.

I found my name as the leader of one team of agricultural experts who were to formulate a project for Intensive Agricultural Development. I was selected as the team leader as I had the experience of managing the project of Intensive Agricultural Development in Shahabad district of Bihar. Another friend of mine from Bihar, Mr. Amaijit Singh Sodhi, was the team leader for starting a quality seed multiplication project in Iraq. We flew by the Iraqi Airlines flight, direct to Baghdad from Delhi. Professor Goyal of the IIPA was also with us in the plane. He was going as an advisor on economic planning. It was a happy coincidence that in the same flight I had another friend who was in business in Bihar, Mr. Nanak Singh Kohli. He had bagged an order of the Iraqi Government for the supply of woolen great coats for the Iraqi Army. We stayed together in the same hotel for some time in Baghdad. All the teams got busy with their assignments. I had a preliminary discussion with the Iraqi counterpart and the members of my team, after which we finalized a framework for preparing our Project Report. Members of the team were allocated specific areas on which they were to submit their reports. I kept with me the overview of the project and the responsibility of coordination. I was comparatively free to sit with Mr. Kohli and sample different beers of Baghdad. It was revealing for me that being an Islamic country there were bars and pubs galore in Baghdad when there was a clear prohibition prescribed for the Muslims in the *Quran*. Ladies with black veils could be seen but most of the Iraqi women wore Western skirts and blouses. We toured the whole length and breadth of Iraq. Iraq is one of the few countries of the world that were inhabited by human societies from the earliest period of human history. Mostly it is covered by the delta formed between the Euphrates and Tigris rivers. It must have been a very fertile land. It had loamy soil and easy availability of water. These very assets proved to be its undoing because the uncontrolled irrigation from the rivers made the soil waterlogged and the rising water table brought harmful salts up, destroying its fertility. The soil can again be made fertile for agriculture after the salts from the soil were leached out. We found the Iraqi farmers to be lazy and incompetent. They had set up a sugar factory near Amara and the farmers were encouraged to grow sugarcane. The farmers had gone for ratooning cutivation for more than five years with dwindling produce every year rather than fresh plantation or crop rotation. It was a problem to formulate a viable agricultural project in Iraq. Our stay in Iraq got extended to three months which was a prospect that was welcome for us, as we were being looked after well and we could make a good saving from our daily allowance. We were able to give a report recommending two intensive agricultural projects, one in the North near Mosul and the other near Basra in the South. My friend Mr. Kohli also spent about two months in Iraq, in two spells. He always found me available for sharing a bottle of beer but Mr. Sodhi, the other team leader could rarely be found free. He asked me as to why it was like that. I explained to him that Mr. Sodhi was a perfectionist, who would like every page of the group report to go through him. My principle in life was that if I found that there was anyone other than me who could take an assignment, may not be so well, I would prefer letting him do that and backing him up for that. It saved me from a lot of botheration and fostered a sense of confidence in the subordinates, who stood by me if the situation so required. We did not lag behind in our project but the division of work that we had left enough time to socialize and take care of the other needs of the team. Professor S.K. Goyal of the IIPA had come to the Iraqi Planning Commission for a longer deputation. He had taken a house on rent near our hotel. His son Samir and daughter got attached to me. They would come every Thursday and insist that I should spend the night with them at their house. Even before I agreed to their request they would pack my toothbrush and a change in a bag. Mr. Goyal was close to D.P. Dhar and the so-called young turks in the Congress. Chandra Shekhar, who later became the Prime Minister of India, has continued to be his close friend. Professor Goyal took the initiative to organize a school for the children of Indians in Baghdad. He asked me to send a consignment of text books for the school. I sent the consignment immediately after my return to India. Mrs. Gandhi had been invited by the Iraqi President to visit Iraq after India had exploded their first Atomic Bomb. I was able to get the consignment of books sent for the school as a part of the baggage of the Prime Minister's party.

India, especially the Congress party, seemed to have enjoyed a special position with the Baath party. We met a number of Indian teachers during our tours. We had the Indian Air Force training Iraqi pilots in Habbaniya. We could locate the place near Baghdad Railway Station where Guru Nanak had stayed. We started assembling there every Friday for reading *Gurbani* and a get together. We had a Sikh First Secretary, Mr. Gill, in our Embassy. He was a Mussoorie boy. His assistant was one Mr. Talha, who spoke fluent Arabic. He was of great help for us in resolving various small problems with the Iraqi administration. We had one Bihar IPS officer on deputation with the Research and Analysis Wing, under the Cabinet Secretariat, which was another name for spying. He was Mr. Satya Narain Rai.

His name was changed to S. Narain. He was posted as a Counsellor in the Embassy. His living and perks caused a lot of heartburns among the regular diplomatic staff. His budget for partying was munificent whereas the regular diplomatic staff had to go by some niggardly budget allotment. I attended a few of the parties hosted by Mr. Rai. As usual Scotch whisky and other drinks flowed like water and in one of the parties Mr. Rai passed out. The other diplomats in the Embassy alleged that the RAW officials could hardly ferret out any real secrets in a dictatorial environment as prevailed in Iraq but they caused enough nuisances to the other diplomatic staff. They would bribe drivers of other diplomats from their secret service funds and send reports against them alleging sale by them of their duty free quota liquor and other indiscretions.

One good thing about the Iraqi administration that I found was that they did not have a file system. The officer authorized took a decision on the basis of the facts presented without having to cite precedents. I had gone to meet the officer in some other connection when I happened to mention that we were senior officers entitled to travel first class. He immediately upgraded our entitlement but the same officer declined a similar request from other groups and their citing our precedent cut no ice. The Iraqi Airways had one weekly flight from Baghdad and everyone had to go to Delhi by that flight since the passage was paid by the Iraqi government. All of us wanted to go via Kuwait that was a duty free city, from where we could buy whatever was needed by our families. The exemption to travel by other than Iraqi Airways could be given only by the Minister for Civil Aviation. My friend from the Embassy accompanied me to the Ministry in order to get the exemption from the Minister. We were asked to wait. We were given a small cup of very strong black coffee as was the custom with most of the high officials on whom we had called although the popular drink with most of the people was black tea with sugar. When the Minister did not turn up we started getting restive on which one of the Minister's personal staff told us that the Minister recently got a young lady on his staff and he had got infatuated by the lady. He said that he generally took her to his official residence on the plea that he had some sensitive official work which he would prefer to do in the privacy of his house. We took his address and knocked at the house. A bit embarrassed middle-aged gentleman opened the door a chink. Mr. Talha straightaway launched in Arabic that I was a very important expert lent to the Government of Iraq by Mrs. Indira Gandhi. He said that she had called me back immediately and there was no flight of the Iraq Airways for the next four days, so we should be permitted to go by Kuwait Airways to enable us to reach in time. He immediately wrote 'Approved' on my letter and closed the door shut again. His order was not authenticated by any official of the government unlike the practice in India. The paper, as signed by the Minister, was honoured by the airlines and we traveled First Class by Kuwait Airways with an overnight stay in a hotel in Kuwait. We shopped like mad in Kuwait. All of us bought TV sets and the like. My subordinate officers from Super Bazar were there to receive me along with Sukhdev, and to help me to get out of the Indian customs after paying custom's duty.

I returned home quite happy but soon after landing in Delhi I found that the ground from under my feet had slipped. Savita Behan, the Chairman came to realize that there was patronage and power in being the Chairman that was being denied to her by me, so I had to be removed from Super Bazar. Her principal detractor in the Management Committee Mr. Balraj Khanna had died having committed suicide. I found that I had to answer a Parliament question tabled by the Marxist M.P., Mr. Jyotirmoy Basu, making filthy and false allegations against me, linking me to the death of the wife of Mr. P.S. Gill, my Assistant General Manager. Gill had a love marriage with a Goanese Christian girl, Teresa. She was a pretty lady and taught in a convent school. He had an affair with a young Sikh widow, who would often come to Super Bazar and declare that she was the *defacto* Mrs. Gill. I did not know about this aspect of his life till after the death of Teresa. Considering his three small children, I had advised him to marry the lady with whom he had the affair. I attended his marriage also but there was no reason or suspicion about the death of Teresa. Mr. P.S. Gill was the brother of a batch mate of mine, Mr. T.S. Gill, whom we called *Tochi*. Their father was the veteran Akali leader, Sardar Mangal Singh, who was the founder of the well-known daily newspaper of Delhi, the '*Hindustan Times*'. We had known each other since my training days. I had given him a quick promotion and I had placed him in-charge of the Groceries and Toiletries Department, considered to be the backbone of Super Bazar. He started being perceived as the *alter ego* of the General Manager. Even Sukhdev felt that my closeness to Gill was not very desirable. When the Union aimed their guns on him I got the same silenced through the girlfriend of the Union President. I was able to satisfy the Government on all the points made or implied in the question.

Another development that had taken place was that through a backdoor, local politicians had acquired a foothold in the running of the Super Bazar. When Mrs. Gandhi was virtually under siege due to the J.P. Narayan agitation, especially after the Allahabad High Court judgment, her supporters organized mobilization of crowds from the slums of Delhi to come on to the streets in support of Mrs. Gandhi. One of the persons who came into prominence in this activity was a cycle mechanic, Mr. Arjan Das. He carried so much access to the PM's house that people started calling him the third son of Mrs. Gandhi. He got Mrs. Menaka Gandhi, the newly married wife of Sanjay Gandhi, to inaugurate a sale of cheap wheat flour for the poor by the Super Bazar. I did not consider it appropriate to interfere with what had been started but I pulled up the manager concerned that it was not right. I got a telephone from the same manager around 9 p.m. in the night that Arjan Das wanted an additional centre to be opened by the Super Bazar the very next day. I told him that nothing doing and banged the telephone. Next day I got late in reaching my office as I had to attend a meeting. There was a lot of excitement in the Super Bazar when I reached. The deputy general manager, Mr. V.P. Gulati was in tears. He said that Arjan Das has told him that the new centre must start functioning by 12 o'clock.

He was told that the General Manager had not approved the proposal. He said that thereafter he received a telephone from R.K. Dhawan, threatening him that if the new centre did not start by the time given he would get him placed under suspension and similar would be the fate of the General Manager, who was coming in the way of public work. He said that he was scared by the threat and therefore he carried out what he was ordered to do. I was livid with anger on hearing the story. I rang up Mr. Tandon, the Joint Secretary to the Prime Minister to pull up Dhawan. Unfortunately, he was not available on telephone.

I dictated a letter to Tandon giving all the details of the action and I was sure that whoever Dhawan was, he would get his wings clipped, as had happened a little earlier when the Private Secretary to Bhola Shastri, the Central Minister for Works and Housing, had tried to pull his weight to get a sacked manager reappointed. I had known the Minister personally as one of the few scrupulously honest ministers in the Government. I wrote to him and in reply I was informed that the Private Secretary concerned had been given marching orders. Mr. R.K. Dhawan stood listed in the telephone directory as the 2nd Additional Private Secretary to the Prime Minister. I started hearing rumblings of what I had done. One member of the Managing Committee who was beholden to Dhawan told me that I was in for trouble. Mr. Tandon himself, it seems was a bit fed up with complaints against Dhawan's activities. He found my letter handy to do him down. Mrs. Gandhi, I was told, gave a dressing down to Dhawan but then he was able to turn the table on Tandon and on me. He produced Mr. Ajmera, the member of the Managing Committee before Mrs. Gandhi to say that bureaucrats were very difficult to get on with and according to him I was one of the worst examples as the case of the lady manager showed. He said to get such bureaucrats moved, sometimes they had to use the name of the Prime Minister, as was done in my case. The bureaucrats all over were always together, as was proved by the support of Mr. Tandon of my complaint. I was told that Mrs. Gandhi wrote a one page note in her own hand absolving Dhawan of all that was alleged against him and brushing aside all other points that Tandon had raised in his note. She also asked him to convey her displeasure to me. I knew that despite all my record breaking achievements, my goose was cooked when I received a peculiar reply to my letter from Mr. Bishan Tandon. One of the points made in my letter was that the orders that officers in the Super Bazar received were oral orders in the name of the Prime Minister. Our Government rules were that oral orders must be confirmed in writing. Not only we did not receive any orders in writing, we were not sure if the orders being conveyed to us were really the orders of the Prime Minister and the person conveying the orders could be accepted as authorised to convey the PM's orders. Mr. Bishan Tandon wrote back obviously on the orders of the Prime Minister that the PM was a very busy person and many times she passed oral orders on the requests of various persons who met her and whosoever happened to be present with her was asked to convey her orders to the officials concerned. This was a ridiculous clarification coming to us from the Prime Minister making a complete mockery of the system of the Government that we were following so far. The episode made me a bit morose. Mr. Kishore Lal, a Congress leader in the Municipal Corporation of Delhi came to see me during the phase of my despondence. He congratulated me on my achievements and he said that he was very impressed by the various charts and graphs displayed in my office room showing a clear upturn in the working of the Super Bazar in all fields. He enquired from me if Indira Gandhi had those charts in her office. I replied in the negative. He said that he had come to tell me that just as in the olden days the barbers and servants of kings were important because they had access to the king, similarly in the present set up Arjan Das and Dhawan were important. Mr. R.K. Soni of Ludhiana had got quite close to R.K. Dhawan. He felt concerned about me. He observed as to what a pity it was that despite the fact that my ex-trainee N.K. Singh was so close to Dhawan and having done so well, I was on the wrong side of Dhawan, the new power centre in Delhi. He said that sitting in Delhi I should have known about it. He said that the South Indian Brahmin bureaucrats had a stranglehold on power at the Centre. It was according to him Dhawan who had broken their grip at the Centre. He said that it was well-known that Dhawan helped all Punjabi officers. I was one of the few who had come to some harm at his hands. He advised me to apologize and beg for his mercy otherwise my name would be struck off from the list of officers who could be considered for an appointment under the Central Government. I told him to not to worry about me as I came from a village where a *tehsildar* is considered to be a big officer and I was of the rank of a Commissioner. My people back home would be happy to know that I had reached that far. I thanked him for his concern. He got Mr. J.K. Kohli appointed as the Chief Secretary of Delhi and also there was a clearance for his appointment as a successor to Mr. Tandon. The hitch was that Mr. Sathe had given him some adverse remarks on his performance in the Academy. J.K. Kohli asked me if I could be of help in that. I was able to convince Mr. Sathe to give his comments on the representation of J.K. Kohli in a manner that resulted in his adverse comments getting expunged. I was happy that decks were cleared for Kohli's appointment to the powerful position in the civil services as the Joint Secretary to the Prime Minister. J.K. Kohli also tried to retrieve my position in the eyes of Dhawan.

When it gets around that one was on the wrong side of the powers that be, even small issues assume a sinister proportion. A food inspector had lifted a sample from a sealed bottle of honey from a branch of the Super Bazar for testing. It was found in the food laboratory that the ash content of the sample of honey was a bit higher than what was the standard. The Super Bazar had a warranty from the manufacturer against any departure from the standards prescribed. Normally only the manufacturer should have been prosecuted for it. A notice for a show cause against prosecution was received in the Super Bazar, of which no notice was taken. The manufacturer called on me and sought my clearance to bribe the food inspector and get the matter closed. I ticked off the gentleman saying that since he was the manufacturer he should face the music if he had violated the prescribed standards and showed him the door. He muttered while leaving that if he had to go to jail, he would not go alone. The Lieutenant Governor of Delhi was one Baleshwar Prasad, a Bihar cadre officer and the Chief Secretary was another friend Mr. K.K. Srivastava. I wrote a letter to him explaining the collusion of the inspectors in the food department with the manufacturers who violated food standards. I was called for a meeting. The case had become *sub-judice* as the inspector had rushed to file a case against me and others as soon as he came to know about my letter to the Chief Secretary. Mr. Baleshwar Prasad was on the receiving end in the media over allotment of some plots of land to a few of his relatives. He felt almost shaky in taking up my complaint in a matter that was technically *sub-judice*. Nothing came out of it. One fine morning the Security Officer of the Super Bazar came to my office on the fifth floor to inform me that an Inspector from the Delhi Police had come with a non-bailable warrant of arrest against me. He advised me to go away from the back door. I straight went to the office of the Secretary, Mr. Qureshi and apprised him of my predicament. He wrung his hands in anguish but he also could do nothing. I surrendered in the court on the next date of hearing and pleaded for the complaint to be quashed against me. The Magistrate turned down my plea but he granted me bail. I appealed against his order in the High Court that put the issue on the back burner. It saved me from the danger of a political vendetta against me if the complaint was inspired by my complaint against Dhawan. The High Court too upheld the order of the Magistrate. I decided to file an appeal in the Supreme Court of India through my Aligarh friend, Mr. O.P. Sharma, Senior Counsel in the Supreme Court. The Supreme Court did not reverse the lower court orders but the judges gave me relief by observing that if there was a warranty given by the manufacturer, the Government could consider withdrawing the case against me. The new Government had no *animus* against me, so the case finally got withdrawn. My case is still a case of the Supreme Court that is cited as it defines what is meant by the term 'Public Servant'.

The father of Mr. N.K. Singh, Mr. T.P. Singh, ICS, was our neighbour in Vasant Vihar. He had recently retired as the Finance Secretary from the Government of India. I found that he had retired with a little bitterness against the Government of India as perhaps he was not made the Cabinet Secretary or he was not considered for appointment as a Governor after his retirement. He confided to me that things in the Government of India had really changed. He said that the erstwhile Private Assistants like Yashpal Kapoor or R.K. Dhawan had come to acquire a clout where they had become the arbiters of destiny. He noted with sadness that many of the high and the mighty were kowtowing to the new power centers and prospering. He said that since he did not cultivate the new court manners so he got passed over. I too considered myself a misfit in the new environment. I thought that before going back to Bihar I should see for myself as to how the new system was working. I rang up Arjan Das, telling him that I wanted to see him. He was overjoyed to receive a call from me. He lived in a small house in Laxmibai Nagar with his family. Everything in the house and around it suggested a lower middleclass living. His wife brought a cup of tea for me. I told him that I was going to Bihar because of him. He said that he did not know me, so he had complained to Dhawan because the Super Bazar had refused to carry out his program. I told him that it was his overbearing manner and threats that made me stand up against him. I found that he genuinely felt sorry and he promised that he would try to undo the damage that got caused to me because of his complaint. I also spoke to my ex-trainee, Mr. N.K. Singh, who was the Private Secretary to Mr. Chattopadhyay, the Commerce Minister. My colleagues in the Commerce Ministry told me that the Minister always went by the views of N.K. Singh, whose friendship with Dhawan was well-known. N.K. Singh had a hearty laugh when I told him that I had just come to know about his closeness to R.K. Dhawan. He said that he was keeping a track on what was going on. He exclaimed that he had seen many Secretaries in the Government of India trying their utmost to simply come to the notice of Mrs. Gandhi and here was I, who sitting in a place like Super Bazar, got one page written by Indra Gandhi in her own hand, describing my qualities of course from the negative side. I said that what had to happen, had happened. He promised that he would try to soften Dhawan about me. Arjan Das came to the Super Bazar a few days later. He asked me to accompany him to the Prime Minister's house and straight went to Dhawan's room. He introduced me to him and we sat down discussing pleasantries when Rajiv Gandhi, who was a pilot in the Indian Airlines, entered the room. Both of them got up to listen to what he was saying but I remained sitting as I had not been introduced to Rajiv Gandhi although I could recognize him, having seen his photographs off and on. Dhawan did not consider it appropriate to introduce me to him. He was in the room only for a few moments. Dhawan also apologized for the harm caused to me but he justified it that I had left him no alternative after he saw my letter to Tandon. He said Tandon was trying his best to undermine his position and from my letter he thought that I was a co-conspirator against him. He said that he helped many Punjabi officers, some even out of the way and he named a few whom he had helped but in my case he admitted that he had harmed me but he said that it was done in self-defence.

He wished me best of luck in Bihar and enquired from me if he should put in a word for me to the Chief Minister of Bihar. I told him that it was not necessary and left him after thanking him for the courtesy and consideration shown to me. I had a friend, Mr. D.N. Kotwal, who was with me in Aligarh University. He joined the IAS via the State Civil Service of Jammu and Kashmir and currently he was posted as a Deputy Secretary in the Ministry of Home Affairs. He told me that the Minister of State in his Ministry, Mr. Om Mehta, was the whole and sole authority there, having a direct access to Mrs. Gandhi. He said that the Cabinet Minister for Home Affairs, Mr. Brahmanand Reddy was only a figurehead. Mr. Om Mehta, he claimed was his personal friend. He asked me to not to give up as extensions of deputation of IAS officers were decided by him in the Ministry. I told him that it was going to be of no use but I did not stop him from trying. He came back to me after a day or two with a long face blaming Om Mehta that he was such a close friend of his and so far he had never asked him for any favour yet he could not oblige him in so small a matter like a small extension in my deputation. It was clear, as I was told by Mr. R.K. Soni, that my name had been put on a list who were not to be called back to the Government of India. had mainly two concerns. One was to find a way to oust the Congress supporters from the control of many important cooperative

14

To Bihar Again

My first deputation to the Government of India was coming to an end. I was going back to Bihar with a mixed sort of feelings. I was happy that I did well in whatever was assigned to me. I had goofed up my credit for it as had happened to me in my first district in Bihar. Perhaps sky could have been the limit for my success only if I had developed the art of taking care of the hangers-on around the Prime Minister. I have to admit that perhaps what *Waheguru* does is for the best. I did not know that Emergency was going to be imposed on the country soon after my reaching Bihar. Had I remained with the Central Government I could have got picked up for some executive assignment and consequently involved in committing excesses or in a risky fight against the powers that be. I had an ambitious Punjabi colleague in Bihar who could not do well in the service right from his Sub Divisional Officer days. I met him in Delhi while he was on some unimportant assignment. I told him about the new power centre of Delhi. He threw himself at the feet of R.K. Dhawan and he did not have to regret it. He enjoyed being at the centre of the stage in Delhi for some time, thanks to the patronage of Dhawan. There was surely one way to succeed as I could see it being demonstrated before me, but definitely it was not my cup of tea, come what may. The Government of Bihar, on coming to know of my return, posted me as the Food and Civil Supplies Commissioner. The Chief Minister was

Professor Jagannath Mishra, the younger brother of late L.N. Mishra, who was said to be very close to Mrs. Gandhi. He was for some time the Railway Minister in the Government of India. Later, he was the Commerce Minister in the Government of India. He had Mr. N.K. Singh as his Special Assistant.

Mr. L.N. Mishra was the fund collector for the Congress. He was known to travel with briefcases full of currency notes. He was known also to be very generous. He would dole out a bundle of notes to anyone who he felt was in need. There were a number of poor Bihar Brahmins who were grateful to him for money that he gave them to enable them to marry off their daughters. Karpuri Thakur, a socialist leader in the opposition had a son with a hole in his heart that could be rectified by a surgical operation abroad for which he did not have the resources. Mr. L.N. Mishra paid for the boy's passage as well as the operation as a gesture of goodwill for a fellow politician. A friend of mine, Mr. Suresh Kumar, who was posted as a Counsel General in our Embassy in Germany, told me about the style with which L.N. Mishra conducted himself abroad. He was received by him at the airport. He told Suresh Kumar that while he would be busy with his official work, he wanted him to buy gifts for his friends, many of them being the leading members of the Delhi Press Corps for which he just handed over a bundle of currency notes and the list of gifts that were to be bought. He always carried a bottle of Royal Salute Scotch whisky for General Sam Manekshaw whom he claimed to be his friend from the days when he was a junior minister in the Defence Ministry. He never counted the money that he gave Suresh Kumar nor did he bother to count the balance that Suresh Kumar returned to him. Mr. N.K. Singh was completing his tenure under the Central Government and he wanted to stay on in the Government of India. Mr. L.N. Mishra took him to the Bihar Chief Minister who had come on a visit to Delhi. He told him that he must permit extension in the deputation of N.K. Singh. The Chief Minister immediately called the Chief Secretary Mr. P.K.J. Menon to write a letter to the Government of India to that effect. Thereafter, he asked N.K. to go back to his office as the errand for which they had come had been completed. Mr. L.N. Mishra, immediately after N.K. left, launched a tirade against him accusing him of being a spy placed by his detractors in the PM's house to report on his activities to them.

He really wanted him to be called back to Bihar but he could not say that while N.K. was present. Mr. Menon was quickly called back to issue revised orders but fortunately for N.K., Mr. P.K.J. Menon well-known for his fast decision-making and quick execution, had already signed and posted the earlier instructions of the Chief Minister. Mr. L.N. Mishra, when he was the Railway Minister, was badly injured in a bomb explosion at Samastipur. He could have been saved as the external injuries did not appear to be serious but he insisted that he should not be taken to a Bihar hospital for his treatment as his relations with the Bihar Chief Minister, Mr. Gafoor, had soured. He was given first aid in his special train and the train was taken to Dinapur where there was a railway hospital. The delay in journey, with perhaps some internal bleeding, took his life before he could reach Dinapur. Dr. Jagannath Mishra came to the forefront in politics of Bihar after his death. I found Jagnnath Mishra to be very courteous and considerate to officers although there were whispers about his corruption too. He was a learned person and a good orator in Hindi. He could reel out statistics about Bihar like the back of his hand. My Minister was Ramashray Prasad Singh who was a *Bhumihar* by caste. Everyone in Bihar knew about my fight with S.K. Sinha, the first Chief Minister of Bihar, who was a *Bhumihar* too. There were some who tried to poison the mind of the Minister against me. Among them was his caste man S.N. Sharma, a promoted IAS officer, who was a favourite during the time of Dr. S.K. Sinha. I had succeeded him as the Deputy Commissioner of Dhanbad. He was the Managing Director of the Bihar Food and Civil Supplies Corporation, a state government undertaking under the Food Department. It was cited as the only state undertaking in Bihar that was in profit. Mr. Sharma had carried a book written by Noorani, on corruption in India, which had an excerpt from the Aiyar Commission Report, critical of my action in temporarily transferring two and a half lakh of rupees from one fund to another. Anyhow, nothing happened in all that went on before I joined.

Bihar happened to be a marginally food deficit state. India, during the sixties, was plagued by hunger. The 1966 famine could be tackled through the generosity of the USA, who fed India through PL480. The PL480 wheat was distributed mainly in the urban areas and some was earmarked for the rural poor although very little reached the villages. All state governments were required to contribute food grains to a central pool at a price fixed by the Central Government to supplement what was received under PL480. It so happened that in surplus states the market forces brought down the price to levels below the procurement price fixed by the Government and for that end movement of food was prohibited from one state to the other. Punjab had no problem in contributing more than two million tons of food grains to the Central pool while Bihar could contribute almost nothing. Bihar administration was under pressure from the Central Government to contribute at least some food grains to the national kitty. The practice in Bihar was to ask the district officers to impose a compulsory levy on bigger farmers that they must sell to the government at the procurement price and to use force against the farmers who were recalcitrant. The food levy led to a lot of resentment against the government without really contributing any significant quantity of food grains to the national pool. I was handed over, by the Minister, a complaint made by a close relative of the Minister against alleged high handedness by Mr. G.S. Kang, IAS, the District Magistrate of Aurangabad, for an enquiry and appropriate action. I decided to hold the enquiry personally. I went to Aurangabad and asked Kang about the facts of the case. He frankly said what he had done was a deliberate act as most of the farmers were looking to the complainant who was also related to the Minister, as to what he did on receiving the notice of levy of paddy against him. He did not respond to the notice, so there was no collection of levy rice in his district. He, therefore, decided to make an example of the farmer concerned and raided his house and the grain store to forcibly collect the levied quantity of rice. This action enabled him to fulfill his quota of the rice levy. I then met the farmer complainant. He was very angry at what he had suffered. He resented the humiliation that the raid had caused to him and his family in the district. I explained to him the rationale of the district administration for choosing him for the raid. I told him that what the District Magistrate did was an official act to carry out the orders of the Minister. His feelings were assuaged by the fact that I had held the enquiry personally and secondly that the District Magistrate considered him to be the most important farmer in the district and he had nothing personal against him. I took him along with me to Mr. Kang, where both of them shook hands and the matter was agreed to be dropped. The Minister complimented me on my getting an issue so amicably resolved that was otherwise so delicate for him because of his relatives being involved in to it. I learnt to my horror that despite so many complaints of harassment there was no law that authorized the government to impose a levy of food grains on the farmers. I succeeded in persuading the Solicitor General of India, who was a Bihari, to suggest a draft for an ordinance, to be promulgated retroactively, to cover the legal lacuna in our policy. I was able to make a record procurement in Bihar that year touching fifty thousand tons through the simple device of cordoning the surplus districts of Shahabad and Purnea and mopping up whatever reached the market when the price went below the fixed procurement price. The second easy source was the realization of the levy quota from the rice mills. Everyone was happy that we could avoid unpopularity with the farmers of the state.

We had to wait for some time for the regular allotment of the house to us. We were given temporarily a suite of rooms in the State Industrial Guest House that used to be the house of the Bihar Chief Minister, Dr. S.K. Sinha. He was the Chief Minister from 1937 to 1961 with a short break, during the Quit India Movement, of about 4years. Somehow none of his successors could stay on as Chief Minister for a full term. The house was pronounced as unlucky and it was converted as the guest house. Another officer who had also returned from deputation with the Central Government was Mr. P.S. Appu, who was also similarly in the guest house. I used to go to office about an hour before the official opening time of the office. My office was in the Old Secretariat, a stately mansion built by the British when Bihar and Orissa were separated from Bengal. It was about the end of Monsoons. There had been heavy rainfall for the last two days. I saw a trickle of rain water on the road while I was driving on the road. I did not take much notice of it and went ahead to my office. Sukhdev rang up about an hour afterwards that rain water had flooded the compound of the guest house. I got down for having a look and on finding that water, about one foot deep, was there in the portico of the Secretariat, I rushed back home and near the Assembly building on the way, the jeep had to be manually pushed as there was deep water where the engine of the jeep had stopped. By the time I reached the guest house the whole compound was full of water and water was just entering the ground floor. I parked the jeep at the highest point on the ground and went to our suite on the first floor. It was clear that Patna was getting flooded. Patna was always known to be flood prone. I am told that Buddha had predicted that the town, then known as Pataliputra, would always stand in danger of being flooded. It is surrounded by three rivers, Ganges on the North and Son on the West and Punpun in the East. The problem always arose if the Ganges was in flood as then it could not take water from Punpun and sometimes from even Son. The water that could go into the Ganges would flood the city. One side of Patna was protected by the high embankment of the railway line. The flood water was constantly rising. My children were having great fun playing in water. I got a slip from the Speaker of the Assembly, who was occupying the house adjacent to the guest house, informing me as the Food Commissioner, that they were about ten persons in the house and that they had no food. I told him that even the Food Commissioner was without food and at that moment I did not know what could be done.

All the telephones were dead. We heard the All India Radio telling us that flood waters had entered their studios and they were going off the air. I dressed myself in a swimming trunk and decided to walk up to the Chief Secretary's house that was nearby. The Chief Secretary was Sardar Saran Singh, a very devout Sikh of the 1948 batch of the IAS. His house also had got flooded with water having entered the ground floor. They had a wireless set through which he was trying to reach the police headquarters. Mrs. Saran Singh seemed to be more worried about the prospect of having to feed the section of their residential security guards whose meals from the police kitchen could not reach them. I enquired from the Chief Secretary if I could be of any service in the situation. He seemed to be flustered fully and said that what he could tell me when he knew nothing as to what had happened. There was no point in waiting there. I decided to survey the situation myself. The situation was atrocious as all the houses was under water. My friend, Kamla Prasad, had returned from a deputation with the FAO at Rome. He had brought a new Volkswagen Beetle car and he had put it in his garage along with the lift van of his household articles. His car engine was badly damaged when flood water entered his garage. When he opened the door of the flooded garage he found his costly appliances and other items floating and flowing away in water. I found on my way a dead body being pushed in the water, being taken to the banks of the Ganges for cremation. I walked about two kilometers in water.

I had to swim for a short distance where the water was deep. I was pleasantly surprised to see that Patna Junction Railway Station was functioning as the railway line remained unaffected by the flood. I had tea and snacks in the refreshment room. I took a rickshaw from the railway station to the office of the District Magistrate, Mr. V.S. Dubey, who had been a trainee with me in Ranchi. There was a control room functioning under the Commissioner Mr. A.U. Sarma. He was simply shocked to see me. He assured me that my services were really not required at that time. He asked me to relax and he arranged a change of clothes for me. I went to the nearby Bankipore Club located on the Southern bank of the Ganges. I found that the club was going on and popular officer, Mr. Shashi Shekhar Sinha, sitting alone in the bar and enjoying his gin and lime cordial, oblivious to all that was going on in the New Patna and the rest of the world. I joined him and soon the Commissioner also joined us. He told me that he had called the Army to assist him in flood relief work. The Army boats were expected to reach Patna during the night. Mr. Sarma was a great company any time and after a drink one really enjoyed his jokes and lighter observations about men, women and matters. He arranged for my stay in the Control Room for the night, a decision which he later regretted, as he could not have a wink of sleep due to my snoring.

The Army boats arrived during the night. I was sent on the first Army boat that was going to bring the Chief Secretary and other senior officers to the Control Room. Patna had been under water for almost 24 hours. When people saw me going alone on the boat, on what was earlier the Bailey Road, they started shouting to me to get necessities for their children or to take them on the boat. They even abused me but I could not help them. I was to pick-up Suresh Kumar who was the Works Commissioner. He was staying in a two floor apartment. I found that the ground floor of his house was completely under water. The boat got parked by the first floor. His mother-in-law, Mrs. V. Shankar, ICS, was staying with him. She had some chlorine tablets with her that she gave me for adding to the drinking water. We were to pick up Mr. Zubeiri who as the Relief Commissioner was responsible for Disaster Management in the state. I was told that when water entered his house he got so upset that he started crying. He then shifted with his family somewhere out of Patna and he had been traceless since then. I got dropped at the Industrial Guest House. The water supply to the guest house had got disrupted. Luckily for us we found that just outside the guest house, the fountain in front of the statue of Dr. Rajendra Prasad somehow remained connected to the town water supply. All the residents of the Industrial Guest House survived on that water supply for almost a week. It was surprising that the flood water level almost reached the plinth level of the colonial Old Secretariat but the water did not enter the building and in the New Secretariat, that had come up during the sixties, water had destroyed all papers and files on the ground floor. Mr. S.N. Sharma, the Managing Director of Bihar Food and Civil Supplies Corporation arranged a boat load of essential supplies and got his daughter, our Minister and me to accompany him in reaching those supplies to the people marooned by flood water. The Army undertook relief supplies in a big operation using their transport aircraft and helicopters. The flood waters almost took more than a week to recede as Patna did not have a proper drainage system.

The Food and Civil Supplies Department was notorious for corruption, especially among the lower staff particularly at the level of Inspectors. Mrs. Indira Gandhi had declared Emergency in the country in June 1975. The civil rights of the citizen as well as the service privileges and rights of the employees were curtailed. State governments were asked to weed out the employees who were reputed to be corrupt or inefficient. We had committees of officers to scrutinize employees at all levels for weeding out. There were many who got axed or were compulsorily retired. The declaration of Emergency had a salutary effect on the administration at all the levels in the beginning but the effect started wearing off soon. Everywhere we had employees reporting to their offices very punctually and the railway trains running on time. The upkeep of the office premises and sanitation everywhere visibly improved. Employees who had remained posted at one place were shifted. We had one Supply Inspector who was reputed to be the top astrologer in Bihar, Mr. Ram Lochan Pande, who had never been posted out of Patna. He was transferred to Gaya. Even the Minister advised a relaxation for him. My friend, Mr. L. Dayal, who had become the Principal Information

Officer in the Government of India, recommended his transfer back to Patna. I thought that discretion was better than valour and reversed his transfer orders. Sukhdev was also happy that I did not make it a prestige issue because she was also impressed by his astrological forecasts. I still have the birth charts of my children that Ram Lochan Pande had cast. When I had left Bihar in 1967 we had the practice of touring officials, looking after themselves for their meals while they were on tour. They either carried provisions for their meals that were cooked by the caretaker or watchman of the Inspection Bungalow or they paid the *Khansamah* of the Circuit House for their meals, on rates that were fixed by the District Magistrate. The change that had come about was that meals were got cooked by the subordinate field staff of the touring officer at their cost. I was shocked when in one district the Supply Inspector had arranged a bottle of Scotch whisky for me. When I saw the bottle, I called for the Inspector but he ran away without facing me. I did not pursue the matter but I left the bottle untouched.

Mr. S.N. Sharma got a posting that was of his liking but no decision was taken about his replacement in the Corporation. He was keen to take up his new assignment. He persuaded the Minister to draft me to relieve him till a regular Managing Director was posted in his place. I held the charge of both the assignments but the work in the corporation was light. I was struck by the caste phenomenon in Bihar. We had a Minister who was a Bhumihar.

The Chairman of the Corporation who was an MLA was also a Bhumihar. My both the deputy secretaries in the Food Department were Bhumihars. Mr. Sharma was a Bhumihar and almost all the district managers were Bhumihars. Bhumihars are less than five percent of population in Bihar. I had no problem about the loyalty of Bhumihar officers during my tenure in the Food Department even when I had a straight fight with the minister. I am puzzled at the Bihar environment where all persons of one caste feel secure only when they were with men/women of their own caste. We, who were outsiders, had an advantage because all the castes could repose confidence in us. Here also, I could clearly perceive that Bihar Rajputs considered me to be closer to them because as a Sikh my name ended with 'Singh' like the Rajputs and the Sikhs were recognized as a martial race at par with the Rajputs.

I received a notice from the Income Tax officer, Patna to pay an installment of advance income tax as the Food Corporation was said to be in profit. The Chief of Accounts of the company put up a cheque for me to sign. I asked him to show me the balance sheet. I saw the balance sheet but I was not convinced. I enquired that if the company was in profit, its bank balance must reflect the same in some way. It seemed that he got suspicious about my intentions. He informed S.N. Sharma about the enquiries that I had made. S.N. Sharma told the Minister that his fears about me had got confirmed and I was about to do him down. He said that I did not belong to Bihar and I had no feeling for the interests of Bihar. He alleged that my reason for questioning the profit made by the only successful government company of Bihar was to besmirch the image of Bihar in the eyes of the Government of India. The minister spoke to me somewhat rudely about it, unlike his earlier behaviour with me. I made a thorough study of the finances of the company and I also consulted the chartered accountant of the company. I recorded a note arguing that the company was in loss for the reasons recorded by me. I requested the Minister, if he disagreed with me, to pass orders disagreeing with me and I shall pay the income tax as demanded. The file never came back to me. I had to guard the interest of the company under the Company Law.

When the income tax officer threatened *ex-parte* imposition of tax, I filed a return of income-tax showing loss. My action became the headline news in Bihar. The Chairman of the Corporation called a meeting of the Board of Directors for the purpose of getting my decision reversed. Unfortunately for him all the other directors of the Corporation were official directors who endorsed my stand. The Minister then tried to use the State Legislature against me. He got a discussion initiated on the working of his department in the state legislative assembly. He started giving replies to various questions that were inspired by him in a manner as to cast aspersions against me. The Speaker of the House was Dr. Hari Nath Mishra, who had been earlier the State Cooperative Minister. He had been an admirer of mine and had openly held that I was an outstanding officer. He intervened mildly on my behalf in the debate that was on. The Leader of the Opposition, on getting a hint from the Speaker, went hammer and tongs against the Minister and his cronies, turning the table on them. One or two inspired news reports also appeared against me in the newspapers. I called on the Chief Minister and requested for a change in my assignment. He appreciated my position and posted me as the Commissioner for Health and Family Planning.

The Minister and S.N. Sharma did not give up, even after my transfer. A three member committee headed by Mr. N.D.J. Rao, the Member, Board of Revenue, was constituted to go into the justification or otherwise, of my decision to file a loss return of income tax. The new Managing Director of the Corporation was Mr. Arun Pathak whom I considered to be a friend of mine. I met Mr. Rao casually on my morning walk. He made an observation that Mr. Pathak was of the view that the Corporation was in profit. This remark immediately alerted me. I gave him a copy of the note that I had given to the Food Minister. This stopped the conspiracy that was planned and the report of the committee completely vindicated me. The storm in the tea cup that was sought to be raised finally disappeared.

The Department of Health and Family Planning was headed by Mr. Bindeshwary Dubey, who was the Health Minister. The Health Commissioner was the Secretary and the executive head. The health professionals had Dr. H.N. Singh, designated as the Director in Chief as their professional chief and the family planning side had a commissioner from the Civil Service and the technical side had Dr. M.P. Singh as their head. The Family Planning Commissioner was A. Wati Ao, an IAS officer from Nagaland. He was a Catholic Christian, but when he was appointed as the Commissioner, Family Planning, the first thing that he did was to get himself vasectomised so that he could advise others to do the same with a moral conviction. Mr. Bindeshwari Dubey had a trade union background. He was known to be one of the close associates of Mr. K.B. Sahay. He knew about me from K.B. Sahay days and in the beginning he was vary of me. He was leaning a bit too much on Dr. H.N. Singh. Dr. Singh was also *ex-officio* Additional Secretary to the government which enabled him to obtain orders of the Minister directly, bye-passing the Health Commissioner. The system required that in such cases the files would go back through the Health Commissioner. One could, therefore, always know as to the game that he was up to. The Health Commissioner had a Private Secretary, Mr. Lakhan Prasad, who knew the Health Department like the back of his hand. He sometimes would express concern about the hold of Dr. H.N. Singh on the Minister. I told him the words of Mardana, the bard who had accompanied Guru Nanak on his expeditions all over the world. He faced innumerable hurdles on his way. Every time Mardana would ask as to what would happen next. Guru Nanak always said, '*dekh mardanya rang kartar de*', meaning that Mardana must wait for the God's design to unfold.

The Health Department was full of problems. The government was committed to free healthcare for which neither they had the resources nor the wherewithal. Whatever provision of funds was made, it was sought to be distributed equitably among all those who needed. The result was that whatever little got made available, got grabbed by the unscrupulous. The state hospitals had no mattresses, no surgical instruments and no medicines. I was shocked to see a surgical operation being performed in the Darbhanga Medical College Operation Theatre in sultry hot season without any air conditioner. The surgeon and the students watching him were drenched in perspiration. The State Government provided some paltry three per cent of its budget for the health sector out of which a major chunk went to the three Medical Colleges in the state. There was corruption, pilferage and mismanagement all over, about which nothing much could be done. All proposals for charging fees for the services did not find favour with the governments either at the Centre or in the States. The governments have deliberately fostered a situation where those who can afford go to the private hospitals and only second class medical care could be expected by an ordinary citizen. The most powerful and influential group in Patna was that of government doctors who were minting money as they were allowed private medical practice. One popular doctor had long queues of patients waiting to see him. The waiting time for the patients, sometimes, became the whole night. An enterprising Bihari had set up a tea shop outside the clinic of the doctor to cater to the patients and their attendants who had to wait in the queue. What could the learned professor be expected to teach in his class next day? The students were not assessed on their merit but on their capacity to mobilize patients for their teacher. I was told that Dr. H.N. Singh, who was earlier the Professor of Medicine in the Patna Medical College, was notorious in this regard. He was facing allegations that as the Director in Chief he had tampered with the MBBS examination results in order to give top marks to his daughter, who was a candidate.

Bihar is the state with the lowest per-capita income. Most of the population is undernourished. Diseases like Filaria and Kalazar, both mosquito borne, are endemic to Bihar. According to pharmaceutical manufacturers, Bihar contributed the highest sale in drugs in India. The only thing that I did was to give a plan for the future of healthcare in the state where primary health centers and dispensaries would be linked to a chain of referral hospitals in place of the sub-divisional and the district hospitals. The main focus during my tenure was the Family Planning Program. Mrs. Indira Gandhi had taken her son, Sanjay Gandhi, to assist her in various programs of national development. Sanjay Gandhi gave top priority to the program of Family Planning. Mr. Bindeshwari Dubey joined in the drive, putting his heart and soul into it. The program aimed at mainly sterilization of males and females in the childbearing age groups. The direction and monitoring of the program at the level of the Central Government was with Mrs. Serla Grewal, known to be a very result oriented officer who was pejoratively called '*hunterwali*' or the lady with a horsewhip. Sanjay Gandhi became a terror for the Congress politicians and in turn Serla Grewal became for the officials as a sort of arbiter of their fate. The Government policy prescribed an elaborate package of incentives and disincentives for the men and women who accepted family planning as also for the officials who motivated them to accept family planning. The backwardness and social conditions were ignored with the result that it were the women who got pushed for tubectomy rather than men for vasectomy despite the fact that vasectomy was a much simpler operation. I felt acute revulsion when I saw doctors conducting operations in filthy conditions, making the patients to lie on paddy straw, as there were no beds in the hospital. Bindeshwari Dubey was an effective speaker too. I found that he would quote quite often from the Hindu epics like *Ramayana* and *Mahabharata* to sway the villagers in favour of the family planning programme. The pitch however, got queered by the targets that were given to each government functionary mostly because of the pressure from the Central Government. It led to a mad race among the officials to fulfil the targets given on fear of losing government service or even of going to jail in extreme cases. There were cases of minors or old persons being operated to meet the targets. Some overenthusiastic executive officers even raided cinema houses to catch hold of men and women who could be sterilized. We were lucky that our anxiety to meet our targets did not result in such excesses but the quality of our performance left much to be desired. All this led to a record achievement for Bihar exceeding a million sterilizations during 1976-77. One fall out of this achievement was that Bihar could get 15 to 20 million rupees from the Central Government as a reward, to be spent on the improvement of healthcare infrastructure in the state. The reward from the Centre had not been claimed in the earlier years as the achievements were insignificant or the officers concerned were ignorant about it.

I came to know about our entitlement around November 1976. Serla Grewal said that the reward had to be utilized before the 31st March of 1977. I consulted the Minister. We sat down with the Director in Chief to finalize the list of items that were needed most in our hospitals. I got a Secretary of the Finance Department associated with the purchase of those items. All purchases were to be made by a High Powered Committee. We arranged that all operation theatres, up to the district level hospitals, got equipped with air conditioners, buying something like two hundred air conditioners. The Government of India had a system of rate contract with the manufacturers of various items, according to which they had a commitment that the items manufactured by them would not get sold at rates lower than what had been offered to the Government. We could get air conditioners at rates lower than even the rate contract because of competition among the manufacturers. I kept monitoring the pace of the expenditure. My engineer assistant reported that we had been able to spend all the reward money except about an amount of a few lakhs of rupees. I knew that the air conditioner purchase was something that could not be questioned and the payment to the manufacturer could be made by a cheque. He prepared an antedated paper for creating a demand of the additional air conditioners. I did not care to read what he had written and signed on the dotted line. The engineer lacked the training of clerks in the office with the result that anyone reading the file could not help perceiving that something was fishy in the whole affair. The file became the cause of a minor headache to me.

Mr. Bindeshwari Dubey was a competent and honest Minister and I had no doubt that he would be the Chief Minister one day. Dr. Jagannath Mishra did not like that any other Congress leader should come to acquire such a stature as would pose a threat to his position in the state. He assumed from my fight against Ramashray Prasad Singh in which the Minister had suffered a loss of face that I would create a similar situation in the Health Department. He also once told me that I was keeping a low profile against Dubey. The closeness of the Director in Chief with Dubey was known to the Chief Minister. I received a private complaint from the Chief Minister's office for a report in which an allegation was made that Dr. H.N. Singh had made a purchase of a drug 'neurobion' from a grant for the rural dispensaries in order to get commission from the manufacturer. The purchase was worth about 20 lakh rupees from a total allocation of 21 lakh rupees for the rural dispensaries. I held, firstly, that the diversion of funds from the rural dispensaries was not justified and secondly, the priority given to 'neurobion', over much needed other drugs, could only be called motivated. I sent the file to Dubey for being marked to the Chief Minister. He considered it appropriate to show it to the Director in Chief who told him that my note was uncalled for as I was a merely a generalist. How could I challenge his discretion as the technical head of the Health Department? When I went to the Minister to discuss some other matter with him, I found the Minister occupied with the whole team of Dr. H.N. Singh, who were trying to help him in formulating his comments on what I had written. I asked the Minister as to what all the flurry was about. He said that he was trying to dictate a note for the Chief Minister. I told him that he might go ahead with it but my request would be to listen to me for a minute before he gave his dictation. Mr. Dubey turned out all the people from his room. I told him that the action of Dr. H.N. Singh was indefensible. He could consult any doctor in whom he had confidence.

I further told him that Dr. H.N. Singh had taken his decision without consulting him nor he had cared to seek his approval on the file. He was, therefore, solely responsible for the action that had been questioned, but if he wrote anything in the defence of Dr. H.N. Singh, the responsibility for the action would come on him. He later consulted two or three reputed medical experts who endorsed the views that I had recorded. He decided then to merely mark the file to the Chief Minister. The file did not come back to the Health Department. Meanwhile Mrs. Serla Grewal came on a visit to Patna. She visited our unit that supplied vaccines to our immunization program. The unit was found to be in shambles. She asked me to get a meeting fixed for her with the Chief Minister. I learnt that Mr. Om Mehta, the State Minister for Home, had come to Patna and the Chief Minister was busy with him. I was told that they would be having their lunch with the Governor. Mrs. Serla Grewal just gatecrashed there along with me. She complained about the incapacity of the Director in Chief of Bihar because of whom the whole program was suffering. Om Mehta enquired from the Chief Minister as to how such an incompetent person was permitted to hold such a key job during the Emergency when everywhere such persons had been weeded out. Mr. Jagnnath Mishra told him that he too had received complaints against Dr. H.N. Singh. We did not stay on there to hear what transpired further. I was woken up by a telephone call from Bindeshwary Dubey around 1 a.m. in the night. He wanted me to meet him immediately at his residence that was close by.

When I reached there, he told me that he had just returned from dinner at the Raj Bhavan that was in honour of Mr. Om Mehta. Om Mehta told him that he was convinced that Dr. H.N. Singh was not fit to be retained in the government service. He asked the Health Minister to remove him from his position or he would order the police to arrest him under the Emergency laws before he took the plane for Delhi the next morning. He said that we had to find a way in which he could tell Om Mehta that Dr. H.N. Singh was no longer the Director in Chief of the Health Services of Bihar. I woke up Dr. H.N. Singh and asked him if he would like to go on a voluntary retirement or to jail. He opted for the former. I asked him to come forthwith and apply for his voluntary retirement. Mr. Bindeshwari Dubey could show the letter of Dr. H.N. Singh to Om Mehta when he went to see him off at the airport. Dr. M.P. Singh, the Director of Family Planning, started fearing for his future after the unceremonious exit of Dr. H.N. Singh. He ran to Mr. Satyendra Narain Singh, the leader of the Rajputs in Bihar, who rang me to say that I should spare Dr. M.P. Singh. I told him that I had no enemity against him and that I had no intention to harm him in any manner. I knew Satyendra N. Singh from Dhanbad and our relationship has continued to be guided by mutual respect and consideration for each other. His informal telephone call to me on almost a non-issue only confirmed that we could trust each other in public affairs. Mr. Bindeshwari Dubey, after this episode, lost whatever reservation earlier he had about me.

Bindeshwari Dubey had utter contempt for most of the Bihar doctors because of their rampant corruption and mercenary behaviour. He took a bold step of prohibiting private practice for the government doctors. Overnight, he became extremely unpopular among the doctors. The doctors had the sympathies of the Chief Minister with them. I found that doctors worked like a freemasonry. They kept track of the doctors who treated some key personalities like the Chief Minister in the state, and whatever problem the brotherhood had, they had no difficulty in getting themselves heard in the relevant quarters. I discovered the freemasonry brotherhood operating in Delhi when I had to deal with the Central Government doctors' strike in 1986 in the government of Rajiv Gandhi. The Bihar doctors resorted to subterfuge in evading orders of ban against private practice.

Some doctors got their wives or husbands to open private clinics in their names where they would examine patients on the sly. Some, like my friend, Dr. K.K. Singh, resigned from government service. Bindeshwari Dubey remained unrelenting. I initiated a minor change in the nomenclature of the teacher doctors of the medical colleges of Bihar that made me popular in the medical fraternity. The teachers in Bihar Medical Colleges had four tiers in their ranks. The junior most were called tutors, next came lecturers followed by readers and professors. I got the pattern changed to Assistant Professors, Associate Professors and Professors, to fall in line with the All India pattern. This order I passed after the Bihar doctors had lobbied for it for quite some time. My father from Gharuan had come for his cataract operation to Patna, to be operated upon by the eye surgeon Dr. Pande, who as a junior doctor, had treated my eyes after my jeep accident in Deoghar in 1957. He was by then well-established as a leading eye surgeon of Bihar. It was a coincidence that the relevant file came to me while I was spending the night with my father in the Patna Medical College Hospital. The operation had gone on well and that had given me a happy frame of mind.

Biharis are a very intelligent people whose work culture seems to have gone awry. They remain on the lookout for making a quick buck without having to work for it. The government employees and their families under the rules were entitled to free medical care. They could buy the medicines prescribed by their medical officers from the market for which, later, they could claim reimbursement. We received a complaint from Muzaffarpur that the doctors there were prescribing medicines to the government employees or their dependents at a scale that the concerned departments found to be beyond their budget allocations. I asked my number two officer to hold an enquiry. The enquiry unearthed a full scale fraud. A group of crooks formed a gang. They would prepare bills as government employee patients and get the same approved by a doctor gang member. A fictitious drug company would issue fake cash receipts and the money would get drawn from the government treasury. One of the worst cases discovered was that of a peon who earned about six thousand rupees a year and in the same year he drew ninety-two thousand rupees as medical reimbursement. The gang had siphoned off about eighty million rupees in the course of one year. Their modus operandi was that they would go to an office on a pay day and get sheets of blank medical reimbursement bills signed from the employees, on the understanding that fifty per cent of the amount drawn in their names would be paid to them and the rest would get shared among the gang members. One Regional Deputy Director of Health Services, who was related to Bindeshwary Dubey, was identified as the kingpin in the fraud. When the report was placed before the Minister he passed orders that the kingpin be compulsorily retired forthwith and the matter be handed to the police. The Bihar Government, on his recommendation, ordered recovery of all the fraudulent amounts of money drawn and prosecution of the employees who had participated in the fraud. The action sent shockwaves among the government employees in Bihar. Their unions got mobilized, presenting the employees as innocent victims of exploitation by the gang members of a gang of cheats. My ex-cook Hanuman, who was a peon, came to Sukhdev for helping him. She said that she could not speak to me for a guilty person. He disarmed her completely by telling her that he was ready to face action for his deeds. The only favour he was seeking was that in the list of employees, against whom action was to be sure, the government would be compelled by the unions to relent. At worst, some action might be taken against a few names on the top of the list or may be at the bottom but others were sure to escape. He proved to be prophetic in that. The government revised their policy on reimbursement of the medical expenses of the employees by permitting free treatment in the government hospitals as indoor patients and by fixing a ceiling of one hundred rupees for a family in a year.

It was announced in the Bankipur Gurdwara, Patna that they had been asked by the SGPC, Amritsar to sponsor names for a pilgrimage to "Panja Saheb" Gurdwara at Hasan Abdal in Pakistan. The *gurdwara* is associated with the visit of Guru Nanak, who had reached this small place situated below a small hill. There was a Muslim Pir Vali Kandhari doing penances with his abode up the hill, near a source of water. Guru Nanak asked Mardana, the Muslim minstrel with him, to fetch some water from above the hill. Pir Vali Kandhari refused to part with even a drop of water. Mardana returned emptyhanded. As he was reporting the failure of his effort the water from the pool above broke its embankment and started flowing to where Guru Nanak was sitting. Vali Kandhari seeing the water flowing down felt enraged and hurled a huge stone towards Guru Nanak. Guru Nanak remained unmoved and when the stone reached him, he just put out his hand. The hurtling stone came to a stop and the hand of Guru Nanak left an impression of his hand on the stone. There is a gurdwara adjoining the spot that commemorated the event. Pakistan government permitted about a thousand Sikhs to visit the *gurdwara* on Baisakhi every year. I got a visa for my visit along with other Sikh pilgrims. The group was led by an Akali leader and there were two IAS officers of Punjab who were accompanying the group as observers. I was visiting in my private capacity. Mr. G.S. Lamba, a young Sikh advocate from Patna, was the only one who knew about me. I had let my beard to flow down which made it difficult for people to recognize me. I knew quite a few in the group but I avoided meeting them as I wanted to visit in complete anonymity. When we assembled at Attari Railway Station for crossing the border, I was shocked that many of the pilgrims were going for the purpose of smuggling goods into Pakistan on which there was a premium in Pakistan and vice versa on the return journey. There was no sense of religious devotion evident among the pilgrims. They rushed like mad, on crossing the border, to occupy seats in the special train. Some of those who made it earlier to the train occupied whole berths and they had stretched themselves on those berths while those like me did not have a place even to sit. When I requested a fellow pilgrim, who was stretched out on a full berth to make room for me to sit, he point blank refused. What was worse was that no one among the pilgrims thought that there was anything wrong about what was happening. Evidently, everyone was for one's own self and devil take the hindmost. I had to make do by sitting on my bag for the overnight train journey. I could recall my journey in 1947 on this very route, when I was returning from Risalpur in the NWFP in a military train, trying to hide at every station because of my being a Sikh. There were many among the pilgrims who had lived at places that the train was crossing without stopping. They would get excited on seeing their old towns/villages passing by. It was night during which most of our journey was covered but I could make out that villages in Pakistan were not as prosperous as the villages in Indian Punjab. Electricity did not seem to have reached every village. Their agricultural productivity was low. Pakistan seemed to have done well in growing kinu, a cross between orange and malta. There was a melee, when the train reached Hasan Abdal Railway Station, for occupying rooms meant for the pilgrims in the gurdwara premises. I slept on the floor in a hall. There was the usual Akhand Path of the *Guru Granth Saheb* and *kirtan* singing of *Gurbani* but most of the pilgrims were interested in the impromptu market that grew up outside the *Gurdwara*. I found that imported rags consisting of secondhand woolens, etc., from the USA were popular with the pilgrims in addition to selected contraband goods that were being purchased for business. I had a bath in the pool of water flowing from over the hill as a water-fall. I swam to the place where the imprint of the hand of Guru Nanak was there on the stone. The stone seemed to be in a position of having been stopped during its hurtling down and the imprint of the hand, to me, appeared to be genuine despite some doubts that have been cast about it by scholars like Dr. McLeod. We returned by a special train on the third day, after the conclusion of the Akhand Path of the *Guru Granth Saheb*. The pilgrimage left a bad taste in my mouth and I decided never to go for such a pilgrimage again. I disclosed my identity after crossing the border. Both the IAS officers of the Punjab Government turned out to be my trainees from Mussoorie. One was Mrs. Rupan Bajaj, a very talented officer from a family having army background. Her father had set up the

Minerva Academy that had coached a large number of young men for a career in the armed forces. Rupan was a good singer. She kept us enthralled with her songs during the journey by car from Amritsar to Chandigarh.

It came as a bolt from the blue when Mrs. Gandhi decided to lift the Emergency in the country in early 1977. Those who had been arrested were ordered to be released. It was like uncorking a bottle of fizz. There were demonstrations and demands from all the comers. The field staff of the Health Department was the first to take to the streets, so far as I was concerned. They pitched a camp in front of our house. Sukhdev was very upset at their slogans which were like, if their children would die of hunger, we would not be permitted to sleep in peace. I had to ask the District Magistrate V.S. Dubey, to remove them by force, to get peace restored in our neighbourhood. The next group that got active was of students from the five medical colleges, demanding a takeover by the government. These colleges had come up as teaching shops, attracting students from all over India, for awarding medical degrees that had no value because the Medical Council of India did not recognize those colleges due to their lack of prescribed minimum infrastructure and qualified teachers. The general elections were perceived to be round the corner. The Chief Minister decided to please the Patna doctors by restoring their private practice. On the day the matter was to be discussed in the state cabinet, Bindeshwari Dubey told me that he was disgusted at the sellout before the corrupt doctors. He asked me to convey his opposition to the move to the Chief Minister and to remain available for the Cabinet on his behalf. There was no discussion in the Cabinet on the subject. I told Dr. K.K. Singh and other doctors who had resigned in protest, to come back if they so liked. Dr. K.K. Singh came back and soon became the Head of the Department of Physiotherapy or Physical Medicine, as he would like to call it. The result of the general election was a foregone conclusion. The Congress party was wiped out in the whole of North India.

15

Imposition of Emergency

Emergency was imposed in June 1975 by the Central Government when Mrs. Indira Gandhi was pushed to the corner, by the opposition parties, who would not accept the electoral verdict for one reason or the other. Her election to the Parliament was set aside on a technical ground by a High Court Judge as it was found that one of her Private Secretaries, who became her election agent, resigned from his erstwhile government position, a day or two after Mrs. Gandhi had filed her nomination papers, due to a bureaucratic lapse in the acceptance of his resignation. She had appealed to the Supreme Court against the decision of the High Court. The opposition parties were not prepared to wait for the decision of the Supreme Court of India and took to the streets. This was countered by the counter demonstrations in her favour by crowds mustered by leaders like Arjan Das and others like him. J.P. Narayan threw his lot with the opposition. J.P. Narayan had his base in Bihar but he had a public image like that of Mahatma Gandhi as he had chosen a path of self-abnegation in public life. He had in the process developed an ego that could not be handled by Mrs. Gandhi in a manner that could have satisfied or assuaged his feelings about his own importance in the country. J.P. Narayan made the eradication of the prevailing corruption in the country as his objective and gave a slogan for a partyless government. He adopted the movement for a revolution to usher in a partyless democracy that had been initiated by students in Gujarat. He gave the slogan but he did not work out a system through which such a government could function. The movement ruined the education system of Bihar, which could not be put back on the rails till date, but it produced a crop of grassroot leaders that came to rule Bihar, after destabilizing the old established Congress leadership of Bihar. Laloo Yadav is a product of the J.P. led student's movement and he continues to dominate the public life in Bihar. However, there can be no two opinions about the decision to impose a state of emergency in India being a bad decision, all the more deplorable as it came from Mrs. Gandhi, the daughter of Jawaharlal Nehru, who is acknowledged as the founder and the foster father of the Indian democratic system.

The decision to impose the state of emergency was kept a closely guarded secret between Mrs. Gandhi and a small coterie of her confidants, the principal among them was her son Sanjay Gandhi. Sanjay Gandhi had married Maneka Gandhi, the daughter of Colonel Anand, who was married to Mrs. Amteshwar Anand, daughter of late Sardar Datar Singh, who could be equally at home with the Congress leaders. He would off and on drop at the Super Bazar to have a chat with me and his friend Agya Singh, whom I had taken on deputation as the Assistant General Manager. He seemed to be a simple and straightforward army officer. He had consulted me in buying a shawl for Mrs. Gandhi, for giving a gift to her on the occasion of the marriage of Maneka to Sanjay Gandhi. He had honoured me by inviting me to the marriage reception but by that time I was in the blacklist of Mrs. Gandhi. I regretted my inability to attend the marriage reception. I remember that Arjan Das, who described himself as the third son of Mrs. Gandhi, had arranged the first public function to be presided over by Maneka through Super Bazar, in getting her to distribute cheap wheat flour in a cluster of huts of the poor in a Delhi suburb, soon after the marriage. It was Sanjay Gandhi, who had finally approved the action that was to be taken against the opposition leaders and the press, prior to the formal declaration of the state of emergency in the country. The necessary instructions were personally passed by Sanjay Gandhi to the Chief Ministers and the Lieutenant Governor of Delhi, Mr. Kishan Chand. The Chief Ministers were cryptically told that they were to put the plan, given by Sanjay Gandhi, into action during the night. Zail Singh, who was the Chief Minister of Punjab, was foxed by the cryptic message of Mrs. Gandhi. He ran to Rashpal Malhotra, the Director of the Centre for Research in Rural and Industrial Development at Chandigarh, as he was known to have been close to Mrs. Gandhi. He too was not a privy to the plan of action, but both of them decided to visit Bansi Lal, the then Chief Minister of Haryana, who was close to Sanjay Gandhi. They found him busy in instructing police chiefs in the districts of Haryana, to arrest all the opposition leaders in their districts and to physically ensure that no newspapers came out the next day. Bansi Lal was surprised to see them at his house in the middle of the night. Zail Singh, like a poker player, said that after ordering the action that was required, they had come to have a cup of coffee with him. They quickly finished their coffee and on return to his house, Zail Singh called the police chief and the Chief Secretary, to undertake arrests of the opposition leaders and to cut the electricity lines serving the newspapers so that there was a blackout of the news the next day. The Akalis were already agitating and courting arrests. Mrs. Gandhi did not seem to have felt threatened by the Akalis, as they were left unmolested. They were the only political party who could carry on a program of courting arrest by their volunteers throughout the emergency period. The Akalis got acknowledged in the country as great fighters for freedom, for their role during the emergency. Delhi Police was most active in carrying out arrests during the night. The election of Indira Gandhi had been set aside on the petition of Raj Narain, a perfect demagogue, who suddenly found himself catapulted to the centre of stage in Indian politics. When the police went to his house to arrest him, he came out and sat on the road in front of the house. He refused to sit in the police van as he said that he wanted to create a scene for the press when he would be physically lifted by the police and put into the van. The concerned police officer whispered in his ear that no press would cover his arrest as the Prime Minister had ordered a gagging of the press. Raj Narain uttered a filthy abuse against Mrs. Gandhi and quietly sat in the police van. The action in Bihar was swift and smooth, sans any dramatics. The Union Cabinet was informed of the action only the next morning. The Cabinet approved the required suspension of the Fundamental Rights under the Constitution, without a murmur. It was rumoured that Sardar

Swaran Singh in the Cabinet had said if it was really necessary to take such drastic measures. This query from him was enough to get him dropped from the Cabinet in the next reshuffle. The President, Mr. Fakhruddin Ali Ahmed, just signed on the dotted line, taking India to a new uncharted phase of political development and an uncertain future.

The initial impact of the new dispensation was good in all appearances. Trains and airplanes were running on time. There was a sudden quiet in the country after a long cacophony of demonstrations and agitations. The *babus* or the clerks in the government offices started reporting punctually. Mrs. Gandhi launched her 20-point development programme to which Sanjay Gandhi added his 5-point programme which included aggressive implementation of the Family Planning Program, slum development and tree plantation. However, the momentum could not be sustained for long. The absence of freedom of the press and the opposition gave rise to rampant corruption and abuse of power. It became worse with the passage of time. The power of the coterie around Mrs. Gandhi overshadowed all legitimate authority. I found my friend, J.K. Kohli, in the small group of junior officials who started calling themselves as the kitchen cabinet. They were all satellites of R.K. Dhawan. N.K. Singh, as a Special Assistant to the Minister of Commerce, had virtually become the Minister of Commerce. J.K. Kohli became the Joint Secretary to the Prime Minister, considered a key appointment in the Government of India. I would often stay with Kohli on my visits to Delhi. Despite holding such an important assignment I found that he remained tense. His brother-in-law R.K. Soni, initially prospered, as he became a manufacturer of ammunitions and defence supplies, but soon his relationship with Dhawan soured because of some misunderstanding. Thereafter, his defence orders got cancelled and even Kohli got sidelined. The end of the Emergency and the defeat of the Congress came as a relief to them. Mr. Kohli admitted before the Shah Commission that he found the atmosphere around Mrs. Gandhi to be somewhat tense, which sealed his fate when Mrs. Gandhi returned to power in 1980. He reverted back to his parent state of West Bengal never to return to the Government of India. The coterie of small men around Mrs. Gandhi indulged in small petty vindictive acts. A film called '*Kissa Kursi Ka*' was released. The film was considered critical of Mrs. Gandhi. The then Minister for Information, V.C. Shukla, and Sanjay Gandhi got the film from the Censor Board and got it destroyed in the Maruti factory owned by Sanjay Gandhi.

The Inspector General of Delhi Police, P.S. Bhinder, got some boys arrested from the campus of Delhi University because they had teased Maneka Gandhi. Surprisingly, the reaction against Mrs. Gandhi remained confined to North India, where there were wild rumours spread about the excesses committed during the Emergency. One of the rumours that went from house to house in Patna, concerned forcible sterilization of a Hindu *Sadhu*.

The announcement of early elections and lifting of the emergency came as a sudden surprise. All political leaders were released. Jaya Prakash Narayan was hailed as Lok Nayak. Jagjiwan Ram who had remained with Indira Gandhi during the emergency suddenly defected and formed a new party with Bahugana called 'Congress for Democracy'. This did shock Mrs. Gandhi who had entrusted him with virtually the position of number two in her cabinet. I found that in the whole of North India there was a wave of resentment against Mrs. Gandhi and Sanjay Gandhi. Almost all the government employees had turned against the Congress. The Inspector General of Intelligence, Bihar was a Congress sympathizer. He was trusted so much that the Congress party entrusted him with the responsibility to distribute the allocated party fund to the Congress candidates in the field. He had the facility of traveling in the Bihar Government plane which he used for the quick delivery of the party funds. N.K. Singh also had his finger in the pie. N.K. Singh boasted that the Congress party had worked out a foolproof strategy to win the Parliamentary elections hands down. He had managed to get a Congress ticket for his mother, who had been a housewife all her life. She came from the family of a big landlord of Purnea called Maul Babu. Excitement ran high in Patna once when counting of votes started. The Bihar daily '*Indian Nation*' had put up a board giving minute-by-minute results of the countrywide elections. All over there were crowds of people watching the election results. The trends clearly showed that in the North, the Congress was doing badly. Everyone was waiting with baited breath the result from Rae Bareily. I decided to take a round of Patna around midnight when it was announced that Mrs. Gandhi had lost from

Rae Bareily. The announcement was greeted with great acclaim but the people wailed for the result of Sanjay Gandhi. It was announced soon after that he too had lost. The Congress symbol for the election was 'cow with calf'. The whole crowd started shouting that the calf, meaning Sanjay Gandhi, had been dispatched where he deserved along with the cow. They formed themselves into a procession and proceeded to the house of Jaya Prakash Narayan forcing him to come out and address the crowd late in the night. It seemed, with the crowd, that something like a revolution had been brought about and like the French Revolution, they could greet in the words of the English poet Wordsworth that 'bliss was in that dawn to be alive and to be young was very heaven'. The Congress party however, had done well in the South of India but all the same because of the debacle in the North, the Congress was in no position to form a government at the Centre for the first time.The Congress also lost in the State Assembly Elections in Bihar. Jay Prakash Narayan and others hammered out a coalition government at the centre with Morarji Desai, a very strict Gandhian and a teetotaler, as the Prime Minister, pipping Jagjiwan Ram for the position in the last lap. Jagjiwan Ram held it against J.P. Narayan and others, as he accused them of a bias against the erstwhile untouchables. Choudhri Charan Singh, a *Jat* leader of Uttar Pradesh, became the Home Minister. The combination of two rigid minds proved to be fortunate for Mrs. Gandhi in staging a come back so soon after losing the general elections. We had Karpuri Thakur, an erstwhile socialist as the Chief Minister of Bihar.

The new government in Delhi had an Akali minister in the Cabinet, Parkash Singh Badal, who had joined as an Akali minister in the Central Government but soon prefered to go to Punjab, as the Chief Minister, to be replaced by Surjit Singh Barnala. I had a new minister in Bihar. He was a young Muslim minister, Mr. Jabir Hussain. He was well-educated and a pleasant person. He tried to keep a distance from me. I was also not keen to force myself on him. Both of us remained on a wait and watch relationship. The Central Government somehow started on the wrong foot. They started targeting Indira Gandhi. The media went on giving lurid details of the excesses committed during the emergency. There is no doubt that in the implementations of the various family planning measures and slum development, many aberrations could be noticed. Individual functionaries here and there could be faulted. The Government decided to appoint a Supreme Court Judge, Justice Shah as a Commission of Enquiry, to enquire into the allegations of various excesses and irregularities which were committed by Indira Gandhi. Justice Shah started public hearing on the charges against Indira Gandhi which kept the focus on her in the media instead of any positive achievements of the government. One of the important areas on which Indira Gandhi and Sanjay Gandhi stood charged was the allegations of excesses during the implementation of the family planning programmes. We were asked to prepare a comprehensive report on the subject for submission to the Shah Commission. I collected all the facts about the progress of the program in Bihar and prepared the brief for the Shah Commission. I clearly brought out the weaknesses of the program in my brief, in the context of the pressures of targets and threat of action against the officials during the emergency regime, in order to protect witchhunting of individual officers here and there. I was glad to see that the Shah Commission accepted our rationale and reasoning fully in their report.

Karpuri Thakur was an out and out politician. He had an agenda of promoting castes considered to be backward in Bihar. He had no patience for the nitty-gritty of the administration. He picked up my friend, Mr. P.S. Appu, for the position of the Chief Secretary. Mr. Appu was known to be an officer of great integrity, known for his penchant for development, land reforms and social justice. Mr. Appu asked me, before accepting his appointment, if I could join him as the Additional Chief Secretary to take care of the maintenance of law and order in Bihar. I had, in the meanwhile, been sounded if I could join the Central Government in the Ministry of Agriculture under Mr. Barnala. I had to decline that offer. The new government too had reservations about my being the Additional Chief Secretary but on the insistence of Mr. Appu they approved the proposal. The Chief Secretary functions as the Secretary to the Cabinet. Mr. Appu had gone on a weeks' casual leave, asking me to mind the store in his absence, when a paper landed on my table purporting to be from the Chief Minister, for inclusion in the Agenda for the next Cabinet Meeting.

The paper concerned reservation in the government services for the backward classes. I expressed my inability to oblige the Chief

Minister, as I felt that the paper must be seen by the Chief Secretary before it was considered by the State Cabinet. I marked the paper for Mr. Appu. He opposed the proposal tooth and nail but he was overruled as it was an important political agenda of the party in power. Karpuri Thakur had no private or personal life. He even made his bedroom accessible to the public. Sometimes, his visitors would eat away all the food from his kitchen. It was difficult to get him alone for any serious discussion. Sometimes, one had to go with him into the bathroom to discuss a point. He selected some little known forest resthouses for the disposal of official files that would pile up in his office. Once, Mr. Appu and I had to issue orders in an important matter. We learnt that he was locked up in the airport resthouse, to dispose of some official papers before he left for Delhi in the Bihar State plane. We made a dash to the airport. His P.A. blocked our entry on the door requesting us to wait for a few minutes. He said that Karpuri Thakur's son had been waiting to see him for the last two days and he had just gone in to see him. We went in after he left, all the time wondering about the sort of life that Karpuri Thakur had. He went after many populist measures. He ordered appointment of engineers in the Bihar State Electricity Board regardless of vacancies, creating a problem for the Board for years to come. Mr. Appu ultimately got fed up and asked me to find a berth at the Centre. Luckily for me, the position in the Ministry of Agriculture as Secretary of the Indian Council of Agricultural Research, was still open.

Financially, this was a bad time for the family. The Central Government had sanctioned a Dearness Allowance for all the government employees. However, in order to appear socialistic perhaps, the Dearness Allowance stopped at a salary of Rs 2500/- per month, with the result that I was drawing the same salary while the inflation, because of deficit financing and other mismanagement, was playing havoc with the fixed income group employees. There were some perks in my job, like the availability of the official car for going to office. I also got a house allotted to me soon after joining. I had preferred to go for an old house, opposite to the Wellingdon Hospital, which was renamed as the Ram Manohar Lohia Hospital by Raj Narain, who was the Union Health Minister. It happened to be close to Gurdwara Bangla Saheb, which I tried to visit daily. My son, Birendar, had successfully completed his training at the Khadakvasla

National Defence Academy. I was happy to see him at the NDA during his training. He had been functioning as the Sergeant of his company. He had mastered the art of enforcing discipline without being harsh and he enjoyed respect and affection from the boys in his company. I had taken Dipender, my younger son, for the passing out parade at the NDA. The parade was a very impressive show. I went to my old primary school, Anjuman-e-Islamiya in Poona Cantt. I was surprised to see that the building was as I had last seen, without any alteration. It happened to be a holiday. I could not meet any of the teachers, we drove down to Bombay where we celebrated the success of Birendar at the Taj Hotel. Birendar moved to Hyderabad for his training as a fighter pilot which was his life's passion. Rosy, my elder daughter, took a shortcut in her vacation as she sat for the school matriculation examination as a private candidate while she was studying in the Convent school in the 9th standard, she joined the government college for girls at Chandigarh for her higher secondary class. She had a first rate mind. She could have done well in academics. She was able to get admission to the famous Miranda House Girls College in Delhi. She was a very sensitive girl. Seeing our tight financial state she decided to go for a professional course to enable her to stand on her own feet at the earliest. She joined a course on dress designing. Noni had completely recovered from her suspected epilepsy which I think was due to the intense prayers of Sukhdev for her recovery. Noni was however, not so sharp in her studies. Sukhdev took extra care in looking after her and she plodded along. My younger son Dipendar, was not very clever nor ambitious. We could get him admitted to the Modern School by pulling some strings.

The Akalis were in power in Punjab. It was the time when Jarnail Singh Bhindranwale appeared on the Sikh scene, almost like a meteor. He was associated with a traditional Sikh seminary called Damdami Taksal. The seminary had been producing Sikh *granthis* and priests. The head was Kartar Singh Khalsa. He enjoyed respect as a Sikh preacher. He had moved to Chowk Mehta near Amritsar. He came across the activities of Sant Nirankari Mandal in the area who believed in a living Guru. He felt that they were misleading the simple villagers for bringing them into their fold and there were a number of senior Punjab government officials who were covertly helping them in that mission. He died in a road accident. The branch of the

Taksal at Chowk Mehta opted for Jarnail Singh Bhindranwale. His installation ceremony at Chowk Mehta was considered important enough by Mr. Badal, the Chief Minister of Punjab. He came to attend the function personally. Jarnail Singh showed his colors in the ceremony itself. Mr. Badal, in welcoming his selection as the head of the Taksal, had offered him all help on behalf of the Punjab government. Bhindranwale in his response to the offer had said that Taksal was in no need of help from the Punjab Government but if the Punjab Government asked for help from the Taksal, the same would be provided at their mere asking. Bhindranwale undertook whirlwind tours of the villages in Punjab, appealing to the youth particularly, to take arms and give up drinking, meat eating and drugs. He somehow fired the imagination of the Granthi and very soon he became a power to reckon with. The Nirankari Mandal decided to hold their annual get together at Amritsar on the Baisakhi day, 1978. They selected the Railway Sports Stadium near Amritsar Railway Station, as the venue for their conference. The Punjab government did not perceive any threat to public peace due to the Nirankari get together. The blessing of the Guru from the *Granth Saheb* from the Golden Temple is generally explained and commented in detail at Manji Sahib, which also became the venue of public meetings. The place is conveniently located near Teja Singh Samundari Hall which houses the offices of the SGPC and the Shiromani Akali Dal. This venue got taken over on that day by Bhindranwale and the Akhand Kirtani Jatha. The Akhand Kirtani Jatha owes its origin to Bhai Randhir Singh, who was sentenced to serve a jail term in the Andamans by the British for supporting an abortive attempt by the Ghadar Party to instigate the Sikh troops to rise against the British. He and his followers are counted as hardliners among the Sikhs and they follow a stricter code of conduct than what is prescribed for the Khalsa. They move about armed with more than one weapon and for them participation in *kirtan* is also a participation in a battle with a double-edged sword. Fiery speeches were delivered against the Nirankaris and during those speeches Bhindranwale taunted that the Nirankaris were indulging in calumny against their Gurus and any Sikh who heard such calumny has to go and get it stopped physically and punish the culprits. Mr. Jiwan Singh Umranangal, who was a Minister in the Badal cabinet, tried to intercede for peace and order but his appeals were ignored.

An impromptu group formed themselves into a body of protestors, ready to march to the venue of a Nirankari Conference, about 3 to 4 kilometre away. It is interesting, that a group from the Damdami Taksal did not permit Bhindranwale to accompany the protestors. They told him that they had issued a '*hukumnama*' asking him not to go to the Nirankari Conference. Surprisingly, there was no activity all this time from the district administration of Amritsar, to stop this armed group anywhere on the way.

The tragedy that is considered to have been responsible for the turmoil in Punjab did come about when this armed crowd, brandishing swords and other weapons, ran towards the venue of the Nirankari Conference. The Conference had a cordon of police security and their own armed volunteers who fearing the worst, opened fire killing 13 persons, including Fauja Singh, the leader of the Akhand Kirtani Jatha. It is said that the group that reached the venue of the Conference happened to be armed, as all true Sikhs are expected to be armed, but they had no intention to be violent. It could be true but from their behaviour of running to the Conference venue and the earlier speeches at Manji Saheb would not brook a risk on behalf of the police or the security of the Conference. The Amritsar administration or the Punjab Government could not move into action before the Nirankari Guru, Gurbachan Singh left the venue after the Conference ended. He had left by car and he safely reached Delhi before hell broke lose in Punjab. The reaction of the Akali government in Punjab was a typical knee jerk reaction. They got together a few veteran Punjab police officers to file a manifestly false case trying to pin responsibility on the Nirankari Guru, for the carnage and in-order to assuage the feelings of the Sikhs over the killing of the Akhand Kirtani Jatha and the Taksal supporters, they got the *granthis* under the SGPC, calling for a boycott of the Nirankaris by the Sikhs all over India. All routine get-togethers of Nirankaris in Punjab got cancelled and there were violent Sikh demonstrations in places like Kanpur, Jabalpur, etc. The Sikhs tried to prevent a get-together of the Nirankaris in Delhi and came to confront the police. The police led by Kiran Bedi, faced the armed Sikh demonstrators boldly and effectively despite the fact that the Akalis were coalition partners in the Central Government. The Akali reaction against the Nirankaris was mainly to cover their ineptitude in preventing the tragedy at Amritsar when they had the political power. The Nirankaris were singled out for their heresy of claiming a living Guru, but the same was the case with Namdharis and Radhasoamis of Beas, who were left unmolested. Nirankaris were accused of circulating some writings critical of the Sikh Gurus on which the Nirankaris explained that they had no such sacred writings and if it could be pointed out as to where any passage in their books was objectionable, they would be prepared to delete the same from any of their books that were said to have offended the sensitivities of the Sikhs. No official response was made on the offer by the SGPC. The Nirankari Guru, in this environment got the case against him transferred to a court in Haryana, where the judge honorably acquitted him.

The Sikh anger got all the more roused against the Nirankaris. Bhindranwale announced that if any Sikh killed the Nirankari chief, he would weigh him in gold. The leading chain of newspapers under Lala Jagat Narain of Jalandhar generally had supported the Nirankaris incurring the wrath of Bhindranwale.

Two Sikh youth, on motorcycles, had shot him dead when he was going in his car on the G.T. Road. The Nirankari Guru who lived under very high security in Delhi, was also killed soon after by a Sikh carpenter who had succeeded in smuggling a pistol in a piece of wood into the residence of the Nirankari Guru. The killer escaped after shooting him at point blank range. He was later found in the Akali camp in the Golden Temple Complex at Amritsar, clearly signaling that despite their declarations of non-violence, they, like Bhindranwale, endorsed the killing of the Nirankari Guru. There seems to be a shortcoming in the Indian legal system, where the leaders who inflame the feelings of a section of the people to commit crimes like murder do not get booked for murder, which needed to be corrected before long. Anyhow, I watched the events from the sideline as I was not directly involved in any matter. Another matter concerning the Sikhs that became a public issue was a Canadian measure which required all drivers of motorcycles and scooters to wear helmets while driving such vehicles. The Sikhs everywhere demonstrated against the implementation of this measure for the Sikhs as it was said to be violative of the code of conduct prescribed for the Sikhs by their Guru. Mr. Barnala, the Akali Minister in the Union Cabinet called the First Secretary of the Canadian High Commission to his office to convey the resentment of the Sikhs against the Canadian Government. The First Secretary agreed to convey the feelings of the Minister to his government but he left the Minister speechless when he asked him about the practice in the Indian Air Force regarding wearing of helmets by Sikh fighter pilots where wearing of helmets was mandatory.

One of the acts of the Moraiji Desai government that outraged the entire civil service was the prosecution and the arrest of Mr. B.B. Vora, IAS, who was the Secretary of the Petroleum Ministry. He was accused of favouring a private company in award of some contract. Mr. Vora enjoyed a reputation of high integrity. He was not given an opportunity to explain and the police arrested him from his office. He was not allowed to speak to his family, even on telephone. Later, it turned out that the police did not have any material to even chargesheet him. All the IAS officers were upset about the cavalier manner in which a serving secretary had been treated by the police. A meeting of the IAS Association was convened in the hall of the Vithal Bhai Patel House. The younger elements wanted some drastic action by the Association but the seniors advised caution, as according to them it was a new government. Ultimately, the seniors prevailed but the anger of the younger officers made the early rehabilitation of Mr. B.B. Vora feasible and perhaps it made the *Jat* Home Minister, Chaudhri Charan Singh, tread carefully in matters involving the civil services. Chaudhri Charan Singh got catapulted as the Home Minister of India but he had a mind of only a village *Sarpanch* with a hyper ego. He next thought that he should teach a lesson to Mrs. Gandhi and he got the police to arrest her on some flimsy charge. Mrs. Gandhi made full use of her prosecution hogging media limelight to the full in the process of reaching the court premises. The court did not find the case fit even for a remand and acquitted her on her appearance before the court. It was clear from the way charges against her were being pursued before the Shah Commission and the latest prosecution that she was on a comeback trail. Surprisingly, it was the vanity of Charan Singh which she used, to drive a wedge in the Morarji government, by sending a bouquet of flowers to Chaudhri Charan Singh on his birthday which he celebrated in great style at a public function. I found Chaudhri Charan Singh sometime later sitting next to me in a plane journey, quietly reading a book on life after death. I started a dialogue with him on the subject. He had read a few articles on the subject in some popular Hindi journals but he had not made any deep study of the subject. I brought the subject of discussion to the arrest of Mrs. Gandhi. He gleefully replied that she had challenged the government to arrest her as she was sure that none in the government had the guts to lay hands on her. He said that he accepted the challenge and got her arrested. My observation, on his remark that the arrest helped her to stage a comeback as the leader of the Indian masses, came as a shock to him. He fell silent for some time and then he said that he agreed with me and blamed some senior police officers for letting him down, as they had not done the necessary homework that was required for the arrest of Mrs. Gandhi.

My work in the Ministery of Agriculture was mainly to provide the administrative support for a chain of Agricultural Research Institutions and Universities spread over the whole of India. The ICAR had Mr. Swaminathan, a brilliant scientist and administrator, as its Director General with the Minister of Agriculture as the President of the ICAR Society. Dr. Swaminathan had sat for the IAS examination but could not make it. I found that the failure still rankled. He had married the daughter of an ICS officer, Mr. Bhoothalingam, and perhaps felt that his failure to make it to the IAS affected his position before his wife, and by becoming a Secretary in the Government of India before his batchmates of the IAS, he would be vindicating his position. He did not like any interference from the administrators in the ICAR, as it was considered to be his private preserve. He generally did not encourage my participation in the technical programmes of the various divisions of the ICAR nor would he favour my visits abroad in any scientists' delegation. My first visit abroad came about when the ICAR had negotiated a MOU with the World Bank. My deputy, Mrs. Rathi Vinay Jha, was involved in the discussions but even she was excluded from the delegation that went to Washington for finalizing the MOU. Finally, the only formality left was of signing for which the Law Department pointed out that the only legally competent authority who could sign the MOU on behalf of the ICAR was the Secretary of the ICAR. I was therefore, asked to go to Washington to sign the MOU. I demurred on it that it would sound ridiculous for me to go to Washington, all the way to attend the signing ceremony of five minutes and come back. The ICAR then found some work for me in the Commonwealth Agricultural Bureau in London which gave me a trip of about ten days. It was during this visit to Washington D.C. that I ran into my old friend, Mr. Nanak Kohli, who had moved there for business and he was apparently doing well. He took me to his beautiful house in Mclean, VA. He was negotiating to buy a nightclub. He took me there. Everyone knew him there. The girls, in bikinis, of the club started coming to our table, to dance on our table. It was fun but I was somewhat embarrassed. My Mussoorie assignment proved to be beneficial as I was having some problem in drawing my allowance from our High Commission in London. I was disappointed that despite being located in London our High Commission was a replica of a typical office of the Government of India, manned by clerks from Delhi, who were inefficient, rude and unhelpful. They reacted like the typical *babus* and told me that nothing could be done. I saw at the reception, the name of one of my trainee from Mussoorie listed as the First Secretary. I spoke to him telling him that I was at the reception and that I was facing a minor problem. The First Secretary, Mr. Jawahar Lal, immediately came down and took me to his room and did what was required to be done to help me. I found that our diplomatic staff were not paid adequate allowance for their stay in foreign countries where the cost of living was high. The rate of allowances was fixed by a team from the Audit and Accountant General, who instead of being liberal, considering the ever rising inflation, pegged the allowances a bit lower even at the current rate, as jealousy guided the *babus* recommending those allowances with the result that the diplomats had to cut corners for living, except for those who were provided with secret service funds belonging to RAW.

16

Agricultural Research

The Sikh agricultural experts, who were there in the ICAR in considerable numbers, felt that in his patronage, Dr. Swaminathan favoured the South Indians. My induction in the ICAR was for the purpose of balancing that suspected tilt. Dr. Swaminathan was completing his five years as the Director General of the ICAR. He made a move for identifying his successor but I suspected that he wanted to be considered for appointment as the Secretary of the Agriculture Ministry. I shared my suspicion with the Minister. Mr. Bamala was pleasantly surprised when Dr. Swaminathan reacted positively to the proposal. Dr. Swaminathan had written a paper, which was the subject of considerable excitement in the academic circles, called '*India — From begging bowl to bread basket*'. His prognosis in the paper that the periods of food shortages in India was gone, has stood the test of time. The credit for this change was sought to be given to Mr. C. Subramanian, the earlier Minister, and to himself. It was only partially correct, as basically the change came about by the development of dwarf varieties of wheat in Cymmit and the 1R-8 variety of paddy in IRRI. Both were international research centres supported by the Consultative Group on International Agricultural Research. The role of Dr. Subramanian was to speed-up the import of the new seeds for multiplication in India and Dr. Swaminathan got the administrative task of seed multiplication completed without any delay. The other important contribution came from the Punjab farmers who went like mad in adopting the new seeds with Ludhiana district in Punjab giving the highest productivity of wheat in the world. Same was the case with cultivation of paddy which was a new crop for Punjab. Punjab soon surpassed the per hectare yield of the traditional rice growing states like Tamil Nadu.

Mr. Barnala was respected as a gentleman minister. He was always polite and straightforward. No whiff of rumour about his integrity ever touched him. He worked on his papers like a lawyer on his brief. He, however, did not display the originality or boldness in decision-making or vision in any area as one came across in a minister like Jagjiwan Ram. Mr. Barnala I found got accused of favouring Sikh officers in various appointments under his ministry. Such an allegation was made by one Mr. Bagri, Member of Parliament, in a letter addressed to Morarji Desai. The letter was replied to but there was something behind it which came to light a bit later. We had a post of the Chairman, Agricultural Scientists Recruitment Board that was responsible for the recruitment of personnel and their promotions to the various positions in ICAR institutions. A Committee was constituted under Dr. M.S. Randhawa, ICS, to recommend a panel of names for the position. The Committee recommended the name of Dr. Sukhdev Singh as number one and Dr. Arakeri as number two. The appointment was to be made by the Minister after prior approval of the Prime Minister. The Prime Minister was requested to approve the appointment of Dr. Sukhdev Singh. I was surprised when I received orders of the Prime Minister, approving the name of Dr. Arakeri on the ground that the age and qualifications of Arakeri appeared to be in favour. I recorded a note for reconsideration of the Prime Minister, showing that on both the counts Dr. Sukhdev Singh was better placed than Dr. Arakeri, and added that his only disqualification could be that he happened to belong to the same community as Mr. Barnala. Mr. Barnala did not consider it appropriate for me to make such an observation on an official file. I stuck to my position, that it was the truth that had to be stated. This happened to be the time when Chaudhri Charan Singh, tempted by Mrs. Gandhi, had taken the step to part ways with Morarji Desai, and his government was likely to fall. I asked Mr Barnala to sit on the file for a few days and leave the rest to time. He was too good a gentleman to fall for it. He made a plea for reconsideration to the Prime Minister without sending the file to him so that he did not have to endorse my observation. Pat came the reply that the Prime Minister saw no reason to change his earlier recommendation and within a week the Morarji government fell.

My father was getting old. He had an angina problem with his heart. The programs of village development and a newly established college at Fatehgarh Saheb called Mata Gujri College kept him active but slowly various systems in his body started running down. He came on a visit to us in Delhi and he got a severe pain in his heart while I was on tour out of Delhi. Sukhdev took him to the Willingdon Hospital nearby where they admitted him without much attention or treatment. He was most unhappy. Sukhdev remembered that my cousin General S.S. Dhanoa was commanding the local Military Hospital. She contacted him on telephone and got my father transferred to the Military Hospital where he got a VIP treatment. He regained health in about a week.

He expressed a wish to stay with us in Delhi but my mother did not agree, as she felt that sitting idle in Delhi would not suit his health for long. He wrote to me after reaching the village that I should try to get Maan Singh posted to some Air Force station nearby. This happened to be his last letter written to me. His handwriting was beautiful but his hand could not complete the letter and he had mailed it unsigned. I spoke to the Director, Personnel of the Air Force for the posting of my brother Maan Singh to Chandigarh. He was good enough to accommodate him. His being near helped my father when he needed some extra attention. We were at a dinner one night in January 1979 in Gymkhana Club when my daughter Rosy rang up late in the night that there was a telephone message received from Chandigarh that my father had expired. I whispered the information to Sukhdev and after some excuse to the guests, we left for home. I travelled overnight to reach Gharuan early in the morning. My mother, Maan Singh and other near ones had kept a vigil over the dead body of my father for the whole night. I was happy to see that they had not followed the Hindu custom of laying the dead body on the floor. They had left lying him on the bed, as if sleeping. I sat down immediately to recite '*Sukhmani*' a long verse of the 5th Guru. After finishing the recitation I offered prayer for the departed soul in which every one joined. By that time other villagers joined and we took the body for bathing under our hand pump. The body was dressed in a new set of clothes and laid on a funeral bier where ladies of the families, near to us or related to us, bowed at his feet and everyone had a last look at my father's face. The body was covered by a coffin cloth and a shawl. My mother's brothers and their wives, from Dhamot, joined us at that time. As per the custom, it was my mother's family that made the arrangement for firewood on the cremation ground nearby. Four of us lifted the body on a wooden bier made like a small ladder, singing verses from *Gurbani* and distributing candy on the way. We had started with head of the body facing forward but midway we were asked to reverse the body as per some Hindu custom. We placed the body on the funeral pyre. Some purified butter and some pieces of sandalwood were put on the body. I and my brother, Maan Singh, lit the funeral pyre. After fire had caught the wood fully, we were asked to stoke the burning firewood near the head which was meant to drive the soul out of the skull. A verse from *Gurbani* called '*Sohila*' was read. Thereafter, everyone moved to the gurdwara where '*ardas*' was said and '*krah prasad*' was distributed. Women did not accompany for the funeral. Next day we went to collect the remains of bones, etc., from the ashes. The ashes were tied up in a small sack and taken away to Haridwar for immersion in the Ganges from the cremation ground itself. My *mama ji* took the ashes by calling my father by name to accompany him. The Hindu belief is that the journey to the next world started from Haridwar. A family priest there read some '*mantras*' and consigned the ashes to the flowing current of the Ganges River. They also entered the name and other details of the deceased and the family in the register maintained by them from generation to generation. The Sikhs under Singh Sabha influence have started taking the ashes of their dead to Kiratpur Saheb for immersion in a small current of the Satluj River. However, no system to replace the recordkeeping of the family Brahmins has been developed. I think that it is a needless innovation that has been sought to be introduced. We arranged for the reading of the *Granth Saheb* to be completed in about ten days at our house. The '*bhog*' ceremony was attended by all the villagers and relatives and friends or well-wishers of the family. A number of persons spoke about my father, eulogizing his services for the village. I also felt like saying a few words. As I stood up and started, I broke down and I could not complete what I wanted to say. There is no doubt that my father had been a great human being who had started from the village, virtually an orphan at one time. My wife's family had brought a turban that I wore over the turban that I was wearing. This ceremony symbolised my succession as the head of our family after my father. A community lunch was hosted by the family for all the guests. Another personal loss that I suffered was the death of my dear friend and well-wisher, J.S. Grewal. He had moved to Delhi after the nationalization of the coal mines. The Government had taken him as the Deputy General Manager of the government company, Bharat Coking Coal Company Limited, but he found it difficult to adjust to the new culture, where salaries were low but underhand earning was plentyful. He started a business of a refrigeration contractor and soon established himself in the business. He used to be there at the centre of everything in Dhanbad. He had slightly changed in Delhi, becoming a bit more religious and less gregarious. It was only towards the end of his life that I learnt that he was suffering from cancer. He was admitted in PGI, Chandigarh when I went to see him. He was in acute pain but he talked to me as if he was normal. It was very painful for me, sitting with him. I could not muster words for a conversation as I felt that I would breakdown any moment. The excruciating pain of cancer was compelling him to end my interview. I left PGI with the promise that I would visit him again. That again never came for me as he died before my return.

Chaudhri Charan Singh was promised support by the Congress from outside. Morarji Desai stuck to the office till the last and resigned only when it was found that in his list of supporters submitted to the President he had included names that should not have been there. Chaudhri Charan Singh was sworn in as the Prime Minister. It was said with some pride that on the coming 15th August the son of a *Jat* farmer, meaning Charan Singh, would be hoisting the National flag on the ramparts of the Red Fort, as per the tradition in India following Jawaharlal Nehru, who hoisted the Tricolour Indian flag for the first time there on the 15th August 1947. Mr. Charan Singh, knowing fully well that his existence depended on the goodwill of Mrs. Gandhi, was vain enough to declare that he was the Prime Minister on his terms and there would be no let-up in the prosecution of Mrs. Gandhi or Sanjay Gandhi, provoking Mrs. Gandhi to pull the rug from under his feet. Mr. Charan Singh is one unique example in India where he remained the Prime Minister without having to face the Parliament even once. He vowed that he would get Sanjay Gandhi convicted for his role in the destruction of the film '*Kissa Kursi Ka*'.

The Government got a direction issued to the court that they should hold hearing of the case on a day-to-day basis. It was in handling this crisis that Sanjay Gandhi displayed the originality of his mind. It was obvious that political winds were blowing their way. The objective was to strangle the court process of trial in a manner that the prosecution got tied up in knots.

Mr. Anthony was the advocate defending Mrs. Gandhi in most of the cases that she was facing. Mr. Sanjay Gandhi personally took charge of the defence. He made his base in the chamber of my friend and class fellow, Mr. O.P. Sharma, a senior advocate of the Supreme Court. He found his chamber to be ill-equipped and badly furnished. He got an air conditioner installed in the chamber and got the furnishing changed to his liking. He got a lady lawyer as a Secretary and virtually turned O.P. Sharma into his assistant. He got his lawyer to file a petition on the date of hearing, stating that he would like to withdraw from the case. The court had to give adequate time to Sanjay Gandhi to find another lawyer. His new lawyer was an expert at getting the proceedings in the court stalled on one pretext or the other. When the court still showed determination to proceed, his lawyer created a situation where the prosecution lawyer alleged that while copying, Sanjay's lawyer had torn 11 pages from the case record. The charge was contested by his lawyer. The judge had to stop the proceedings and order an enquiry into the incident that was alleged. Nothing came out of it as was expected, but in the meanwhile, the dates for the Parliament elections came and the people of India elected Indira Gandhi as the Prime Minister, with a clear majority. The first order that was passed by her on coming back to power was to send Mr. Raj Dev Singh, IPS, the Special Prosecutor for the cases against her, back to his parent cadre Bihar. Sanjay Gandhi having married a Sikh girl Maneka, was favourably inclined towards the Sikhs. I was told even before the election results came out that the caucus around Sanjay Gandhi had decided that the next Cabinet Secretary would be Mr. S.S. Grewal, an IAS officer of the Punjab cadre and Giani Zail Singh became the Union Home Minister in the new Cabinet. Sanjay Gandhi ordered about the new ministers, more or less like his subordinates. He passed on instructions to Zail Singh that Mr. P.S. Bhinder, IPS, be appointed the Inspector General of Police in Delhi. Bhinder had appeared before the Shah Commission and he had boldly accepted before the Shah Commission that he had arrested the students of Delhi University whom Maneka Gandhi had accused of having teased her by passing some remark while she was passing. There was no direct communication between Mrs. Gandhi and her ministers.

They had to depend on one member or the other of the caucus around Mrs. Gandhi and act on the basis of the instructions received. Zail Singh, in a confessional mood, had admitted that he had collected funds for the party when he was the Chief Minister but he said that he had passed on all that he had collected to Sita Ram Kesari, a Bihari veteran, who was the Treasurer of the party for very long, as he knew that if he had kept any portion for himself he would have been given the boot. It was well-known that Lalit N. Mishra, a fund collecting minister from Bihar, had been keeping the key staff of the PMO in his pocket to get the news of the happenings in the court circles of Mrs. Gandhi. He too rendered account of his collections to Mrs. Gandhi and his special assistant Mr. N.K. Singh kept R.K. Dhawan informed. Mr. Bhinder did not happen to be senior enough for the position but all the same, Zail Singh was asked to carry out the order within forty-eight hours. He had to manage the bureaucracy if it came in the way. Zail Singh had picked up his erstwhile Secretary from Punjab cadre, Mr. S.P. Bagla, who happened to be my next door neighbour, to assist him in carrying out such tasks that were many and very pressing often. Mr. Bagla was later appointed by him as the Establishment Officer in the Government of India where he had a hand in all senior placements in the Government of India. This sort of remote control of Sanjay Gandhi would have sooner or later resulted in trouble but unfortunately soon after coming to power of Indira Gandhi, he dıed in an air crash.

We had a minister in the short interval of Charan Singh. He was a Delhi *Jat* politician, Choudhri Brahm Prakash. He was a fine well-off gentleman. I went ahead with my task of assisting the Government in locating a successor of Dr. M.S. Swaminathan. Our shortlist had one Dr. J.S. Kanwar, the Deputy Director General of the

International Crops Research Institute for Semi-Arid Tropics located at Patancheru, Andhra Pradesh, as number one candidate. He was a soil scientist who was earlier working as a Deputy Director General with the ICAR. I had gone to sound him about the proposal before initiating a formal proposal for clearance of his name for the post of the Director General of the ICAR. He gave his consent and met the Cabinet Secretary. I felt badly let down, when after clearance of his appointment, he used the offer to get his pay and perks improved in the ICRISAT instead of joining as the Head of the prestigious national agricultural research organization like the ICAR. We had to go to the number two in the panel for the position of the Director General. He happened to be Dr. O.P. Gautam, who was the Deputy Director, looking after the agricultural universities in the country. He was a scientist of limited capability, somewhat jealous of Dr. Swaminathan. The first task he had was to oversee the celebrations of the Golden Jubilee of the ICAR, with the inaugural function being held in Ashok Hotel, New Delhi, along with an International Conference. The whole thing had been planned by Dr. Swminathan and the details were left to me for implementation. I had been assigned the duty of welcoming the distinguished guests among whom was Charan Singh, the Prime Minister. The only thing that was not tied up was the inaugural function lunch in hotel Ashok. Dr. Gautam threw up his hands, leaving me alone to hold the baby. I approached Dr. Swaminathan to help me. He was good enough to speak to Nanda of the Escorts, who offered to host the lunch for the inaugural function that was attended by more than one thousand guests.

We had a hardy annual in the ICAR so long as Dr. Swaminathan was associated with the ICAR. This was a question by Dr. Bhai Mahavir in the Parliament regarding a false claim alleged to have been made by Dr. Swaminathan as a breeder of wheat in developing a variety Sonora 64 that was claimed to have a lysine content equal to that of the cow's milk. He had made this statement in an address to a World Vegetarian Conference and not in any paper of scientific research. It was found that the initial evaluation of lysine content in the particular variety of wheat, done at the IARI laboratory was also higher than what was actually found later. Dr. Austin, who had conducted this evaluation, had publicly apologized for his mistake in the initial reporting of the lysine content. It was alleged that the whole thing had been stage managed by Dr. Swaminathan for earning international acclaim on the basis of a false achievement. Every year the same question in one form or the other would be framed. Since the question related to an issue concerning Dr. Swaminathan, its answer was left to him for final approval. Meanwhile, a British magazine called *New Scientist*, carried a series of articles about scientists who made false claims of achievements in various fields and among them, the magazine named Dr. Swaminathan, as one of the main actors. The question came for answering in the Parliament and the draft answer was put up before Dr. Gautam, for approval. He showed no intrest in rebutting the charges leveled. I felt bad that the loyalty for the erstwhile chief should be so skin deep. I got all the papers concerning the issue and prepared a comprehensive reply on all the aspects of the issue, so that once for all this ghost was laid to rest. I could show that in none of the scientific papers a claim had been made that the particular variety of wheat developed by Dr. Swaminathan had lysine content higher than the actual. I informally showed the answer to Dr. Swaminathan, who cleared the draft and felt obliged to me for that. The hardy annual ceased to appear thereafter, once for all.

My friend Mr. Bagla, the Establishment Officer, tried to get me fixed up as the Chief Commissioner for the Union Territory of Chandigarh. I consented for being considered for the appointment as it was a virtually independent position with a lot of salience in Punjab. I had very few contacts in Punjab except for my close relatives, among whom I was the most eminent person. I had to find suitable marriage partners for my children, who were fast reaching marriageable ages. It was necessary for the arranged marriages to be known in the social circles outside ones immediate kinship group. I later found that Bagla was trying to kill two birds with one stone. One IAS officer of the Assam cadre of 1952 batch, Mr. B.S. Sarao, who was the Chief Secretray, had received a shabby treatment from the Assamese politicians, having been summarily removed from the position when he was mourning the death of his wife. I happened to be visiting Guwahati on that day and I had gone to him to convey my heartfelt sympathies. His father's mother came from Gharuan and he had always treated me as a sort of a relative. His record of service was not bright and he had not been selected for empanelment as a Joint Secretary in the Government of India. The promotional system for the IAS was that having joined the service, one got promoted to the higher grades on the basis of the length of service, regardless of the quality of one's performance. The Government of India had introduced the system of empanelment to qualify for appointments under the Government of India at the level of joint secretaries and above. This system was sometimes abused when, for some extraneous reasons, some IAS officers were not included in the panel but the abuse was an exception and it came after the coterie around Indira Gandhi started influencing her judgment in the matter of placement of officials. Perhaps it would be correct to say that Mrs. Gandhi trusted this small group of junior officials in matters of placements, more than her Secretary of Personnel Department. A Prime Minister has to have trust in someone close to her for the nitty-gritty in administration where an obstructive or mischievously inclined official placed in a strategic position sometimes could become an extreme source of embarrassment to the Prime Minister. It is not clear to an outsider like me as to how stalwarts like Haksar failed her in this concern but she started relying on the small group of officials considered personally loyal to someone enjoying her trust after she found out that there was no sure way of locating committed officers other than depending on such small coterie. Perhaps this is one gap that the Indian bureaucracy and politicians have failed to bridge. We adopted the Westminster Cabinet Model in our constitution which required civil servants to be neutral, impartial and anonymous, whereas our society and conditions required the civil servant to be an activist and an agent of social change. It was necessary in our environment for civil servants to foster and nurture empathy for the political agenda of the ruling party without permitting any animosity against the programs of the political parties in opposition. Some civil servants were able to fine tune such adjustment in our system but they were not inclined to share their experience to enable the system to evolve a code for propriety in relations between the civil servants and politicians. The dividing line between what is appropriate and what is not appropriate between the civil services and the politicians in power has continued to elude the Indian polity.

Punjab since Independence has been politically dominated by *Jat* Sikhs. Partap Singh Kairon was the first one among the *Jat* Sikhs to become the Chief Minister of Punjab. Giani Zail Singh was a carpenter by caste and for him to become the Chief Minister of Punjab was made possible by the backing of Mrs. Indira Gandhi and his own native skills in managing the Akalis and dividing the Sikh *Jats*. He wanted to assuage the Sikh *Jats* before the assembly elections in Punjab. He got persuaded by Amarinder Singh, the ex-Maharaja of Patiala, to post Mr. B.S. Sarao, as the Chief Commissioner of Chandigarh. Mr. Sarao's father used to be the Congress candidate against the Akali candidate, Sardar Baldev Singh, from the Sikh constituency of Ambala district before 1947. Unfortunately, Mr. Sarao was not in the panel of names approved for the position of Joint Secretay or its equivalent in the Government of India. Mr. S.P. Bagla sponsored my name on the ground that I satisfied both the criteria of Zail Singh and that of the Government of India. I was called by Zail Singh to see him. Mr. Sarao met me in the corridors of the North Block that housed the Home Ministry and complained that I was coming in his way.

I assured him that I had no such intention and I did not know as to why I had been called. I found Zail Singh to be a friendly person. We had just exchanged pleasantries when my friend O.P. Sharma, who had been earlier his lawyer in a case of election petition against him, just walked in as he had kept himself informed about the visitors who were to meet Zail Singh. He somewhat embarrassed me when he asked Zail Singh for my posting to Chandigarh. Zail Singh mentioned about the plight of Sarao. I immediately said that I knew his plight and I would not like to come in his way in the matter of posting. Zail Singh felt happy on hearing me, but both of my friends, i.e., O.P. Sharma and S.P. Bagla were cut up with me that I let them down.

The ICAR was the administrative department through which ICRISAT corresponded with the Government of India. The team from the World Bank, that had negotiated with the Government of India, thought it necessary that they should always have the services available of an IAS officer at an international salary, at par with the scientists to enable them in dealing with various local problems and in issues that they had to take up with the Government of India. ICRISAT asked the ICAR to get for them a panel of names of IAS officers of the Additonal Secretary level for their consideration, as the current incumbent was about to complete his tenure. I saw that the opening could solve my financial problems of always living from hand-to-mouth. I started praying for my selection in my daily prayers. I asked Mr. Bagla to put my name on the panel that he had been requested to send for ICRISAT. My name was one of the two names that the Government of India sponsored. I was called for interview by Dr. L.D. Swindale, the Director General. He was a scientist from New Zealand. He strongly believed that it was their compulsion to have a senior IAS officer on their staff but he was dead set against any import of the bureaucratic *babu* culture into ICRISAT.

He made it clear that he would like to have an IAS officer on tap instead of being on top, as was the custom for the IAS. He explained his ideas in the interview. I told him that I was attracted for the job mainly because of its salary and perks and not its content. I plainly told him that if he wanted to pay me the international scale salary for doing nothing, I would not be averse to it. I did not object to his redesignation of the position from 'administrator' to being 'special assistant to the director general'. The other candidate perhaps was not in so desperate straits. I think that Dr. Swindale had consulted Dr. Swaminathan about my selection. It was the only positition after joining the IAS for which specifically I had prayed to *Waheguru* and I consider that I got it only through His grace as otherwise I had done a lot to rub Dr. Swindale the wrong way while handling their files in the ICAR.

I admired the basic structure of the Government of India, as it functioned well. The upkeep of papers was in good order and the office was generally able to put up a case on the basis of past precedents on which one could rely in decision-making, unlike the Bihar Secretariat where one's capacity to manage a Department depended more on one's personal capability and mastery of the secretariat procedures. Some bright efficiency expert in Bihar introduced the single file system where the Government and the Heads of Departments operated on a single file avoiding duplication in paperwork. Apparently it looked good, but in reality it meant that neither the Head of the Department was accountable on any subject nor the Government assumed responsibility for anything, as important papers that once came before the Government got lost when the same file moved to the Head of the Department. The strength of the system lay in the framework of the Central Government being provided by the Central Secretariat Service recruited on the basis of the same competitive examination as provided recruitment for the IAS, the only difference was that the candidates for the CSS came from the lower-end of the merit list. Mr. V.P. Menon, who had a hand in the amalgamation of states with India in 1947, was an outstanding example of a CSS officer making to the rank of a Secretary to the Government of India. The position of the CSS had somewhat gone down since then. The maximum that a CSS officer could aspire currently was the post of a Joint Secretary to the Government of India. One Mr. Hariharan was working with me in the ICAR as a Director. His name got cleared for the panel of Joint Secretaries. According to the prevailing procedure, the panel got circulated among the Secretaries for being picked up as a Joint Secretary. Mr. Hariharan had only six months of service left before his retirement and for that short period no Secretary was prepared to pick up his name. I talked to the Cabinet Secretary about it and offered to go on leave for three months so that he could become a Joint Secretary before he retired, giving him a certain prestige and some pecuniary benefit in his pension. My proposal was accepted and after a long time I had a real holiday with my family. We had a whale of a time in traveling to South India. The ICAR had a network of Research Stations all over where we could stay in their guesthouses. We had a memorable sea journey in a regular coastal ship in their state room from Goa to Cochin. We had sea bathing on the beach of the CPCRI at Kasargode in Kerala, staying there for a week.

Sukhdev, Rosy, Nony and Dipy really enjoyed this holiday which became an experience which they would always remember.

ICRISAT was a new experience. Though we lived in Hyderabad we got our salaries in US dollars. The centre was located at Patancheru, about 30 kilometre outside Hyderabad on the Hyderabad-Bombay road. We commuted daily in automatic gear Nissan cars. Our offices had no peons or attendants. We had our lunch in an American style cafeteria where we carried our own tray to the table. I was literally given no work for the first two months. I had a Personal Assistant who was a retired commodore, Cdr Ratnagar of the Indian Air Force. The lack of work seemed to worry him a lot. We had a system where we had to go and pick up our mail and other papers from a central desk. He would walk to it every hour and come back to tell me that there was no mail for me. I selected a beautiful four bedroom house for myself in Banjara Hills area. It was a newly constructed modern house which I consider to have been the best house that our family had in my service career. The ICRISAT provided separate cars for the wives and families of the international staff so that wives of the scientists remained happy and they did not have to depend on their husbands for their mobility. The climate and the cosmopolitan atmosphere of Hyderabad was something that the family really enjoyed. I became a member of the Secunderabad Club, one of the best clubs set up by the colonial *Sahebs* in the whole of India. Salary and perks were such that we could indulge in all that we had a fancy for. Slowly, I started getting a lot of work relating to coordination of ICRISAT research with extension to the field and linking up with the research that was in hand in the Indian research centers. We had some ongoing problems, partially created by me when I was in the ICAR that had to be resolved. One related to the privileges of the international grade staff who had been equated with the World Bank staff rather than the U.N. staff. I had to get the Cabinet Secretay to intervene in favour of the ICRISAT for that purpose. Dr. Swindale had asked me to accompany him to Washington for the meeting of the CGIAR in which funds were pledged for the research activities over the coming year. Sukhdev accompanied me on this trip that lasted about a month. We were staying in a hotel in Washington D.C., very near the White House. We decided in the evening to walk to the White House and visit downtown, As we came out of the hotel my attention was drawn to a taxi outside the hotel that had the name of its driver 'Mohinder Singh' written boldly above the front window. As I came near the taxi, the driver who was otherwise clean-shaven, greeted me with a loud '*Sat Sri Akal*'. He enquired as to who I was and where were we going. I told him about me and my wife. He greeted Sukhdev as his sister as he said that he came from a village very near Bassi Pathana, where she had studied in school. He invited us to sit in his taxi and virtually forced us to accept his hospitality. He said that it was unwise to walk on foot in the downtown as strangers were in danger of getting mugged and robbed by the black hoodlums. I asked him as to how he was surviving in Washington D.C. which was a black majority town. He said that as a principle he never took a black passenger in his taxi. He mentioned in the taxi that Ganga Singh Dhillon, a lawyer from Bassi Pathana lived in Washington. Ganga Singh Dhillon had caused quite a furore in India when he had been invited to address the All India Sikh Educational Conference in Chandigarh, by raising the issue in his Presidential Address that the Sikhs are a separate nation. Sukhdev rang him up as Ganga Singh Dhillon, as a junior, had worked with her father, Sardar Kartar Singh Tiwana. Dhillon said that he was delighted to hear from her and invited us for a dinner at his house. He personally came in a Cadillac to take us to his home in Georgetown, a prestigious residential area in Washington. I was a bit disappointed on meeting him, as he did not seem to be well-versed in the Sikh tenets or the Sikh tradition. I could see from the pictures in his drawing room and photo albums that he was quite close to Zia-ul-Haque, the Pakistani dictator. He and his wife were very affectionate and hospitable but I could not help returning from his house with an uneasy feeling that his speech at the Sikh Educational Conference was a plant of the CIA or the ISI, or both.

I had arranged to send my daughter, Rosy, for a course in Fashion Designing in London. She stayed there with my sister, Mohinder.

I had a responsibility for liaison with the state governments. This enabled me to visit the interior of states like Andhra Pradeh, Maharashtra, Karnataka, Madhya Pradesh, Haryana and Punjab. Wherever I could, I traveled by car as I liked to drive the automatic gear Japanese Datsun car. Birendar was posted as a Flying Officer at Sirsa, flying MiG 21 fighter planes. I heard, on my visit to Punjab, from Principal Kartar Singh of Moranwali, whom I held in some esteem as a devout Sikh, that there was group among the Sikhs who were able to transform a person by getting the indwelling Divine in him to awaken during their administration of *Amrit*, The group was built around Hardyal Singh of Dodra in the interior of Malwa. I got persuaded to join the *Amrit* ceremony although I had taken *Amrit* earlier. The new group asked me to become a vegetarian and a teetotaler. I also started wearing a *kirpan* too. After *Amrit* I went to Sirsa which happened to be on the route which Guru Gobind Singh had taken, when he left Damdama Saheb near Bhatinda, to meet Aurangzeb the Emperor, in Deccan. He had halted at a place called Sahewa in Rajasthan where there is said to be a '*peepal*' tree growing in a '*palas*' tree. It was said in a book called '*Sau Sakhi*' or hundred tales ascribed to Guru Gobind Singh, that when the '*peepal*' would fully enclose and cover the '*palas*', it would be the time when the Khalsa would rule. We reached the place in the night. There was a gurdwara to commemorate the visit of Guru Gobind Singh. There was no Sikh family in the village. Saheva was the last halt of Guru Gobind Singh enroute to the Deccan where regular gurdwaras came up at each halt. Thereafter, gurdwaras are there in large towns enroute, but not on every halt. Sahewa was also said to be a halt from where a large number of the Sikhs accompanying Guru Gobind Singh deserted him during the night including the Rai Kalha, the Chaudhri of Raikote, who had been his constant companion after he met him somewhere on reaching Alamgir from where he had started travelling on horseback for the first time after leaving Chamkaur in 1704 CE. It is said that as usual the first thing in the morning, Guru Gobind Singh called for Rai Kalha but there was no response even after when the call was repeated. It is said that at Saheva there was a Muslim *faqir* who responded to the Guru's call, saying that there was neither *ballah* nor *kallha,* and henceforth Guru was *Kalla*, meaning alone. It was clear that, '*Sau Sakhi*' was a compilation containing many tales ascribed to Guru Gobind Singh that served the ends, either of the British or the Namdharis. Similarly, the *Amrit* I found did not make for any recognizable transformation in me. The tall claim made about it was only propaganda of the group.

I accompanied Dr. Swindale and Mrs. Swindale to a tour of Madhya Pradesh where we were guests of the Madhya Pradesh Government. My friend and batchmate, Madneshwar Singh, was the Chief Secretary. We visited the beautiful National Park of Bandavgarh. The National Park was teeming with wildlife. We rode an elephant along with the Madhya Pradesh Minister, Mr. Digvijay Singh, who later became the Chief Minister of Madhya Pradesh. After a week long tour we returned to Hyderabad. Thereafter, I went with my sons, Birendar and Dipender, to Bombay by car, staying on my way at Poona with my cousin, Major General S.S. Dhanoa, whose son, Pinchu, was of the same age as Birendar. He had joined the Merchant Navy and also worked for Bollywood films, mostly in the role of a villain where his name was Dan Dhanoa. I did not know much about Bombay roads. We reached Bombay by the evening, guided mostly by road maps. I do not know as to how it happened, but after a session of drink and dinner at the Taj Hotel, when I started for the Port Trust guesthouse, I found myself on the pavement near the Gateway of India. I was about to drive into the sea when Birendar shouted of danger and physically took the steering of the car from me. We thanked our stars for having been saved in the nick of the time. My batchmate, Mr. K.K. Uppal, was the Chairman of the Bombay Port Trust. He had got his posting on his request through R.K. Dhawan and as the Chairman of the Port Trust, he seemed to have done well. He was able to clear all the backlog in the unloading of ships, as Bombay had become notorious for delays in handling ships, making the loaded ships wait in queues lasting weeks. All of us were touching the seniority where we would become due for consideration of appointment as Secretaries in the Govemment of India, provided we made it to the panel of Secretaries kept by the Cabinet Secretary. It was ironical that the first of our batch Mr. A.D. Samant, of the Maharashtara cadre did not make it even to the panel of Joint Secretaries. Mr. K.K. Uppal showed me a letter, personally signed by Indira Gandhi, congratulating him on his Achievements as Chairman of the Bombay Port Trust. I told him on seeing that letter that whoever else might make it to the panel of Secretaries, it was certain that he would be one of them. He seemed to be very happy with himself and the world. Little did I suspect that he was a split personality like the story of Dr. Jekyll and Mr. Hyde. It seemed he had a crush for the wife of his deputy, Mr. K.B. Srinivasan. He typed out stealthily, an anonymous letter, almost lifting out a paragraph from some pornographic book, describing how her husband was having an affair with some lady employee of the Port Trust. Srinivasan had some contact with the police, having earlier worked in the Home Department of the Maharashtra Government. He requested the police to investigate about the author of the pornographic letter. It was found that the anonymous letter had been typed on the Chairman's typewriter. The house of his P.A. was raided, as also his office. It was found in a drawer that there was a copy of the letter lying and also a bank passbook, showing deposits in foreign currency in the name of the Chairman that clearly appeared to be kickbacks. My poor friend Mr. Uppal got suspended and chargesheeted. It only showed that one only got what Waheguru designed for him. All contacts and cleverness was of no avail. When I look back on my career I find that there were many indiscretions which were committed by me but Waheguru, in his mercy provided His cover to those indiscretions.

There was, however, one difference in my indiscretions from what Mr. Uppal had done. It was that all my indiscretions got committed without any design or cold-blooded pre-planning. Franklin Roosevelt had said about some of his actions, that God's angel for justice judged the actions of the warm hearted in a scale different from that by which actions of the cold-blooded calculating persons were judged. *Gurbani* also makes it clear that God judged one from what was in the mind and what was intended rather than from what really happened.

We generally went to the gurdwara on Sundays. We had a choice of three gurdwaras. Two were in Hyderabad and one was in Secunderabad. The gurdwara in Secunderabad was better attended as it attracted the army personnel because of the location of an old British cantonment there. Quite a few Sikhs had moved to Secunderabad-Hyderabad after 1947, most of them were from the business classes. It seems that during the days of Maharaja Ranjit Singh, the Nizam of Hyderabad had secured the services of a Khalsa brigade for his army. The descendents of those Sikhs later settled in Hyderabad. Many of them were in the Nizam's police force that got taken over by the Andhra Pradesh Government. They had an old gurdwara near Begampet Airport. One thing that struck me about the Sikh communities outside Punjab was the similarity of the mind set. The leadership of the Sikh community had moved from the earlier urban educated classes to the rural, comparatively less educated class, dominated by the Punjabi *Jats*. However, the refrain in the community was that the Sikhs had not been treated fairly in India after 1947, despite the fact that the community had done well in services, business, and Punjab had the highest per capita income in India. We had Bibi Rajinder Kaur, M.P., the daughter of Master Tara Singh, visiting and addressing the Sunday congregation in the Gurdwara at Secunderabad. The audience listened to her with rapt attention. Her speech sounded more or less like a tirade against the majority community in India. She gleefully mentioned that how the Sikhs and Hindus could be considered equal.

The return of Mrs. Gandhi brought a new Minister for Agriculture. He was Mr. Rao Birendra Singh, an Ahir politician of Haryana, who was a scion of the family of Rao Tula Ram, who had taken a prominent part in the 1857 revolt against the British. He was a man with literally a stiff neck. He liked that when he went abroad or returned from official visits abroad all senior officers of the Ministry should receive or see him off at the airport. I had never done so. His Private Secretary noticed my absence and next time rang me up to say that the Minister would be expecting to meet me at the airport. He was clearly a very vain person. One new dispensation that we noticed in the new set up of Mrs. Gandhi was that all the Private Secretaries of the Ministers were handpicked by R.K. Dhawan, who had proved his loyalty to Mrs. Gandhi and her family during the period of Janata Government of Morarji Desai and Charan Singh. He was a bachelor and ostensibly lived for the well-being of Mrs. Gandhi and her family. It was he whom Mrs. Gandhi had trusted when Maneka Gandhi decided to leave her house as she felt that her political ambitions were being stifled while living with Mrs. Gandhj. It was known that Dhawan had made no money while being in the powerful position of her trusted Private Secretary. He did not have a house of his own to live when he had to resign from his service as Mrs. Gandhi had lost in the 1977 elections. It was Mr. C.P.N. Singh of Bihar who gave him the keys of his Golf Links house to live. C.P.N. Singh of course was soon rewarded when Mrs. Gandhi returned to power, by being appointed the Governor of Uttar Pradesh. Anyhow, there was no doubt that there was nothing wrong in Dhawan being called a 'Hanuman' of Mrs. Gandhi. Mrs. Gandhi of course could rely on Dhawan but she could not bestow on him the vision of India that Jawaharlal Nehru had. It remained a handicap with Mrs. Gandhi that she did not have with her, among her close advisors, a replacement of P.N. Haksar, with whom she had to part company when he did not go along with her in grooming Sanjay Gandhi as her successor. I was soon to discover that with the return of Mrs. Gandhi there was the return of the unofficial black list of officers who were to be kept away from important positions. I got the first hint about it when the PMO showed their displeaure to Rao Birendra Singh and Mr. S.P. Bagla, on my having been sent on deputation to ICRISAT without a clearance from the PMO. Luckily for me, the rules did not require such clearance. I had already joined ICRISAT by the time the PMO came to know about it. I was accused of having approved some extension of deputation of a scientist when it was said that only the Minister had powers to grant such extensions. The issue was raised again and again, even after I reported back in Bihar. ICRISAT proposed an extension of deputation for me for six more months, which to the amazement of all, was turned down by Rao Birendar Singh. I still hoped that I would find a berth for me in Delhi as I was meeting the Cabinet Secretary Rao Saheb Krishnaswamy fairly often and Mrs Krishnaswamy felt quite at ease to ask for various small errands from our local Delhi guesthouse. I proceeded to Delhi on the 1st of February 1983, and parked myself in Bihar Bhavan. Mr. Rao Saheb assured me that he would fix my posting in a day or two. It seemed after two days that he had hit a road block. He asked me if I could take leave for a week or two to enable him to find a suitable placement for me.

Mr. Rajiv Gandhi had become the General Secretary and the leader of the Youth Congress after the death of Sanjay Gandhi. Mr. Chenna Reddy was replaced by a Harijan leader, Mr. Anjaihia. He thought that the only qualification that he had was his loyalty to Sanjay Gandhi. He was a person with limited knowledge and limited capacity. There were many stories about his capers. One such story was about his going to a girls school function. A small girl presented him a bouquet of roses. Anjaihia said to her while accepting the bouquet that he loved her. The girl student responded by saying that she loved him too. Mr. Anjaihiah said that he loved her three which made everyone laugh. An average Andhra felt that they had been humiliated by putting such a clown as their Chief Minister. This got further compounded when the Chief Minister laid out a grand reception for Rajiv Gandhi on his visit to Hyderabad against specific instructions of Rajiv Gandhi, who wanted the visit to remain a low key affair. When he saw all the show that was put up for his reception, he got wild and rebuked Mr. Anjaihiah publicly, in front of all the people and the media. Andhra people were furious over the insult to their Chief Minister. The Congress that had held Andhra Pradesh like a pocket borough suddenly got challenged on the slogan of restoring Andhra honour by Mr. N.T. Rama Rao, the well-known film actor. He led his party to a landslide victory in the Assembly Elections that were round the corner.

I was neglectful about my future although I was completing 25 years in service. I would have to find a roof on my head soon. The Delhi Development Authority had announced a scheme of constructing self-financing scheme flats for about one and a half lakh rupees for a three bedroom flat. Sukhdev did not wait for me to apply as she was not sure if I would be interested. She borrowed rupees ten thousand for the initial deposit from our family friend from Dhanbad, Mr. J.S. Grewal, and handed over the receipt to me for applying for loan from the Government, which I could not avoid doing thereafter. Earlier, I had goofed up in investing my Provident Fund money in a plot of land near Chandigarh. I got persuaded by my two friends from Aligarh to join them in that project for living together after retirement. I failed to realize that after Aligarh our lives had gone on completely different courses. They had taken to legal profession facing the rough and tumble of a struggle for existence in the legal profession, whereas I had joined the top civil service of the country. I soon discovered that we were no longer on the same wavelength and it was not feasible to live together as friends of the old. The property prices remained stagnant for a few years. I got out of the project as soon as I could get back the investment made. The flat that I had applied got allotted to me in Munirka Enclave. I got a loan of about 70,000 rupees from the government for the flat and I had to put in about 70,000 rupees of my own for the flat. I had an option to go for a servant quarter and a garage for about an additional rupees 30,000. I opted out of it as I thought that I would not be able to find the amount of money that was needed. Little did I know that going to ICRISAT would solve my problem. I have regretted these decisions ever since. True to her magnanimous character, Sukhdev did not ever hold such foolish decisions in life against me, even when we quarrelled over many petty issues in life. We got the possession of the flat just on our return from ICRISAT. My wife, Sukhdev, opted to stay behind in Delhi to get the flat ready for occupation which required considerable running round. I left my car also with her.

17

Last Innings of Bihar

I felt humiliated when I did not get my posting in Delhi after I had put in more than 25 years of creditworthy service. Perhaps all that was required for me was to call on R.K. Dhawan, who had promised that he would help me after I had completed my tenure in Bihar but somehow this option never entered my mind as I did not like to interact with my boss via any intermediary after I had burnt my fingers in my first district tenure. The Government of India is like something of an ocean where a petty civil servant like me did not count and perhaps my style of functioning would not have worked. However, I was confident that Bihar, where I had spent the best part of my service career, would surely be remembering me and they would receive me with open arms. I had a joining period of ten days. I decided to report to my parent state cadre for duty. I did not bother to inform the Government of Bihar nor did I get any transport arranged to meet me at the Patna Airport. It was perhaps on 3rd February 1983 that I boarded the morning flight from New Delhi. As was expected I found some Bihar officers travelling in the same flight and one of them was Dr. Miss Tirkey, who was the Director-in-Chief of the Health Services. She was the lady doctor back in Deoghar who had done the delivery of my son Birendar. She was delighted to see me. I told her that the Bihar Government was unaware about my return to state. She dropped me at the Patna Circuit House where it seemed that I was well-known. The caretaker of the Circuit House immediately allotted a room to me. I put my bags in the Circuit House and decided to walk to the Bihar Secretariat, which was about a kilometer away, instead of asking for a car to reach me to the Secretariat. I walked straight to the room of the Chief Secretary, Mr. Subhash Mukherjee, IAS, one of the brightest Bihar officers. He had worked in his younger days as Joint Secretary in the Ministry of Information and Broadcasting when Indira Gandhi had joined as a Minister and later he had moved to the PMO. He had mastered the Geology of India as a hobby. He had come to be recognised as a sort of an authority on the Geology of India. He had a fad of collecting topographical maps of India and he was a very interesting storyteller who could keep one spellbound for hours. We took to each other on our first meeting. He told me to visit him daily at 5.30 p.m. when he closed his office and he would sit down for an hour to chat with me. It was mostly one way, as his stories never ended. All the same, he was a bit eccentric also because of which he got kicked out of the Government of India. He got me to sign the joining report and told me that he would have to talk to the Chief Minister about my posting. I told him that I was not in a hurry about my posting. Meanwhile, a yellow light in his room started flashing indicating that the Chief Minster Dr. Jaganath Mishra had become available in his office. He spoke to him on the intercom and asked me to see him. His office was just across in the Secretariat. I was meeting him for the first time. He happened to be the younger brother of L.N. Mishra and an erstwhile Professor of Economics. He was very courteous and aplogised that he was not ready with my posting as I had surprised him by my sudden arrival. He said that till March 31st he did not want any transfers of senior civil servants, therefore, I had to make do with a special position that he had contemplated creating in his budget speech that would be called Commissioner for Reservation in Services. I thanked him for his courtesy and told him that it did not matter to me as to what the nomenclature of the position was, so long as I got the salary as per my seniority. My erstwhile SDM from Ranchi, Mr. B.P. Verma, was the Finance Secretary in the Government. He immediately placed a staff car with a driver at my disposal. I retired to the Circuit House in the staff car and I thought that I should have a wash before asking for my meal from the Circuit House. I opened my briefcase for taking out soap, etc., when I was shocked to see that instead of my things lady's lingerie, bras and blouses started coming out of it.

I thought for a moment that perhaps my wife had packed her things too in my briefcase but I soon realised that it was not my briefcase that I was holding although it looked exactly similar to mine. My briefcase was very important for me as it contained all my important papers without which I could become a non-person. I realised that the mix-up must have taken place at the airport luggage belt. I picked up a police officer from the Secretariat and rushed to the airport. The manager of the airport was visibly relieved on seeing me as the lady whose bag I had taken with me was abusing them from the morning and accusing them of robbing her. She had left behind my bag which she had picked up earlier. I thanked my stars and returned to the Circuit House to relax.

The news that I had joined spread in the civil service circles and I started having a chain of callers in the Circuit House. It was like a home coming for me too. My friend, Mr. G. Narain, virtually smothered me with his hospitality. It became a routine, that once a week I would have dinner at their house. I was staying alone in the Circuit House. I did not like the food that was provided by the Circuit House *khansamah* or the cook. The British *sahebs* adopted this title for their cooks from Mughal nobles as in their establishment *Khan-e-Saman* stood for the Lord of the Hospitality Department. There was an attendant provided by the Bihar government who was prepared to cook for me but I cared more for my privacy than the help from the attendant. There was a small kitchenette attached to the room. I got a connection of the cooking gas and started cooking my meals. I found that it was not much of an errand, as for breakfast I had a toast and boiled eggs with a cup of coffee. I had some snack for lunch and I could make a gruel of rice and lintel called '*khichri*' for my dinner or sometimes I would order dinner from a Punjabi restaurant nearby. Soon my room became a centre for get-together of friends who liked me to join for a drink in the evening. I made a study of the Cabinet paper on the basis of which my position was created and I saw Dr. Jagnnath Mishra about it. I apprised him about my understanding of my job on the basis of which I wanted to proceed ahead. I told him that there were many appointments in the state government that had been made in violation of the Reservation regulations. All such appointments would have to be terminated. He heard me but he did not like my proposal as it amounted to setting the cat among the pigeons. He said that I was there in the job for only two months at the maximum so I should let thesleeping dogs lie. I could see the reason for his reluctance to go whole hog for the policy that he himself had announced because the base of the Congress party in Bihar happened to lie in castes that would be affected adversely by the policy. I spent a week in Delhi in trying to understand the picture at the All India level. I found that there had been a Commission chaired by a Bihar politician, Mr. B.P. Mandal, that had gone into the position of representation of various castes in the services of the government. The Commission found that Brahmins mostly occupied almost all the higher echelons of services in the Central Government. The Brahmin hegemony in services was likely to continue because of the Brahmin's initial advantage in education and a built-in bias in recruitment, in favour of the Brahmins. The Commission had recommended reservations in all recruitments on the basis of backwardness of the various castes in India. The report was considered to be explosive and the same was kept under the wraps. I got unofficially a copy of it and found that as and when it was made public it would act as a bombshell in the Indian political scene which actually did happen when Mr. V.P. Singh announced that his government would implement the Mandal Commission Report.

Dr. Jagannath Mishra called me in early April and he had two positions in mind for me. He said that the first was the post of Chairman of the State Transport Corporation. This was another disastrous decision that had become a millstone around the neck of the State Government. The running of public transport was one activity that should never have been taken over by the government as the necessary expertise and capital for it was available in the private sector. There could be some justification for the urban sector where transport fares could not pay for the cost of the services unless fares rose substantially which affected the poorer sections adversely. The Bihar State Transport Corporation was an unmanageable behemoth, reeking with corruption and saddled with mounting losses every year. I offered to take over the management provided the Chief Minister agreed to permit me to get the corporation wound up. Dr.

Jagannath Mishra was apparently not prepared for it so he made the other offer of my taking over as the Development Commissioner. I took over the new job and soon thereafter we had the meeting of the National Development Council presided over by the Prime Minister. I saw Dr.Jagnnath Mishra at his best in this meeting. He put across the case of Bihar extremely well. His about one hour speech, was full of statistics concerning different sectors of Bihar's economy but he delivered his address extempore. Mr. Rajiv Gandhi, who was a professional pilot in the Indian Airlines had been drafted by Indira Gandhi to assist her in managing the Government and the Congress party. He was spoken of well as a pilot.

I got an infection in my groin that gave me a lot of trouble. The infection did not go even with strong antibiotics. The doctors in Patna advised surgery. I decided to get the surgery done in Patna by Dr Ram Sharan Sinha who was the Head of the Department of Surgery in the Patna Medical College Hospital. I found that the official operation theatre of the Hospital could not be used for my surgery for one reason or the other. Some times the hospital lacked anesthetic support, some other time there appeared another obstruction. Meanwhile, I was going through excruciating pain. The surgeon proposed that he could undertake the operation in his private clinic where all facilities were available. Taking it to be a minor surgery I neither informed my friends nor my family in Delhi about my intention to go for surgery. I went to the clinic of Dr. Sinha with only an attendant of mine with me. The doctor found that the infection had spread a bit and it would not be amenable to operation with local anesthesia. I agreed for general anesthesia, there and then. My attendant got alarmed over the situation. He rang up Mr. A.U. Sarma, my friend, who would often drop in the Circuit House to join me for a drink in the evenings. He was there when I regained consciousness.

I was told that the infection in my groin had got so bad that the surgeon had to remove one of my testicles. A.U. Sarma, known for his ready repartee and humour said to me that he would like to congratulate me on this operation as the operation had qualified me as fit for promotion to the rank of the Chief Secretary because the Government could not make a person a Chief Secretary if he had both his balls intact. Luckily, it turned out that whatever growth had appeared was not cancerous. The doctors called it benign. A.U. Sarma rang up Sukhdev about my operation. She was shocked to know about it.

She reached Patna the next day. I moved to the Circuit House in the meanwhile, but still convalescing. My ex-secretary in the Health Department, Mr. Lakhan Prasad, became a daily visitor. He was totally against my drinking. He convinced my wife that my problems were there because I was taking two alcoholic drinks in the evenings. Both of them, in my somewhat weak state, extracted a promise from me that I would give up drinking. I refrained one day from touching alcohol. The doctor came for a routine check-up in the evening. He found my blood pressure to be low. I asked him to come back after two hours. Meanwhile, I asked Sukhdev to make me two stiff drinks of whisky. When the doctor came after two hours, my blood pressure was found to be normal. He enquired if I had taken any medicine for it. I told him that the medicine was my whisky. The doctor told my wife that whisky up to two pegs was good for me. Luckily, Lakhan Prasad was not there that evening. He even now holds that the whole thing was stage managed by me and the doctor, although it is not true. Anyhow, this convinced Sukhdev and she stopped objecting to my drinking.

I was entrusted with the responsibility of directly looking after the Home Department and the Department of Personnel which were directly under the Chief Minister. I was authorized to remain in attendance during the Cabinet Meetings. There were certain matters that required me to go through the Chief Secretary. The Chief Secretary, Mr. K.K. Srivastava, was an old style dyed-in-wool bureaucrat who neither saw what was on his left nor what was on his right. Chandra Shekhar Singh got disenchanted with him within two months and started more and more leaning on me. He was more like a civil servant in his lifestyle and dealings. His wife was the daughter of a senior railway official. She was more at home with the wives of senior officers than with the politicians or their wives. She told my wife, when she had come on a visit to Patna to plan to move to Patna as I was slated to take over as Chief Secretary very soon. I got a house allotted on Hardinge Road that was earlier occupied by the Chairman of the Bihar State Electricity Board. The house had the advantage of having uninterrupted supply of electricity even during breakdowns.

We got an *Akhand Path* of the *Guru Granth Saheb* performed in our new house, prior to our shifting there.

Mr. Chandra Shekhar Singh called me and said that since he had personally got Mr. Srivastava to come to Patna as Chief Secretary, he was biding time to tell him to shift elsewhere but he had no patience with him and he did not like his style of functioning. He asked me to formulate a distribution of work in which all the work of the Chief Secretary except vigilance got looked after by me. I told him that it would not look nice and desirable for him and me to undermine the position of the Chief Secretary in the state as it would adversely affect the morale of the services in the state. We decided to let the matter rest at that for the time being. The Chief Minister confided to me that on his last visit to Delhi he heard that some stories were being spread about him in circles close to Indira Gandhi that he was favouring officers of a particular caste by posting them in important positions in his government. It was alleged that because of the JP agitation and the Allahabad High Court judgement, Mrs. Gandhi was suspicious about officers who were Kayasthas. It was said that General S.K. Sinha, who was the seniormost General in the Army, was not made the Army Chief, as he happened to be a Kayastha. I told him that I would try to get the issue settled in the PMO. I got an appointment with Mr. V.S. Tripathi, an officer of the Madhya Pradesh cadre, who looked after placements in the PMO. I met him on behalf of the Chief Minister and accosted him with the stories that were being spread about the Chief Minister. He confirmed that there were some whispers like that doing the rounds in Delhi.

I told him that I looked after the placements of senior officers in Bihar and the Chief Minister had desired me to know from him if there were any guidelines to be followed in the matter of placements. I told him that the stories of his favouring the Kayastha officers were false. I showed him the civil list of the Bihar IAS officers, where from 1948 to 1957, the only Bihari officers who made it to the IAS were Kayastha officers. It was natural that at the senior levels there would be only the Kayastha officers for some years to come. He seemed to have been satisfied with my explanation. He confirmed that there was some screening by the PMO in important placements. He said that those IAS/IPS officers, who at one stage or the other had tried to harm the interests of Mrs. Gandhi, were not to be considered for positions considered important or salient by the public like, he named my friend Mr. L. Dayal, who was the Principal Information Officer in the Government of India during Emergency. He had deposed before the Shah Commission that he found the atmosphere in Mrs. Gandhi's government to have been suffocating. Here was a confirmation for me of the blacklisting of certain officers in the government, who at one time or the other, happened to be on the wrong side of the powers that be. I was one of them from my Super Bazar days. It was really the reason for the refusal of the extension of my deputation with ICRISAT.

I found that Bihar had lagged behind in promotions, in both the IAS and IPS. The Chief Minister agreed to bring the promotions at par with the Central Government. The decision benefited me as I got promoted to the rank of Secretary in the Government of India and my friend Mr. G. Narain got promoted as an Inspector General of Police. I remained working as the Additional Chief Secretary but my pay was drawn against an ex-cadre post in the scale of a Secretary designated as Chairman of the Bureau of Public Undertakings. All the backlog of IPS promotions was cleared, which made me somewhat popular among the IPS circles. Another backlog that I came across in the Home Department was the action to be taken on the various Commission of Enquiry reports which had been appointed by the Bihar Government to look into the causes that had led to communal riots in places like Jamshedpur, Bihar Sharif and Bhagalpur, etc. I could not help feeling, in all the cases, that the officers in Bihar had become professionally inefficient and unable to face difficult situations. The problem became worse because of the lack of competent leadership, both in the administration and political level. The JP led agitations made the police neglect their crime control duties, as they had to go out chasing crowds in the streets. The investigations of cases suffered in the police stations so also was the patrolling of the police constables on their beats and their identification of bad characters in their beats. The normal process of booking criminals and their trials got clogged.

We had a situation where we had to close down industries in jails, as the requisite number of criminals convicted by courts was no longer going to the Central jails. The district jails everywhere got so crowded by the undertrial prisoners that in some places prisoners had to take turns for stretching themselves to sleep, all at one time.

I got to order summary release of prisoners whose offences carried less punishment than the time that they had spent in jail. Similarly, there was a backlog in training of personnel at all levels. We had a large number of police constables who were not trained to fire a rifle. A regular program was worked out to take care of the backlog in training at all levels.

One peculiar case that had hogged media headlines at the national level came before me while framing a reply to a query from the Central Government. The case also brought out the ugly face of politics of no holds barred. Mr. Prem Shankar Singh, son of Bhisham Narain Singh, who was the Central Minister for Urban Development, lived at Daltonganj, Palamau, looking after his farming and other businesses. Bhisham Narain Singh was a low profile Congress leader with a clean record. Mrs. Gandhi, when she lost elections in 1977, started trusting him and she used him for some delicate Congress party assignments. He was made a Cabinet Minister when she came back to power in 1980. He could be a candidate or rival for the position of the Chief Minister of Bihar. Dr. Jagannath Mishra would not permit a rival in public life. He got an officer posted as a Deputy Commissioner, who had got promoted out of turn. He thought of repaying his debt to Dr. Mishra by getting a prominent rival eliminated. There was a report lodged by a petty mechanic with the local police that Prem Shankar Singh had threatened to physically harm him. The police officer got active on that report and reported that Prem Shankar Singh was evading arrest because he was the son of a Central Minister. The report raised the hackles of the district police chief. He raided the minister's house at midnight and arrested Mr. Singh from his house. There was widespread coverage of the arrest along with exaggerated accounts of the complaint against Mr. Singh appeared in the press. The very widely circulated weekly journal from Calcutta, '*Sunday*', gave a very coloured version of the incident, inspired by the Deputy Commissioner. The matter was raised in the Parliament. Mr. Bhisham Narain Singh got painted as the bully of the area, who thrived on holding people in awe through intimidation by the goons of his son. The damage was done.

The case was said to be *sub-judice*. The district police chief, who had felt so concerned as to personally lead the raid on the minister's house, could not find enough material to get the accused chargesheeted for trial in the court. I pointed out to the government the immensity of the crime that the police had committed in besmirching the reputation of a public figure and got the then police chief punished and finally got the file closed in the Home Department and in the Home Ministry of India. Often, in the Indian administration, I have come across ambitious officers, who in order to advance in their careers, became willing instruments in the hands of one or the other unscrupulous politician, and the administrative system has not yet evolved any system of accountability for such officers, even when exposed at any time later on.

The one matter that was causing me anxiety was the tragic march of events in Punjab. Bhindranwale was in the headlines of the newspapers in India and even abroad. He projected forcefully that the Sikhs in India had been made into second class citizens with their self-respect having been trampled under the feet of the Hindu Government and Hindu bureaucracy. He lifted the Akali political agenda, used by them to create their constituency among the Sikhs and projected that in so telling a manner that most of the Sikhs started believing in what he was saying. His speeches turned more and more into fulminations against the Hindus, who were the majority community and ridiculing leaders like Indira Gandhi. He was also a missionary who projected himself as the 'messaiah' who has come to rescue the Sikhs from their enemies and to restore their honour. He openly advocated violent ways for the redress of acts that offended the Sikh sensitivities, advising the Sikh youth to spend money on buying motorcycles and guns. He praised killers, who inspired by his fulminations against the Hindus and Sikh toadies, committed murders. He openly moved about in a caravan of vehicles full of armed Sikh youth. The inaction of the Government led people to believe that he enjoyed patronage at the highest political quarters in the country because of which he was roaming scot free in the whole of India. Biharis were one community who were very supportive of the Sikhs. They took pride in the fact that Guru Gobind Singh was born in Patna. A Sikh in Bihar was synonymous with patriotism and someone who was always in the forefront for the cause of the Hindus. I discovered that Sikhs in Patna too had an appreciation for what Bhindranwale was holding out as the post-partition Sikh psyche suffered from a complex of having been cheated from enjoying the gains of freedom of India due to manipulation of Congress leaders.

The Akali leaders, either because of demoralization or expediency, were reconciled to playing a second fiddle role in the *Dharam Yudh Morcha* that had been launched by them in 1982.

Patna happens to be one of the five places from where edicts can be issued for the Sikhs by the head priest called *Jathedar* of the Takhat Patna Saheb. Jathedar Maan Singh, a native Bihari Sikh was the head priest. The gurdwara is managed by a Committee appointed by the District Judge of Patna. The various Sikh organizations in Bihar, the SGPC, the SAD, had their nominees on the Committee in addition to three nominees of the Bihar Govemment. The Bihar Government never took any interest as to who was nominated to the Gurdwara Committee. The Committee in 1983 had Mrs. Nirlep Kaur, an Akali politician and a daughter of Gian Singh Rarewala, who flitted between the Congress and the Akalis, as it suited him. The Secretary was a serving judicial officer, Bhagat Singh Hora. I generally visited the Patna gurdwara once a week. There was one Sardar Pritam Singh Sohi, who owned a fleet of trucks. He had a big house, very near the Gurdwara in Patna City. He was a nominee of the SGPC on the Gurdwara Committee. I talked to him about getting Maan Singh to issue an edict to distance the Sikhs from Bhindranwale. I found that his understanding of Sikh religion only meant to blindly accept what was doled out by the Akali leaders or persons like Bhindranwale, who enjoyed the tacit endorsement of the Sikh community. I then spoke to Bhagat Singh Hora. He did not say anything to me in reply, but promised to check-up with Maan Singh and let me know. It seems that he consulted the President who lived in Delhi and told me that Jathedar Maan Singh was a recluse, who kept himself away from worldly events and agitations. He would not like to involve himself in any controversy. I thereafter decided to see Maan Singh personally. I went to see him at the Takhat Saheb Gurdwara. I found him to be an old man, not in full control of his faculties. The local people, particularly the Sikhs would touch his feet as they considered him to be a Saint. Apparently, he had been briefed about my visit, so I drew a blank. Meanwhile, the events moved fast, the first straw in the wind of the pent-up anti-Sikh feelings among the Hindus came from Panipat in February 1984 when Hindu mobs attacked the historic gurdwara on the G.T. Road which is associated with the visit of Guru Nanak to Panipat.

We had a visit of Indira Gandhi to Bihar on 1st May 1984, when she came to address a public rally of the INTUC affiliated trade unions. A last minute agenda was introduced in her program to address the troops at Ranchi. I had deputed the Inspector General of Police (Intelligence) to represent the State Government for her visit. He told me that in her address, Mrs. Gandhi devoted her speech, almost entirely, to the Punjab situation and her efforts to resolve the crisis. He said that he was puzzled by one exchange in the car between the Army General and Mrs. Gandhi. Mrs. Gandhi had enquired from the General as to how was his Communications. His reply that was baffling to him was "Excellent madam. We have a direct train to Amritsar from Ranchi." Later, it got deciphered when I discovered that the particular Division of the Army was earmarked for duties for Operation Blue Star in Amritsar. I felt sad when I heard about Operation Blue Star on 5-6 June 1984. I felt that it was a tragedy that was avoidable.

I blamed the Akalis and Bhindranwale for it and in a way the whole Sikh community, who permitted themselves to be led by such leaders who had brought this tragedy about. It might have politically suited Mrs. Gandhi but I could not blame her, as she acted only when the entire country came to believe that for her there was no alternative. This was the contingency about which I had forewarned the Akali leadership in December 1982 through my letter to Sardar Surjit Singh Barnala. One can say that the day for launching the Operation was wrong, as it happened to be near the Martyrdom Anniversary of the Fifth Guru, when a lot of pilgrims were present inside the Golden Temple Complex. These are operational details which must have been decided by the Army Generals, most of whom were Sikhs. I think all the Generals involved in Operation Blue Star or Operation Woodrose, were Sikhs except for one. I had a visitor a day after Operation Blue Star. The visitor was Mrs. Nirlep Kaur, who had rushed to Patna and got hold of Maan Singh to go with her to the Governor of Bihar, to protest against Operation Blue Star. Maan Singh, who had claimed to be a recluse, had meekly accompanied her. She knew me slightly. She came to see me in the Circuit House. She gleeful told me that Khalistan was around the corner. General (Retd.) Jaswant Singh Bhullar and some others, she told me, had reached USA, where shortly Khalistan was going to be declared. She virtually said that instead of worrying about the Government of India, I should worry about my future in the new set-up. She was considered to be in the higher echelons of the Akal leadership. I was left wondering by her that if the Akali leadership was so wooly headed, then God save the Sikhs. I told the Chief Minister that our failure to influence Takhat Patna Saheb had resulted in the Central Government being blamed for having committed a holocaust against the Sikhs. I looked into the constitution of the committee of management for the Gurdwara Takhat Patna Saheb and got the nominees of the Bihar Government changed. I also got a policy decision taken that in nominations to the Managing Committee the Bihari Sikhs, who had kept the torch of the Guru's teaching burning in Bihar through all the turmoil and troubles in Punjab, they should receive preference over other Sikhs who came to Bihar mainly after 1947. One of the young Sikhs, who had been a leader of the Student's Congress in Calcutta, Sardar Surinderjit Singh Ahluwalia had impressed me a lot with his intelligence, personality and behaviour. His family had set-up some ancillary industries around Barauni Oil Refinery. I got him nominated to the Takhat Sahib Managing Committee. As expected, Takhat Saheb Patna soon started singing a different tune. It seemed that some of the Akali hardliners got wind of this change. They decided to abduct Maan Singh to Calcutta, so that he remained away from the influence of the Government of Bihar. I was tipped one morning that Maan Singh was being taken by a superfast train in the morning from Patna Junction. I asked the police intelligence chief to prevent the abduction. A police officer came to report to me after the train had left Patna that they had checked the passenger list and they did not find the name of Maan Singh in the passenger list. It shocked me to know that a police officer could be so naive as to not to know that a person who was being abducted would not be travelling on his real name. I found that the train that they had selected for taking Maan Singh was a train that stopped only at Asansol in West Bengal after Patna. The police sought my permission to intercept the train before it reached Asansol. I decided to avoid unnecessary sensation to let Maan Singh reach Calcutta. Maan Singh was met at the Howrah Railway Station by Ahluwalia and the Bihar Police and he agreed to come back with them.

In my capacity as a Sikh citizen of India I had been giving my unsolicited advice to the Government of India on various Punjab related issues. The Akalis were a political party with a political agenda but they operated from gurdwaras. I could see that Mrs. Gandhi was handling the Akali agitation in a manner that the Akalis got isolated and while negotiating with them she wanted to ensure that they could get no political mileage out of the various concessions that sometimes she announced on the demands of the Shiromani Akali Dal. She drafted almost everyone who felt concerned about Punjab in her negotiations with the SAD including the Communist leader Harkishan Singh Surjeet and Sardar Swaran Singh, the veteran Akali leader, who had moved over to the Congress in 1957 when the SAD had announced a merger with the Congress for their political agenda. She decided to visit Gurdwara Bangla Saheb in Delhi to announce conceding most of the religious demands of the Akalis in order to give credit to the Delhi Sikh leader Santokh Singh, aligned with the Congress and a confidant of Bhindranwale. I cannot fail to notice that the views of the bureaucrats like Sir Malcolm Hailey, who had successfully handled the Akali *morchas* without permitting them from gaining any political mileage from the situation must have influenced Government of India. I wrote to the Home Secretary, Mr. M.K.K. Wali, after Operation Blue Star, that there was a lot of anger against the Government of India among the Sikhs but also an overwhelming support for Operation Blue Star in the rest of India. I drew a parallel with the situation that the Mughal administraion faced after defeating Banda Bahadur. A sizeable section among the Sikhs, that came to be known as the 'Tatt Khalsa' had disassociated from Banda Bahadur and they had been rewarded by the administration. The Mughal rulers calculated that after the defeat of Banda Bahadur they did not need to placate the 'Tatt Khalsa' and they started prosecuting them for the excesses committed by them when they had joined Banda Bahadur. This j forced the Khalsa to the wall and they decided to fight the Mughal regime in Punjab. The struggle lasted almost three decades but during this period they got the Mughals uprooted in Punjab. I also wrote a paper titled "*Wither Khalsa*" for circulation among the Sikhs so that a process of introspection could be initiated among the Sikh community after the holocaust of the Operation Blue Star.

My batchmate and friend, Mr. K. Ramanujam, was the Director at the L.B.S. National Academy of Administration at Mussoorie. He invited me to visit the Academy for a series of lectures to the IAS trainees. I had just given my introductory lecture when I got a wireless message from the Government of Bihar that I must return to Patna post haste as jawans at the Sikh Regimental Centre at Ramgarh, having been upset with Operation Blue Star, had revolted, marshalling whatever transport they could lay their hands on and moved by road to reach Amritsar post haste after killing their Commanding Officer, Brigadier Puri. It was a case of impressionable minds of young recruits being carried away by the rhetoric of Bhindranwale, who made such irresponsible statements in Punjab saying that if the police or army was ordered to enter the Golden Temple complex, the soldiers should turn the guns on the officers giving them such orders. The Sikh soldiers had carried their weapons and ammunition with them. It was not possible for the Bihar police to take them on. They were allowed almost to cross the Bihar border beyond which troops commanded by the Sikh Sub-area Commander, Brigadier N.P.S. Bal from Dinapore near Patna intercepted them before they could reach Mughal Sarai. Their leader realized, when the troops had surrounded them, that it would be a suicide for them to fight the regular troops. He advised his followers to surrender and shot himself dead. There were other Sikh troops too that had revolted here and there in India but the bulk of the Army including the Sikh troops remained loyal. The Army had apparently debated about the attack on the Golden Temple and a strong group of Generals was opposed to the attack but General Vaidya, the Army Chief and General Sunderji, the Chief of the Western Command, gave a green signal for it. All the Sikh soldiers who had rebelled were sacked and court-martialled. As expected from their past conduct, the SAD did nothing to defend the overenthusiastic Sikh recruits and soldiers, who had risked their lives and careers on the call of the politicians, to whom the emotional appeals to the Sikh soldiers was nothing more than an additional weapon in their armoury to fight the Government of India. Many of them served life imprisonments and for all one knows some may still be rotting somewhere in various jails in India. The price that these soldiers have paid is far more than what the rebels of the Indian Army who joined the Indian National Army of Subhas Chandra Bose had paid. Jawaharlal Nehru and the Congress leaders had roused the whole nation to defend the INA soldiers with the result that they got rehabilitated and got their names included as freedom fighters. One off and on hears about the plight of the 'Blue Star' Sikh rebels from some odd mention in magazines like the '*Spokesman*' of Chandigarh where they are described as the '*dharmi fauji*'.

I visited Delhi in July. I had functioned as the Additional Chief Secretary for a few months. The Chief Minister was waiting for a suitable moment to induct me as the Chief Secretary but the prospect did not appeal to me. I would surely be hurting K.K. Srivastava, who was sought to be sidelined. I have generally, in my career avoided treading on anyone's toes or depriving a colleague of his due. I thought that I should try my luck again for a deputation under the Central Government. I saw Rao Saheb Krishnaswamy, the Cabinet Secretary and reminded him of his promise to get me fixed up in Delhi when I had come back from ICRISAT. He promised to help me since I had completed my prescribed cooling-off stay in the state which was one and a half years at the level of my seniority. I also went calling on officers in the Ministry of Home Affairs. I met my friend and batchmate, Mr. Surat Das Srivastava. He had a very friendly temperament. He was delighted to meet me. He said that he was the Secretary of a High Powered Committee that was going into the causes of the failure of Punjab administration leading to Operation Blue Star and they were to suggest measures for strengthening the Punjab administration. The Committee was chaired by Mr. R.V. Subramanian, a retired IAS officer, and it had two retired IPS officers as its members in addition to the Secretary. He introduced me to the other members of the High Powered Committee. I did not realize at that time that my meeting, by coincidence, would turn out to be an interview for me for the position of the Chief Secretary of Punjab, as one of their important recommendation was about induction of an IAS officer with a proven track record from outside Punjab as the Chief Secretary of Punjab. After the Committee submitted their report in early August, the Chairman of the Committee was appointed the Senior Advisor to the Governor of Punjab, with a brief that he would be calling the shots in all matters concerning Punjab. He was picked up for the assignment by P.C. Alexander. He did not know anything about Punjab or the Sikhs nor was I impressed about his grasp of the law and order affairs. This was a sad coincidence that in 1984 none of the persons who were heading the administration had a grasp of the Punjab problem nor did they have the reflexes of a successful District Magistrate.

It looked that the army operation in Punjab was like the use of a sledgehammer to swat a fly. One side consequence was that the Army started broadcasting live the hymns being sung in the Golden Temple, which was one of the demands of the Akalis that stood conceded, but the SGPC had dragged their feet in implementing the same. The SGPC *granthis* were not attending to their duties after Operation Blue Star, so the direct broadcast was started through *granthis* of the Army. Giani Zail Singh, the President of India, visited the Golden Temple Complex when dead bodies were still floating in the holy sarovar. Seeing the destruction all round and the damage to the Akal Takhat, he visibly cried.The first angry letter of protest in the press that I saw was from Sardar Saran Singh, my senior colleague from Bihar. In his letter to the editor of the *Statesman*, Calcutta which described the operation more or less a carnage. I found that the very next month he was presiding over a meeting of the Sikh diaspora in New York that was attended by General Bhullar, who was touted as the new messiah, who would organize the Sikhs and lead them to their salvation. There was a lot of sound and fury in the New York meeting about which later on some pro-Khalistan Sikhs said that the meeting was hijacked by the agents of the Indian Intelligence to derail the movement for Khalistan. Sardar Buta Singh tried to take the wind out of the sails of the Akalis by giving a call for a 'Sarbat Khalsa' meet. The Sarbat Khalsa used to be the gathering of all the Khalsa during the 'Tatt Khalsa' days and the Misl period in the 18th century, on the occasion of *Diwali* and *Baisakhi*. The Sikhs in general ignored this call. A hired crowd more or less, was shown on the media as having participated in it. To give some credibility among the Sikhs for this *sarkari* show, Jathedar Maan Singh was intercepted during his journey back to Patna from Calcutta. Sardar S. S. Ahluwalia got him to detrain at Barauni, his home place where a special plane sent by Sardar Buta Singh, took him to the *Sarbat Khalsa* meet. The *Ardas* for the *Sarbat Khalsa* was said by Jathedar Maan Singh. I was amused at seeing this happen after only about a month of having pleaded with me that he was a recluse, who would avoid participating in such affairs.

18

As Chief Secretary, Punjab

I got a telephone call from the Cabinet Secretary to see him in Delhi. I was delighted on hearing from him as I thought that at last I was being considered for some Delhi posting. I met him in his office and thanked him for his having kept his promise to me. He told me that it was not for Delhi that I was being considered but it was for the post of the Chief Secretary of Punjab. I quickly saw the logic of it and in my mind calculated that I would be the senior most IAS officer in Punjab. My batchmate, Mr. Prem Kumar Kathpalia, had joined the IAS as an officer senior to me but he fell down in the order of merit as he had failed in one paper in the final examination for the IAS probationers. Little did I know that such a coincidence was going to matter when time came. Rao Saheb asked me to see Mr. P.C. Alexander, the Secretary to the Prime Minister. Mr. P.C. Alexander appeared to be someone who had clear superior airs about himself. He asked me that I must be having a large number of relatives in Punjab, being a *Jat* Sikh. I mumbled that I had some relatives but not many, as I could not make out the reason for his having made such an observation.

It however, came out a bit later that one of the objectives of sending me to Punjab was that the Government wanted to give a Sikh friendly impression to the people for which my salience as Chief Secretary would be of help. I went back home after calling on Mr. P.C. Alexander. I was to fly back to Patna by the next morning flight.

I got a call from Rao Saheb, well past 10 p.m. in the night, asking me as to what I was doing the next day. I told him that I was going back to Patna. He told me to get my booking of the plane cancelled without telling me the reason for it. There was no time for me to get the booking cancelled but I did not show up for the flight. I got a call again from Rao Saheb that I had an appointment with Mrs. Gandhi at 12:30 p.m. in her office in the Parliament House. I was told to present myself at the appointed time and I was asked to report to R.K. Dhawan, who sat on a side of her office. I duly reached there and found that a number of persons were waiting in a big room to see Mrs. Gandhi. I decided to not to go to R.K. Dhawan. I gave my visiting card to one attendant who took the same inside and I waited to be called. An attendant called me after about half an hour. I entered through the door that opened directly into the office of Mrs. Gandhi. She shocked me by coming to the door to receive me. She escorted me to my chair while smiling all the time. She was exuding all charm and grace. She told me that she was happy over my selection for the tough assignment of the Chief Secretary of Punjab at a time like the present one. She said that she was very concerned about Punjab and she assured me that she had tried her best to find a solution to the Punjab problem. She said that one of the handicaps of being in public life was that one got blamed for everything this or that way, I agreed with her in that observation. She had put me completely at ease during her conversation. I happened to mention a recent controversy in which her name had figured. It was a derogatory reference to her in the book of an Indian expatriate author, Mr. Salman Rushdie. She laughed and said that when the writing appeared people said that if she did not respond to the insinuation made against her, it meant that she accepted what had been slated in the book. She decided to sue the author for damages, on which the author recanted and came out with an unqualified apology. She said that thereafter, she was being accused of giving unnecessary importance to a not very well-known writer. She further said that Salman Rushdie had tried to insinuate that she had neglected her husband, Mr. Feroze Gandhi, and she was critical about his eating habits. She perhaps had looked at my somewhat fat frame when I had entered her room. She smilingly said that Feroze, like the Punjabis, was fond of good food that was doing him no good. She had been, therefore, telling him that he should not let food spoil his figure. Sukhdev, when she heard about the remark that was made by her, said to me that Mrs. Gandhi's remark was equally addressed to me. Perhaps she was right. Mrs. Gandhi said to me that she was disappointed with the Punjab politicians and administration in not being of any help in resolving the Punjab imbroglio. I was told that I had only ten minutes with the Prime Minister when I was getting in. We had already spent more than 30 minutes together. A number of times her staff would peep from outside to check as to what was going on. They must have been puzzled on seeing both of us smiling and chatting like old buddies. She gave me an impression that at that particular time I was the most important person in the world for her. It was I who started fidgeting when we had been closeted together for forty minutes. She told me to go to Punjab and study the situation there and if I could come up with something constructive, she would be willing to give it a try. It was on this note that we parted. She again escorted me to the door but to the door that opened into the room of R.K. Dhawan, who received me very warmly and congratulated me on my appointment as Chief Secretary of Punjab. It was my first one-to-one meeting with Mrs. Gandhi and it turned out to be the last too. Unless I am grossly mistaken in my understanding of human character, I can never accept that there could be anything diabolical about her, as some of her detractors try to present. My selection for the position of Chief Secretary of Punjab also indicated that it were the small men around her whom she trusted who were mostly responsible for bringing a bad name to her through their overzealousness rather than any of her actions. I was also asked to meet Mr. Narashima Rao, who was the Home Minister. I called on him the same evening. We just exchanged pleasantries. It was obvious that he had no hand in what had taken place in Punjab nor was he kept in the picture as to what was going on or what was being thought about for the future. I flew back to Patna the next day. My orders appointing me as Chief Secretary of Punjab reached Patna the next day. The Bihar Chief Minister congratulated me and I was given a warm send off by my colleagues and friends on 16th August when I departed for Chandigarh from Patna Airport.

At Chandigarh I was allotted a suite of rooms in Punjab Bhavan. The upkeep of the guest house and the food served was excellent. I went to the Secretariat and assumed charge of the Chief Secretary because Mr. Vasudeva, my predecessor had already proceeded on leave. The Punjab cadre officers, other than my trainees, did not like my posting, as they thought that it was a reflection on their performance. Punjab was a sought-after state for the ICS during the British period and the Punjab school of administrators had made a name for themselves in maintaining law and order though the Punjab officers faced much less challenge than the IAS officers in Bihar. The Akalis had excelled in launching and sustaining agitations against the government and the administration had developed no expertise in dealing with those law and order problems but no one in Punjab, after 1947, had applied his mind towards tackling this problem at the administrative level. This aspect was left to the political executive, that too mostly of the Central Government. I later surmised that the British colonial set-up had treated the relationship with the Sikhs as something very sensitive to be dealt only in the Central Government except for the day-to-day matters, which were left to be handled by the Punjab officials. The new government after 1947 brought about no change in the policy. I was surprised to find that the Punjab Home Department had no proper file in which the stalwarts of the Punjab cadre might have gone into to identify the causes or into the strategy of handling the frequent Akali upheavals. I could lay my hands on some scrappy notes from the Police Intelligence, mostly summing up all that had taken place up to a particular time and what could be anticipated in the immediate future. There was one paper of the time of Sardar Darbara Singh, who became the Chief Minister after Giani Zail Singh got drafted for the Central Government in 1980. This paper was drafted in the office of the Chief Minister and it was in the nature of almost superficial comments on the 45 demands of the Akalis for the acceptance of which the *Dharam Yudh Morcha* of 1982 was launched. I drew a similar blank about the records from the office of the Governor. I had to play by the ear as the situations developed. Mr. B.D. Pande had resigned as the Governor and in his place came Mr. Satarawala, a Parsi ex-Army Officer, who had worked in the Asiad with Rajiv Gandhi. He seemed to be a non-entity and only a figurehead. Punjab, I found, was run on hotlines of telephone from Delhi, by persons close to Mrs. Gandhi. I could make out that the main person was Arun Nehru. Even the Amritsar Congress leader, Raghunandan Lal Bhatia, had a hotline to Delhi which was installed for him in the Circuit House, Amritsar. The Congress leader, Mr. Fotedar, also seemed to be in the group and so was Mr. Arun Singh, a buddy of Rajiv Gandhi from the Doon School. He was a scion of the Kapurthala rulers' family in Punjab, married to a foreigner.

Mr. R.V. Subramanian had joined as the Senior Advisor and was showing off everywhere that he was really the boss. We had Mr. Surinder Nath, an IPS officer of Punjab, as an Advisor to the Governor along with General Gauri Shankar from the Army. We met in the Governor's office everyday at about 11 a.m. to exchange notes and once a week as a formal Governor in Council where certain policy matters were cleared as per the Rules of Executive Business. When we were not meeting as Governor in Council, we had those who had come on deputation to Punjab like me. I could sense that whoever was pulling the strings from Delhi, the policy was to be tough vis-à-vis the Akalis and the Sikhs. We had to make an appointment of Legal Remembrancer of Punjab. Mr. Subramanian ensured that the decision on the subject was taken on a day, when I was out of station, as the senior most judicial officer, who could be selected for this rather sensitive appointment was a Sikh, Mr. K.S. Bhalla. Mr. Nehra, who was a Hindu and next in order of seniority was selected behind my back after a hush-hush consultation with Mr. Surinder Nath got the tenure of Mr. JS Grewal, the vice chancellor of the Guru Nanak Dev University, terminated as he had got himself identified as a pro-Akali ideologue. We had to prepare a panel of names of IPS officers who could be considered for appointment as Deputy Inspector Generals. We cleared 6 or 7 names on the basis of their performance records. Among those cleared was the name of one J.S. Chahal, who was a devout Sikh. When Bhindranwale had surrendered for interrogation by the police in the murder case of Lala Jagat Narain, Bhindranwale had laid down a condition that he would surrender to only an Amritdhari Sikh police officer. The choice had fallen on J.S. Chahal for taking him into custody. The panel file had to go to the Governor through R.V. Subramaniam for his approval. Mr. Subramaniam would not clear the file. The Director General of Police was under pressure for placement of some of the officers whose names were in the panel. He went to Subramaniam for ealy clearance of the file. He agreed to clear the same if the name of J.S. Chahal was not there in the panel. K.S. Dhillon came to me with the file when Mr. Chahal was not there in the panel. K.S. Dhillon came to me with the file when I was busy in another meeting. He sought my concurrence to remove the name of Mr. Chahal from the list in order to get the promotion process started for the other police officers. I agreed to that in that weak moment which meant endorsing injustice to an honest and a competent officer. I tried to undo the damage and recalled the file for reconsideration but by that time the list got notified. I had only to reconcile myself for having been a party in the commission of a wrong.

It was peculiar situation in Punjab, where on the one hand the government was talking in terms of being keen about applying soothing balm for the Sikh psyche that was hurt by Operation Blue Star and on the other hand more repression was advised against the Akalis and their sympathizers, and consequently against the Sikhs. The Punjab Government was pulled-up if there was any report of defiance of the government by the Sikhs, particularly by the youth. Some of the young men started wearing *Kesri* or yellow coloured turbans as a symbol of protest against the government. The police was instructed to arrest those who were found wearing *kesri* turbans. I brought up the subject in a meeting of Governor in Council. I said that there was no law that banned the wearing of *kesri* turbans and the action of the police was illegal. I, therefore proposed the British way to deal who dealt with the Akali movement in the twenties. The proposal came as a shock to the non-Sikh members in the Governor in Council. They realised that such actions of the Punjab government made the government look ridiculous in the eyes of the rest of the country apart from generating hostility against the government among the Sikhs. I was asked to brief the press after the meeting, that there was no ban on the wearing of the *kesri* turban in Punjab. My statement was carried prominently in all the newspapers. The government encouraged me to appear on TV and address the press on all issues, since I was the only Sikh face that could be legitimately presented by the Punjab Government. I found that my TV exposure was noticed by the people and the impact on the Sikh audience was good. I made this discovery in New York in 1985 on a visit there as the Union Health Secretary. After checking-in late in the night, I went out for a stroll. I found a store open that had a young Sikh boy looking after it. He greeted me and enquired if I happened to be S.S. Dhanoa. I was shocked to hear this question. I asked him as to how he could recognize me. He told me that he had just entered the USA, as an illegal immigrant via Mexico and he was working as the night salesman in that store. He said that he had seen me on the TV in Punjab. Like everyone, newly coming to Punjab, I visited Amritsar in my first week in Punjab after arrival. The Governor had allowed me to use his plane for the visit. I visited the Golden Temple Complex. The Complex was still under the control of the government and the badly damaged Akal Takhat was under repair at the cost of the Central Government, apparently under a cover provided by Santa Singh, the Jathedar of the Buddha Dal of the Nihangs. Sardar Buta Singh was providing the necessary funds and the gold required for the reconstruction and the restoration of the Akal Takhat. I saw as to how massive was the Army operation and the damage that was caused all around. One peculiar omission of the Army was to have left the backside of the Akal Takhat building as unguarded from where about three hundred extremists had made good their escape on the night of 5-6 June. I visited the Durgiana Temple, which the Hindus of Amritsar had got built, after the Sikhs under the Singh Sabha influence, had removed the Hindu idols from the Hindus of Amritsar till this development did not feel the necessity of having a separate temple dedicated exclusively to the Hindu deities. The common Hindu for his worship considers it enough of a religious observance if he could make an obeisance before an idol or a picture of any of the gods or goddesses. The Hindus of Amritsar had gone to Banaras, for advice, to Pandit Madan Mohan Malviya, the founder of the Banaras Hindu University who enjoyed a lot of goodwill among the Sikhs. He advised the Hindus to put up a separate temple for those Hindus who felt the necessity of worshipping the Hindu deities exclusively. The Durgiana Temple is an exact replica of the Golden Temple except that it has doors opening only on three sides. It is to demonstrate that Hindus and Sikhs were equal in one's eyes, that all dignitaries coming to Punjab visited Durgiana Temple also when visiting Amritsar for the first time. I also visited the Jallianwala Bagh Memorial for the victims of the firing while visiting as many districts as possible to have a feel of the administration and the people. Moving about in Punjab one could discern an undercurrent of polarisation between the Hindus and the Sikhs. The Sikhs made no secret of their sense of humiliation about all that had happened. There was bitterness among the Sikhs that the Punjabi Hindu did not feel for their Sikh brothers in distress. The Hindu-Sikh divide had reached even the IAS officers. The Sikh IAS officers has started meeting in separate groups. It was in this context that four Sikh officers of the Punjab IAS cadre applied for casual leave to participate in the '*kar sewa*' of the Akal Takhat that had been destroyed during the Army action. When Bhindranwale was calling the shots from the Golden Temple Complex, the Sikh officers who had access to him were placed in strategic positions. P.S. Bhinder, IPS, was brought as the Director General of Police. Mr. Gurdev Singh was posted as the Deputy Commissioner of Amritsar. When Bhindranwale was to be technically arrested in the case of the murder of Lala Jagat Narain, J.S. Chahal, IPS, an Amritdhari Sikh, was brought in to carry out the arrest. All these officers were at the receiving end after Operation Blue Star. It was a frequent refrain with the Sikh IAS officers of the Punjab cadre that their Hindu colleagues were not loyal and committed to the interests of Punjab, as the Hindus of Punjab had disowned their mother tongue. This was a false impression as I discovered that facts were to the contrary. When I was on way to join Punjab, I had met the Resident Commissioner of Punjab Government in Delhi, who had told me that the Army, on storming the Golden Temple complex had found in one of the rooms, a few young girls who had been kept confined there by the extremists, a canard spread by some mischievous persons in Punjab, which the senior officer had chosen to believe and apprise me, the would be Chief Secretary! It was quite plain that the condition and morale of the civil services was anything but healthy in Punjab.

Punjab was a much smaller state in area and population compared to Bihar. The population was a little more than fifteen million, about 75% being in rural areas divided in about 12 thousand villages. It was, however, the state that was a leader in agricultural production and the highest per capita income in India, being more than double of Bihar. All the villages were connected by road and all the villages had electricity. Punjab had more than 90 percent of land under irrigation. The population of Punjab after reorganization in 1966 was about 60 percent Sikh and about 40 percent Hindu. About 25 percent population were scheduled castes who were earlier classified as untouchables. The Hindus and Sikhs had been living peacefully. Many Hindus considered the Sikh Gurus to be the Avatars in line with Ram and Krishna, who came to save Hinduism from the onslaught of Islam. It was a practice in many families to have the eldest son baptised as the Khalsa. The British policy of reservations in government jobs and preference for the Sikhs in the recruitment for the Army and the stridency of the Arya Samajists favouring strictly, back to Tara Singh a Hindu converted to Sikhism, was acclaimed unanimously as the leader. One could say that Operation Blue Star was a major surgical procedure to cure the persisting pain in the body politic of India and in retrospect it has to be festering sore. It is sad reflection on the capacity and statesmanship of the Indian national leadership that this problem had continued to defy a mutually acceptable solution.

When we look at the general picture of the Sikhs in India, we find that as a community they have fared better than perhaps any other community. We have had a Sikh Prime Minister and for the first time a Sikh Chief of the Army. The Sikhs are there in every walk of life, holding prominent positions. It also remains a fact that most of the Sikhs believe that they have been denied their due and the national leadership has even gone back on the solemn promises which they had made to the Sikhs before Independence. Such allegations were formally made on the floor of the Constituent Assembly by leaders like Sardar Hukam Singh and others. The allegations attracted a forceful response from Sardar Patel in the Constituent Assembly and it is worth quoting from his speech in the Constituent Assembly on 14th October, 1949. "We are not the people to break pledges. Every sympathy and every consideration will be shown to the Sikh community because it is located in a particular area, it is a small community, and yet it is brave, virile and it can stand on its own against anybody. Do not break that spirit by continuously saying, "we are injured, we are helpless, we are in a minority, we are hopeless, we can not do anything". That kind of psychology will injure the community itself and not others, and injuring the community means injuring the nation."

Despite the above exchange and the lack of facts to support such accusation of discrimination, the impression has continued to persist among the Sikhs that the community had been denied justice in free India. This is the space, in the Sikh mind that various aspirants for leadership of the Sikhs, have been trying to fill. When Bhindranwale was succeeded by the Khadkus that is the extremists and the terrorists, the Sikhs turned to them in the hope that they would secure the long awaited redress for them. This is what keeps the phantom of Khalistan alive.

So long as the British ruled India, the Sikhs were happy with the somewhat preferred treatment that they received but after their departure, a feeling got generated among the Sikhs that Muslims had got what they had wanted and had a country of their own in Pakistan, and for them and also as it appeared to everyone that Hindus would be ruling India but the Sikhs, who for some time enjoyed the status of being the third party in the negotiations for the transfer of power with the British, were left high and dry. The Sikh politicians, particularly Akalis, started fashioning a strategy to retrieve the lost ground. The demand for reorganisation of Punjab on the basis of mother tongue got generated from the situation that after the partition an area had emerged that had a narrow Sikh majority which could provide the Sikh state denied to them by the British because before 1947 there was not a single district of Punjab where Sikhs were in majority. It is mentioned in the biography of Master Tara Singh, the sole and undisputed leader of the Sikhs for more than three decades that he read in some book about Israel when he was imprisoned under orders of Sardar Patel for his leading a morcha against the government. A minority group like the Jews could carve out a state for themselves was something unknown to him. He recalled with some remorse that he was not aware about it when he was negotiating with the British Government, otherwise he would have pressed a demand for an independent state on behalf of the Sikhs. With Arya Samaj and the euologising of the Vedas by scholars, Hindus feel somewhat superior to the Sikhs to whom they had earlier been looking for defence decided to oppose them at every step. They would not concede easily that only Gurumukhi script should be used for Punjabi because before partition, Punjabi could be written in Urdu or Devnagri. If the Akalis demanded a smaller linguistic Punjab, they came out with a demand for a bigger Punjab called Maha Punjab. The Akalis demanded that everyone must declare Punjabi as their mother tongue as every one spoke Punjabi. It was countered with the argument that for the Hindus their cultural language was Hindi and spoken Punjabi was a mere dialect for them. The two communities who had stood together for the last three centuries started falling apart and drifting away from each other. The politicians who had an axe to grind on both the sides poured oil on this smouldering heat. This could be summed up as the genesis of the Punjab tangle. The Akalis with their expertise in organising 'morchas', from their base in gurdwaras forced one concession and the other till they were able to have the present Punjab carved out on the basis of the Sikh numbers. Still the Sikh-Hindu ratio of population in Punjab could never give a secure majority in an election if the party appealed only to the Sikhs. This was the cause of the frustration among the Akali leaders and the aspirants for '*raj karega khalsa*' or the Khalsa shall rule. Sadly, one has to admit that the Indian state and the Sikh ideologues so far have failed to come up with a praxis in which this frustration among the Sikhs could be taken care of.

Punjab is one of the most orderly and peaceful states in India. The incidence of crime is one of the lowest. Rioting, taken as a symptom of a disturbed civil society is an exception, so is the incidence of robbery and dacoity. Atrocities against the untouchables are much less heard of in Punjab. The elections to various fora such as village panchayats or to Punjab Assembly or the Parliament have been orderly and peaceful. Urban rioting or communal rioting in Punjab had been rare. There had been one case of rioting by the students in Moga years back in which the police had to resort to firing. The Sikhs are one community who have never become a mob whatever might have been the provocation. I am sure from the record, in the 1919 disturbances, there must not have been any Sikh among the mobs that were reported to have turned out in the streets of Amritsar and other cities in Punjab. In a free for all, individual Sikhs or some Sikh '*jathas*' might have participated in killings and lootings but never as mobs, even during 1947. The great contribution made by Guru Gobind Singh has been the fostering of a strong sense of identity among the Sikhs that comes in the way of becoming anonymous which is essential to mob formation. The Army was called to aid the civil authority through an enigmatic letter addressed to the C-in-C of the Western Command from Mr. A.S. Pooni, IAS, the then Home Secretary, dated the 02 June 1984. The wording of the letter was, "I am directed to say that the Government of Punjab considers it necessary to call in the Army in aid of civil power in view of the deteriorating law and order situation in the state. Immediate action may please be taken in this regard." The letter seems to have been issued on the direction of someone in the Central Government as the state was under the President's rule.

The Government of India need not have resorted to the subterfuge of asking the Home Secretary of Punjab to make a request for the Army aid to civil power, made on the 02 June 1984 when eight Divisions of the Indian Army had already moved in to take positions in various places in Punjab. A curfew was imposed from the 03 June on the whole of Punjab.

The Central Government chose not to spell out the real reasons or objectives for the army action. The Army, which had been inducted in Punjab, was mostly non-Punjabi, although a sprinkling of Punjabi units was also there. The soldiers had spread out all over Punjab. In order to guide them about their task a circular called '*baat cheet*' meaning small talk was issued in which it was said that among the general populace of Punjab the soldiers should be particularly wary of the Sikhs who were '*amritdhari*' as they might most likely turn out to be the extremists. The circular had got leaked out and it caused a furore in Punjab. The Army immediately withdrew their circular and apologised their lapse but the damage was done. What the circular said was partly correct as most of the followers of Bhindranwale were '*amritdhari*' but all '*amritdharis*' were not extremists. There were many units of the Central Reserve Police that had been called for duty and most of them were Hindus. We came across cases where Punjabi Hindus felt more secure if for their security they had contingents of the CRP in place of the Punjab Police and in some sporadic cases there was an exchange of fire between a picket of the Punjab Police and the CRP. There were sporadic cases of selective killings of the Hindus by the suspected Sikh extremists. It was observed that when some important Hindu leader was killed there were spontaneous mob violence committed by the Hindus. It happened when Choudhari Balbir Singh was killed in Hoshiarpur.

However, there was no reaction in kind against the Sikhs when the World Sikh Conference that was called by the Akalis who were not in jail for 2.9.1984 at Gurdwara Shahidan at Amritsar as a counterblast to the 'Sarbat Khalsa' show of Buta Singh for which the Sikh High Priests had excommunicated him. The Punjab Government did everything to prevent it, short of banning it. There was strict checking of trains and buses all over. Tractors and trucks carrying passengers were impounded. Movement on the roads at Amritsar was restricted by passing orders under Section 144 of the Criminal Procedure Code banning assembly of five or more persons in public places. All the pent up anger of the Sikhs about Operation Blue Star, it was found an expression in making the Conference a success. The Sikh house owners in the neighbourhood of the gurdwara broke down their compound walls to enable visitors to reach the gurdwara as the police had blocked the road. More than 50,000 people collected to join the Conference, making it a grand success for the Akalis, virtually making the Akalis and the Sikhs synonymous. One important decision of the conference was that the Sikh High Priests would lead a march of the Sikhs to take over the Golden Temple and the Akal Takhat if the shrines were not handed over to the High Priests by the Government. The Governor and the Advisors to the Governor were summoned to Delhi and given a dressing down for their failure to stop the Conference about which the Punjab Government had been alerted beforehand. I was excluded from the group going to Delhi. I learnt about the dressing down in Delhi in the next meeting of the Governor in Council after their return from Delhi when postmortem of the event was done. The Director General of Police was accused of incompetence. I intervened to say that the general upsurge that was observed during the Conference was such where the police could do nothing except to book the leaders for some later day prosecution. I explained that it was the settled policy for the law and order enforcement agencies all over. General Gauri later busied itself in preparing a report for the Government of India where the whole attempt was to show that only about 15,000 people had responded to the call for the World Sikh Conference. The men/women sitting on hotlines in Delhi had to be assuaged.

The Army action in Punjab must have had considerable planning behind it. Between 5th and 7th June, during the two nights apart from the action in the Golden Temple complex, 37 Gurdwaras, 5 Mandirs and one Masjid were raided and searched by the Army. The Army also undertook a parallel operation of search and apprehend called the Operation Woodrose, targeting the young Sikh extremists in the border districts of mainly Gurdaspur and Amritsar. This operation drove a large number of the youngsters among the Sikhs to seek shelter in Pakistan where they were welcomed by the ISI with open arms. Many of the youngsters escaped to wherever they could go in India or abroad. One such young man called Chhinda had escaped to a village in Ropar district and became a tubewell operator. He lived in an operator's hut on the farm outside the village. It was alleged that he was eliminated in a false police encounter. I happened to visit Ropar at that time. Sant Ajit Singh who was the President of the district Akali Dal came to see me with a delegation of the villagers. They handed over to me a written petition in which these allegations were made. A news item about the allegation had appeared in the daily *Tribune* also. I ordered the Deputy Commissioner, Mr. Kailey, to hold an enquiry into the alleged incident and report to me. Mr. Izhar Alam, who was the Senior Superintendent of Police, saw me in the evening and what he said to me came as a shock. He said that Mr. Surender Nath, the Advisor to the Governor had told the district chiefs of the police that wherever they came across some suspicious character or a fugitive, they should eliminate such persons and show an encounter with the police on paper. I told him that I was not aware of any policy of the sort that Surender Nath might have told him about. I had simply received a complaint on which I considered it my duty to order an enquiry. The action of redressal or otherwise on the complaint would depend on the report that the Deputy Commissioner was to send to me in due course. Technically, my reply to Izhar Alam and the action taken by me was correct but the confession of the police chief about someone having been killed without due process of law left me uneasy. Punjab had been solving their serious breakdowns of the law and order in this fashion had been in vogue from 1950 or so, when dacoity had become widespread, in what was then known as PEPSU. The Central Government had to intervene after the imposition of the President's rule which was perhaps the first President's rule in the country under the new Constitution. Mr. P.S. Rao, ICS, was the Advisor to the Raj Pramukh (Governor). He gave a free hand to the police and in less than six months normalcy had got restored. I ran in to him in Hyderabad where he had settled after his retirement from the service. I asked him as to how did he perform such a miracle. P.S. Rao laughed and said that no miracle was involved in it. He said that he had called Sardar Gurdial Singh I.P., the Inspector General of Police to work out some strategy for tackling the dacoity menace. The dacoits had become so bold that they attacked a group of officers coming from a party late at night on the Nabha-Patiala highway and abducted the wife of an Army Major. Gurdial Singh told him that if he was given two months and a free hand against the suspected dacoits and their harbourers, he could vouchsafe that there would be no dacoits. Rao said that he accepted his condition with a rider that if any time it came to his notice that the police had gone against some innocent person, he would not spare anyone including the Inspector General himself. The same technique was used by the Punjab Police against the 'naxalites' who had become a menace in the sixties when Badal was the Chief Minister. The action of the Ropar police was in line with the tradition of resorting to an extra-judicial process to tackle their law and order problem. Apparently, the extremist violence got tackled by having given a free hand to tackle it to Mr. K.P.S. Gill, the Director General of the Punjab Police by Sardar Beant Singh, the Chief Minister of Punjab.

Mr. Rameshinder Singh, who had come on deputation from the West Bengal cadre, had mentioned in his confidential report about a case where a section of the Army had indulged in the looting of money from a *'kar sewa' dera,* and in order to cover their trail they had killed a Sikh baba and some of his associates in cold blood. The concerned file never came back from the Governor. I am still not sure if I should have done something more in this case. Such extra-judicial measures to mete out an executive justice became necessary in states like Punjab because the judicial system failed. No witness would come to testify that the occurrence was seen by him and no judge would be willing to punish a murderer if no one came forward to depose in the case before him. Professor Tewari, a Congress leader, considered to be pro-Sikh having married a pretty Sikh *Jat* girl, was shot down by two extremists who had come to his house as students visiting their teacher when he was having a cup of bed tea and Mrs. Tewari had gone to make tea for the visitors. She had seen the visitors, yet she did not name them before the police for fear of the safety of her family. That was the reason that the Human Rights groups and the higher judiciary generally tend to gloss over. I am quite clear that I could not have given such orders for extra legal remedies for the Punjab problem because it violated the norm that I adopted for myself when I joined the IAS that I shall do nothing that later on I could not own up in writing but I am also not able to suggest as to what else could be done alternatively to solve the problem.

I had remained outside Punjab in my service career. My coming to Punjab was a surprise to me, as well as to my acquaintances and relatives in Punjab. I happened to be the Chief Secretary when there was President's rule with the bureaucracy ruling the roost. I was flooded with all sorts of requests for favours. I decided for myself that I would generally try to help everyone who came to me with some problem that he or she was facing but I would not listen to anyone who came to recommend some other's case. A number of my friends were disappointed that I could not grant them even small favours for their friends or relatives. One of my college roommate of Amritsar, Sewa Singh, was so upset with my negative response that he stopped speaking to me after that. Another of my roommates, Sajjan Singh Kishanpuri, was a Deputy Director in the Education Department. He had a number of corruption charges against him in the vigilance section. He approached me to help him. I saw his file and decided to do nothing about it. He went to my wife's sister Sarjeet, a devout sort of a person and cried before her that I was not being helpful to him as I was a bit afraid of the Anti-Sikh Central Government and therefore, I was avoiding helping him who was being victimised by his communal Hindu boss. She started pestering me taking his brief as a case of providing a legitimate redress to an innocent Sikh government employee. I had a relook at his case and found his assertion to be not wholly true. I did not quite clear him from the charges but I reduced the severity of the charges which enabled him to get away with some minor penalty. He later became the Director of Education. He had quite a bad reputation in that assignment. A friend who knew both of us blamed me for sparing a corrupt official as he was once with me in the college. The boy from Gharuan, Harnek Singh, who used to drag me to school when I was inclined to play truant came to me to endorse his case for pension as a freedom fighter. His case was pending with the government, nearing final clearance. I knew that he had not taken part in the freedom struggle. He was trying to get the pension sanctioned to him on the basis of a false certificate of someone who was claiming to have been a co-prisoner with him. I regretted my inability to help him. He spread the story in the village that I had become arrogant and totally inconsiderate to my old acquaintances. One lady, somewhat distantly related to me, wanted me to recommend her case to the Vice Chancellor of the Punjab Agricultural University for some appointment. I somehow felt very awkward when I was asked to speak to someone for a favour. I told her that I shall give due consideration to her request. I had every intention to speak to the Vice Chancellor but she seemed to be impatient about it and asked her another relative to check up from me if I had spoken to the VC. He was the son of a judge, who thought nothing of ringing me up at my house. I just told him that he did not know me and he had no business to ring me up. I decided thereafter to not to speak to the VC. One of my cousins from Chanarthal came with a friend complaining that his tyre from the tractor had been stolen by someone known to him but on his complaint the police took no action. I asked the local police officer to help him. The alleged thief was promptly arrested and subjected to third degree torture for three days. The police officer then came to me to report that the complaint against him had been made to settle some private score. I told the police to let him off. The alleged thief on his release went to my mother in Gharuan and showed her the third degree that he had suffered because of me. My mother came to our house in Chandigarh and soundly rebuked me. I had to admit that I had been led up the garden path by my cousin. A school friend rang up to seek my assistance in helping him with the local police. I asked my P.A. to tell the concerned police officer to be considerate to him. Later, I heard from another friend that on my P.A's telephone that school friend got off the hook in a serious criminal case in which their daughter-in-law having been driven to desperation by the treatment of her mother-in-law had committed suicide. I cursed myself for falling into a trap. My brother-in-law was caught by the police for pillion riding on his motorcycle. He got violent against the police officer. The police officer not knowing him gave him the treatment that is given to offenders in Punjab. While he was being roughed up, someone told the police officer that the person being roughed up was related to the Chief Secretary of Punjab. The police officer immediately booked him under the TADA and sent him to the Central Jail, Ludhiana. We could get him out of jail after two days. I thanked my stars that I had served in Bihar where I was free from the pulls and pressures of relatives and friends. These cases and similar others have made me often pray to Waheguru to pardon me for such excesses that unknowingly got committed by me. It is a risk that is there for everyone who wielded an executive authority in the administrative set up that we have in India. I could, of course provide genuine redress and help in many cases. I got the school building of Gharuan renovated and repaired. I got a scheme for drinking water sanctioned for the village. The water supply project proved to be a boon as after the Bhakra Canal Project, the groundwater in the village had ceased to be potable. The district administration put up a sports stadium in the village and they got all the village streets paved. However, my first visit to Gharuan after taking over as the Chief Secretary was a bit awkward for me. I had intended the visit to be private as I wanted to see my mother to take her blessings. Little did I realise that nothing was going to be private for me. Because of the security consideration the visit could not remain secret. I found that there was a full reception committee outside the village, waiting for me with a brass band. All sorts of people were crawling around our house and they had taken over the house. My mother was confined to an inner hall in the house. I could meet her only after I rebuked the gathering for not permitting me to meet my mother. The whole visit left a bad taste in my mouth. One of the retaliatory acts committed after Operation Blue Star was the breach in the Bhakra Canal at a spot not far from Gharuan. I visited the site of the breach that resulted in stoppage of water flowing to Rajasthan. I was amazed to see how a small cut on one of the banks had expanded into a long breach due to the force of water in the canal. The repair work was going on at full speed as there was acute need for irrigation water in Rajasthan. I returned to Chandigarh after reviewing the progress of the work with the Chief Engineer and his team.

I had to watch my step in my decisions. Mr. G.K. Arora who was the Joint Secretary in the PMO recommended to me the case of the release of grant of funds to the Centre for Research in Rural and

Industrial Development (CRRID). The centre was set up on the basis of 50:50 support by both the Punjab Government and the Government of India. Mr. P.N. Haksar, the former Principal Secretary to the Prime Minister was its Chairman and Mr. Rashpal Malhotra was the Executive Director. While the Central Government had released their part of the grant but the Punjab Government was dilly-dallying on it. I found that my predecessor had referred the matter to the Committee of Secretaries that was an informal group consisting of all the Secretaries of the Government of Punjab. I brought up the subject in the next meeting of the group. It was there that I perceived that Mr. P.H. Vaishnav who was a Financial Commissioner rank Secretary had got the group lined up against me. He said that he was opposed to the release of the grant to CRRID that according to him this was nothing but a private estate of Mr. Rashpal Malhotra. It was insinuated that till some time ago he was only a small time salesman of a private firm and later a caretaker at the Institute of Advanced Study Shimla. He generally had the house with him because inwardly most of the IAS officers resented Mr. Malhotra's rise to prominence. They ascribed it to the patronage of Mrs. Gandhi. Many suspected that he was serving RAW. It was, however, a fact that when Mrs. Gandhi visited Chandigarh, generally she was received by the Governors and Chief Ministers of Punjab and Haryana, she would spot Rashpal Malhotra waiting somewhere in the crowd at the back and call him by name to her to talk for a minute or so before she moved out of the airport. This was a signal enough for the observers to note that Rashpal enjoyed her confidence. Sometimes such closeness could become a source of embarrassment also was brought out by what happened to a Patna professor, Mr. Harbans Singh, who happened to be with her in London during his student days. She spotted him in the crowd at Patna Airport. She hailed him by name and asked him to accompany him to Muzaffarpur in her plane. He very happily travelled with her to Muzaffarpur and came back to Patna with her, very happy with himself, basking in the sudden importance that got thrust on him till he received a bill for a hefty amount from the Defence Ministry for payment as airfare for travel in the government plane. This however did not happen with Rashpal Malhotra, whose services she had used as her special emissary to talk to the Assam student agitators. The IAS is like a free masonary structured strictly according to the seniority in service, so much so that even on informal occasions if they queue up for a lunch, the queue would be formed strictly according to the seniority in the civil list. They instinctively did not like anyone who jumped the queue or happened to be an interloper. Rashpal Malhotra was both. I countered the arguments against him by saying that one saw in all the academic institution in the private sector that there was a distinct and a distinguished individual behind those institutions. The individual's personality was not the subject for discussion. It was the work done in CRRID that mattered. Some of the books that had come out from CRRID were lying on the table out of which one covered the "Punjab Crisis". I said that I would like them to tell me if the work done in CRRID was of some merit. All agreed that the work done did a credit to the Institution. I therefore, ruled that I was in favour of releasing the grant. All other Secretaries agreed but Mr. Vaishnav insisted that in the minutes of the meeting his note of dissent must be recorded which I did. This encounter resulted in my general acceptability in Punjab cadre of the IAS. Mr. Vaishnav belonged to Gujarat but in the true spirit of the IAS he had identified himself completely with Punjab. He could speak better Punjabi than me. He had completely accepted the Akali thinking about Punjab. He was of the view that it was the failure of the Indian statesmanship that stood in the way of conceding small things that could meet the Sikh aspirations as articulated by the Akalis. It was the sheer cussedness of the majority community in India that had compelled the Akalis to launch their morchas from time to time. He, of course, felt strongly that I had got Mr. Vasudeva ousted from the position of the Chief Secretary for no fault of his. However, he went a little beyond the role of an advocate for the cause of the Punjab IAS cadre when he surreptitiously got the proceedings of the meeting splashed in a news item in a daily newspaper in order to malign me. However, in the long run the item in the newspaper harmed him only. I had the ready goodwill of five batches of the IAS officers who had been trained by me. The position of the Chief Secretary was viewed on a higher pedestal than the Chief Secretary in Bihar. One of the important function of the Chief Secretary happens to be the placement of the civil service personnel. I felt a bit handicapped in discharging this function as I had not watched the performance of various officers accountable to me and I had to go mostly by the advice of my Secretary

Personnel, Mr. P.K. Verma, who was not only my trainee but he had also learnt Punjabi from Sukhdev. He proved to be very good and a dependable support. Mr. N.N. Vora was the Home Secretary. He was a workaholic and dependable, who performed his duties well during those difficult days. We had a Director General of Police, Mr. Dhillon, a clean shaven *Jat* Sikh from Moga, on deputation from the Madhya Pradesh cadre. Mr. K.P.S. Gill from the Assam cadre had just joined as an Inspector General of Police but Mr. Dhillon seemed to be a bit wary of him. He came into his own much later as a supercop around 1990. The IAS cadre in Punjab had different ethos than the IAS of Bihar. The IAS officers and their wives lived in style. Most of them seem to have done well for themselves. Many of them had farm houses in the villages that they would visit on the weekends. They had a supportive climate about each other and great respect of their seniors. They were more go-getters and performance oriented. Orders once given were generally carried out to the satisfaction of the officials passing the orders. The administration was more orderly and effective. The Punjab officers were more responsive to the public and much more at ease with the politicians compared to the Bihar officers.

Operation Blue Star was accompanied by a statewide curfew. Normal life in the state appeared to have remained disturbed for almost the whole of 1984 because of the sporadic violence by the Sikh extremists and riots that followed many killings. We thought that we should prepare a case for assistance from the Government of India for all the losses that Punjab had suffered. When we started collecting data for preparing our case, we discovered that there was something in Punjabi character that comes into play in the face of manmade or natural calamities. It is their will to survive and come on top. We found that workers in factories and other establishments would adjust their working hours to fit into the curfew times. Quite often, if the nature of the work permitted, they would take the raw material home to turn out production from their homes. The production we found had actually increased during the period of disturbances. The Hindu-Sikh divide did not affect either the social interaction of the two communities nor did it have any effect on their relationship at the workplaces. One indirect consequence of the prolonged phase of extremism and terrorism was that the Hindu reaction on the killings by the Sikh extremists got muted. Imperceptibly, the Punjabi Hindus withdrew themselves from confronting the Sikh extremist or fundamentalist demands or agitators, permitting the Indian Government to sort it out with the Sikhs. They even voted for the Sikh extremists led by Simjranjit Singh Mann in 1989, signifying the fact that for them peace in Punjab was the foremost priority and no longer the fear of the Sikh domination which had been their bug bear for more than forty years after Independence.

There are many facets of Operation Blue Star that have puzzled me. The launching of the operation on the martyrdom anniversary of Guru Arjan Dev when a large number of devotees were at the complex paying homage to his memory denies understanding. There have been Army Generals posted at Amritsar and one posted there could have been chosen for commanding the operation but we had the newly drafted General Brar from Meerut, hastily brought and placed in command of a very sensitive operation for which planning must have been so naive as stated by Gurdev Singh, the then Deputy Commissioner of Amritsar that he believed that he would have Bhindranwale surrender to him in about two hours. The back of the Complex behind the Akal Takhat was left unguarded. As told by General Sunderji personally in a meeting that they had only one string on the bow for the success of the operation and that consisted of the use of the imported stun guns on Akal Takhat so that the extremists operating from there were rendered unconscious and the plan failed as the extremists in the Complex had SLR and AK-47 guns having a range much longer than the range of the stun guns. They had to use tanks, mortars and howitzers for the assault finally, causing extensive damage to the Akal Takhat and very heavy human casualties inside the Complex. Many were killed and injured in the operation as per the White Paper of the Government of India. Those who were arrested from the complex by the Army included women and small children. Some of the children were released by the Army only on the orders of the court. We had taken up the case with the Army of a lady related to one of the Advisors to the Governor, Sardar Harbans Singh, IAS, who got arrested as she had gone to the *Darbar Saheb* to pay her obeisance as per her daily routine and got trapped inside the complex. She was a simple housewife. It was said that when she was questioned by the Army about her presence, she seemed to have been shocked to see the carnage all round her and said that although she had come only as a devotee but what she had seen happening, made her feel like taking a gun and shoot at all those who were engaged in destroying the Akal Takhat. The Army had categorised her 'black', the highest risk security category and refused to budge even when her release was recommended by the Governor of Punjab. No next of kin or relative was allowed to claim any of the dead bodies for performing the last rites. Some persons from the Punjab police had got some shroud put on the body of Bhindranwale but his body was not handed over to anyone of the family although his brother Harcharan Singh Rode who was in the army en-masse. It was an internal security operation against mostly the civilians. Incidentally, I met one Mr. Sodhi, the Suprintendent of happening at Amritsar for quite some time. He was of the firm view that Bhindranwale had surrendered to the Army on June the 6th. He was eliminated thereafter, on order from Delhi. He had with him a photograph of Bhindranwale with his hands tied. This was a phase when the army action added to the alienation of the Sikhs favouring Khalistan from the Indian state. It was demonstrated visibly when all the detainees from the Golden Temple Complex were moved in a special train in daytime from Patiala to Jodhpur in Rajasthan. All of them were blindfolded with black cloaks covering their faces and in handcuffs under a heavy Army escort.

We in the Punjab Government merely watched these developments, more or less as bystanders from a distance. The Akalis had resumed courting arrests from around 15th July 1984. It was decided in Delhi to withdraw the Army to the barracks after handing over the Golden Temple Complex to the Sikh high priests. The negotiations for that purpose were conducted in Delhi. I could not know as to who represented the Akalis or who was talking on behalf of the Government. I suspected that one Akali leader involved was Balwant Singh who had not been arrested in the wake of the arrest of the Akali leaders after Operation Blue Star. He was a Block Development Officer before coming to the Akali politics. He had done well for himself after joining politics having amassed enough wealth, making him counted as an industrialist in Punjab. The reconstruction of the Akal Takhat under the supervision of the Punjab Government Chief Engineer, Mr. Malhotra, was nearing completion. The funds for the project were provided by Sardar Buta

Singh and the gold for goldplating the top dome was ferried from Delhi by a Punjab IAS officer close to Buta Singh, Sardar K.S. Bains, Baba Santa Singh, the Budha Dal Nihang Chief provided the cover for the reconstruction calling it "*kar sewa*" which is the term used for the voluntary community service in the various projects of repair and reconstruction of gurdwaras among the Sikhs. Nihang Sikhs are an order among the Sikhs who remain always fully armed and wear a dark blue dress. They derive their origin from Maan Singh, one of the '*panj piaras*' from Chamkaur who had escaped from the mud fort there along with Guru Gobind Singh in the night on 22nd December 1704 to Machiwara from where till Alamgir he was carried by Ghani Khan and others in a palanquin disguised as '*Uch Da Pir*' wearing a dark blue dress. Guru Gobind Singh discarded his dark blue dress on the way to Damdaṃa Saheb. It is said that Maan Singh kept a piece of dark blue dress and wore it on his turban. The name Buddha Dal was taken when the old '*Dal Khalsa*' had its first division with the younger members becoming "*Taruna Dal*" and the older generation Khalsa became the Budha Dal. The Nihangs have been something like the *Kami Kaze* of the Japanese. They drink a lot of *bhang* or 'marjuana'. They enjoyed a lot of importance during the reign of Maharaja Ranjit Singh. Their leader was Akali Phula Singh who had died in the battle of Nowshera in the NWFP. They were intensely anti-British. They were used as the suicide squads of the Sikhs like the Japanese *Kami Kaze*. They had controlled the Akal Takhat till the advent of the British. They got completely marginalised during the British period, turning almost into an order of mendicants. Their leader had been given some limited powers to grant licenses for bearing arms by the Government and they enjoyed a certain privilege to demand fodder and rations for themselves and their horses from the gurdwaras. Many Sikh farmers would welcome the grazing of their crops by the horses of the Nihangs. The Punjab Government had no hand in Santa Singh having taken over the '*kar sewa*' of the Akal Takhat. Sardar Buta Singh had told me that he had not inducted Baba Santa Singh. His guess was that it was K.C. Pant, a Central Minister who was a member of a group of ministers that had a hand in policymaking on Punjab. I could sense that negotiations were afoot to hand over the Golden Temple Complex to the Sikh High Priests. I felt that in the process Baba Santa Singh would be made the sacrificial goat. He had stuck his neck out for the Government incurring the wrath of the Sikh High Priests for undertaking the government sponsored '*kar sewa*'. Sardar Buta Singh and Baba Santa Singh had been ex-communicated from the Sikh Panth and declared '*tankhahia*'. The term came into use for the Sikhs who joined the service of the Mughal emperor. Such persons could come back to the Sikh brotherhood after they tendered an apology for their lapse and carried out as a penance the punishment that was prescribed by the High Priests. Giani Zail Singh was also threatened with the spectre of ex-communication. Sardar Tarlochan Singh and Sardar Rawail Singh, an Akali leader, unofficially met the High Priests and sought a reprieve for him. We got a message that he was visiting Amritsar by his official plane. We rushed along with Governor Satarawala to receive him at the Amritsar Airport. We heard that Giani Zail Singh was visiting Amritsar against the advice of the Prime Minister. We received him at the airport and escorted him to the Golden Temple. Giani Zail Singh was met by Giani Kirpal Singh, the *Jathedar* of the Akal Takhat and other clergy. He was taken inside a room on the Darshini Deorhi where he was closeted with the priests. I was also present. He came out and addressed the gathering after Giani Kirpal Singh. Giani Zail Singh was also the Supreme Commander of the Armed Forces of India. He had no alternative but to listen to the tirade against his Army, perhaps as the price of his not being declared a '*tankhahia*'. I thought of interceding on behalf of Baba Santa Singh. I sought an interview with Mrs. Gandhi on the subject and waited for an appointment for a week. I heard nothing. I then thought of going through the official channel. Mr. Prem Kumar, my batchmate was the Special Secretary, Home for Punjab. I met him and told him that it would look bad for the Government of India to leave Baba Santa Singh in lurch. The alternative could be to hand over the charge of the Golden Temple Complex to Baba Santa Singh before 30th September which was the deadline for the threatened Sikh March to liberate the Golden Temple. Baba Santa Singh could settle the modalities for its restoration to the SGPC and his own honourable exit from the complex. Prem Kumar seemed to have been impressed and he spoke to someone on his Rax telephone and left his room post haste leaving me sitting in his room. He returned after a few minutes and said that the arrangements to hand over the Complex to the High Priests had gone too far from where the Government could not turn back. The Senior Advisor, Mr. Subramaniam and I were called to meet Mr. P.C. Alexander, the Secretary to the Prime Minister in Delhi. We were given a cup of tea and a paper containing about ten conditions prescribed for handing over of the Golden Temple Complex, including the newly built Akal Takhat to the Sikh High Priests. We were not told as to who were involved in any discussion or meeting in which those ten points were worked out. We were also not told if those points were open to discussion. The Sikhs officially have no clergy. The person who read out the *Guru Granth Saheb* in the gurdwara is called a *granthi*. The exigencies of the Akali Politics brought about the transformation of *granthis* of some important gurdwaras who started being addressed as *Jathedars*. The Gurdwara Act called them 'Head Priests'. They were designated as *Jathedars* only lately. Kirpal Singh was the first one to be officially designated as the *Jathedar* of the Akal Takhat. It suited the Government to deal with the Jathedars instead of the politicians of the Sikhs.

We reached Amritsar the next day. We called on Baba Santa Singh who was camping in the Nihang Chhawani near Gurdwara Shahidan. He offered us a 'marjuana' soft drink that Mr. Subramaniam politely declined but I gingerly drank it. Santa Singh was a bit cut up but otherwise in high spirits perhaps due to the 'marjuana' drink that he had taken. He said that he was happy that all the work in the Akal Takhat had been completed. He said that he would be leaving the Akal Takhat after performing 'ardas' on the 1st of October. Thereafter, we went to the Golden Temple to meet Giani Kirpal Singh and the other High Priests to discuss the modalities of the handing over of the complex. Apparently a word had reached that we were on our way to the Golden Temple. A crowd of Sikh youngsters greeted us near the entrance shouting slogans like that the Khalsa had won, etc. We went inside, Mr. Subramaniam could not speak Punjabi so it was left to me to talk to the High Priests. I explained to them the 10-point charter that was given to us by Mr. Alexander. It seemed that they were aware of the conditions and they nodded their heads in approval as I read that paper to them after translating the same to Punjabi. They started fidgeting when I insisted on a written undertaking from them that they had accepted all that I had read out to them. They pleaded that we should accept their word for it. Mr. Subramaniam decided to not to make it an issue. It was decided that we would have the handing over ceremony the next day in the morning. Next day, as soon as we reached and sat down to sign the handing over formally, I received a message that Mr. Prem Kumar from Delhi wanted to speak to me. I showed the message to Mr. Subramaniam. He asked me to wait a few minutes as the necessary papers were being brought for signatures. The papers were duly handed over with the keys of the *Tosha Khana* where valuable articles received as gifts for the Golden Temple were kept. The *Tosha Khana* lock was opened and the valuables displayed. Everything was as it had been originally stored. One stray cannon shot had struck *Tosha Khana* that had set on fire a valuable canopy presented by the Nizam to Maharaja Ranjit Singh. The canopy was reduced to ashes in no time but no other article was damaged during Operation Blue Star. The burnt remains of the canopy were packed in a gunny bag and handed over to the High Priests. Again I received a message that Mr. Prem Kumar wanted to speak to me. I went to the telephone in the gurdwara office to speak to him. He enquired from me specifically if we had obtained a written undertaking from the High Priests accepting the 10-point charter that was given to us. I replied that we had accepted their oral acceptance as sufficient. He did not seem to be satisfied with my reply. As soon as I returned a message was received that someone higher up in Delhi wanted to speak to Mr. Subramaniam. Mr. Subramaniam returned after listening. He had received orders to not to hand over the Complex to the High Priests. I told him that we could not take back the keys. We had not yet handed over the portion housing Teja Singh Samundri Hall and Guru Ram Das Sarai although the paramilitary personnel in anticipation had got their bed rolls loaded on to the trucks waiting for a signal from us to move out. We asked them to unroll their beds and stay put. There was a bit of consternation over our decision to not to hand over the Sarai area to the High Priests. Baba Kharak Singh who had announced that the *kar sewa* of the sarovar would start immediately after the take over declared that the *kar sewa* could start only after the sarai area was vacated by the government. Mr. Subramaniam and General Gauri Shankar were summoned to Delhi, apparently for a dressing down. They did not tell the full story about what had happened. One of the remarks made by Subrmaniam was that the morning edition of the *Indian Express* carrying a photo of a Sikh youngsters shouting anti-government slogans on the first page had upset Mrs. Gandhi. She felt that such a demonstration should not have been permitted. It did not seem to be the whole truth. I pointed out that holding on to the sarai area was bringing a bad name and it was counterproductive. Santa Singh left the next day after the complex was handed over. The musicians in *Darbar Saheb* specially picked up selected verses from the *Granth Saheb* denigrating persons of low character occupying high offices. We quietly withdrew from the sarai area after a few days. Once again Subramaniam had to face the wrath of Mrs. Gandhi. This time on her learning about the humiliation that was brought on Baba Santa Singh. No one in Delhi owned up before Mrs. Gandhi, the responsibility for having left Baba Santa Singh in the lurch. Mr. Subramaniam was made the scapegoat for the same. Mr. Subramaniam tried to retrieve his position with the powers that be in the Central Government by issuing a strongly worded circular order superseding the 1981 order that had strictly forbidden the police in uniform from entering gurdwaras. He sought to emphasize that if the situation so warranted the police could enter the Golden Temple Complex too under the orders of the local officers. I objected to the wording of the circular by pointing out that even during the British times the Police had refrained from entering Akal Takhat when some members of the then illegal SGPC were to be arrested from a meeting taking place there. The Circular was slightly revised and issued. It was pointed out by some one that the road separating the Golden Temple Complex from the 'sarai' area was a public road. Mr. Subramaniam ordered the district administration to regularly patrol the road in order to establish that the road was a public road. He was very happy when the Deputy Commissioner of Amritsar reported that they had started patrolling the road twice daily. Mr. Subramaniam was very happy on getting such a report and gleefully showed the same to me. I was intrigued at not receiving any protest about the patrolling from the SGPC. When I visited Amritsar the next time, the mystery got solved. The police chief had introduced the practice of the plainclothes policemen walking from one gate of the complex to the other on the connecting road every morning and evening, in an arrangement settled between the local police and the SGPC. The same was being reported as a compliance of the orders of the Punjab government. It was clear that the local administration was taking the higher ups in Chandigarh for a ride since they were ignorant about the Sikh tradition or history.

A coordinated plan was worked out between the Army and the Punjab government for the return of the Army to the barracks in three phases. Army was to withdraw from the whole of Punjab except Amritsar and Gurdaspur by the 31st October and from these districts the withdrawal was planned by the 30th November. The Army's presence provided a lot of confidence to the people particularly the Hindus of Punjab but the Army did not prove to be of much use for internal security purposes as it lacked local intelligence about the miscreants to be watched. We had a civil-military liaison meet in the Western Command Headquarters at Shimla for the Northern region covered by the Command. The Conference was presided over by Lt. General Sunderji. I found him to be very intelligent and articulate. He was good enough to explain to me the planning and the execution of Operation Blue Star. We had a briefing from Lt General B.S. Dayal, who was in overall command of the Operation. He was Advisor to the Governor of Punjab too for some time. I was glad to attend this conference that had started under the revised manual on Aid to Civil Authorities that had taken into consideration the recommendations that I had made as the Deputy Commissioner of Ranchi. One incidental benefit that accrued to our area was in the inclusion of the Chandigarh-Ludhiana road in the list of the Defence Strategic Roads that are to be maintained at the cost of the Central Government. We had another sensitive problem regarding the release of water for the cooling tower in the newly constructed Ropar thermal power station. The water was to be taken from the Bhakra Canal through a cut on the side and the water after cooling the plant was to flow back to the canal. No water can be taken for any purpose from the Bhakra Canal unless the Central Government and the Governments of Haryana and Rajasthan agreed for it. Punjab has been quite vociferous about Bhakra water going out of Punjab to states considered non-riparian to the rivers of Punjab. This matter was to be finalised quickly as the thermal plant was nearing completion. Rajasthan insisted that for taking the water for cooling, the cut on the canal bank should not be more than three feet deep in order to ensure that the canal should always flow full for the sake of the thermal plant. Mr. S.S. Sidhu as Advisor to the Governor of Punjab had signed this agreement that would have led to a closure of the thermal plant whenever there was some shortage of water for the canal. Mr. Tejinder Khanna was the Irrigation Secretary who brought the dangerous portent of the agreement to my notice. Mr. Subramaniam was the Advisor to the Governor who looked after the Irrigation Department. We discussed the issue with him and we agreed that while cutting the canal bank for taking out the channel of water for the cooling tower, we should cut the canal bank right up to the bottom. It was also decided to not to make the Governor Mr. Satarawala privy to this violation of an inter-state agreement. As soon as the news about the cut reached Jaipur the Rajasthan Government asked the Central Government to effectively intercede with the Punjab Government. The Chief Secretary of Rajasthan, Mr. Anand Mohan Lal, was my batchmate. He protested to me that he did not except such an action from a friend. I promised to look into his complaint. It was a lie like the lie of Yudhistra in *Mahabharat* on the death of Ashwathama, the elephant and not the son of Dronacharya of the same name. Mr. Satarawala was pulled up by the Central Government. He ordered me to call for the explanation of Mr. Tejinder Khanna and he also ordered that the *status quo ante* should be restored immediately. I passed the order on restoration of the cut to the Chief Engineer who responded in a note that for restoring the cut the canal would have to be closed for a month. I advised the Governor to apprise the Central Government and the two state governments of it. The canal had been dry for a month due to the extremist action a little earlier. The prospect of the closure of the canal for a month more made them see wisdom in letting things in accepting the fait accompli. I consider the action of Mr. Tejinder Khanna to have been in the best tradition of the IAS in which one identified one self with the interests of the state of ones allotment even to a point of peril to one's career and service. I came across the similar instances of total identification with the interests of the state among other Punjab officers. One was Mrs. Shyama Mann who was the Secretary Planning, Punjab. She took upon herself to almost coach me like a schoolboy when I was to attend a meeting in the Planning Commission at Delhi lest Punjab might lose some of the legitimate grant that should be coming from the Central kitty. Luckily for me, Dr. Manmohan Singh was the Secretary of the Planning Commission, who knew the Punjab situation very well. He warned me about the mounting expenditure of policing and administration which could become a millstone around the neck of

Punjab in future. He also advised mobilising of some extra resources especially measures like raising bus fairs during the President's rule. I think that it was another failure of the Punjab civil services that sensitive subjects like the Hindu Sikh issues were not allowed to be examined in depth by the civil services and subjects like the dispute on sharing of the river waters or territorial adjustments on the basis of the language spoken were handled by individual officers more or less in their personal capacity regardless of their posting. The criteria for the selection of these officers was that they enjoyed the trust of some politicians mainly Akali and they happened to be Sikh officers.

All the officers concerned with the law and order were provided with high security. I had a police van following wherever I went with one officer sitting with me in the car. I intensely disliked it but I was helpless. Whenever I had an opportunity like going for shopping with Sukhdev or for social calls. I would go in my personal car without my personal security till one day my security officer came and begged me to take him with me as he had been threatened by his commandant that if he found me roaming anywhere without the security guard, he would get him sacked from service. I had to acquiesce into permitting him to travel with me. I did not like the invasion on my privacy and I did not have any fear that I could be killed. I believed that only the bullet that had my name on it could kill me. It happened once when I had gone shopping for something while I was walking alone window shopping in another direction. She overheard a boy talking to another Sikh boy telling him that the Chief Secretary was walking alone nearby who could be a good target for them. The other boy questioned as to how he could be certain about my identity. Sukhdev panicked on hearing the exchange between the two youngsters and came running to where I was. She pulled me to the car without telling me anything. It was only after reaching home that she told me what she had overheard. The danger still did not register in me. I did not ask for any security when I moved to Delhi. One day when I was on tour in Bombay, my newly wedded daughter-in-law, Kamalpreet, picked up phone on a ring. The caller did not identify himself but said to her to tell Dhanoa that they were going to kill him for having been associated with Punjab administration after Operation Blue Star. She rang me up in panic in Bombay. I told her to not to worry as I had received such threats often from the day I joined. I remember the first threat came in an anonymous letter posted from Calcutta soon after my joining at Chandigarh, advising me either to resign from the service or to go on leave as no Sikh was expected to serve the evil Government of India. I strongly suspect that Simranjit Singh Mann a Punjab Pro-Bhindrawale police officer who was at that time hiding in Calcutta, was behind the letter. I generally ignored anonymous letters but in this case I thought that Delhi Police should become aware about the danger from the Sikh extremists, so I told Kamalpreet to inform the Delhi police about the telephone call that she had received which was my undoing. I found a personal security guard waiting for me on my return from Bombay. I could not get free from him till well after my retirement from service on 31 August 1988 and that too after persistently writing to the Police Commissioner that I had become a private citizen after my retirement from the service and as a private citizen I was prepared to face the risk, if any, from any quarter, if my security guard got withdrawn. I was trying to familiarise myself with different facets of the administration in Punjab. All the high security prisoners including those arrested from the Golden Temple Complex were kept in the Central Jail at Nabha. I decided to visit the jail to see the conditions there myself. I met many youngsters listed as extremists in the jail. None of them complained of any ill treatment although they insisted that their incarceration was unjustified. The younger brother of Bhai Amrik Singh, Sardar Manjit Singh, was there. He was an employee of the SGPC when he was arrested. He became a leader of the All India Sikh Student Federation. I found that he was not very knowledgeable about the Sikh tradition or the Sikh tenets. He was grumbling that he was arrested because he happened to be the brother of the late Bhai Amrik Singh, who was close to Bhindranwale. I also met Rachhpal Kaur, the wife of the driver of Bhindranwale. She had a small baby in her lap when she had been caught in the crossfire during the army attack. A bullet had hit her baby in her lap that had pierced through the baby and got lodged in her tummy. The baby died on the spot. I asked her as to why did not she escape when the Army had made an announcement on the PA system for all pilgrims to vacate the Complex. She confirmed that she had heard the announcement but she did not go out as she believed that the police would kill her in any case, being the widow of Rachhpal Singh who must have been their target along with Bhindranwale. She decided to leave it to Waheguru and as she decided to remain sitting in His lap in the Golden Temple. I was not aware during my visit that the Punjab government had been carrying on an illegal covert operation in Nabha jail by having a portion declared as an interrogation centre where the suspected extremists were tortured for information in the name of interrogation. The centre got hastily closed on hearing about my visit and the same did not reopen after my visit. The sympathisers of the extremists and the human rights activists somehow thought that I had visited the Nabha jail on purpose for that reason. They had raised the matter in a Public Interest Petition in the Punjab and Haryana High Court. When the petition came for hearing before the court, my name was suggested by the petitioners for holding enquiry into the alleged violation of human rights in Nabha jail. The court accepting their suggestion issued a formal order appointing me as the enquiry officer. May be, that my name came up because after Operation Blue Star, against the police advice, I had paid a visit to the Chowk Mehta gurdwara, which was the headquarters of the Damdami Taxal. Damdami Taxal had not accepted that Bhindranwale had been killed in Operation Blue Star. I had not taken my official security with me while visiting the gurdwara. There was no one to receive me. I saw an old man near the gate. I enquired from him as to where I could keep my shoes. I entered the gurdwara and bowed before the *Granth Saheb*. I then enquired if there was a *granthi* who could read out the '*vak*' of the day from the *Granth Saheb*. The old man himself read out the '*vak*' and before I left he presented me a '*siropa*' or a robe of honour. Every one was surprised at it including myself. The number of pilgrim casualties in the Golden Temple Complex has continued to baffle me. The Director General of Punjab Police was Mr. Sawhney when Bhindranwale was doing his capers. Mr. Atwal was the Deputy Inspector General of Police who was in overall charge of the area for law and order purposes. He probably was to meet some police informer within the precincts of the Golden Temple or he might have gone there as a devotee. Mr. Atwal was coming out with '*krah prasad*' in his hand when two extremists shot him dead near the entrance and cooly walked back into the complex. This was a time when the police should have stormed the Golden Temple Complex in hot pursuit of the killers. No one would have raised a finger over the police entry into the gurdwara, even if they had gone ahead with the arrest of

Bhindranwale. The police seemed to have panicked and the district police chief dithered. It was perhaps that the Punjab Government had issued a circular order in 1981 asking the police to not to enter gurdwaras. The matter went to Mr. Sawhney for a decision. He in turn asked Sardar Darbara Singh, the then Chief Minister who sought instructions from Mrs. Gandhi direct. Sardar Darbara Singh told me that Mrs. Gandhi advised him against entry into the Complex to arrest the culprits who had killed Mr. Atwal. The demoralisation of the police force in Punjab was there for everyone to see.

I ran into Mr. Ahluwalia from Patna at Hotel Janpath in Delhi where he was staying. He told me that with his involvement in the '*Sarbat Khalsa*' that was organised by Sardar Buta Singh and Takhat Patna Saheb, he had got himself dragged into the Sikh affairs and politics of the Congress party. He had been off and on meeting Rajiv Gandhi. He got called to meetings frequently. He was therefore, staying at the hotel in order to remain available for the meetings. It was proving to be a bit heavy on his purse. My wife, Sukhdev, had moved with me to Chandigarh. Our flat in Delhi was lying vacant. I invited him to move there. He gladly accepted my offer. He was aware that financially I was not very well-off, so he would pay my wife some money which he considered reasonable as rent for which we had no lease or deed nor did we ever discuss. I heard from him that he had lost his mother on the 22 October and her '*bhog*' ceremony was to be on the 1st of November. I got an air ticket for going to Patna for 31 October. We had a meeting of the Governor in Council in the morning. It is there that we received a message that Mrs. Gandhi had been shot by her security guards, who were Sikhs. Officially it was stated that she had been taken to the All India Institute of Medical Sciences for treatment but from the details about the incident that we learnt on telephone it was clear that she could not have survived the shooting at point blank range. Mr. N.N. Vora, the Home Secretary alerted all the districts to be prepared for the eventuality of her death when announced. There was no question of my going to Patna. I did visit Patna after a fortnight. The Patna Sikhs had gone through the trauma of violence in the wake of Indira Gandhi's assassination. The Patna Sikhs were no different from other Sikhs in their emotional attachment to the Akalis in Punjab. They were incensed at the role played by Jathedar Maan Singh and my friend S.S. Ahluwalia in helping Sardar Buta Singh with the '*sarbat khalsa*'. They tried to get the local community to boycott Ahluwalia at the time of the *Bhog* ceremony after his mother's death. It were the contacts of Ahluwalia with the local Congress leaders due to his perceived closeness with Rajiv Gandhi that saved Patna from a holocaust like the one in Bokaro or Delhi, although many shops owned by Sikh traders got looted. However, no one was killed in Patna. It led to an exodus of Sikhs from Patna to Punjab. Mr. G.S. Lamba, who was an open admirer of Bhindranwale packed his bags and moved with his entire family to Jalandhar in Punjab. There were many others who had packed their bags and they were waiting to move to Punjab. I addressed a Sikh congregation in Takhat Patna Saheb, advising the Sikh community to not to act in haste and stay back as the storm had blown over. Patna was the birth place of Guru Gobind Singh which the Sikhs could not think of abandoning. My address to the Sikh community was widely applauded in Bihar and it was given a good coverage in the Bihar media. The '*Searchlight*' English daily from Patna wrote an editorial praising me. He also connected my visit and address to the Sikh truck drivers back in the sixties. The press also reported that after hearing me the Patna Sikhs had decided to stay back.

Indira Gandhi was universally blamed by the Sikhs for Operation Blue Star. She was continuously being demonised all over the world by the Sikhs ever since June 1984. There were press reports that said that Jagjit Singh Chauhan, an ex-Minister of Punjab and other abroad had announced handsome rewards for anyone who killed Indira Gandhi. The Sikh personnel in her security were taken off duty by the officials responsible for her security. It was Indira Gandhi who noticed the absence of the Sikh security guards and ordered them back to duty as she felt sure that she was in no danger from the Sikhs. A person who as alleged had designs to destroy the Sikhs as a community like the Nazis had against the Jews as some of the Sikhs try to prove against Indira Gandhi, could not have passed such orders. Whatever the hatred that might have been generated against Indira Gandhi among the Sikhs, she had succeeded in having the rest of India behind her so far as Operation Blue Star was concerned. There was not even a ripple about it in the Parliament. The protest were there only from the Sikhs like Khuswant Singh, Amrinder Singh, Patwant Singh, Harinder Singh from the Indian Foreign Service and many others that only showed that the Sikhs as a community stood isolated from the rest of the country on this moment of great trauma. The publicity received by the anti-Hindu outpourings of Bhindranwale accompanied by the indiscriminate killings resorted to by his followers completely submerged the feelings for the death and the sighs of the innocent pilgrims to the Golden Temple on a Gurpurb so far as the conscience of India was concerned.

By noon the whole of Punjab was abuzz with rumours about the assassination of Mrs. Gandhi. It so happened that both the President Zail Singh and Rajiv Gandhi who was being groomed to succeed Mrs. Gandhi were not in Delhi. The announcement about her death was made only in the evening after Rajiv Gandhi and Giani Zail Singh had reached Delhi. The trouble ahead for Delhi could have been clear to anyone when in the evening the mob at the AIIMS had attacked Giani Zail Singh's car who had come to see Mrs. Gandhi there. A friend of mine who was secretary with Mr. Shankranand, the then Health Minister, who was present at the AIIMS along with all the senior Congress leaders, told me that it was Mr. Arun Nehru who had virtually taken over as the boss who in one of his outbursts said that killers of Mrs. Gandhi deserved to be taught a lesson. Apart from the outbursts of Arun Nehru, spontaneous anger against the Sikhs had started erupting everywhere in India immediately with the announcement for her death through shooting by her Sikh security guards. There was a subdued and at places overt jubilation over the killing of Indira Gandhi among the Sikhs. Some pictures appeared on the TV of the Sikhs opening bottles of champagne in London. Some of my Sikh relatives or friends rang me up to tease me over her death. It was missed by almost all the Sikhs that the Sikh security guards were guilty of a great sin in abusing the trust of Mrs. Gandhi who had trusted them to protect her life. It seems that conscience was something that had disappeared from India with Mahatma Gandhi. Generally, there was a pall of gloom in the Hindu houses. The Hindu-Sikh emotional divide in Punjab was there for all to see. The same night of 31st October a group of IAS trainee officers of Punjab cadre had detrained at Arrah station in Bihar for a stint of training. They travelled in a van to their place of stay. There was one young Sikh officer, Mr. Sidhu among them. He was spotted by the people when he got down from the van. There was a shout that there was a Sikh.

A mob collected on hearing the shout and started pelting brickbats. Mr. Sidhu got injured. They were saved by the timely arrival of the police. The incident was narrated to me when Sidhu came to see me later. As far as Madras, a Sikh friend had to spend a night in the police station when his house got attacked on 31st night. Any number of Sikhs travelling on trains got attacked and many got killed by mobs at various railway stations in India. However, the spontaneous anger got played out by the 1st November. Generally, the non-Congress governments proved to be better in controlling the anti-Sikh outburst. It was the worst in Delhi where the administration instead of doing anything to control it actually seemed to have connived at it. My daughter, Rosy, had got stranded in Delhi. I rang up a senior police officer about her safety and enquired as to what was being done to control the situation in Delhi. His cryptic reply was as to who was bothered about the situation in Delhi. The anger against the Sikhs got fanned by the live show on Doordarshan of the people filling past the body of Mrs. Gandhi. Some could be heard on T.V. shouting blood for blood. My daughter described to me how the Hindu neighbours, mostly Punjabi Hindus joined together to help and protect Sikhs. There were only 5 or 6 families in Munirka Enclave having about more than 200 flats. The Hindu neighbours advised the Sikh families to not to move out of the Colony. They arranged to get milk and vegetables, etc., for them. Rosy saw that two bus loads of ruffians wielding sticks and iron rods appeared in front of the colony around noon but they were not allowed to enter the colony. They went to the market targeting Sikhs shops. The police was nowhere to be seen. Rosy spent the day with her Hindu hosts but insisted that she would sleep alone in our flat. The colony people named her '*Punjab di Sherni*' or the lioness of Punjab. The Punjab police escorted her to Chandigarh the next day.

There was no retaliation or back lash in Punjab against all that was happening in Delhi and the rest of India. Whatever tension might have been there between the Punjabi Hindus and the Sikhs, either of them could not go so far as to take to killing the members of the other community. Bhindranwale in one of his speeches during his last days at the Akal Takhat had appealed to the Sikhs that if the armed forces attacked the Golden Temple it was the duty of every Sikh to kill the Hindu nearest to him. I checked up from the crime records in the whole of Punjab only one mad cap Sikh had acted on that appeal. No Hindu was harmed by any Sikh in the wake of the anti-Sikh riots elsewhere in India. The euphoria on the assassination of Indira Gandhi had been replaced by a sombre realisation that the Sikhs were so vulnerable. As the details of atrocities committed against the Sikhs trickled in Punjab there was widespread anger against the Central Government. This was made worse by the statement of Rajiv Gandhi, the new Prime Minister that the earth shook when a big tree fell. It was read as a justification for the pogrom against the Sikhs. When the dust had settled a bit I went to Delhi and met K.C. Pant, who was one of the Ministers in the Committee overseeing Punjab affairs. I told him that it would help assuage feelings of the Sikhs if it was announced that an enquiry into the riots following Mrs. Gandhi's assassination would be held by a judge. K.C. Pant showed no remorse at what had happened but asked me a question with a bit of sarcasm as to what I thought of the people's feelings for Mrs. Gandhi. I came away from him quite disappointed. I could not persuade the Governor to make a formal suggestion to the Government of India for a judicial enquiry.

Indira Gandhi died much revered by the people with the exception of the Sikhs. Majority of the Sikhs have continued to associate her name with Operation Blue Star. Perhaps she had planned general elections immediately after Operation Blue Star but due to faux-pas in Andhra Pradesh, the same could not be ordered. Rajiv Gandhi ordered the general elections in which the Congress party was returned to power with a thumping majority. One achievement of Operation Blue Star, though not explicitly articulated, has been a lesson for the Akalis that Sir Malcolm Hailey wanted them to learn when they were leading the gurdwara reform agitation. It was to instill among them a sense of modernisation and understanding about the rights and sensitives of other human group that has rendered the *Dharam Yudh Morcha* as the last Akali morcha of the class that had provided a laboratory for Gandhi to fine-tune his strategy of '*satyagrah*'.

Rajiv Gandhi started personally interviewing Secretaries to the Government of India, soon after taking over. One of the persons who faced him in the first set of personal interviews was Mr. C.R. Vaidyanathan, the Union Health and Family Planning Secretary, who was from the Bihar cadre of the LAS. He had gone fully prepared for the interview, armed with all the facts and figures that showed that every year the Health Ministry was giving an improved performance. Mr. Rajiv Gandhi, it seemed had done his homework even better. He brought out the figures of the birth rate per thousand couples that despite the increasing expenditure every year the position became worse. Mr. Vaidyanathan had apparently not studied this aspect of the program. He fumbled for an answer and along with one or two more Secretaries he was reverted back to the state. The story was received with a sense of terpidation among the civil services. I was called to a meeting of the Chief Secretaries of the states, to be addressed by Rajiv Gandhi soon after. He elaborated before us his views about the civil services. He felt that the civil servants were attaching more importance to forms and procedures and not to the real objectives of their programs. He illustrated this point by describing his disappointment with the Union Health Secretary. The other important point that he made was that the civil servants suffered from an unwarranted sense of complacence and their thinking was hide bound and out of date as they never went for training after joining service. His both observations I found to be valid. I came away highly impressed by the youthful handsome Prime Minister. He appeared to me to be a breath of fresh air causing a flutter in the dovecots all over. He started showing his hand about Punjab immediately with his victory in the elections. The Akali leaders started being released from jails. The action in the Central Government started without involving us from the Punjab Government. Sant Harchand Singh Longowal, the dictator of the Akali morcha was released after bringing him to Delhi. He went around with Sardar Paramjit Singh Sarna, a Delhi Akali leader seeing what the Delhi Sikhs had suffered during the disturbances that followed the assassination of Indira Gandhi. He was literally horrified to see the plight of the Sikhs. He heard stories as to how the Punjabi Hindus got mobilised for the rescue and relief of the Sikhs. However, his statements on reaching Punjab were highly critical of the Central Government. I was an outsider in Punjab. I did not know any of the Akali leaders except Sardar Surjit Singh Barnala. Since the political atmosphere was hotting up in Punjab, I thought that I should meet Sant Longowal for making my own assessment, so that I was in a position to advise the government on the new situation that was unfolding in Punjab.

The Deputy Commissioner of Amritsar told me that Harbhajan Singh Sandhu, an Akali leader of Amritsar was his close confidant. I asked him to arrange a meeting with Sant Longowal that was to be kept secret. I was told that Sant Longowal would be glad to meet me at the Sangrur PWD Inspection Bungalow. I had to take the Deputy Commissioner of Sangrur, Mr. Piara Ram, into confidence. When I reached the Inspection Bunglow, I found that a caravan of cars was going out. Not finding Sant Longowal I was wondering about as to what to do next when the Deputy Commissioner reached to tell me that Sant Longowal did not feel safe at the Inspection Bungalow, so he had gone back to his village gurdwara Kaimbowal but he had given time for me to meet him there at 10 p.m.

I found Sant Longowal in good cheer. We greeted each other. He asked me to sit down beside him. No one else was there with us. I made the purpose of my visit clear by telling him that my visit was more in a personal capacity as I did not know him, having all along served in Bihar. I told him that my experience as a civil servant had been happy. I did not come across any discrimination against the Sikhs nor did I found anything so objectionable in India that could give a feeling to the Sikhs that the Sikhs were not secure in India. I also said that the *Dharam Yudh Morcha*, of which he was the dictator, in my view was a folly that had harmed the Sikhs more than any benefits that might have been seen in its launching. I of course admitted that having somewhat shelterd life of a civil servant might have deprived me of some perceptions that the Akali Dal might have acquired from their participation in the public affairs. I, therefore, requested him to throw some light on his current stance of being quite bitter about the Indian Government. He was quite frank in his reaction. He said that the Sikh community was seething with bitterness against the Government of India. He said that no one would permit him to go on the stage if he did not articulate that bitterness. This gave me the opening that I was looking for. I said that he must have felt the Hindu-Sikh divide that had come about due to their agitation. The logical end of the road in the direction in which he was taking the Sikhs would be what the hardliners were calling Khalistan. I asked him if the Sikhs had not suffered enough by pulling out of the West Punjab and Haryana/Himachal. I challenged him to convince me if he had any other alternative than repairing the damage that already had been caused to the unity of the present Punjabis. He was good enough to immediately agree to what I had said but expressed his helplessness in moving forward in that direction under the prevailing conditions. I told him that he was the leader of the Sikhs and an opinion maker. He need not sound so pessimistic. He confessed to me that he had visited Delhi after his release. While he had felt very sad on knowing all that happened to the Sikhs but he was moved by the stories as to how the Hindus, particularly the Punjabi Hindus came out in support of the Sikhs in distress. He said that he came to Punjab with a resolve to restore the Hindu-Sikh fraternity in Punjab which would be his number one priority. He requested me if I could help him to obtain two assurances from the Government. It would give him the strength to undertake the mission of peace that he had in mind. I told him that I had come strictly in my private capacity but I could sense the Government mind to some extent and say that the Government would be prepared to meet him more than half the way on this mission. We were quite relaxed in our conversation and we were left totally undisturbed. I asked him if he shared any of the views of Bhindranwale. He replied in the negative and said that Bhindranwale was like a dead snake put round the neck of the Akalis by the wily Congress. He said that all they were doing was to put the snake back around the neck of the Congress. He admitted that in that attempt they did not succeed. I asked his views about another self-appointed ideologue of the killer squads of Bhindranwale, Bhai Kanwar Singh Dhami, who was operating from the Golden Temple Complex. When on a signal from the Akalis, the Sikh High Priests had issued a *hukumnama* prohibiting killings within the precincts of the Darbar Saheb, it was Bhai Kanwar Singh who had issued a rejoinder explaining that during confrontation with the government, the Sikh gurdwaras became their forts. It was lawful to mete out punishments to culprits in forts during a war. Sant Longowal said that Kanwar Singh Dhami was a dangerous person whom the govenment should not touch, even with a barge pole.The two demands that he gave me for conveying to the government; were firstly, that the Central Government must announce that a judicial enquiry would be held into the anti-Sikh disturbances that followed the death of Mrs. Gandhi and secondly, the government must lift the ban that had been imposed on the working of the All India Sikh

Students Federation. I told him that I could make no commitment on behalf of the government but I would surely convey his request to the Governor. We shook hands and parted, little realising that like Indira Gandhi this would be my first and last meeting with Sant Harchand Singh Longowal.

I received a wireless message about the visit of Sardar Buta Singh to Chandigarh that also said that I was expected to receive him at the airport. I felt that the wording was odd as the Chief Secretary was not required to go to the airport to receive a Central minister. I therefore, ignored the message, I got a telephone call around lunch time from Sardar Buta Singh personally that he was at the airport lounge waiting for me. I immediately left for the airport where I found Sardar Buta Singh accompanied by his family and my friend Sardar S.S. Ahluwalia, having tea in the airport lounge. He asked me to join them for a cup of tea. All of us came out ostensibly to leave for the Punjab Government Guest House. I found that Sardar Buta Singh, instead of going to his car came with me to sit in my car. As we sat, he said that he was on a secret visit and that he would like to visit Anandpur Saheb incognito in my car. He had been declared a '*tankhahia*' after the '*sarbat khalsa*' and he faced a constant threat from the Sikh extremists whose activities were on the rise, more so after the Delhi riots, when many victims of Delhi violence increasingly joined their ranks. The *ragis* in the gurdwaras were playing havoc by singing verses that emotionally disturbed the listeners, instigating them to violent revenge. It was only the other day that on the advice of the local I.B. chief I had called Ragi Professor Darshan Singh to my house, to warn him that if he did not desist from provocative '*kirtan*' the Government would be compelled to put him under arrest. I was, therefore, in a dilemma to permit him to go alone in my car. I decided to accompany him in my car. I alerted the Deputy Commissioner of Ropar about my own visit to Anandpur Saheb so that a security cover was available. Sardar Buta Singh told me that he was to meet Jathedar Mahalon of Takhat Keshgarh Saheb. I could guess that he must be negotiating some way out from his ex-communication by the High Priests that was apparently hurting him, especially after Giani Zail Singh had made a deal with the High Priests.The Deputy Commissioner received us at the Inspection Bunglow. He was surprised to see Sardar Buta Singh with me. I got dropped at the gurdwara to listen to the hymns being sung in the gurdwara, leaving the car with Sardar Buta Singh, who went to the house of Jathedar Mahalon. I was informed after about an hour that the meeting was over. When I came back I found that Sardar Buta Singh was riding the Deputy Commissioner's car. I was told that for some reason my car did not start from Jathedar Mahalon's house. We had to leave the car behind. I cautioned the Deputy Commissioner about the sensitivity of our visit and ordered him to get my car repaired immediately so that it reached Chandigarh in the night itself. The furore caused by the local officers in locating a mechanic for the car in the night blew away the secrecy of our visit. The first thing that I did in the morning was to apprise the Governor about the secret visit of Sardar Buta Singh. The story of the secret visit broke out in the daily press the next day almost as a headline news. Rajiv Gandhi did not like, firstly, that Buta Singh should have gone on that mission and secondly, my name being associated with the visit. My having apprised the Governor before the story broke somehow saved me plus some explanation on my behalf by one of my well-wishers, who had access in quarters close to Rajiv Gandhi.

The Punjab issues that were on the back burner till the general elections were brought on the centre of the stage by Rajiv Gandhi who seemed to be in a hurry to be done with it. He appointed Mr. Arjun Singh as the Governor of Punjab in place of Mr. Satarawala who was more or less a figurehead as Punjab was run through the hotlines in Delhi except for routine matters. I read out the appointment order of the Governor in the swearing-in ceremony for the new Governor. Mr. Arjun Singh read out his oath of office in Punjabi. He read out the wording before me in his office to check if his pronounciation was correct. The oath was administerd to him by the Chief Justice of Punjab and Haryana High Court. I found Mr. R.V. Subramaniam to be in very low spirits after the swearing-in ceremony. He asked me to enquire from the Governor if he needed any briefing from him. It was a strange request coming from him who had always acted as if he was the de-facto Government of Punjab. I went to Arjun Singh to make that enquiry. He told me that he was in no need of briefing and all of us could go home. He had brought two of his trusted IAS officers from Madhya Pradesh as his secretaries. We learnt the next day that Mr. R.V. Subramaniam was given the marching orders.

Arjun Singh had come with a brief to resolve the Punjab crisis. The hotlines from Delhi went dead from the day he took over. Mr.

P.K. Kaul from Uttar Pradesh cadre had taken over as the Cabinet Secretary. He told me that Arjun Singh had been given full authority to handle the Punjab situation. The Cabinet Secretary and the Home Secretary were specifically told that they were not to call any Punjab officer for any discussion. I was told to visit Delhi only when absolutely necessary. Mr. Arjun Singh was given full authority over the central agencies like the Intelligence Bureau, RAW and others in matters concerning Punjab. Arjun Singh set about building his communication network among all concerned sections of the Sikhs. A large number of Sikhs had set up big farms in Madhya Pradesh. He had known quite a few of them. He used them to build his contacts with the Sikhs. Gurbir Singh, son of the ex-Akali Chief Minister Sardar Gurnam Singh, was one of his principal link in Punjab. Another person who moved to the center stage was Daljit Singh Pannu, son of Sardar Mohan Singh, who had served as the Chairman of the Punjab Public Service Commission. He was a member of the ICAR Society when I was the Secretary. He showed a lot of affection for me. He would invite me for a drink often in the evenings when he visited Delhi. Daljit Singh Pannu, I found was quite knowledgeable about officials serving in Punjab. I asked my P.A. about what was important about Pannu. He said that he did not know anything but he testified that the gentleman, when he visited my predecessor, would sit with him for hours and Mr. Vasudeva would call him inside immediately on being informed that he had come. I liked Daljit Pannu a lot for his information and his manner of presenting a case. I found that on one or two occassions Arjun Singh kept us waiting while he was closetted with Mr. Pannu. I had gone to see Arjun Singh in an official matter at the Raj Bhavan in Sector 6 of Chandigarh whereas I was staying in a sprawling minister's house in Sector 2. The meeting with Arjun Singh ended sooner than expected. I had some time to spare. I decided to see Pannu at his house on my way back. Mine was to be a surprise visit. I found his house full of various people in more than one group. Pannu was attending to them group by group when he saw me. He greeted me and escorted me to his drawing room. He introduced me to the young man sitting there as Mr. H.S. Gill, who was the leader of the hardliners in the All India Sikh Students Federation. His statements often appeared in the press but he was supposed to be underground. I had asked about him from the Inspector General Intelligence only a day earlier and he had told me that they had information that he was in Jalandhar and they were keeping a watch on him to nab him when he tried to move out from there. It was a surprise for me to see him there. I found him to be a pleasant person to talk to. His criticism of the traditional Akali leaders appeared to me to be a bit harsh. He did not seem to have much understanding about what was going on in the world nor did I find him to be articulate about the Sikh tenets or tradition. I sent a note to Arjun Singh on my chance meeting with the activist of the AISSF, Mr. Gill. I found shortly thereafter Mr. Pannu barging into my house with a long face. He complained to me that he was dragged over by Arjun Singh for having introduced Mr. Gill to me. He said that he had just got out of the jam by telling a lie that Mr. Gill had not met me at his house. He then confided in me that he was exploring the possibility of the AISSF fighting elections under their own banner and he had arranged a secret meeting of Mr. Gill with Arjun Singh. The police had instructions to not to check the car in which Mr. Gill had travelled.This episode at least explained to me the reason for Pannu enjoying priority over officials like me. I had got my meeting fixed with Sant Longowal when Satarawala was the Governor but the meeting had materialised after Arjun Singh had joined. I went and briefed Arjun Singh about my meeting with Longowal. I conveyed to him the two demands of Sant Longowal. It was within the next 48 hours that I heard an announcement on the All India Radio conceding both his precondition. Thereafter, secret parleys started between Longowal, the Governor Arjun Singh and Rajiv Gandhi without involving any of the civil servants of Punjab or of the Government of India. I was told to remain out of it and avoid seeing Longowal. Longowal often came to Chandigarh but he never went to the Raj Bhavan for the meetings. The secret meetings were held mostly at the house of his South Indian Secretary, Mr. Narayanan. Sant Longowal had hesitated about attending these meetings when invited after his two preconditions had been met. He went for the meetings only after he had consulted the *Granth Saheb* and felt that the negotiations with the Government had the blessings of the Guru.

One of the points that was highlighted by Rajiv Gandhi in his address to the Chief Secretaries was about the lack of response and the lethargy that was associated with the Indian administrative process.

Generally, the people did not know about what relief they could get and from where. The lavatories, urinals and the surroundings of the government offices were marked by filth. The stink of urine was the distinguishing mark of a government office as soon as one entered it even in Lutyen's North Block and the South Block and no senior officer ever bothered about it. Surprisingly, when this aspect of our set-up was highlighted, it came out that the Punjab Secretariat had no separate restroom for the lady officers. It fell to my credit to provide a portico in front of the Punjab Secretariat where we got down from the cars and a separate restroom for the ladies. I wrote a general letter to the senior officers that they were also expected to ensure that the environment and facilities in their offices were kept spick and span. One of the senior officers protested that it was not the tradition in Punjab where senior officers were called upon to attend to such trivialities. There was one innovative young officer of Ahmednagar in Maharashtra, Mr. Lakhina, who initiated a transformation of the district office where the working of the office was made transparent and public friendly with the active cooperation of the lower category staff who were otherwise notorious for fleecing the people. I called him to address a meeting of the Punjab officials hoping that someone from Punjab would take the torch from him. I, however, found that this aspect of the administration did not interest the Punjab officials. We had a meeting of the District Officers and Commissioners in which we reviewed the achievements in the field of administration in the past year and prepared a milestone chart for the future. The meeting was addressed by Mr. Arjun Singh, who spoke for a future of peace and prosperity for Punjab. One achievement was that it was decided to bring the position of the district officer in Punjab at par with the position prevailing in the rest of India in the matter of initiating of the annual performance report of the district police chief. Everywhere except Punjab the performance report of the police chief was initiated by the District Magistrate. Mr Arjun Singh who had come from Madhya Pradessh saw no objection in it. I gleefully issued a circular in this regard causing an uproar among the Punjab police circles. The police in Punjab at that juncture was too important to be trifled with. Arjun Singh next day asked me to withdraw the circular. I still hoped that I would be able to convince Arjun Singh to let the order stand. I merely issued a letter staying action on the circular.

Mr. Arjun Singh called me the next day and said that what I had done was not a compliance of his order. Seeing that his mind was made up, I quietly withdrew the circular. I found Arjun Singh to be a very intelligent and sharp Governor who was an accomplished political player who would not let his left hand know what his right hand was doing. He spoke very little and he never raised his voice. He would send two liner notes to officers in his own hand for compliance. He had gone to Punjab Bhavan at Delhi. He gave a particular time for his breakfast. He was punctually present on the dining table at the given time. The bearer had kept a bowl of breakfast cereal on the table, he followed his practice of heating up the milk for the cereal after the guest came to the table. Arjun Singh sat on the table and took a spoonful of the cereal on his plate. He left the dining table before the milk arrived, without uttering a word. He sent a oneliner note to me on his return to Chandigarh to immediately transfer the Director of Hospitality whom I had rated as one of the very competent officers of Punjab. I proposed his transfer to a slot that I thought he deserved. The file came back to me with an order to speak to the Governor. I went to him and he told me that he had ordered the officer's transfer to punish him but what I was proposing amounted to rewarding him. I told him that I rated the officer highly. It had no effect on him nor would he tell me his reasons for punishing the officer. I had to obey the orders. The reason for his punishment, I came to learn when I visited Delhi the next time. Next time I received another list of officers whom he wanted to be transferred. This list had two officers who were not due for a transfer. One was the Sub Divisional Officer of Rajpura and the other was Jasbir Singh Ahluwalia, whom I considered as one of the outstanding officers of the state civil service. I had actually recommended him for out of turn promotion. I requested Arjun Singh to reconsider his order. He said that he was ordering the transfer of the SDO on the request of Vinod Sharma, the Congress MLA of the area. I called Vinod Sharma to know as to what he had against the SDO. He said that he had nothing specific against him but he could not trust him in elections which appeared to be round the corner. He said that he had found the SDO friendly with the likely candidate of the Akalis. I could not persuade him to withdraw his request. I called the SDO and told him that I could not prevent his premature transfer from Rajpura but he could choose his next posting. He was very happy at my offer and he got posted to the place that he wanted. Arjun Singh was not prepared to consider any stay of transfer of Ahluwalia. I could guess that it was because Ahluwalia had a dubious reputation of playing one group of Akalis against another. He was rated as an important Sikh intellectual and an ideologue. When it suited the Akalis to emphasize the separate identity of the Sikhs, he brought out his book called '*The Sovereignty of the Sikh Doctrine*'. It was claimed by him that the official Anandpur Saheb Resolution had been drafted by him in place of the draft given by Kapur Singh in 1973. He is a clever and worldly wise officer. He has almost converted the Guru Gobind Singh Foundation that was set up to commemorate the three hundredth birth anniversary of Guru Gobind Singh with hefty financial endowments from the Government of India and the Govenment of Punjab and others into a sort of his private estate, enabling him to enjoy certain perks and doing nothing. Apparently Ahluwalia was not in the good books of Balwant Singh, the Akali leader considered to be close to Arjun Singh. Arjun Singh did not like anyone who questioned his decisions and he started showing signs that he did not like me. He was of course always polite but he had his own way of showing his likes and dislikes. He would make me wait indefinitely when I went to see him even after an appointment given by his Secretary. I had come across a similar behaviour at the hands of the Raja of Ramgarh in Bihar. Arjun Singh was also from an old feudal Thakur family like him. It was perhaps a way with the rulers of the states to show their displeasure to important functionaries of the state. I asked the Cabinet Secretary to shift me from Punjab as the Governor did not seem to trust me. Arjun Singh was one step ahead of me in this. He had proposed that I be kicked upstairs as Advisor to the Governor carrying a higher rank and emoluments. The Chief Secretary is a statutory position through whom important papers have to go where he had an opportunity to express his views but an Advisor could be by-passed at will. Arjun Singh was good enough though to allocate almost all the important departments that were held by R.V. Subramaniam to me. Mr. P.H. Vaishnav was appointed as the Chief Secretary in my place.

Mr. Surinder Singh Kairon, the elder son of Sardar Partap Singh Kairon, came to see me for some help or the other. He was often a source of embarrassment for Kairon when he was the Chief Minister.

He tried to make some quick money through the abuse of the clout of the local officials in cahoot with his mother. Dr. Ghai who was Kairon's physician, in his autobiography, had described a Kairon family row of which he was a witness. The argument was over the advice of Kairon that his sons should take to social service from where they could come into public life in the tradition of their father and grandfather, the sons and their mother were saying that those times were well past. What was required currently was money for the public service. They said that they should first make money. These activities of Surinder and his brother Gurinder had led to the appointment of the Das Commission of Enquiry against Kairon. It was the adverse finding of the Das Commission, though only for a minor indiscretion, that had led to the resignation of Kairon as the Chief Minister of Punjab. He was a very dynamic person and a true Punjabi. He is the founder of the modern Punjab, that came to be known as the most advanced state with the highest per capita income. Surinder had set up some industry for producing DDT that was dependent on the Government for orders as the entire output of his factory went for the anti-malaria program. His son married the daughter of Mr. Prakash Singh Badal, the Akali leader. Badal was ridiculed and often taunted by Bhindranwale over this marriage alliance of the Akali leader with the family of a leader of the Congress led by Mrs. Gandhi against whom they were having the *Dharam Yudh Morcha.* I had never met Badal. He arranged a private dinner at his house in which apart from the family I was the only guest. He kept himself busy in looking after the guests while the ladies, as is the Indian tradition, congregated in one group talking among themselves. Mr. Badal and I were left alone to talk to each other. I found Mr. Badal to be somewhat aloof with me. He did not open out with me for quite some time. He seemed to be deliberately avoiding sharing his perceptions or ideas with me till Surinder joined in and put in a word in my praise. Badal liked his Black Label Scotch whisky but more so the tender, well marinated, Punjabi style Tandoori chicken. The negotiations had got started between Arjun Singh and Sant Longowal but Badal had not agreed to take part in those talks. I asked Badal as to why he had not joined Longowal in this effort to restore peace in Punjab. Badal said that he had refrained from joining the talks as he felt that the youngsters who had become so strident in their demands, would not allow any agreement to work. This answer from him clearly indicated to me that Badal stood for what was expedient and not necessrily for something that was desirable or right whereas Longowal realised as to what was correct and he was prepared to take a risk for what he saw as the right course. He was in a freer frame of mind after we had had one whisky each. We discussed many generalities and during that freewheeling discussion, I asked Badal about the Anandpur Saheb resolution of the Akali Dal. I said that the wording of the resolution did not make sense to me. How was it expected from the Government to do something for the '*bol bala*' of the Khalsa in a state that was declared to be a secular democratic republic? He laughed and said that he too did not understand much that was written or read in the Anandpur Saheb resolution. He, however, said leaving aside the wording of the resolution, the Akali Dal wanted to tell the Government of India that they should recognize that the Akali Dal had a committed following and they were the third party to the transfer of power by the British and by virtue of that the Akali Dal must be permitted to wield political power at least in Punjab.

He said that so far either the Central Government did not permit the Akalis to come to power through various tricks and strategems or if at all they got voted to power, their government was never allowed to complete its tenure. I told him that he was in public life and a leader of long standing, so he was in a better position to find a solution to the problem that he had raised. I further said that being in a position to know what was cooking in the government, I could tell him that for the time being Rajiv Gandhi had decided to place the Akali Dal in power in Punjab. He asked me to elaborate what I had said. I said even he could see the first straw in the wind in that direction which was the selection of Rajinder Singh Sparrow, a retired Army General as the President of the Punjab Pradesh Congress. It was an indication that the Congress was to play a friendly match against the Akali Dal in the coming elections with the intention of losing the elections. He laughed and said that there was some merit in my assessment. Rajinder Singh was a hero of the 1965 war against Pakistan during which he had commanded an armoured division on the Punjab front. He had joined the Congress party after his retirement. He had kept himself to his army lifestyle even after joining a political party. He lived in the style of senior army officers. He lived in a bungalow type of a house. He kept two large pet dogs and he daily went for a morning jog. He generally met people by appointment. Someone described his experience of meeting him. He asked for an appointment from the General. Sparrow said that his calendar for the day was full but he could join him in his morning jog and talk to him. The visitor joined him in the jog but the General kept the pace of jog so fast that the visitor all the time remained out of breath and unable to talk. The General offered to take him in his car as he was going to Ludhiana after his breakfast. His experience in the car was no better as the General's two bull dogs accompanied him in the car and the visitor remained petrified all the time because of the dogs sitting next to him. Such a person could not be expected to campaign for the victory of the Congress party in the elections. Anyhow, it was an enjoyable and useful dinner for me that recompensed me for the small favours that I might have shown to Surinder Kairon. Another benefit was that his son, Adesh Pratap Singh, became a bit of my admirer.

The Rajiv Gandhi-Longowal accord was signed on 24th July 1985. The accord was unique in many ways. It was one accord that was signed by the Prime Minister of India with the leader of a political party. Unlike earlier times no other parties were involved in discussions for working out the draft of the accord. The bureaucracy and the Home Minister were given the final draft only in the forenoon of the day when the accord was to be signed with a stipulation that the draft worked out would not undergo any further change. The draft was worded in a manner that it appeared that the Government was prepared to concede everything that the Akalis had been demanding. Chandigarh was conceded to be given to Punjab without specifying the Hindi speaking villages that would be transferred in lieu thereof. This was left to a Commission to identify the area from the Abohar Fazilka sub divisions that were Hindi speaking provided that such areas were contiguous to Haryana with village as a unit. The Akalis knew that village Kandukhera, which was Punjabi speaking, broke the contiguity for Haryana, so the whole area though not Punjabi speaking, the same could not go to Haryana.

Similarly, for the river waters a clause was inserted that the water to go to Punjab would never be less than a particular figure which was considered to be the maximum that Punjab required. I believe that there was a real meeting of minds between Sant Longowal and Rajiv

Gandhi. It seems that the unwritten expectation from the Akalis was that they would not let the extremists assume control of the Golden Temple Complex. The Punjab Government and the Akali Dal resisted the attempts of the Sikh Students' Federation and Damdami Taxal in early 1986, but unfortunately the Akali split came in their way. Gurcharan Singh Tohra, the SGPC President, publicly decried the use of force to oust the Taxal and the SSF activists. I am sure that Sant Longowal would have been able to carry out fully what was expected from the Akalis and the Accord would have survived but after his demise there was no one in the Akali leadership whose writ could run in the Sikh community.

The situation in Punjab improved rapidly after the accord. Arjun Singh left no opportunity to win over the Sikhs. He formally installed the equestrian statue of Maharaja Ranjit Singh in Ram Bagh, Amritsar, fulfilling a long pending aspiration of the Sikh community. He announced that all those who got killed in Punjab during the various police or army actions since 1.8.82 would be compensated by the Government at an enhanced rate.

A Committee was constituted under my Chairmanship to identity all the beneficiaries. The Committee had received, by 3.8.1985, only 668 applications after full publicity had been given in the media about the scheme. 495 applications had come from Amritsar and 52 from Sangrur. When exorbitant numbers are given for the Sikhs killed by the police and the army, I think one cannot take them without a big pinch of salt.

Longowal took it as his mission to explain the accord that had been signed by him with Rajiv Gandhi. He travelled from village to village, explaining and asserting that the accord signed by him was the best that the Sikh community could have extracted from the Government. I was impressed when in one of his public speeches he had distanced himself from Beant Singh and Satwant Singh, the assassins of Indira Gandhi. He said that they were carried away by emotion but their action was morally wrong. He seemed to be succeeding which perhaps alarmed those who were looking to Punjab to become like Bangladesh for them. The elections to the Punjab Assembly had been announced. Longowal set himself a schedule that was punishing for a human being. He would leave home early and visit village after village till late in the evening. The security guards even could not keep pace with him. So, it came about that when he started addressing a meeting in Gurdwara in village Sherpur on 20th August, 1985, his security guards were taken to the 'langar' for their meals. This seemed to be what the assassins were waiting for. The first shot fired missed. The first assassin disappeared in the melee but before the security guards could come, the other assassin Gian Singh posing as a security guard shot Longowal dead at a point blank range. The second assassin was nabbed on the spot. His interrogation revealed that he was a young man of impressionable age who was moved to tears by the hymn singing of Darshan Singh Ragi covering events in the Sikh history and Operation Blue Star. Someone who saw him crying told him that the Sikhs of Guru Gobind Singh did not cry like women, they fought the oppressor and took revenge. He said that he was seething with anger against the enemies of the *Panth* and if he had a weapon he would prove his worth. He was picked up some time later and given a revolver gun. He did not know how to use it. He was told that he was only to press the trigger after reaching the target. That was precisely what he did.

The elections to the Punjab Assembly were postponed for a few days due to the assassination of Longowal. The new date announced was 22nd September, 1985. I was provided a helicopter to oversee the conduct of elections in the Patiala and Ferozepur Divisions. We had not anticipated any trouble during the elections but the decision for the Advisor to the Governor to go on hopping helicopter flights, overseeing the process of elections all over Punjab were taken by Arjun Singh as perhaps to patronize the entrepreneur running the helicopter company. I visited as many places as I could on one day. I found that elections everywhere were peaceful and orderly. There was a lot of excitement in the constituency from where Bimal Khalsa, the widow of Beant Singh, was fighting her election. All her polling volunteers were Sikh youngsters with *Kesri* turbans.

I was to oversee counting of votes too after two days or so. It seemed on a visit to the counting centers that the SAD would be winning hands down. Bimal Khalsa as an independent candidate also seemed to be winning. I was surprised in the evening when I learnt, at the end, that she had lost by a narrow margin. A look at her voting figures indicated that the Returning Officer of her constituency had rejected a large number of votes caste in her favour on grounds of being invalid. This sort of thing cannot happen with the electronic voting machines. The results of the elections were unique in the sense that for the first time the SAD won a majority of seats in Punjab on their own.

19

Secretary, Government of India

Sardar Surjit Singh Barnala took over as the Chief Minister on the 29th September, 1985. The next day I joined as the Secretary, Health and Family Welfare under the Central Government. The Governor of Punjab permitted me to travel in his plane for reporting at Delhi. I stayed in the room of the Chief Secretary of Punjab in Punjab Bhavan. Sukhdev had stayed back to do packing, etc., for moving to Delhi. The Minister for Health was Mrs. Mohsina Kidwai from Uttar Pradesh. I had to join on the 30th as the former Health Secretary, Mrs. Serla Grewal, who had moved to the PMO as the Secretary to the Prime Minister, had fixed a meeting of all the Deans of the medical colleges in India, to arrive at a consensus on the 15% reservation in admissions to the medical colleges on the basis of merit in pursuance of the orders of the Supreme Court of India. I was virtually thrown before the wolves in the meeting as I had been given no briefing about the issues involved. It was my Bihar experience as the Health Commissioner and as the Reservations Commissioner that helped me in handling this important and ticklish issue. We discussed the subject the whole day but towards the evening I found that some lines were emerging on the basis of which a consensus looked feasible.The problem got complicated as the State Governments had prescribed varying reservations for admission to the medical colleges ranging from zero to 85 percent. Our consensus decision was that for our calculation for every state the ceiling for the reservation would be 50% and from the remaining 50% we would presrcibe 30% reservation on merit. There were some murmurs from states like Tamil Nadu but at the end of the day the consensus was endorsed. I decided to approach the Central Board for Secondary Education for administering a test for admission to the medical colleges and for allocating the particular medical colleges for admission to the students. We evolved a formula on the lines of the formula that the Government of India had for allocating states to the newly recruited IAS officers. We reported the whole package of our decisions to the Supreme Court of India who put their stamp of approval without any further fuss as no state had contested any clause of the package. I am glad to say that these decisions still guide the admissions to the medical colleges of the Government. My Joint Secretary dealing with the subject, Mr. P.P. Chauhan was a bright officer who belonged to a Scheduled Caste. He tried to smuggle in the caste reservation in this formula meant for the meritorious. I overruled him. He took the file to the Minister who also agreed with me. He gave up only when the Supreme Court endorsed the package. This only illustrates that in the Government environment, if one felt strongly on any issue, one had the freedom to fearlessly write it and take it to its logical end. I must also mention that some civil servants also got it into their neck when they touched on too sensitive a subject in a routine manner. One of my acquaintances suffered a lot when he stated certain facts about the land acquisition proceedings of the Maruti car project in his draft for a reply to a question in the Parliament. His house had got raided by the police. Nothing was found in his house except two bottles of Scotch whisky that he had brought with him from his foreign visit as his legitimate baggage but it was found that keeping more than one bottle in the house was an excise offence. It was a hell of a task for him to get out of the jam. However, such vindictive acts were very rare.

I found that the Health Ministry was one of the ministries that was among the priority areas selected by Rajiv Gandhi. We had change of ministers soon. Mr. Narasimha Rao became our new Minister. He was a known intellectual in the Congress. He had a sharp mind and he could articulate his thoughts well. He was appointed Minister of Health while he was in New York, attending a UNESCO meeting. We also had a young dynamic Minister of State Mr. Krishan Kumar, an ex-

IAS officer of Kerala cadre. He made a name for himself as the District Magistrate of Ernakulum for organising camps for mass sterilization or vasectomy that had become an example for the country as a whole. It seems that he was hand-picked by Rajiv Gandhi for galvanising the family planning program in India. Mrs. Serla Grewal was a very alert officer who could read the writing on the wall. She had been associated with the family planning programme almost all through when it was found that the medical professionals who had been presiding over the program did not have the necessary dynamism to lead the program. She was retained in the program during the stormy tenure of Sanjay Gandhi. She had survived the Janata Party phase too. Mr. Raj Narain, the victor from Rae Bareili against Indira Gandhi, had started relying on her. There was a funny anecdote about both of them going together in the official car to attend a meeting. Raj Narain had sat on the front seat, next to the driver, while Serla Grewal sat alone on the rear seat. Raj Narain liked himself to be addressed as '*Neta Ji*'. Someone asked him about his sitting on the front seat, in his own official car. His reply was that he was a '*brahmachari*' or the one who guarded his chastity. How could he even think of sitting next to Mrs. Grewal who was a young pretty lady. She had given the best that was in her for the family planning program in the country. She was also well aware of the sacking of C.R. Vaidyanathan for his failure to satisfy Rajiv Gandhi. Rajiv Gandhi was really proving difficult for the civil services by raising questions that the civil services in India were not equipped to answer. It appeared that he was also a bit in awe of the civil servants for their being highly educated while he could not claim himself to be a graduate.

I noticed that he would avoid eye contact with the civil servants in meetings. He, however, very much liked the civil servants to shiver in their pants before him. The action against Vaidyanathan had that purpose in mind. Similarly, sometime later he announced the sacking of the Foreign Secretary, Mr. Venkateshwaran, during a press conference. Mrs. Serla Grewal's appointment as his Personal Secretary was also to serve that very purpose as she was known in the civil services circles as the '*Hunter wali*' or the lady with the whip. Mrs. Grewal, before she moved to the PMO, had called the main advertising firms in India. She had entrusted them to come up with a project in which family planning could be marketed and sold to the people as they sold tea, soaps or other consumer products. Rajiv Gandhi and his Doon School friend, Arun Singh, had blessed the idea. The advertising firms asked for a time for presentation of their schemes as a trial baloon before they came up with the project. I was somewhat overawed by the famous names from the advertising world who came for that presentation session. I felt myself inadequate in handling them. Luckily for me they had some differences among themselves that came to the surface during the presentation. It was decided that a revised presentation would be made before a bigger house in which our Minister of State, Mr. Krishan Kumar, would be present. The next session made Mr. Krishan Kumar take over the subject, completely as his baby. He sat through the presentation and he held series of discussion with the advertising firms after which he prepared a presentation of his own. Rajiv Gandhi was requested to preside over the presentation which turned out to be a mixture of the traditional strategies and a few ideas lifted from the advertising agencies. Krishan Kumar was quite happy with himself. However, it was obvious that the presentation did not jell with Rajiv Gandhi. Krishan Kumar, in desperation, asked Rajiv Gandhi as to what he wanted and where he had gone wrong. Rajiv Gandhi's reply was that Krishan Kumar was the Minister in charge of the program and it was for him to come up with a formula that would solve the problem. He on his part could say that what he had presented would not give the program the break through that he was looking for. Mr. Krishan Kumar was quite disappointed and confessed to me that the whole exercise had left him demoralised. The fact clearly emerged in this meeting that in a country like India, with such a diversity of languages, communities, tribes and religions in our democratic framework of functioning, we could not work out a consensus to enable us to solve our population problem. We had burnt our fingers trying the Sanjay Gandhi model of coercion and monetary incentives. We could not adopt the Chinese model as we did not have a monolithic party like the Communist Party of China along with an autocratic authoritarian model of administration that functioned under a controlled press. Neither any bureaucrat nor any academician nor any family planning professional nor any media baron nor any politician had an answer to the question raised by Rajiv Gandhi. The only answer that one could cite as a success to be replicated was the example of Kerala state where a real impact could be seen on the birth rate where the target of NRRI had almost been achieved. The causes for that were cultural, female education and the empowerment of women. A major factor was the availability and the tradition of institutional facilities for child birth instead of dependence on untrained midwives. All these deliberations spread over more than six months resulted in a sort of windfall to two personalities. One was Professor Ashish Bose, an academician from the Indian Institute of Economic Growth. He had exposed the hollowness of the achievements claimed for the Family Planning Program through his studies and writings. He showed as to how giving targets to different levels of officials had completely distorted the program. He brought out the glaring failure of the program in the Hindi heartland of India. The rise in the population growth continued to be above two percent in these states when the aim was to reach zero growth or NRRl in 2001. He coined the acronym BIMARU for the area which in Hindi meant "Sick". BI was for Bihar, MA for Madhya Pradesh, R for Rajasthan and U for Uttar Pradesh. Dr. Ashish Bose became the most sought after academician on Family Planning. The other person who got recognized by Rajiv Gandhi was the pretty journalist, Mrs. Rami Chhabra. She had a charming personality and she was an articulate journalist. She had been doing pieces on Indian women and family planning. Her columns appeared in all the prestigious newspapers and magazines in India and abroad. She was appointed as a Media Advisor in the Ministry of Health in the rank of an Additional Secretary to the Government of India. It seemed that the offer of appointing her had emanated directly from Rajiv Gandhi. Serla Grewal when conveying orders of her appointment to me cautioned me that she was suspected of having CIA links. She advised me to keep a watch on her and also to not to allocate the subject of dealing with the International Organisations and AID to her in my order of distribution of work in the ministry.

S.S. Ahluwalia had been able to build himself up in the eyes of Rajiv Gandhi. He had come in contact with Rajiv Gandhi as a colleague of Sardar Buta Singh but slowly he moved closer to Rajiv Gandhi. Rajiv Gandhi had appointed him as a Member of the Committee that had been constituted for providing relief to the victims of the anti-Sikh riots. The Committee had Sardar Gurdial Singh Dhillon as the President but he was more or less a figurehead. Ahluwalia kept a low profile and rendered very useful service in organizing relief for the victims. Rajiv Gandhi, recognizing his merit and usefulness, selected him as a Congress candidate for the Rajya Sabha from Bihar. The rise in the importance of Ahluwalia was not to the liking of Sardar Buta Singh. My relationship with both of them, however, continued to be cordial. Ahluwalia told me that Rajiv Gandhi felt that the Secretaries in the Government of India really occupied crucial positions from where they were in a position to make or mar a program. He felt that, as he saw them, only a few of them applied themselves seriously to making the programs under them a success. Mostly they remained satisfied with being only file pushers. He told him that he was planning an exercise for a few Secretaries where they would have to personally make a presentation before a Committee of the Parliament. He said that those who failed in the exercise would be reverted back to their states on the spot. He thought that the proposed exercise would shake the Secretaries out of their complacence. Rajiv Gandhi had picked up five areas of administration for what were called Technology Missions. The progress in these areas was to be monitored by the PMO. These missions had a component of technology and its application on the ground. These missions were spread of telecommunications, provision of drinking water in the remote and rural areas, production of oilseeds, universal program of immunization for children and compulsory primary education. The universal child immunization program fell on the Ministry of Health. Serla Grewal called the five concerned Secretaries and told us that we had to make a presentation of our respective programs before the Parliamentary Committee attached to the Department of Science and Technology which would be presided over by the Prime Minister with respective Ministers in attendance during the presentation. We were given one month to prepare ourselves for the presentation. Thanks to Ahluwalia, I had some idea as to what to expect in the meeting. We went to Serla Grewal to know as to how we should go about it. She told us that Rajiv Gandhi would like the presentation to be as far as possible audio-visual so that members attending could easily grasp what was being planned. Apparently she was not privy to what was in the mind of Rajiv Gandhi for this exercise. My other colleagues hired professionals for their presentations perhaps due to the advice of Serla Grewal. I went to Narasimha Rao and apprised him about the ordeal.

He listened as usual with a poker face and asked me as to what I had thought about it. He did not seem to appreciate the whole idea of the exercise that we had to go through. I am sure that if I had displayed some reluctance in undertaking the exercise, he would have got me exempted as he had done for the Education Secretary for the Mission on Compulsory Primary Education. I showed my willingness to take the test. I told him that since the Secretary was required to make a presentation personally, so I would make a presentation through photographic slides on a screen. He desired that I should show him what I had finally decided to present. I presented the slides that I had got prepared a day or two before I was to appear in the Parliament House. He made one or two suggestions that were good and helped to improve the presentation. It was like the day for me on which I had appeared for the IAS interview in 1954. All of us sat quite tense as the Ministers and MPs trooped in followed by Rajiv Gandhi. Mr. Bandyopadhya the Secretary for Rural Development was the first to rise for his presentation on rural water supply. His presentation opened with a musical showing a beautiful Rajasthani lass carrying a water pitcher on her head. Mr. Rajiv Gandhi intervened within the first two minutes of the presentation upbraiding the Secretary, saying that the whole group was sitting there for understanding from him a serious national program and not to watch a cinema show. He asked him to make a presentation without the frills of the audio-visual presentation. He asked him to recast his presentation in the light of the observations that he had made. He asked for the next presentation from the Telecommunications Secretary. The Secretary seemed to have been well-prepared and his presentation went without a hitch. Later, I came to know that the success of the presentation was due to Sam Pitroda, an NRI entrepreneur friend of Rajiv Gandhi. The whole idea of technology missions was his brain child. He was the executive behind the ambitious expansion of the telecommunication network in India. The presentation of Mr. Krishnaswamy, the Agriculture Secretary was next but he had developed cold feet after seeing the fate of Bandyopadhyay's presentation on rural water supply. He requested me to make my presentation before him to give him more time for revising his presentation. I gladly agreed and it was announced that the next would be my presentation. Mr. Narasimha Rao, who was sitting next to Rajiv Gandhi, called me to the high table and asked me loudly so that Rajiv Gandhi could hear it to confirm that I was going to make the same presentation as I had earlier made before him, to whom I replied in the affirmative. No one interrupted me during my presentation. It was only after I had completed that Najma Heptulla, MP, tried to score a point by asking me a question. I got away from it by promising to enquire into the matter though I knew that what she was alleging was not true and she had asked the question only to impress Rajiv Gandhi. Mr. Krishnaswamy inspite of the extra time that he got failed in his presentation completely, so much so that Rajiv Gandhi said that he was being reverted to his state of Andhra Pradesh forthwith. He asked the Cabinet Secretary who was sitting there to issue orders to that effect before the day was out. It made Serla Grewal run to the high table to say something to Rajiv Gandhi. We could not make out what the exchange was between them. It was announced at the end of the meeting that Mr. Krishnaswamy would be making a presentation to him in the afternoon and if he could satisfy him in that, he would be permitted to stay on. Mr. Gurdial Singh Dhillon, the Agriculture Minister sat through the entire session completely silently. I later learnt from a friend that he was quite upset at the treatment that was meted out to the Secretary of his Department. He straightaway went to meet Giri Lai Jain, the Editor of the *Times of India*, who was his friend. He cried over his shoulder over what he saw as his humiliation. Giri Lai Jain asked him if he would resign from the Cabinet on that issue. Dhillon's reply was in the negative as he said that he would not like to embarrass Mr. Rajiv Gandhi by resigning. Giri Lai Jain wrote an Editorial in the *Times of India*, the next day, castigating Rajiv Gandhi for his immaturity. The surprise of the whole affair to me was as to why Rajiv Gandhi had not taken his ministers or Serla Grewal into confidence about the purpose of the exercise, which to me seemed to be unexceptionable. Could it be because he was an airplane pilot who always sits almost alone in his cockpit and takes all his decisions on the basis of his assessment and judgment? I think that he never learnt the lesson that in public life even for legitimate decisions one had to build acceptability for the same among the articulate sections of the people affected by such decisions.

One more trait that I observed in Rajiv Gandhi was his change of mind on many issues. I asked Mrs. Sheila Dixit, who was a MoS with the PM. She observed that his change of mood was due to his discussion with the last person whom he met that day. Her hint was clear that it was Mrs. Sonia Gandhi.

We had an excellent officer in Dr. L.S. Bisht, the Director General of the Health Services. He commanded a lot of respect in the medical profession. He was very devoted to his work and he could be depended upon fully in any situation. He got selected for an appointment under the World Health Organisation. He remained with me for about two months to enable me to find my feet in the Health Ministry but he had to go ultimately. The next candidate according to the gradation list was Dr. Vishwakarma, an Orthopaedic Surgeon who was the Medical Superintendent of the Safdarjung Hospital in Delhi. I happened to discuss this matter with Mr. Narasimha Rao. I told him that the Director General represented the medical profession for the Government of India. Although the health services was a subject in the state list under the Constitution of India but all the states looked for guidance from the Director General of the Health Services. Secondly, it was in the field of public and preventive health that the Government of India was expected to initiate policies and programs that the state governments could implement. A specialist in orthopaedic surgery would be a misfit. The Government, in appointing him as the Director General, would be losing the expertise of a competent orthopaedic surgeon, and in him they would have a person unfit to provide leadership in the field of preventive and public health. He welcomed the idea of revising the rules of recruitment for the post of the Director General of the Health Services. I got busy in the matter of consultation at various levels in order to evolve a consensus about the qualifications for the post. The exchange of notes between me and the Minister got leaked out. There was a news item in the press that I was playing some sort of game for the purpose of getting a favourite of mine selected as the Director General. I ignored the insinuation and went ahead in working out the revised draft rules of recruitment for the post of the D.G. The lobby that wanted Dr. Vishwakarma, consisting of some MPs and some senior doctors then directly accused Narasimha Rao of trying to ignore seniority and merit in the matter of the appointment of the D.G. The complaint was directly addressed to the Prime Minister. When I next met Narasimha Rao to discuss the draft further, I found that he had developed cold feet. He said, after dilly dallying for a few days, that we had started the process of the revision of the recruitment rules a bit too late, therefore, he felt that we should drop the matter and go ahead with the appointment as per the existing recruitment rules. Dr. Vishwakarma was well aware of our move to block his appointment as the Director General. Dr. Vishwakarma had a tenure of about three years, almost coterminous with my tenure as the Health Secretary. I decided to accept his appointment with a good grace. I told him that I had valid reason to oppose his appointment but once his appointment got cleared we had to work together as a team. He assured me that he would never give me a cause for a complaint against him and I found him to be a man of his word.

I had gone to attend a meeting in the WHO at Geneva for a week. When I returned I found that the doctors of the Central Health Service had gone on strike after giving a charter of their demands. The thrust of their demands was that the pay and prospects of the medical officers belonging to the Central Health Services should be no less attractive than the pay and prospects of an IAS officer. Mr. Umashankar, my Additional Secretary, was handling it by meeting the leaders of the doctors on strike and the officers of the Finance Ministry, who had the final word about how much could be paid to the medical officers. Generally, Dr. Vishwakarma had accompanied him in all the meetings. The negotiations were reaching nowhere. It was suspected that Dr. Vishwakarma was queering the pitch for the government in those negotiations by leaking out the content of the discussions to the striking doctors. It had been decided in consultation with the Cabinet Secretary and the Finance Secretary to drop Dr. Vishwakarma from the negotiating team. I was briefed about the situation on my arrival back. I thought of taking my Minister into confidence. He arranged a meeting with Mr. V.P. Singh, the Finance Minister and his officials. I was disappointed with the outcome of the meeting as no new ground could be broken in the meeting. Meanwhile my old detractor Mrs. Promilla Kalhan, from the Super Bazar days, put out a story in the *Hindustan Times* that I was proving to be a disaster as the Secretary of the Ministry of Health. She presented me as a crony of Sardar Buta Singh, who according to her was responsible for bringing me back to Delhi after having been found incompetent in my earlier assignment in Delhi. She concluded that there was no hope of the matter getting resolved so long as I was the Health Secretary. One curious new development was the appearance of Dr. Wats on the scene as the leader of the striking doctors. He made no secret of the fact that he was affiliated to the Congress party and that he had some links with the PMO. As soon as Mr. Narasimha Rao got a wind of the PMO being in some way involved in the matter, he made himself unavailable for any discussion or guidance. This in a way was a repeat of his performance of 1984 when he was the Home Minister. The strike had gone on for more than two weeks. I decided to step-in at that stage. I invited the leaders to meet me at a neutral venue. Some press reporter asked me if I had something special to offer for the striking doctors. I replied to the question in the negative. The newspapers carried the story of the striking doctors being called to meet me along with my statement that I had nothing new to offer. This was the first time that I had a telephone call from Narasimha Rao at my residence, early in the morning when I had gone to seek the morning blessings from the *Granth Saheb* installed in a room in our house. He seemed to be a bit upset over my statement that I had nothing to offer to the striking doctors. I told him that my statement to the press was a deliberate ploy to test as to how rigid or flexible the striking doctors would be on the negotiating table and I was sure that the leaders of the doctors would come to attend the meeting all the same. I had discarded the policy of keeping Dr. Vishwakarma out of the discussions concerning the demands of the CHS doctors. The leaders of the doctors came for the meeting as was expected. They talked tough which I considered to be good. The meeting had from the government side the representatives of the Ministry of Finance apart from the officials of the Ministry of Health and the Director General of the Health Services. I frankly told the leaders of the striking doctors that they had to convince me about the legitimacy of their demands and we would try to explain to them our compulsions in acceding to their demands and we had to ensure that in solving their problems we did not create problems elsewhere and that conceding to their demands did not have a cascading effect on other services in the country. We had a discussion on every aspect of their demands for the whole day. We agreed to meet in a smaller group, as and when it became necessary. One clear gain of the meeting was that the doctors were able to shed their prejudice against the bureaucrats. The other was my education that as Secretary Health it was my duty to stand for the cause of the doctors in the government.

I enjoyed the position in which I found myself. It reminded me of my district days, handling tough law and order situations. When it really became hot in the districts, it was experienced that the politicians, the senior officers and the police chief would welcome me taking upon myself the responsibility for tackling the problem threatening the public and permitted them to watch from the sidelines. The Minister and his associates, after showing some initial interest, decided to wait and watch. Mr. Narasimha Rao took shelter behind the principle that he said he had always followed in his political career. He said that he could never negotiate with a group of employees while they were on a strike. I personally thought his real reason for remaining away was his uncertainty about the PMO. After all he was known to be a great survivor in the Congress who had come to occupy the position of the number two in the Central Government. Unexpectedly, I found that in handling the issue in the Government of India, I had a free hand to the extent that I could carry the Finance Ministry and the Cabinet Secretary with me. I was meeting them frequently. I came to acquire a good idea about the limits of tolerance on both the sides.

The flexibility on the Ministry of Finance side was obtained by me when I cited the example of a popular medical specialist who was about to retire. I said that under the present dispensation he would retire in the rank of a Director that was below the Joint Secretary rank whereas an IAS officer became a Joint Secretary after putting in only 19 years of service. I could see that the example quoted went home with both the Cabinet Secretary and the Finance Secretary. One of the hitches was that the doctors were demanding a system of time bound promotions for the doctors regardless of the vacancies.

I had an experience of working the system in the ICAR. The operation of a time bound promotion system affected performance very adversely. It was like equating the horses and the asses in which excellence in performance became nobody's concern. We had many sittings together in our effort to work out a formula that could be acceptable to both the sides. I had kept Serla Grewal apprised of the progress that we were making. She rang me up one day telling me that Rajiv Gandhi was going to Sri Lanka the next day and it would be a feather in his cap if I could get the doctors to agree to sign a settlement before his departure. We had almost hammered out an agreed deal. I called on the Finance Secretary Mr. Venkataraman due to a last minute hitch. His Joint Secretary was B.P. Verma from Bihar. He was of great help to me in finally getting Mr. Venkataraman to endorse the package that we had worked out. We sat through the night to finalize the agreement. I told Mr. V. George that we would be able to report a success by about 2 a.m. He said that the Prime Minister would be waiting to hear from me till then. As sometimes happens one mad cap among the doctors put a spanner in the wheel at the last minute where our talks broke down. I told my Secretary to close the office as I was going home. I informed George that we could not agree at the last minute. Dr. Vishwakarma, the Director General, got wind of my leaving the office. He came to me and asked me to give him five minutes before closing the office. He went across to the room where the leaders of the striking doctors were also preparing to go home. Dr. Vishwakarma roundly abused the leaders and said that what I had worked out was the best deal possible for them. They were being bloody fools in turning it down. He gave them a dressing down in the real sense. The leader of the striking doctor sheepishly came to say that they accepted the deal that had been worked out but formally they would like to say so in the presence of the Prime Minister. He requested me to take them to the Prime Minister. I rang up George to tell him that we were on way to the PM's house. I suddenly remembered that we had to get a formal nod from Narasimha Rao too. I took the doctor's delegation to 10, Moti Lal Nehru road, the residence of Narasimha Rao and woke him up. He gave his blessings to the deal and all of us trooped in to 7, Race Course Road. Rajiv Gandhi was awake and looked fresh. He received us cordially and expressed his happiness that a bad chapter in our relations with the doctors was going to be behind us. I could not help feeling that the striking doctors had enjoyed a sneaking sympathy from Rajiv Gandhi who felt happy in conceding to the demands of the doctors which the Government otherwise would never have granted to a single category of employees in such an adhoc manner. The doctors felt that what they achieved by way of improvement in their pay and promotional prospects and other service conditions was the best so far. Much later I happened to meet one of the leaders of the doctor's strike as my consulting physician, Dr. Agarwal, in the Lohia Hospital. He was very solicitous about my health and said that the whole doctor community would remain indebted to me for the deal that I got from the government for them. He confirmed my suspicion that Rajiv Gandhi had been convinced of their case before they had gone on strike. It was he who hinted that even he could not get all from the system that they were expecting. They had to get the administration into a situation where the administration got compelled to grant them what was their legitimate due. This was a new facet of the personality of Rajiv Gandhi that the public hardly knew.

I attended a meeting of the Secretaries of the Government which was called by Professor M.G.K. Menon, Member of the Planning Commission and Professor Gowarikar, the Secretary for the Department of Science and Technology. The meeting was addressed by Mr. Rajiv Gandhi. He said that he was keen that we should think about ourselves in 2001. He had taken the initiative to get each of the Secretaries connected to a countrywide computer network extending up to the district level. He, however, found that the Secretaries, mostly, were not computer savvy nor he found them having a scientific temper. He said that the scientific temper was a must if we had to keep pace with the Western nations. He said that during the discussions Secretary Railways had claimed that in rail coach manufacturing they had the most advanced technology, equal to the best in the world. Yet, he said that a few weeks after the discussion, he got a file from the Railways proposing a technical collaboration with some foreign concern for upgrading our technology which was getting obsolescent. He posed the question to all as to why this was happening. No one got up to answer his question. He then gave out his own opinion about it. He said that our situation demonstrated the lack of scientific temper in our people. He gave the example of the speaker that was before him. He showed that there was a slight shredding of the wire that was going into the speaker which was likely to crack if left unattended. He was sure that it would be attended here only after it got cracked. Whereas in cultures that had the scientific temper the janitor who came for dusting the office in the morning would have noticed the defect and given the necessary feedback to the maintenance section or may be even to the manufacturers. I could not help feeling that we had amongst us someone who was before his times.

I had gone to attend a meeting of the National Development Council when I received a paper on which something was scribbled through an attendant sent by Serla Grewal. I found the paper that was addressed to the Health Minister on which there was a note written by Rajiv Gandhi in his own hand. It was a letter from Dr. Ramlingswamy, the Director General of the Indian Council of Medical Research, informing the Health Minister that six prostitutes had been found HIV positive. These were the first known cases of AIDS in India. Rajiv Gandhi in his own hand had written that he had been cautioning the health authorities since quite some time but the Health Ministry had just been dithering over it. He had written that since AIDS had officially appeared, so he would like the Health Ministry to come up with an emergency program to deal with AIDS in India. He wanted the Health Ministry to work out a crash program and put up to him for his approval within a week. I continued attending the meeting as if nothing had happened. Serla Grewal walked to me from her seat on the high table to ask me if I had read the note that she had sent to me. I told her that I had read the letter and I was trying to collect my thoughts about the crash program that we were required to prepare. She also asked me to inquire as to how the letter addressed to the Health Minister had reached the Prime Minister. It was obvious that it was the overenthusiasm of Dr. Ramlingaswamy that had made him endorse a copy to the Prime Minister and the same was sent by him through his personal physician.

I learnt that the freemasonry of the doctors functioned in that manner throughout. This made the medical profession to have the ear of powers that be, no matter who was in power. There were certain aspects about the Indian discovery of the AIDS which were confusing. The expert said that the AIDS got communicated either through sharing of injection needle of the affected person or through the blood transfusion from an affected person. The second source was through unprotected sex with an infected person or through promiscuous sex. With all these factors that the first case discovered from Salem in the interior of Tamil Nadu was difficult to grasp. The second doubt arose from the fact that none of the HIV positive cases had developed any symptoms of AIDS in India so long as I was the Health Secretary. When these questions were raised, it came out that the HIV virus in India was a strain different from the one that was found in the Western countries. It was, however, clear that AIDS was a new enemy that we had to be prepared to fight. I got a Committee of Experts set up to give us a crash AIDS control program within the framework of one week that was given to us. We were able to meet the deadline in that. The program involved a massive investment in our blood testing laboratories to screen all the vulnerable sections of the people. A lot of foreign exchange was involved as we had to import all the blood testing kits for AIDS from abroad. The WHO also set up a special directorate for AIDS in Geneva. A World AIDS Awareness and Control Conference was convened by the WHO in London. The Conference was attended by me and Narasimha Rao, on behalf of India. It seemed that the WHO was aware about the standing of Narasimha Rao in the Indian Government. He was unanimously elected as the Vice Chairman of the Conference. I was taken in the Drafting Committee. We made a provision in the Draft for a resolution by the Conference in which slight variations in approach in devising the control program were permitted to the participating countries according to the particular conditions prevailing in those countries. One African delegate in an aside said to me that 'Africans in many countries were dying like flies of many diseases and epidemics about which the WHO had never bothered but since AIDS was affecting the White races more, so they wanted the resources of the healthcare programs to be diverted to AIDS all over the world'.

The Secretary Health, I found had to go abroad almost once in two months to attend some meeting or the other. The World Health Assembly met in Geneva during the first fortnight of May every year. The Minister of Health generally attended in the first week and the Secretary Health in the next week. Hindujas were the leading members of the Indian community. Srichand Hinduja invited me for tea at his house. I consulted the First Secretary of our embassy in Geneva, Mr. Malhotra, the son of General Malhotra, the Army Chief, if it would be appropriate for me to accept the invitation. He said that the family was well-respected in Geneva and it was the practice with the Hindujas to invite the visiting ministers and senior officials for a meal or tea at their house. I accepted the invitation. Hindujas lived in a villa overlooking the world famous Geneva Lake. The view of the lake and Geneva city from their house was breathtaking. He had a charming but simple Indian wife. They were strict vegetarians and teetotalers. They had a cellar full of all the rare and choicest wines. The tea was a simple afair. It came in an elegant and a shining silver service.

They also served us Alfonso mangoes that had come from India. Hindujas were excellent and affectionate hosts who could put a guest at ease and feel at home. Srichand overheard me talking to Sukhdev in Delhi. She had asked me to enquire about the possibility of bringing a small microwave oven. Mr. Hinduja enquired from me if I needed anything for our house or children in Delhi. I had replied to that in the negative. It was a meeting for which Narasimha Rao too had come to Geneva. He was staying in the same hotel called Hotel DeBergue. I got a telephone sometime in the afternoon from Chandraswami whom I did not know. He invited me to come to his place for dinner. I told him that I was with the Health Minister in Geneva; therefore, I could not be sure if I could be free for dinner or not. Chandraswamy said that Narasimha Rao would be going to his place for the dinner. I told Chandraswamy that if the Minister so liked I could accompany him. Somehow, Mr. Narasimha Rao preferred to go alone for the dinner which saved me from an awkward situation. Mr. Srichand Hinduja came to see me off at the airport when I was leaving. I found that along with my baggage there was a cardboard package containing a microwave oven on the scale. I thought that it was placed on the scale by mistake and advanced to remove it when Srichand Hinduja signalled to me that it was for me, for my wife with his compliments. I tried to argue over it with him. He said that he had been giving such gifts and much more to most of the Indian VIPs who had been happily taking. He said that I was unnecessarily haggling over something so trivial. It appeared a bit awkward at the airport to create a scene. There was another scene at the Delhi airport created by the Protocol Officer of the Health Ministry. The cardboard box of the microwave oven was the original packing of the product with 'microwave oven' boldly written on it. It was an item under the baggage rules for which 120% customs duty had to be paid but the Protocol Officer, as usual, took it in a trolley passing through the green channel. The Customs Inspector knew the Protocol Officer, so he did not stop him. There was a Customs Officer just near the exit gate, who looking at the trolley pointed out that a Duty had to be paid for the particular item. He turned to another Customs Officer reminding him that only the other day he had come to receive the Minister of State, Ms. Saroj Khaparde, returning after attending the same meeting. He said that she had 14 bags with her. The Customs Officers did not question her about her baggage at all. He said that the Secretary had only one bag and a small cardboard box for which he was being stopped and asked to pay the Customs Duty. He relented but again at the gate the same officer stopped the trolley and asked the Protocol Officer to accompany him to the Assistant Commissioner. I intervened at that stage, offering to pay the Customs Duty as was due. Some 1600 rupees was levied as the Customs Duty. My Protocol Officer was incensed at my being made to pay the customs duty. I pacified him telling him that the Customs Officer was only doing his duty. I told Sukhdev that for fulfilling her desire I got myself put into a somewhat compromising position. I reminded her of our Deoghar days when she had returned the silk sari that was brought to her by Burman of the Dabur and later when I had sought permission from the Bihar Government to accept a coffee percolater. Now I found myself accepting a gift in clear violation of the IAS conduct rules and doing nothing about it. Was it because of a flexibility in standards that had come about in me or was it reflecting the change of times with the passage of 30 years in service or both?

Saroj Khaparde was from the Rajya Sabha. She belonged to Maharashtra. The allocation of work, which was made by Narasimha Rao had not given her any authority over the personnel in the Ministry. She had an access to Rajiv Gandhi. She complained to him that as Minister of State she had no work. She got some say in postings and transfer of the doctors after her complaint. She was guided more by prejudices than principles in her decisions. She did not like the Medical Officer of the Parliament Medical Centre, allegedly because of the airs that the doctor had about herself. She ordered her transfer. Narasimha Rao, in an earlier decision taken by her, had refused to interfere on the ground that he would not reverse the decision of his Minister of State as a matter of principle. The lady medical officer of the medical centre in Parliament was a favourite of Mr. Balram Jakhar, the Speaker of the Lok Sabha. He pulled up Narasimha Rao for transferring the Medical Officer without the courtesy of even consulting him. Narasimha Rao enquired from me as to how the transfer was made. I sent the file to him. Saroj Khaparde had bypassed me in ordering that transfer. Mr. Narasimha Rao did not have the courage to defy an important politician like Balram Jakhar. He asked me to meet him and explain the position. Balram Jakhar insisted on having his pound of flesh and asked me to get the transfer cancelled. Mr. Narasimha Rao had no alternative other than to depart from his self-imposed principle and over rule Saroj Khaparde. Wherever Saroj Khaparde had an opportunity she would snipe at me and give vent to her anger against me but because of her limited capability she could not do much except stop one or two of my proposed visits abroad. We were together in the Commonwealth Health Ministers Conference in Nassau, Bahamas. Our leader of the delegation was Narasimha Rao. I got ticked off by Narasimha Rao by giving him a draft for a speech to be delivered by him that was prepared without much thought by a Joint Secretary. He spent all the travelling time in preparing his speech. He sat through most of the night dictating and correcting his speech. I felt bad for having let him down. We had stayed in a beautiful hotel on the sea beach. I could not resist the temptation of bunking the meeting like my student days and splash into the sea for a swim. We had an official reception in the evening.

We had a change in our Minister with the reshuffle of the Central Cabinet. Mr. Moti Lal Vora became our new Minister. He was the Chief Minister of Madhya Pradesh after Arjun Singh. He was a quiet sort of a gentleman who was friendly and courteous. He seemed to be a bit jealous of Arjun Singh. I had mentioned to him that there was a project for child welfare in Churhat in Madhya Pradesh patronised by Arjun Singh. They had applied for assistance from the USAID. Mr. Arjun Singh, in his Punjab style, had sent me a two liner slip written in his own hand to help in getting an early clearance of the project. I had told Ms. Lata Singh, the dealing Joint Secretary, to keep an eye over it so that it was not caught in some routine bureaucratic exchange of notes. We were able to get the project through in about three months. Moti Lal Vora expressed a desire to see the relevant file. Moti Lal Vora observed that the field conditions were not as good as had been described in the file. The other case in which he had taken a direct interest was in the recommendations of a Technical Committee which was considering laying down standards for *Paan Masala*. The Committee was cosidering banning of tobacco as a constituent of *Paan Masala*. *Paan Masala* is a multi-crore business in India and its sales were feared to plummet if tobacco was excluded from its ingredients. Moti Lal Vora entrusted the task of restoring tobacco as an ingredient of *Paan Masala* to Dr. Vishwakarma bypassing me. Dr. Vishwakarma sought my advice on the issue. I said that I was not personally involved in the issue either way. It was really a decision for the experts to take. If the experts in the Committee wanted to oblige the Minister, I was not interested in making it an issue to fight the Minister. The Minister ultimately tried to justify his action to me as perhaps he was trying to assuage his guilty conscience. Moti Lal Vora, by virtue of his position as the Minister for Health, was the President of the Governing Body of the PGI, Chandigarh. The post of the Director of the PGI was falling vacant. Generally, the seniormost Professor was appointed as the Director. Professor B.N.S. Walia who was the Dean was the seniormost with a good performance record. It was expected that his appointment would be cleared by the Governing Body. I happened to be out of India when the meeting of the Governing Body was held. Later, I discovered that the item concerning the appointment of Dr. Walia was not cleared in the meeting. I asked Moti Lal Vora if there was any reason behind the postponement of the consideration of the item in the meeting. He said that Mr. Kaushal, MP, and former Governor of Bihar had alleged in the meeting that Dr. Walia was communally biased in his decisions, so unfit for the appointment. He said that others remained silent over the allegation, so he had to postpone the item. He also said that he had nothing against Dr. Walia, if I could find some way to rebut the allegation made against him. I was in a quandary, more so as I too happened to be a Sikh. I wrote to the Director Generals of the CBI and the Intelligence Bureau, as also to the Inspector General of Police, Chandigarh. All of them replied that they had no information or complaint from which they could endorse the charge against Dr. Walia that he was suffering from any communal bias in his dealings. The Intelligence Bureau report said that the only thing that they had heard against Dr. Walia was that during the November 1984 riots Sikh doctors of the PGI often were seen visiting Dr. B.N.S. Walia. I put up the replies received before Moti Lal Vora, recommending clearance of Dr. Walia's appointment and adding in my note that 1984 was a period of great stress everywhere and during that period if the Sikh doctors of the PGI visited for solace their senior Dr. Walia, the same could not be held against him. Thus, his appointment as the Director PGI, Chandigarh got cleared. This was about the end of my career as a civil servant in free India. The last episode in my career vindicated my faith in the Indian democracy and the acceptability and recognition of all communities in it. The Sikh community seemed to have harmed themselves by listening to shortsighted political leaders, a prospect against which Sardar Patel had cautioned the Sikh leadership in the Constituent Assembly. I wish and pray that the Sikh community is able to reclaim the leadership role in the Indian society as was assumed by the Sikh Gurus and their ancestors not so long ago.

20

As Election Commissioner

I was physically and mentally quite fit when I retired. My friend O.P. Sharma, who has studied Law with me at the Aligarh Muslim University, was a Senior Advocate of the Supreme Court of India. He persuaded me to join him in his legal practice. I was required to undergo an internship of one year before being admitted to the Bar. This was waived in my case because of my experience as a District Magistrate. I got a black coat stitched and acquired the prescribed collar and the gown of the lawyer. Mr. O.P. Sharma got an extra table and chair put for me in his chamber where sometime earlier Sanjay Gandhi had sat. I watched hearings of some important cases in the Supreme Court. One morning I saw a person in Mr. Sharma's chamber, accompanied by a client. Mr. Sharma signaled to me to leave his chamber. It shocked me to know that Mr. Sharma had touts to bring clients to him. Having walked always a straight path during my service tenure, I could not make myself a partner in a calling that required touts. I told Mr. O.P. Sharma that the legal practice was not my cup of tea. I have continued being a non-practicing member of the Supreme Court Bar Association that entitled me to the use of the Supreme Court Bar Association sticker for car parking. The sticker saved me from challans by the traffic police for minor traffic rule violations apart from enabling me the use of the Supreme Court Car Park during the Trade Fairs in Pragati Maidan.

Mr. R.K. Sinha, a Joint Secretary in the Ministry of Industrial Development requested me to accept chairmanship of a one-member Review Committee constituted by the Ministry of Industrial Development to review the working and performance of the National Institute for Research in Cement and Building Materials that was earlier known as the Cement Research Institute. The Research Review was a ten yearly review. I was chosen by the Industrial Development Ministry for this review because of my experience in the ICAR and ICRISAT. I was provided a car with a driver and a personal assistant and a secretary. I was paid a daily allowance of 400 rupees for my labour. I toured whole of India to visit cement plants and to meet industry executives for my report. I completed my report in September 1989. When I had retired from the IAS in August 1988 I had demitted office after making a request to Mr. V. George the Private Secretary to Mr. Rajiv Gandhi to get me an appointment with Mr. Rajiv Gandhi to enable me to say good bye after more than 34 years of service in the IAS. I heard nothing till my demitting of the office. Again I was having an office and a PA as the Chairman of the Review Committee. I dictated a letter to Mr. V. George reminding him of my request before my retirement from the IAS. I promptly got a call from him informing me of the time and date of my appointment with the PM in his office at the 7, Race Course Road. I went there and I was ushered in to see him. He greeted me and enquired about my well-being. I thanked him and told him that I had come there to say a formal goodbye. He smiled and said that I looked hale and hearty so why should I not do something for the Government. I said that I would be happy if I had an appropriate assignment from the government. He promptly asked me if I had any assignment in my mind. I told him that throughout my service, I had been accepting postings as the government had ordered for me. I told him that my entire record of service performance was with the government. I would, therefore, leave it to him to give an appropriate assignment to me. I shook hands with him and left. Some of my friends blamed me for having let a golden opportunity slip from my hands. Sardar Buta Singh, the Home Minister rang me up and told me that the GOI was considering making the Election Commission a three member Constitutional body. He said that my name was one name that was under consideration for that appointment. However, I heard nothing from the GOI for quite some time. Mr. A.U. Sarma was the Chief Secretary of Bihar. He met me some time in August 1989. He told me that the Chief Minister of Bihar, Mr. Sateyndra N. Singh had asked him to seek my consent for appointment as the Chairman of the Bihar Public Service Commission. I felt overwhelmed at this recognition given to me, a Punjabi, by the Bihar Chief Minister, when all over the country parochial winds were blowing. I gave my consent to Mr. A.U. Sarma. I received orders of the Bihar government appointing me as the Chairman of the Bihar Public Service Commission in September. My wife advised me to ascertain from Buta Singh about the Election Commission before I went to Patna. I was, however, riding a high horse. I went and joined as the Chairman of the Bihar Public Service Commission. My numerous friends and admirers in Bihar were happy on my being back in Patna. I thanked Mr. S.N. Singh for selecting me for the prestigious job in Bihar. I had a dinner with Mr. G. Narain and other friends. There was only one working day before the ten day long Puja Holidays. I signed the list of the successful candidates for the Bihar Civil Service batch of 1989 and flew back to Delhi for the Puja holidays. I went to my village in Punjab for a family function in my village. The local Superintendent of Police came there to convey an important message from Sardar Buta Singh, who wanted me to talk to him. I contacted him from Chandigarh. He asked me to come to Delhi and join the Election Commission. I told him that I had already joined as the Chairman of the Bihar Public Service Commission. He asked me to resign immediately and join the Election Commission. I pleaded with him that it would not be fair for me to let down the Chief Minister of Bihar by resigning from the post for which he had resisted all pressure from the lobby of the 'sons of the soil'. He then said that he would ask Mr. S.N. Singh to advise me to resign. I received a call from Mr. S.N. Singh as soon as I reached Delhi. He said that he would be sorry to lose me but he had to bow before the priority of the Prime Minister. He came to Delhi to receive and accept my resignation from the BPSC. I went to meet Sardar Buta Singh. He took me to meet Mr. Rajiv Gandhi. I thanked Mr. Rajiv Gandhi for my appointment as the Election Commissioner. I asked him as to what was his expectation from me in my new assignment. He said that the government had decided to make the Election Commission a three member constitutional authority. All the members would be equal. He said that I would have to be tough. Next day, i.e., on the 16th October, I reported at the office of the Law Secretary, Mrs. Rama Devi. The third member Mr. S.V. Seigell also joined there. She escorted both of us to the room of the Chief Election Commissioner, Mr. R.V.S Peri Sastri. Mr. Peri Sastri greeted us with the remark that both of us, the new Election Commissioners had been appointed against his wishes and against his advice. He further added that there was no work for us in the Election Commission as he had completed all preparatory work for the general elections which were expected to be announced soon. However, he added that we were welcome to join. He apologized to us as there was no room yet in the Election Commission for our office. He promised to arrange for rooms for our office in a day or two. He offered us a cup of tea after which we left. Next day when I entered his office, I found Peri Sastri engaged in a discussion with Mr. B.G. Deshmukh, the Principal Secretary to the Prime Minister. The exchanges between them became hot as I sat down on a chair next to Mr. Peri Sastri. Both of them continued their discussion with Peri Sastri shouting that he would not accept what was being conveyed to him and that he would go public to denounce the Prime Minister. I intervened at that stage by remarking that Mr. Peri Sastri in his remarks was overlooking the fact that the Election Commission had two other members who had to join him in any decision that he was contemplating. Mr. Peri Sastri stopped in his tracks and angrily remarked that he understood as to why we had been appointed. I told Mr. Deshmukh to leave the message of the Prime Minister with the Election Commission and wait for our decision. Although I wondered as to why the Prime Minister had sent his Principal Secretary to convey his message instead leaving it to the Cabinet Secretary. I learnt later from a newspaper article written by Mr. Deshmukh that Mr. Rajiv Gandhi felt that his decision about the date of the general elections without consulting Peri Sastri would upset him. The Cabinet Secretary, Mr. T.N. Seshan was an abrasive personality, who could make matters worse. The other thing that he and his Principal Secretary had overlooked was the fact that the GOI had made the Election Commission a three member body. Mr. Deshmukh said that the Prime Minister desired a decision from the Election Commission by 2 p.m. and left. Mr. Peri Satri told us after Mr. Deshmukh had left that the Prime Minister had announced without consulting the Chief

Election Commissioner that the next General Elections would take place from the 22nd November. The news had already been reported by the SSC. We agreed with him that the Prime Minister had violated an established tradition and that his announcement also violated the law. But the problem was that if after his public announcement the Election Commission did not accept the date announced, it would mean a confrontation with the Prime Minister for which the Prime Minister had to either resign or remove the Election Commission members for which he had the required two-third majority in the Parliament. While we were debating the issue the press corps of Delhi came to know about it and they had trooped into the Election Commission building called *Nirvachan Sadan*. I found our corridors teeming with press reporters. Buta Singh rang me up on the telephone of the Secretary of the Election Commission as I did yet have an office or a telephone. He was anxious about our decision. I asked him to wait as our discussion was still going on. I ventured to ask him the reason for bypassing the Chief Election Commissioner by the Prime Minister. He said that the Prime Minister had lost trust in Peri Sastri as on an earlier occasion he had passed on a one-to-one conversation with the Prime Minister to a friend, who had leaked it to the press. Anyhow, by about 2 p.m. Mr. Peri Sastri came round to the idea of lodging a formal protest to the Cabinet Secretary and accepting 22nd November as the date of poll for the Lok Sabha Elections. I asked Peri Sastri to inform the press who were outside, making a noise in our corridors. Mr. Peri Sastri asked me to wait as till 5.30 p.m. was the '*Rahu Kalam*' during which no important work could be undertaken. I informed the press reporters that our decision would be announced at 5.30 p.m. I, however, informed Buta Singh about our informal decision. Our conference room was full with the TV and press reporters when all three of us walked in to announce our decision. I was surprised to discover that a photograph of ours was published in the US Time International Magazine along with the news about the elections to the Lok Sabha. The manner of our appointment as Election Commissioners followed by the announcement of the general elections got a lot of adverse publicity for us and for the Prime Minister Rajiv Gandhi. Mr. Seigell was from the Indian Police Service. It was Mr. Narayanan the Director General of Intelligence, who had got him appointed as an Election Commissioner. He would not open his mouth in the meetings of the Commission. He generally supported me on all issues till it became known that the Congress party might not come back to power. Mr. Seigel had confided to me that he had been appointed an Election Commissioner to reward him for his services in getting Sheikh Abdullah to soften his views about Jammu and Kashmir independence and accept office of the Chief Minister under the Constitution of India. Mr. Seigell had spent a few months at Ooty where Sheikh Abdullah was kept under detention. Mr. Seigell said that Sheikh Abdullah could be brought around after a series of informal meetings with him. It was mainly the concern for the future of his son and family that made him to come around to accept office as was proposed by Mrs. Gandhi. Mr. Buta Singh's telephonic call to me in July had indicated that at the political level, a decision had been taken to make the Election Commission a three member body by July 1989. I cannot say if it was the failure of the Cabinet Secretary, Mr. T.N. Seshan or Mr. Rajiv Gandhi's lack of concern for the public opinion that delayed the announcement of an important decision of the Government of India making the Election Commission into a constitutional authority, for the first time. I was shocked to discover that the civil servants had drafted the proposal to make the Election Commission a three member constitutional authority in a slipshod manner. The justification given for the proposal was that due to the expected general elections the work load of the Election Commission had increased whereas the real reason was that the nature of the issues that the Election Commission was required to handle were such where a single member could not be trusted for exercising an impartial and correct discretion, therefore, a three member body had become necessary.

The second reason though not stated was the distrust that Rajiv Gandhi had about Mr. Peri Sastri. Mr. Peri Sastri, on his part often regretted his inability to have a rapport with Rajiv Gandhi. He mentioned that his predecessor, Mr. R.K. Trivedi, had been rewarded by appointing him as the Governor of Gujarat but he would be just retired when he completed 65 years. It was all the more necessary that the Government of India should have projected the decision to make the Election Commission a three member body as a step in the right direction. I consider the ham-handedness displayed in otherwise legitimate and correct decisions to a personal blind spot in Rajiv Gandhi. He constantly overlooked the fact that as a popular elected leader he had to take decisions that appeared fair and correct and he had to ensure that the general public perceived and viewed those decisions in the same light.

I went home after the announcement of the general elections leaving Peri Sastri and the Home Secretary to work out the nitty-gritty of the schedule for the general elections in different states. It came out, during our preliminary discussion that the elections in Uttar Pradesh would start a day later as there was a holiday falling on the date fixed for scrutiny of the eligible candidates. I was contacted by Sardar Buta Singh around 10 p.m. with a request to get the date of the poll changed for Uttar Pradesh as Mr. Rajiv Gandhi, perhaps on the advice of his astrologer, insisted that the date of the poll in his constituency must be the same as announced for the general elections. I then recalled that it was due to a public holiday falling on the date of scrutiny that was responsible for the change in the schedule for Uttar Pradesh. Since I could not be contacted for some time Buta Singh approached Mr. Peri Sastri to accommodate the change in the date of polling for Uttar Pradesh. Mr. Peri Sastri told him that he was helpless in the matter. Mr. Buta Singh then pleaded with me to help him. I told him that he should get the local holiday of Uttar Pradesh exempted from the Negotiable Instruments Act so that it did not come in the way of scrutiny of the nomination papers. Mr. Buta Singh rang me up to convey that the Uttar Pradesh government had passed the necessary order. I then requested Mr. Peri Sastri to convene a meeting of the Election Commission to consider the request of the Home Minister. The Commission met at about midnight and consulted the Chief Secretary of Uttar Pradesh about the local holiday. After confirming from him about the holiday denotification, Mr Peri Sastri agreed to restore the date of polling for Uttar Pradesh as was desired. The episode compromised my position as an Election Commissioner as the Home Minister had picked me up to sort out the situation. Unwittingly I continued permitting Sardar Buta Singh to use me as his instrument in the Election Commission. Mr. Peri Sastri made no secret of his animosity to Rajiv Gandhi. He told all whom he met that I was a plant by Rajiv Gandhi to checkmate Peri Sastri. Another incident that made my bonafides suspect before the opposition political alliance related to the Election Symbol for the new political set up called the Janata Dal. Mr. Dandwate, a senior leader of the opposition had submitted a symbol of eight spoke chakra for approval before the Election Commission. Anticipating the approval of the Commission, the Janata Dal released the symbol before the media. Next day when I entered the room of Mr. Peri Sastri, I found Mr. Dandvate sitting with him awaiting a written approval for the Election Symbol. I accosted Mr Peri Sastri with the fact that the Janata Dal had gone to the press already with the symbol that was awaiting approval of the Election Commission. I proposed and insisted that the proposal received from the Janata Dal should be rejected outright on this ground. Mr Peri Sastri was taken by surprise by my onslaught. He murmured agreement with me while Mr. Seigell endorsed my view. Mr. Dandvate quickly left. This was followed by a full delegation of the top leaders of the Janata Dal, led by Mr. V.P. Singh, appearing before us, requesting for restoration and approval of the Janata Dal election symbol. It was left to me to oppose them. They apologized for their premature publicity of the unapproved symbol. Mr. Peri Sastri suggested a slight modification in the proposed symbol and pleaded with me to relent on my stand. Mr. Yashwant Sinha, my erstwhile IAS colleague from Bihar, spoke to me requesting the same. I then agreed to the slightly modified symbol that had six spokes in the chakra instead of the original eight. This incident also damaged my image of neutrality and impartiality in the eyes of the opposition leaders. Somehow, I remained unaware of this aspect right till the end. Buta Singh was the Home Minister. I had developed a rapport with him because of my concern with the exploitation of the Sikh community by the Akali leaders to further their political aims. We had frequent meetings to develop an action plan to checkmate the Akalis. I did not object to his frequent telephonic contacts. He made a request on behalf of Rajiv Gandhi concerning a notification that had been issued by the Election Commission for election to the Rajya Sabha from the Delhi local bodies constituency. It was a seat where the Congress party was sure to win. It appeared that Rajiv Gandhi wanted Sardar Charanjit Singh, the owner of the Meridian Hotel to be the Congress candidate. However, Mr. K.C. Pant too staked his claim for the same seat. Apparently, Mr. Rajiv Gandhi did not like K.C. Pant. He faced a dilemma in deciding about the Congress candidate. Sardar Buta

Singh requested me to withdraw the Election Commission notification if possible. I discovered that the Election Commission had issued the notification in a routine manner when the Delhi Metropolitan Council, the main constituent, had been dissolved. I raised the issue in the meeting of the Election Commission. Mr. Peri Sastri agreed that the Election Commission was in error but he argued that it would reflect badly on the Commission if the notification was withdrawn. I was able to corner him on the issue once he had accepted the fact that the Election Commission was in error. The Election Commission withdrew the notification much to the relief of Rajiv Gandhi.We had adopted the practice of meeting daily over a cup of coffee in the room of the Chief Election Commissioner. It became more and more obvious that I was the Election Commissioner who dominated the exchanges in the meetings. I proposed that the Election Commission should develop procedures for having a formal agenda, a formal distribution of work and a record book of the decisions on the model of the Board of Directors under the Company Law. Mr. Peri Sastri somehow avoided the exercise proposed by me. Mr. Seigell suspected that Mr Peri Sastri was secretly planning to get the Government of India to go back to the one member Election Commission. Mr Seigell had taken legal opinion to contest such an eventuality. Informally, the day-to-day overseeing of the general elections in states like Punjab, Haryana, Bihar, etc., was entrusted to me. All our decisions so far had been unanimous. There were acrimonious exchanges on some issues but in the end the Election Commission would arrive at a unanimous decision. Mr. Peri Sastri, on his part, respected the government decision of the Election Commission being a three member body. He got all decisions endorsed by the three members. There were some media reports about elections in some polling booths in Amethi constituency of Rajiv Gandhi being disrupted. We tried to contact the Returning Officer but he was not available on telephone. We contacted the Election Commission Observer to enquire about the alleged disruption. The Observer was unaware of any untoward incident. He promised to visit the spot and let us know. Perhaps there was pressure from the opposition parties and the media that made Mr. Peri Sastri send an Under Secretary of the Election Commission to Amethi to enquire about the allegations and report to the Election Commission. He informed me about this decision in the evening. I objected to his decision that had been taken by Mr. Peri Sastri alone. I also pointed out to him that the person sent by him was not fit for the purpose for which he had been sent as he happened to be a non-Hindi knowing South Indian officer. Mr. Peri Sastri avoided answering me on the telephone. He convened a meeting of the Election Commission at around 11 p.m. to consider the complaints about the alleged irregularities in the polling in Amethi constituency. I took Peri Sastri to task for his unilateral action in sending an Under Secretary of the Election Commission for enquiry. He could give no plausible reason for his action. Meanwhile, a telephone call was received from the Under Secretary. The call was taken by Mr. Peri Sastri. He said aloud to us that the Under Secretary was recommending a repoll in three assembly segments of Amethi. I took the telephone from the hands of Mr Peri Sastri and asked the Under Secretary to let me know the basis of his recommendation. He said that he had formed his opinion after talking to the people whom he met at various *dhabas* or tea shops and local bazars. I shouted at him that he was merely carrying out the wishes and directions of Peri Sastri and it was nothing but a conspiracy to harm the prospects of Rajiv Gandhi. The plan of the conspiracy became clear to me as a repoll in three assembly segments would require reprinting of ballot papers meaning a delay of more than a fortnight in the repoll. I discovered that Mr. Seigell, for the first time, was joining Mr. Peri Sastri. Mr. Peri Sastri pleaded with me to fall in line as he felt that public outcry and media focus on the irregularities in Amethi poll was such that if the Election Commission did not take a decision like the one proposed, the Election Commission would lose all credibility in the eyes of the public. I lost my temper on this casuistry and told Mr. Peri Sastri and Seigell that they seemed to be playing politics of which I refuse to be a partner. I then walked out of the room of the Chief Election Commissioner telling them to record their decision on which I would record my dissent. Mr. Seigell walked into my room soon after. He enquired from me if I could take a call from Mr. Narayanan, Director IB. I said that he was welcome to talk to me. Mr. Narayanan said that he wanted only to convey a message for me from Rajiv Gandhi. The message was that Mr Rajiv Gandhi would be happy if I did not go for recording a dissent on the issue of election in Amethi and that Mr Peri Sastri and Seigell had agreed to order a repoll in about 100 polling booths. 100 polling booths would amount to less than half of an assembly segment. This meant that repoll could be held on the next day. I protested that such a decision would be arbitrary but since Rajiv Gandhi himself had desired me to be cooperative, I would sign as would be proposed. Thereafter, I walked back to the room of the Chief Election Commissioner. We had a report from the Returning Officer recommending a repoll in about ten booths. To make this number 100 we decided to order repoll in all booths where any complaint had been received concerning conduct of the poll. We could thus reach the number of 95, or so. I signed on the file in token of my agreement although orally I protested that I was signing with a sense of committing a sin. Anyhow, the response of the press to our decision was positive though the decision left a bad taste in the mouth. I was approached, sometime around midnight by my friend Mr. Ahluwalia, when the counting of votes in Uttar Pradesh was going on, for help. He told me that the counting of votes at Amethi had been obstructed by rowdies belonging to the opposition parties with the result that the Returning Officer had ordered a stoppage in the counting of votes. I told him that I alone could do nothing in the matter. He then contacted Mr. Peri Sastri, who convened a meeting of the Election Commission around 1 a.m. When I reached the *Nirvachan Sadan*, I found that a delegation led by Ghulam Nabi Azad, the General Secretary of the Congress was sitting with the Chief Election Commissioner. Mr. Peri Sastri, after hearing them, rang up the Collector of Amethi who was the Returning Officer. The telephone attendant of the Collector told him that the Collector had gone to sleep. Mr. Peri Sastri expressed his helplessness in the matter. I again took the telephone from him and rang up the Chief Secretary of Uttar Pradesh. I told his telephone attendant to wake him up to hear the call from the Election Commission. When the Chief Secretary came on telephone I told him to pull up the Collector of Amethi for stopping the counting of votes in Amethi due to disturbance by some rowdies. He said that he was unaware of the stoppage in the counting of votes but assured me that he would get the Collector of Amethi to restart the counting of votes. We soon got a message that the counting of votes in Amethi had resumed. The Congress delegation left *Nirvachan Sadan* after profusely thanking me. What puzzled me in the episode was the reason for the Congress delegation approaching the Election Commission to get the counting of votes resumed in Amethi instead of asking the Congress Chief Minister, Mr. N.D. Tewari, to get the same action taken! This incident and the incidents concerning repoll in Amethi constituency point to some sort of internal sabotage of the election of Mr. Rajiv Gandhi. The last formality was to present the list of the elected candidates to the President along with the report of the Election Commission. Mr. Peri Sastri tried to have an appointment with the President on his own but later on he decided to take the other two members of the Election Commission along. While presenting the report to the President, he let out his venom against Rajiv Gandhi despite the fact that the results of the General Election had gone against him. There was a lull in the activities of the Election Commission. The two Election Commissioners were given no work in the Election Commission nor any meetings being called. Mr. V.P. Singh had become the new Prime Minister. I went on a holiday to Punjab around Christmas. I returned only on the 30th December. I received a telephone call from the Law Secretary, Mrs. Rama Devi, towards the evening. She told me that the Government of India had decided to revert to the one member Election Commission. If I could agree to resign, I could be accommodated in an equivalent post. She wanted to know my response on telephone. I tried to buy time by telling her that I could reply to her only if I knew about the alternate post that the Government of India had in mind. She disclosed that she was speaking from the room of the Principal Secretary to the Prime Minister, Mr. Vinod Pande. The post that they had in view was the membership of the Board for Financial and Industrial Reconstruction or BIFR. It was a good offer but I declined to accept it on the spur of the moment. I thought that Mr. Seigell also must have rejected such offer as he was preparing himself for facing such an eventuality.

Mr. Seigell however disappointed me by saying that he had agreed to resign. He refused to part with his notes on the issue. The Government of India thereafter issued a notification sacking the two Election Commissioners. The news was flashed on the TV with our photographs being displayed repeatedly. My response to the situation was totally confused. I was told by a friend in Rashtrapati Bhavan that the President had raised some objection to the Government proposal.

I had got a reprieve of at least one day during which I could have moved a court for a stay of the government order. I wanted to go to court to vindicate my position but I was afraid of the cost as I had no money for paying the senior advocate's fees. I talked to a friend, Mr. B.N. Kirpal, who was a Judge of the Supreme Court, about my predicament. He asked me a counter question as to how the Government of India could do such a thing. Mr. Peri Sastri and Seigell who had agreed to resign had arranged a farewell for the Election Commissioners, presuming that I would fall in line. The party was converted to a New Year celebration because of my refusal to resign. I attended the party and our sacking order was served on me at our residence at midnight on the 1st of January 1990. I remained undecided about my future. I called on Rajiv Gandhi who was no longer the Prime Minister. He had with him Mr. Sidharth Shankar Ray, who was an eminent lawyer too. Mr. Rajiv Gandhi also felt that what the VP Singh government had done was illegal. Mr. S.S. Ray felt that the case against the government would have to be argued by some good advocate. I said that I was all for a case against the government but I could not afford the fees of a senior advocate. Mr. Rajiv Gandhi then asked Buta Singh to speak to the former Attorney General to take up my case. I met him the next day and I was asked to give my brief to Mr. Gopal Subramaniam for preparing a draft writ petition. Mr. Gopal Subramaniam told me that he would work for me free. I would be required to pay his advocate on record, Mrs. Tamta and his junior, Mr. Murlidharan, their usual fees. I gave all that had happened in the Election Commission during my tenure in a paper dictated by me. My purpose was to bring out all the dirty linen of the Election Commission before the public to make out a case for a multi-member Election Commission and to show that in all decisions I acted impartially and in public interest. I tried to show that the Government and Mr. Peri Sastri had colluded to get rid of the two new members of the Election Commission. The Supreme Court took more than one year to hear my case after admission of my writ petition. Meanwhile, I had joined as a fellow at the Institute of Advanced Studies, Shimla to study the evolution of the Sikhs in relation to the State. Mr. Seigell was proposed by the Government for a membership of the Central Administrative Tribunal but the proposal was not accepted by the Chief Justice as Mr. Seigell had neither a law qualification nor judicial experience. Mr. Seigell thereafter just disappeared from the scene. The Supreme Court accepted the argument in my case that a body like the Election Commission must be a multi-member body. My conduct was found to be otherwise above board except that I was accused of trying to dominate the Chief Election Commissioner. I was not ordered to be reinstated as the Supreme Court accepted the government plea that the two new posts of Election Commissioners were created to deal with the extra work generated by the General Elections. Since the General Elections were over, the government was justified in abolishing the two new posts of the Election Commissioner. It was the conduct of Mr. T.N. Seshan, the successor Chief Election Commissioner that forced the government of Narasimha Rao to again make the Election Commission a multi-member body citing the judgment of the Supreme Court in my case as the rationale which gave a recognition to me as being the first Election Commissioner in the multi-member Election Commission. I have to accept that this assignment which was my most prestigious assignment was not handled by me with the finesse that was required. I did act correctly and impartially but I had failed to demonstrate it before the media and the public. I fell in the trap of fighting my case directly with the media and made it appear as a personal fight against journalists like Mr. Arun Shorie of the *Indian Express*. What was required was that I had to be correct in my actions and also ensure that I appeared to be correct in the eyes of the public. My having been the Chairman of the Bihar Public Service Commission saved me from being drafted as an Advisor to the Governor of Punjab during its worst terrorist phase. I was later appointed Chairman of the Banking Service Recruitment Board, Chandigarh after my three years at Shimla. I was 65 years in age. Normally no government appointment could be expected for me. Bihar still came forward for my last public service assignment. It was my appointment by the Securities and the Exchange Board of India (SEBI) on the recommendation of the Government of Bihar as the Administrator of the Magadh Stock Exchange at Patna. I resigned from the assignment on June 30th 2000 after the sad demise of my wife.

21

Conclusion

The Indian Civil Services or the ICS was created by Britain to facilitate their rule over India. The Indian Civil Service was neither Indian nor civil and nor a service. It was recruited in Britain mainly to train administrators who would enable the British to successfully rule a very diverse country like India. They vindicated the British trust as the late Mr. Winston Churchill called them the "Steel Frame of the rule in India". Most of the freedom struggle Indian Leaders were not in favour of continuing with the service like the ICS. However, Sardar Patel could see the value of a service recruited centrally but serving in the States/Provinces. He endorsed the creation of a service called the Indian Administrative Service on the pattern of the ICS. The new service had lesser pay and prospects and privileges than the ICS. The entitlement to the home leave for the ICS was not available for the IAS.

It was left mainly for the civil servant after 1947, who were almost all from the ICS, to work out the training and service rules for the IAS. It is in this context that one has to accept that the ICS failed to provide for a training schedule according to the Constitution of India and the requirements of working under that Constitution. They provided for a pre-service training for one year centrally and one year in the States of allotment. They failed to make a distinction that with Independence the Indian Administration has undergone a fundamental change. The training schedule for the IAS mainly provided for teaching of Law, Indian Economics, Constitution of India, Hindi and the regional language of the State of allotment. In a country like India ability to swim is a must for administrators. It is still not in the schedule of the IAS training. The ICS had virtually no experience of working with the political executives, so they were unable to provide any guidelines to deal with the political executives. The result is that till date the IAS is not able to evolve a '*Laxman Rekha*' or the limits of tolerance in the equation between IAS officers and the political executives. The IAS has functioned for more than 60 years and a whole generation of IAS officers have successfully functioned as administrators, adjusting with the political executives. Every IAS officer who went up the ladder in the IAS, worked out his own manner of adjusting with the political executives but no one has yet described that adjustment and fine tuning of the compromises made with the political executives.

I have given out truthfully my account of working with the political executives but I am not sure if I could be justified in all that I did in my service. I had started with the belief that the IAS, as a service will provide me a guideline in tackling various problems that I would be facing. I, however, discovered during my first district that I had to fight my battles alone. The political executives called the shots and all the senior layers of administrative authorities were of no help if one went on the wrong side of the political executives.

I had to device my own strategy of handing problems and serving the people while taking political executives along. All training that had been given to us as IAS officers and the environment of the Indian Administrative Service took it for granted that the political executives were there but in the decision-making of the IAS officers somehow they had to be cajoled or befuddled. The civil service hero in Bihar was a person like C.K. Raman, ICS, who when questioned by a minister's query that he did not understand what C.K. Raman was saying. C.K. Raman's answer was that he was sorry that he could provide only reasons for his views but not an understanding for the honourable minister. I decided that I will function with integrity and for the people and always remain truthful but, as I came to recognize that the political executives did represent the people and they had their own compulsions and it was my duty to provide them an understanding of what was I doing and how it was in public interest, and if possible also show that it was in the interest of the political executives to support me.

I tried my new approach in my second tenure as District Magistrate where the Chief Minister and his party wanted to supplant the leaders of existing trade unions with their own men. I succeeded in getting my position vindicated among the trade union leaders, the public, the civil service hierarchy and the Chief Minister of the State. This approach of mine worked well and enabled me to complete my service career successfully in both the state and the central appointments.

An IAS officer from the very first posting has to supervise a number of subordinates. The British had evolved a system which has continued, in which detailed rules and regulations of handling various papers and issues are prescribed. The common tendency amongst officers is to leave the nitty-gritty of rules to the subordinates and sign on the dotted lines provided by the subordinates. This gives them an opportunity for corruption and for hoodwinking the superior officers. The mastery and enforcement of these rules should be made an essential part of the training of the IAS officers, so that in every position they ensured that what has been ordered by them has been implemented efficiently.Two other elements of my service approach deserves a mention. Among all the positions in the IAS that I got posted I found areas which had been neglected and in which I could excel in performance and also serving the public interest. I avoided trying directly to impress the political executives or local political leaders, letting the people appreciating my services to convey good words about me to the political leaders and others. I decided to stand-up if any expected civil servant or political executive tried to force me to act against what I thought to be right and in public interest. I suffered one or two setbacks on this policy, but in the long run those setbacks enhanced my reputation and worth.The civil service structure in India, in most of the positions, confers a lot of power on the holder of an office. The system, however, does not provide for a communication of the rationale of the decision in the area of responsibility of an officer. It also exposes in retrospect to expose some decision to charges of favouritism or corruption. The remedy that I adopted was to have a system of collegiate decision-making in every position that I had. This also enabled me to pick brains of my colleagues and others for my decisions. This sort of decision-making should be inbuilt in the training of the IAS officer. This is in my view, still a vacuum in the IAS. Finally one aspect of my functioning was to take advantage of the weaknesses and fears of my superior officers and political executives. I was never frightened in taking up a matter or issue on the ground that the required authority was vested with my superior officers. This should conclude my journey through a very interesting and fruitful experience of life.

Index

14th Punjab Regiment, 24
161 Brigade, 54
3rd Armoured Brigade, 41, 45, 46
41st Mountain Battery, 28
5/14 Punjab Regiment, 25, 26, 30, 31, 46
5/14 Punjab Regiment Allotted to Pakistan, 46
8th Indian Army in North Africa, 31

A Wati Ao,
  Catholic Christian, 201
  IAS from Nagaland, 201
Abu Hakim, 180
  Author's Friend from AMU, 179
Academy
  Golden Jubilee Retreat of 1954 Batch, 160
  Hunting Ground for Matchmaking, 167
Administration, 28, 74, 85, 87, 103, 118, 150, 218, 236, 268, 294, 332
  Basic Function, 129
  On Paternalistic Lines, 82
Administrative
  Process, 94
  System, 78
Advanced Technology, 332
Afghanistan, 25, 30
Agricultural
  Export, 164
  Project in Iraq, 181
  Research, 227-247
  Scientists Recruitment Board, 228
  Universities, 234
  University Pant Nagar, 166
Ahluwalia, Surinderjit Singh, 264, 298, 299, 306, 312, 323, 350
  Impressed Author by his Intelligence, 260
Ahmed Shah Abdali (1761), 158
AIDS, 334
  Control Program, 334
  In India, 333
Aiyar Commission, 145
  Report, 193
Aiyar, Venkataraman Rao, Supreme Court Judge, 145

Ajit Singh, Sant, 278
Akal Takhat, 22, 58, 65, 122, 264, 272, 286-290
Akali
  Agitation, 261
  Dal, 39, 278, 304, 314, 314, 315
  Leaders, 42, 258, 258, 303, 304, 309
  Leadership, 259, 260, 316
  Morcha, 302
  Movement, 270
  Party, 121
  Political Agenda, 257
  Politics, 290
Akalis, 22, 23, 33, 35, 40, 116, 214, 220, 223, 237, 264, 268, 269, 270, 274, 275, 277, 284, 287, 312, 315, 347
  And Bhindranwale, 259
Akbar, Mughal Emperor, 78
Akhand
  Kirtan Jatha, 221, 222
  Path of Guru Granth Sahib, 254
Akhauri, BP, IPS, IGP, 146, 147
Akhnoor, 107
Alexander, PC, 263, 265, 290
Aligarh Muslim University, 57, 61, 179, 190
  Became the Brain Trust of Pakistan Ideology, 57
All India
  Congress Committee (AICC), 110
  Sadhu Samaj, 111
  Sikh Educational Conference, Chandigarh, 241
  Sikh Students Federation, (AISSF), 52, 305, 308, 309
Allahabad High Court, 254
  Judgment, 184
Allegations of Excesses/Irregularities, 218
Allied
  Bombers, 31
  Central Services, 64
Allies, 31
Ambala Cantonment, 22, 47
Amin (Draftsman), 80
Amrinder Singh, 299
Amrit, 241, 242
  Ceremony (Baptism), 65
Amritdharis, 276
Amritsar, 41, 42, 47
  Administration, 222
  Founded by 4th Guru of Sikhs, 38
  Historical City, 38
  Railway Station, 46
Anand, Amteshwar Mrs, 213
  Daughter of Sardar Datar Singh, 213
Anandpur Sahib, 306
Anjuman-e-Islamiya, Poona Cantt., 220
Annual Sikh Educational Conference, 94
Anthony, 232
Anti-
  Corruption Department Inspector, 134
  National Conduct, 126
  Sikh Riots, 323, 324
Appu, PS, 195, 218, 219
Arab Socialists, 180
Arakeri, Dr. 228
Arjan (Arjun) Das, 184-186, 189, 213, 307-312, 317
  CM, Madhya Pradesh, 337
Armed
  Forces, 21, 106, 289
  Sikh Groups, 48
  Sikh Youth, 257
  Boats, 197
  Eastern Command, 103

School of Management and Training, Rock Island, 156
Special Course, 26
Station Commander, 147
Arora, GK, JS, 282
Arson and Killing of Muslims in Ranchi, 147
Arun Singh, 269
Rajiv Gandhi's Friend from Doon School, 321
Arya Samaj, 274
Asa-di-Var, 65
Assembly Elections, 141
Atomic Bomb, 182
Attari, 46
Railway Station, 209
Attock Bridge, 46, 50
Aurangzeb, Mughal Emperor, 63, 241
Author
Able to Make Record Procurement, 195
Admission for Graduate Course--, 57
Advice to Govt. of India on various matters, 261
Appearance for IAS, 1953 at Simla, 63
Appointed As Election Commissioner, 342
As Election Commissioner, 340
As Food Commissioner, 196
As General Manager Super Bazar, 175
As Health Commissioner, 319
As Secretary to Govt. of India, 270, 319
As Sub-Divisional Officer Deoghar, 1856, 82
As Union Health Secretary, 270, 319
As Trainee, 68
Attended Meeting of Secretaries, --, 332
Availed Facilities by Joining Tennis and Horse Riding, 58
Called Muslim Opinion Leaders and Their Mullahs, 126
Chairman Bihar Public Service Commission, 342
Changed Four Tier System of Doctors, 207
Chief Secretary, Punjab, 265
Completion of Six Month Training at Laheria Sarai, 78
Congratulated by Bihar CM, 267
Congratulated by RK Dhawan for Appointment as Chief Secretary Punjab, 267
Constituted Committee of Experts in Health Ministry, 334
Dy. Commissioner of Dhanbad, 99, 193
Dy. Commissioner of Ranchi, 101, 293
Dy. Secretary in State Mines Department, 100
Elected Leader Group of Trainees from Ten Countries, 157
Evolved Formula (for Admission to Medical Colleges), 320
Executive Capability, 151
Experience As District Magistrate, 340
First Visit to Simla, 63
Found Bihar lacked Behind In Promotion of IAS/IPS Officers, 255
Friend of BP Sinha, CM, 95
Given Responsibility of Home Dept. and Dept. of Personnel, 253

Got Posting as District Magistrate in 1960, 86
Headquarters During Training in Ex-Zamindari, 79
IAS Interview in 1954, 325
In Aligarh Muslim University, 57
In Black List of Mrs. Indira Gandhi, 213
In His Old Primary School-Anjuman-e-Islamiya Poona Cantt., 220
In List of Agricultural Experts, 180
In Ndola Trade Fair, 179
In Ranchi, 125
Introduced Three Tier System of Doctors on All India Pattern, 207
Introduced - Asst Professor, Associate Professor and Professors in Medical Teaching Pattern, 207
Jeep Accident in Deogarh, 207
Joined Communist Led Students Federation, 37
Land Survey and Settlement Training, 78
Law from Aligarh Muslim University, 340
Main Focus on Family Planning program in his tenure, 203
Meeting with Cabinet Secretary Rao Saheb, 246
Met Accident While Driving Jeep, 85
Moved to Medical Hospital Patna, 85
Mussoorie Assignment, 152, 226
Nominated (Ahluwalia) Takhat Sahib Managing Committee, 260
Offered Job of Development Commissioner, 252
Opted for Deputation—from Ranchi, 151
Order for Summary Release of Prisoners, 255
Posted Addl. Chief Secretary, 263
Posted as Collector of Shahabad, 86
Posted as Dy. Secretary in Finance Department, 91
Posted at Ranchi as Asst. Development Commissioner, 85
Posted Chief Secretary Punjab, 265-318
Posted in Deoghar Sub-Division of Santhal Pargana Division, 81
Posted Relieving Officer for 1957 General Elections, 84
Posting As Dy. Commissioner of Dhanbad, 92
Posting at National Academy of Administration Mussorie, 152
Pre-Occupation with-, 37
Promoted to Rank of Secretary in Govt. of India, 255
Refused for Extension in ICRISAT, 255
Reported to Ram Das Sarai, 35
Responsible for Functional Training, 152
Retired IAS--, 1988, 341
Second Tenure as District Magistrate, 356
Secretary Health and Family Planning in Govt. of India, 319
Senior Most IAS in Punjab, 265
Sent to Darbhanga for District Training, 73

Served As Registrar of Cooperatives Societies, 151
Success in IAS, 63
Super Bazar Days, 255
Sympathizer of Communist, 54
Termed as Sub-Standard Material for IAS, 71
To Bihar Again from Centre (After Deputation), 191-211
Tool of KB Sahay (being said), 149
Toured on Bicycle during Training, 79
Trip to Badrinath and Kedarnath, 163
Trip to London, 220
TV Exposure, 270
Visit of Cement Plants, 341
Visit to Durgiana Temple, 271
Visit to Gurdwara Hemkunt Sahib, 163
Visit to Mughal Sarai, 163
Visit to Panja Sahib Gurdwara, 209
Visit to Training Institutions in USA, UK, Honolulu, Tokyo, Manila and Hong Kong, 156
Visited New York—Manila, 157
Visited Patna Sahib, 258
Was Escorted by Mrs. Indira Gandhi to Gate (after the Interview), 267
Was Nominated for Course in University of Pittsburg, 154

Author's
College Days, 34
Father Expired, 229
Father Gave Gift of Granth Saheb Verses on Passing B.Sc Examination, 60
Father Havildar with Three Stripe, 26
Father in 5/14 Punjab Regiment, 24, 46
Father Posted Intelligence Officer in 161 Brigade, 50
Father Selected Lieutenant at Secundrabad, 31
Fight with SK Sinha, first CM of Bihar, 193
Financial Problems, 237
First Air Travel, 134
Friend Jia Lal Singh, 66
Friend KK Singh, 207
Interest in Current Affairs, 37
Involvement in Sarbat Khalsa, 298
Letter of Appointment for IAS, 67
Marriage and IAS Examination, 62
Mind Wandering and Daydreaming, 37
Name Sponsored for Joint Secretary Govt. of India, 237
School-Khalsa High School, 29
Stinging Letter to Vice-Chancellor, Ranchi, 139
Termination of Probationer in IAS, 69
Testimony before Justice SP Singh-Commission of Enquiry, 152
Visit to Ajanta and Ellora Caves, 70
Visit to Andhra Pradesh—Punjab, 241

Ayub Khan, Gen., 108
Azad, Ghulam Nabi, 350

Baat-Cheet Circular, 276
Baath Party, 182
Baba
Jagga, 32

Kharak Singh, 290
Santa Singh, 288, 289, 291, 292
Siri Chand, Elder Son of Guru Nanak, 32
Babu Rajendra Prasad, 97
First Indian President, 96
Bachan Singh, 29
Backlash Against Muslims, 147
Badal, Prakash Singh, CM Punjab, 221, 279
Badal, Prakash Singh, Akali Leader, 217, 313, 314
Cabinet, 221
Bagchi, 154
Bage, SK, 142
Baghdad, 28, 180, 182, 183
Baghdad, Iraq, 22
Bagla, SP, 237, 238, 245
Author's Friend, 235
IAS Punjab Cadre, 233
Later Establishment Officer of Govt. of India, 233
Secretary to Zail Singh, 233
Baidyanath
Dham, 82, 83
Shiv Temple, 83
Bajaj, BR, 167
Bajaj, Mrs. Rupan, IAS, 210
Bal, NPS, Brigadier, 262
Baldev Singh Sardar, 33, 45, 237
Baleshwar Prasad, Lt. Gov., 187, 188
Baluch Regiment, 47
Balwant Singh Akali Leader, 287
Banaras/Haridwar, 163
Banda Bahadur, 261
Bandyopadhya, Secretary, Min. of Rural Development, 325
Banerjee, Chairman UPSC, 70
Bankipur Gurdwara Patna, 209
Bannu, 25
Bano, Block HQs., 101, 102
Bansi Lal, 214
Bar Association of Ranchi, 139
Barauni Oil Refinery, 260
Bari Doab Sikhs (Majha Sikhs), 21
Barnala, 217, 259
Agriculture Minister, 227, 228
Sardar Surjit Singh, CM Punjab, 319
Bassi Pathana, 30, 62, 63, 240
Basu, Jyotirmoy, Marxist MP, 184
Battle of Nowshera, 288
Beant Singh, 317
Bimal Khalsa Widow, 317
Beas River, 107
Begampet Airport, 244
Bengal Army, 106
Bhadra Lok or the Upper Caste, 80
Bhagat, PS General, 103, 105, 136
Bhai Amrik Singh, Sardar, 296
Bhai Mahavir, 234
Bhakhra Canal, 293
Project, 282
Bhakti Movement, 41
Bhalla, KS, 269
Bharwara, 75, 77
Bhatia, Raghunandan Lal, Amritsar Congress Leader, 268
Bhinder, PS,
IGP Delhi, 216, 233
IPS, 272
Posted Dy Commissioner Amritsar, 272
Bhindranwale, Jarnail Singh, 58, 123, 220-223, 262, 269, 272, 274, 286, 287, 297, 298, 299, 305, 313
Hukumnama Not to Attend Nirankari Conference, 222
Killed in Operation Blue Star, 297
Bhisham Narain, 256
Bhoothalngham, IAS, 225
Bhuller, Jaswant Singh, Retd. General, 259, 264

Bhumihar, 193, 199
  Landowners, 79
Bibi
  Bhani Daughter of Guru Amar Das, 38
  Rajinder Kaur, MP, 244
Bihar
  Administration, 145, 194
  And Orissa, 195
  Border, 262
  Brahmins, 192
  Bureaucrats, 121
  Cadre Officers (1954), 71
  Civil Service, 342
  Civil Service Tradition, 73
  Doctors—Corruption and Mercenary Behaviour, 207
  Farmers, 88
  Food and Civil Supplies Corporation, 193
  Food Deficit State, 193
  Fund 'Bihar Nirmata Kosh', 148
  Highest Sale of Drugs in India, 203
  Land Reform Act, 1946, 79
  Land Reforms Legislation, 113
  Legislative Assembly, 99
  Mounted Police, 88
  Nirmata Kosh, 96
  Police Intelligence, 111
  Pradesh Congress Committee (BPCC), 112
  Public Service Commission, 342, 353
  Regiment, 106
  State Electricity Board (BSEB), 218, 263
  Tenancy Act, 1885, 78
  Treasury Code, 128, 129
  Tribes, 106
Bihar's Economy, 252
Bihari
  Hindus, 119
  Sikhs, 120
Biharis, 106
Bimal Khalsa, Widow of Beant Singh, 317
BIMARU, 323
Bird and Company, 148
Birendar
  And Dipendar, 242
  Author's Elder Son, 85, 97, 243
  Author's Son Joined St. George School, 153
  Born in 1957 Ranchi, 85
  Posted as Flying Officer at Sirsa, 241
  Training for Fighter Pilot, 220
Birhors, Survived on Eating Monkeys, 124
Birsa Munda, Tribal Freedom Fighter, 101
  Statue, 101
Bisht, Dr.LS, Dir. Gen. Health Services, 327
Blood Testing Kits for AIDS, 334
Board of Revenue, 129, 201
Bomb Explosion at Samastipur, 193
Bombay, Commercial Centre of India, 70
Bose, Subhas Chandra, 262
Boundary Commission, 45
Boycott of Nirankaris, 222
Brar, General, 286
Brett, Mr., 77
British
  Army, 44
    Unit, 54
  Cabinet Mission, 36
  Colonial Rule India, 59
  Colonial Set Up, 268
  Empire, 30
  ICS Officers in Bihar, 71
  Indian Army (BIA), 22, 26

Indian Army Mule Battery, 24
Indian Soldiers, 25
Masters, 71
Paramountcy, 28
Policy of Reservation-Govt. Jobs, 273
Preference for Sikhs in Army, 273
Revenue System, 97
Rule, 127
Rulers, 22
Buddha, 196
Dal, 288
Bureaucracy, 81
Burk Sheeran, Prof., 156
Expert Adviser to Pakistan, 156
Buxur, 88

Cabinet Mission, 39
Cairo, 31
Canadian Air Force Pilots, 153
Canal Revenue, 87
Cash Balances to Pakistan, 51
Caste Reservation, 320
Central
Administrative Tribunal, (CAT), 352
Board of Secondary Education (CBSC), 320
Health Services, 328
Jail Nabha, 296, 297
Pool, 194
Reserve Police (CRP), 276
Centre for Research in Rural and Industrial Development (CRRID), 283, 284
Chahal, J. S, 269, 270, 272
Amritdhari Sikh Officer, 269
Chaibassa, 86
Chamkaur, 242, 288
Chanan Singh, 28
Chandigarh, 21
New Capital of Punjab, 134
Chandra Shekher, PM of India, 181
Chandraswamy, 335
Charan Singh, 119, 245
Chaudhury, 217, 228, 231
Chaudhury, Jat Home Minister, 224
Vowed to Convict Sanjay Gandhi, 232
Chaturvedi, TN, 153, 154, 158, 160, 161, 163, 168, 170
Chauhan, Jagjit Singh, Ex-Minister Punjab, 299
Chauhan, PP, 320
Chavan, YB, 160
Chawla, Navin, 175
Chhamb Jaurian, 107
Chhinda, 278
Chief Khalsa Dewan, 94
China's Ambassador to India, 70
Chinese
Aggression, 98
Army, 56
Episode, 95
Chitpavan Brahmins Poona, 26, 158
Introduced Counselor System, 159
Chota Nagpur, 86
Development, 85
Choudhury, Nirad C., 70
Chowk Mehta, 220, 221
Christian
College Lahore, 34
Medical College, 30
Missionaries, 110
Churchill, Winston, 354
CIA or ISI, 241
Citizen Advisory Committee, 128
Civil
Hospital Ranchi, 139
Rights, 198
Services Officers, 151-168

Training of-, 151-168
Supplies, 130
Coal
Mine Manager, 97
Mine Trade Unions, 93
Mines, 92
Coalition Government, 1947, 40
Collector of Ballia, 88
Commander Ratnagar of IAF, 239
Commission for Reservation in Services, 249
Commission of Enquiry (COE), 97, 115, 117, 119, 121, 129, 146, 148, 150, 218, 255
Chairman Justice Shah, Supreme Court, 218
Under Justice Raghubar Dayal, Supreme Court Judge-, 148
Committee of Secretaries, 283
Commonwealth
Agriculture Bureau in London, 226
Health Ministers Conference, Bahamas, 337
Communal
Rioting in Punjab, 275
Riots, 147, 150
Riots in Bihar, 74
Riots in Calcutta, 39
Riots—in Ranchi, 101
Tension, 126
Communalism, 80
Communist, 59
China, 70
Literature, 37
Manifesto, 37
Movement, 37
Party of India, 52, 54, 58, 80
Community
Development, 86
Work, 81
Lunch, 231
Compulsory Primary Education, 324, 325
Congress
Conclave, 113
Leaders, 33, 51, 113, 257, 300
Leadership of Bihar, 213
Legislature Party, 95
Ministry, 49
Party, 90, 91, 93, 111, 135, 141, 182, 216, 302
Party in Bihar, 251
Constitution of India, 69, 345
Cooperative
Movement, 151
Society (ies), 151, 152
Structure, 151
Corruption, 80, 132, 135, 202, 212
Corruption in India Book by Noorani, 193
Cow Slaughter, 75, 111
Banned in India, 111
Criminal Procedure Code, 165, 277
Crop Rotation, 181
CSS Officers, 239
Customary Incentives, 132

Dal Khalsa, 288
Dale Jagjit Singh, 57
Dam Dama Sahib, 241, 288
Damdami Taxal, 297
Sikh Seminary, 220, 222
Danapur, 106
Dandwate, Janata Dal, 347
Darbar Sahib, 292, 305
Darbara Singh, CM, 298
Darbara, Senior, IAS, 167
Darbhanga, 75, 81
Medical College, 202
Das Commission Enquiry Against Kairon, 313
Das, A, Joint Secretary, 170
Das, KK, ICS, 157, 158

Secretary Ministry of Health, 157
Dasgupta, STC, 179
DAV College Jalandhar, 54
Day of Judgment, 126
Dayal, L, Principal Information Officer, 255
Dayal, Lt.Gen. BS, 293
De Nobili Convent School, 97
Death of Mother Teresa, 184
Debacle of
India Against China, 1962, 94
Indian Army Against Chinese, 103, 107
Defence of India Rules, 104
Dekh Mardanya Rang Kartar de (Guru Nanak), 202
Delhi
Cantonment, 57
Base General Hospital, 57
Development Authority, (DDA), 246
Press Corps, 192
Riots, 306
Violence, 306
Delhi—Kalyan, 26
Demands of Akalis--, 268
Deogarh, 82, 83, 84, 85
Desai, Morarji, 95, 160, 217, 224, 228, 231, 245
Gandhian, 217
Prime Minister, 217
Teetotaler, 217
Desertification, 78
Deshmukh, BG, Principal Secretary to PM, 343
Development Commissioner, 252
Dey, SK, 81
Dhami, Bhai Kanwar, 304, 313
Dhamot, 230
Dhanbad, 133, 144, 231
Gurudwara, 94
School of Mines, 92, 97
Sikhs, 94
Dhanoa, SS,
General, Author's Cousin, 229, 295
Maj. Gen, 242, 271
Dhanoa, Mrs. 104
see also Sukhdev Kaur
Dhar, DP, 180, 181
Dhar, TN, 154
Dharm Yudh Morcha (for Sikhs), 258, 304, 313
Dharmshala, 56
Dhawan, RK, 185, 186, 189, 191, 215, 233, 243, 245, 248, 266, 267
Dhillon, Ganga Singh, 241
Lawyer, 240
Dhillon, JS, General, 107
Dhillon, KS, 269, 270
Dhillon, Sardar Gurdial Singh, 323, 326
Digvijay Singh, MP, CM, 242
Dikkus, Hatred of Tribals Against Non-Tribal Population, 125
Dinapur, 193
Dipendar, Author's Younger Son, 135, 153, 220
Direct Action Day, 39
Director General Health Services, 327-329
Disaster Management, 197
District
Administration, 88, 151, 282
Amritsar, 118
Ludhiana, 24, 228
Nazir, 73
Palamau, 86
Public Prosecutor, 90
Purnea, 78
Ropar, 278
Shahabad and Purnea, 195
Singhbhum, 86

Divinity, 36, 37
Dixit, Mrs. Sheila, 326
Drinking Water, 324
Dronacharya, 294
Dubey, Bindeshwari, 201, 203
Dubey, Binod, 204, 206, 207, 208, 211
Dubey, VS, District Magistrate, 197, 211
Duggal, VK, 167
Dumka, 82, 117, 118
Durand Line, 25
Dutt, Sachin, 74, 77
  District Magistrate and
    Professor of Economics, 77

East Bengal, 40
  Massacre in--, 39
  Now Bangladesh, 39
  Riots, 74
East Punjab University, 57
East Uttar Pradesh, 92
Economic Planning, 180
Edict—Against Bhindranwale, 258
Edicts Issued for Sikhs Centres, 258
Edicts,
  Jathedar Maan Singh, 258
  Jathedar of Takhat Patna Sahib, 258
Education
  Of Soldiers, 43
  System of Bihar, 213
Election
  Commission, 343-345, 350, 351, 352
  Symbol, 347
Elections in UP, 346
Emergency, 191, 198, 255
  Imposition of-, 212-226
  Laws, 206
Empowerment of Women, 323
English
  Coal Mining Companies, 97
  Currency, 179
Epic Ramayana, 83
Ex-Raja of Ramgarh, 141

Fakhruddin Ali Ahmed, Indian President, 215
Fakhruddin Ahmed, Cabinet Minister, 170
Family
  Planning, 201, 203
  Program, 215, 218, 321, 323
  Purohits, 24
Famine of 1966, 193
FAO In Rome, 196
Fascist and Nazis, 33
Fellowship Grant of Ford Foundation, 154
Female
  Education, 323
  Infanticide, 24
Field Administration, 129
Filaria and Kalazar, 203
  Endemic To Bihar, 203
Financial Commissioner (Revenue), 129
First Christian Mission, 30
Five Point Program of Sanjay Gandhi, 215
Flood
  Relief Work, 197
  Victims, 78
Fodder Scam, 128
Food and Civil Supplies, 191
  Deptt., Notorious for
    Corruption, 198
Food Levy, 194
Forcible Sterilization of Hindu Sadhu, 216
Ford Foundation USA, 86, 156, 164
Fotedar, 269
Free
  Health Care, 202
  Medical Care, 208

Freedom Fighters, 124
French Revolution, 217
Frontier Province, 44, 46, 49
Fundamental Rights of
 Constitution, 214

Gafoor, Bihar Chief Minister, 193
Ganda Singh, Dr. 37
 Historian on Sikhs History, 37
Gandhi, 46, 51
 And Congress, 23
 Feroze, Mrs. Indira Gandhi
 Husband, 266
 Mahatma, 30, 33, 80, 124, 212
 Assassination of-, 51
 Autobiography- 'My
 Experiences with Truth',
 60
 In Bengal, 45
 Khadi Gandhi Cap, 80
 Mahatma's Techniques of Non-
 Violence, 23
Gandhi, Mrs. Indira, Daughter of
 Jawaharlal Nehru, 110, 122, 135,
 148, 163, 169-171, 175-177, 180,
 182-186, 189, 190, 192, 198, 203,
 211-218, 224, 225, 228, 231-233,
 236, 237, 243-245, 249, 252, 254,
 256, 257,259, 261, 266, 267, 268,
 283, 289, 291, 292, 298-300, 302,
 306, 316, 343
 A Master Politician, 113
 Assassination, 298, 302
 Fed Up with Punjab Politicians
 and Administration, 267
 Government, 255
 PM, 113
 To Lift Emergency, 211
Gandhi, Mrs. Maneka, 184, 213,
 216, 233, 245
Gandhi, Rajiv, 189, 246, 252, 268,
 269, 298, 300, 302, 303, 307, 309,
 314, 315, 320, 321, 323-326, 330-
 333, 336, 341, 343, 345-347, 349,
 351, 352
 Professional Pilot in Indian
 Airlines, 252
Gandhi, Sanjay, 184, 203, 213-215,
 216-218, 231, 232, 233, 245, 246,
 321, 340
Gandhi, Sonia, 327
Ganges, 88
Gauri Shankar, General, 269, 290
Gautam, OP, 234, 235
Gaza, 28
General Elections, 85, 343, 346-348,
 351
George Bharat Singh, 105
George, V, 331, 341
Ghadar Party, 221
Ghai, Dr., Kairon's Physician, 313
Gharuan, 38, 39, 41, 43, 48-50, 54,
 56, 64, 65, 85, 207, 229, 221 *see
 under* Village Gharuan *also*
Ghosh, Atulya, Strongman of West
 Bengal, 110
Ghototkuch, Son of Bhim, 21
Gian Singh Rarewala, 258
Giani
 Kirpal Singh Jathedar, 289
 Sharan Singh Jathedar, 122
Gill, HS, 308
Gill, KPS, DGP, 279, 285
Gill, PS, Asst. Gen. Manager, 184
Gill, TS, 184
Girda, 102
Godse, Nathuram Vinayak, 51
Gold Sheets on Darbar Saheb, 38
Golden Temple (GT), 38, 221, 264,
 297, 300
 Complex (GTC), 35, 58, 223,
 259, 262, 271, 272, 278, 287,
 288, 289, 290, 292, 296, 297,
 305, 316

Important Shrine of Sikhs, 22
Gopalakrishnan, Author's Batchmate, 169
Gosains, 32
Government of India Act, 1935, 33
Goyal, SK, IIPA, 181
Granthis, 222
Grewal, JS, 120, 247
  Author's Dhanbad Friend, 119
  Dy. GM, Bharat Cooking Coal Company Ltd., 231
  Loss of Friend and Well-wisher of Author, 231
  Vice Chancellor Guru Nanak Dev University, 269
Grewal, Serla, 203-205, 323, 324-326, 330, 333
  Called Hunterwali, 203, 321
  Health Secretary, 319, 321
  Suspected CIA Links, 323
Grewal, SS, IAS, 232
Gulati, VP, 185
Gurbachan Singh, Nirankari Guru, 222, 223
Gurbani, Solace to Author, 91
Gurdaspur and Amritsar, 278
Gurdev Singh, DC Amritsar, 285
Gurdial Singh, IP, 279
Gurdwara
  Bangla Sahib, 179, 261
  Reform Agitation, 302
Gurmit Singh, Sikh Scholar, 121
Guru
  Arjan Dev, 286
  Gobind Singh, 48, 65, 122, 123, 163, 241, 242, 257, 288, 290, 299
    Born in Patna, 257
  Granth Sahib, 38, 61, 65, 83, 133, 137, 150, 179, 210, 221, 230, 292, 297, 329
  Harikrishan, 179
  Nanak, 22, 41, 65, 83, 94, 121, 122, 182, 202, 209, 210
  Nanak Dev University, 269
    JS Grewal, Vice Chancellor, 269
  Ram Das Sarai, 35, 42
  Teg Bahadur, 63
Gurdwara (s), 22
  At Secundarabad, 244
  Committee, 258
  Reform Movement, (1921-1925), 22, 23
Gurumukhi Script, 27

H Lal, ICS Bihar Cadre, 162
Hailey, Sir Malcolm, 302
Haksar, PN, 236, 245, 283
Handicrafts, 175
Handsome Rewards for—Killing Indira Gandhi, 299
Harbaksh Singh, General, 107
Harbans Singh, Prof of Patna, 283
Hardliners, Shout 'Long Live Pakistan', 126
Hariharan, Director, 239
Harinder Singh, 299
Hasan Abdal, Pakistan, 209
Hassan and Hussain, 102
Haveli Ram, Astrologer, 108, 109
Hazaribagh and Dhanbad, 95
Health
  Commissioner, 201
  Ministry, 303
Healthcare Infrastructure, 204
Heavy Engineering Corporation, 101
  Complex, 126
  Management, 125
Heavy Machine Tools Plant, 126
Hereditary
  Mahant, 22
  Priests, 83

Rights, 83
High
Powered Committee, 204
Security Prisoners, 296
Higher Education, 56
Hindu
And Sikh Refugees, 47
And Sikhs, 273
Ascetic, 110
Bureaucracy, 257
Communist Students, 58
Customs, 230
Fanatic, 51
Gods, 83
Muslims Communal Angle, 75
Oppression, 121
Religion, 111
Religious Literature, 69
RSS Cadre, 51
Traders, 102
Hinduism, 51, 273
Hinduja, Sri Chand, 335
Hindujas, 335
Hindus
And Muslims, 28
And Sikhs of Lahore, 40
In Calcutta, 39
Hindu-Sikh Refugees, 49
Hindustan Steel, 103
Hitler, 51
HIV
Positive, 333
Virus in India, 333
Holocaust, 47
Hora Bhagat Singh, Judicial Officer, 258
Hukumnama, 305
Human Rights
Activists, 297
Groups, 280

India and Pakistan, 49
India International Centre, 176
Indian
Administration, 152, 257
Administrative Service (IAS), 59
Association, 224
Batch of 1957, 86
Conduct Rules, 132
Officers, 102, 132, 141, 146, 152, 155, 157, 159, 307, 320, 356, 357
Probationers, 68, 154
Trainee, 153, 154, 262, 166, 168
Training Academy, 163
Training School, 67, 68, 69
Agricultural Research Institute (IARI), 234
Air Force, 97
Training Iraqi Pilots in Habhaniya, 182
Ambassador to China, 70
Army, 25, 30, 41, 42, 46, 56, 103, 107, 276
Army Education Corps, 30
Civil Services (ICS), 59, 69, 354, 355
Council of Agricultural Research (ICAR), 175, 177, 219, 225, 227-247, 330, 341
Institutions, 228
Society, 308
Democratic System, 213
Foreign Service (IFS), 68, 299
Hindus, 121
Independence, 45
Institute of
Economic Growth, 323
Public Administration (IIPA), Delhi, 160, 161, 180
Intelligence Bureau (IB), 109
Legal System, 223

Muslims, 33, 51
National Army, 262
Soldiers, 263
National Congress, 29, 39, 44
National Trade Union Congress (INTUC), 93, 259
Police Act, 1861, 165
Police Service (IPS), 64
Promotions, 255
Punjab, 210
Research Centres, 240
Rice Research Institute (IRRI), 227
Soldiers, 26
Indians in Zambia, 179
Indonesia, 31
Indo-Pak War of 1965, 105, 104, 107
Industrial
Development, 341
Development Ministry, 341
Guest House, 198
Industries in Jails, 255
Infrastructural Support in Bihar, 87
Inspector General Intelligence Bihar, 216
Institute of
Advanced Studies, Shimla, 283, 352
Management, University of Pittsburg, 156
Insurgency, 107
Intelligence Bureau, 308
Intensive Agricultural Development, 180
Internal Security Operation, 287
International
Boundary, 107
Crops Research Institute, (ICRISAT), 234, 237-240, 245, 247, 263, 341
Scale Salary, 238
Inter-Security, 293
Iraq, 180, 181
Iraqi
Administration, 182
Airlines, 180
Airways, 183
Army, 180
Planning Commission, 181
ISI, 278
Islam Onslaught, 273
Islamia College Lahore, 40
Izhar Alam, Sr. Superintendent of Police, 278

Jag Pravesh Chandra, 177
Jagjit Singh, Dr. 163
Jagjiwan Ram, 216, 217, 228
Jain, Giri Lal, 326
Jain, Sahu, 90
Prosecutor, 90
Jain, Shanti Prasad, 91
Jaipal Singh, Hockey Player, 106
Jaiswal, Lakshmi Narain, 114
Jakhar, Balram, 336, 337
Jalandhar Cantonment, 54
Jammu and Kashmir, 50, 53, 54, 68, 107
Jamshedpur, 108
Janata Dal, 247
Elections, 347
Janata
Government, 245
Party, 321
Japanese
Attack on Singapore, 31
Hara Kiri, 31
Jaspal Singh, Mrs. 112
Jaspolan School, 41
Jat Sikhs, 64, 236, 237, 265
Jathedar
Maan Singh, 298
Mahalon of Takhat Keshgarh Sahib, 306, 307

Of Keshgarh Sahib, 122
Jathedars, 290
Jenkins, Sir Evan, Governor of Punjab, 40
Jerusalem, 31
Jha, Binodanand, Deogarh, 91, 93, 95
Later Leader of Congress Legislature Party, 91
Chief Secretary, 130
Jharia, 98
Jia Lal Singh, Author's School Friend in Army HQs, 157
Jinnah, Mohammad Ali, 39, 45, 46
Jodh Singh, Principal, 35
Jodhpuri Coat and Trousers, 70
Joginder Singh, Prof., Chemistry Teacher, 37
Josh, Sohan Singh, 35
Top CPI Leader in Punjab, 55
Well Known Communist Leader of Punjab, 35
JP (Jaya Prakash)
Led Agitation, 255
Led Students Movement, 213
Narayan Agitation, 184
Judicial Commission, 145
Justice BP Singh Commission of Enquiry, 152

K Kamraj, 111, 112
Congress President, 110
Plan, 95
Kailey, DC, 278
Kaimur Plateau, 86
Kairon, Partap Singh, CM Punjab, 236
Adesh Pratap Singh, Son, 315
Surinder Singh, 315
Kaistha, IAS Trainees, 167
Kalhan, Mrs. Promila, Author's Old Detractor from Super Bazar, 175, 328
Kalkat, GS, 164
Kang, GS, IAS
District Magistrate of Aurangabad, 194
Kanwar, Dr. JS, 233
Dy. Dir Gen ICRISAT, 233
Kapoor, Yashpal, Private Asstt. To Prime Minister, 188
Kapur Singh,
Ex-ICS, 121
Sirdar Akali MP, 121
Kar Sewa, 272, 288
Of Sarovar, 290
Karma Yoga By Swamy Vivekananda, 59
Kartar Singh, Principal, 241
Kartic Oraon, Chief Engineer in Heavy Engineering Corporation, 125
Kashmir, 107
Kashyap, Nishta, Near to Prime Minister, 175, 176
Kathpalia, Prem Kumar, Author's Batchmate, 265
Kaul, PK, IAS UP Cadre, 308
Kaushal, Former Governor of Bihar, 338
Kaushal, MP, 338
Kayastha Officers, 254
Kesri Turbans, 270
Khadakvasla National Defence Academy (NDA), 219, 220
Khadkus-Extremists, 274
Khalistan, 259, 274, 287, 304
Khalsa
Brigade, 244
College Amritsar, 35, 36, 40, 42, 54
Product of Singh Sabha, 35
Sikh Institution of Learning, 35
Order, 65

Panth, 123
Kartar Singh, 220
Khan
Abdul Ghaffar Khan, 44
Brothers, 44
Khanna, Balraj, Jan Sangh, 177
Khanna, Tejinder, 294
Khaparde, Ms. Saroj, MOS, 336, 337
Kharian, 107
Khem Karan, 108
Graveyard of Pakistani Tanks, 108
Khilafat Agitation, 51
Khizar Khan Hayat Tiwana, Premier, 40
Khosla, RP, 154
Khushwant Singh, 299
Khyber Pass Bordering Afghanistan, 30
Kidwai, Mrs. Mohsina, UP, Minister for Health, 319
Kings Commissioned Officers, 41
Kiratpur Sahib, 230
Kirpal Singh, 290
Kirpal, BN, 352
Kishan Chand, Lt. Gov. Delhi, 213
Kishan Lal, Congress Leader, 186
Kissa Kursi Ka-Film, 215, 232
Kitchen Athlete, 36, 37
Kohli, JK, 159, 162, 167, 215
Appointed Chief Secretary of Delhi, 187
Kohli, Nanak Singh, Author's Friend, 180, 181, 226
Kosi
Canal, 78
Embankment, 78
Krishan Kumar, IAS Kerala Cadre, 320, 321
Krishna Menon, VK, 118, 160
Krishnamurty, 154
Krishnaswamy, Agriculture Secretary, 325, 326
Kuwait, 183

L Dayal,
Author's Friend, 198
Principal Information Officer, 198
Labour
Government in United Kingdom, 39
Union, 174
Laheria Sarai, 73, 77
Lahore College, 52
Lal Bahadur Shastri National Academy of Administration, Mussoorie, 151, 262
Lal, Anand Mohan,
Author's Batchmate, 294
Chief Secretary Rajasthan, 294
Lala Jagat Narain's Murder, 269, 272
Laloo Prasad Yadav, 213
Lamba, GS, 209, 299
Land Grants to, 23
Brahmins, 32
Udasis of Baba Siri Chand, 32
Land
Records, 79
Reform Law, 113
In India, 79
Reforms, 79
Revenue, 78
Surveys, 78
Law and Order, 330
Affairs, 264
Handling, 124
Problem, 268
Situation, 276
Law of Crimes, 69
Lawyers of Ranchi, 139
Le Carbusiers, Famous French Architect, 84
Lee Enfield, 303
Left Leaning Professors, 58
Legendary Ghototkuch, 21

Lenin, 37
Local Congress Leaders, 299
Lockhart, Sir, Governor of Frontier Province, 49
Lohia, Ram Manohar, 135
  Socialist Leader, 87, 110
Longowal, Sant Harchand, 303, 304, 306, 309
  Dictator of Akali Morcha, 303
Lord
  Dalhousie, 122
  Mountbatten, Viceroy of India, 45, 71
  Ram, 102
  Shiva, 83
Lusaka, 178

Maan Singh, 32, 56, 229, 258, 259, 264, 288
  Author's Younger Brother, 97, 230
  Jathedar, 120
  Posted in Air Force, 152
Madhubani Sub-Division, 74
Madhupur, 82
Madneshwar Singh,
  Author's Friend and Batchmate, 242
  Chief Secretary, 242
Maha Punjab, 275
Mahabharata, 21, 294
Maharaja of Patiala, 109
Maharana of Udaipur, 71
Maheshpatti, 75, 76
Malaya, 27, 30, 31
Malhotra, Rashpal,
  Chairman CRRID, 283
  Dr. CRRID, 214
Mall Singh, 23
  QM Havildar, 21
Malviya, Madan Mohan, 271
  Founder Banaras Hindu University, 271
Malwa, 241
Management
  Committee of Super Bazar, 183
  Of Gurdwaras, 23
Mandal Commission Report, 251
Mandal, BP, Bihar Politician, 251
Mangal Singh, Akali Leader, 184
Manji Sahib, 35, 221, 222
Manjit Singh, Indian High Commissioner in London, 122
Manjit Singh, Sikh IFS, 122
Manmohan Singh, 163
  Member Planning Commission, 294
Mann, Simranjit Singh, 296
  Pro-Bhindranwale Officer, 296
Mahants, 23
Mardana, 202, 209
Marjuana, 289, 290
Markham, AF, 139
  Vice Chancellor, 137, 139
Marriage of Maneka to Sanjay Gandhi, 213
Martial Races, 106
Maruti Factory, 216
Marxism, 37, 54, 59
Marxist
  Ideas, 37
  Party Cadre, 80
Mass Sterilization, 321
Master Tara Singh, 22
Mathur, B C, 161
Mazumdar, SJ, Chief Secretary, 117
Mecca And Medina, 22
Media Adviser, 323
Medical
  College of Bihar, 207
  Council of India, 211
  Profession, 321, 327
  Reimbursements, 208
Medieval Rajputs Johar Ceremony, 41

Meerut Riots, 41
Mehta, Kanti, Socialist, 92, 93
Menon, Dr. VKN, 60
Menon, PKJ,
  Chief Secretary, 192, 193
  From Bihar, 169
  Secretary Department of Personnel, 169
Menon, Prof. MGK, 332
  Member of Planning Commission, 332
Menon, VP, 239
  Hand in Amalgamation of States with India, 239
Metcalf House Delhi, 67, 68
MIG Fighters Planes, 241
Military
  Balance, 107
  Hospital, 229
Minerva Academy Chandigarh, 166, 211
Mines Ownership, 93
Mining Industry, 148
Ministry of
  Agriculture, 219, 225
  Home Affairs, 190
  Labour, 109
Miranda House, 220
Mirchandani, 68
Mishra, Hari Nath,
  Earlier State Cooperative Minister, 200
  Speaker of House, 200
Mishra, Jagannath, CM Bihar, 204, 206, 249, 250, 256
  Professor, 192, 193
Mishra, Lalit N, 192, 233, 249
  A Fund Collecting Minister from Bihar, 233
  Fund Collector of Congress, 192
  Rly Minister, 192, 193
Miss Tirkey, Dr., 248
  Director Health Services, 248
Modern
  Education, 94
  School, 220
Mohammad Habid, Professor, Historian, 60
Mosul, 181
Mountain Division, 103
Mughal
  Dynasty, 180
  Emperor, 289
  Nobles, 250
  Suzerainty, 21
Mukherjee, Subhash,
  IAS, Chief Secretary Bihar, 249
  Work as JS in Min. of I&B, 249
Muslim
  Army Officers, 45
  Celebration of Muharram, 102
  Community, 126
  Culture, 58
  League (ML), 33, 39, 40, 41, 42, 47, 49, 51, 57, 58, 74
    Government in NWFP, 40, 46
  League's Call for Direct Action, 51
  Legislators, 40
  Majority Provinces, 40
  Opinion Leaders, 126
  Population, 57
  Provinces, 39
  Refugees, 46
  Sacrifice Cow on Every Bakr-id, 77
  Students, 26
  Sufis, 41
Muslims of East Pakistan, 43
Mussoorie Leaders, 163

Nairobi, 178
Najma Heptullah, MP, 326

Namdharis, 242
Namkum Vaccine Research Institute, 127
Nanda, Gulzari Lal, 108-111
  Faith in Astrology, 108
  Gandhian From Gujarat, 108
  Prime Minister, 109
Narain Singh, 21
  Viceroy's Commissioned Officer, 21
Narain, G, 111, 137, 144, 342
  Author's Friend, 250
  District Superintendent of Police, 104
  IGP, 255
  IPS, 149, 150
Naranjan Singh, Subedar, 24
Narasimha Rao, P., 267, 320, 324, 325, 327, 329, 331, 334-337, 353
Narasimhan, Chief Justice of Patna High Court, 71
Narayan, Jaya Prakash, 130, 135, 148, 212, 216, 217
  Lok Nayak, 216
Narayanan, Dir IB, 349
National
  Coal Development Corporation, (NCDC), 102, 131
  Defence Academy (NDA), 219, 220
  Defence Fund, 94, 97
  Development Council (NDC), 252, 333
  Elections, 135
  Park of Bandavgarh, 242
  Police Academy Hyderabad, 165
  Rice Research Insitute, 323
Nationalization of Coal Mines, 231
Nazis, 299
Nazis and Fascists, 51
Nehru, Arun, 300
Nehru, Jinnah and Baldev Singh, 45
Nehru, Pandit Jawaharlal, 29, 45, 56, 70, 95, 98, 102, 111, 174, 176, 231, 245, 263, 269
  PM, 81
  Ashes, 98
Nihang Sikhs, 288
Nihangs, 48
Nirankari
  Conference, 222
  Mandal, 221
Nirankaris, 222, 223
Nirlep Kaur, Akali Politician, 258, 259
Nizam of Hyderabad, 244
Noni, Author's Daughter (Later Niripjit Kaur), 94
Non-Tribal Teachers, 125
North Bihar, 77, 78
North Western Frontier Provinces, (NWFP), 33, 39, 40, 41, 43, 44, 45, 51, 288
Nowshehra, 50
  In NWFP, 42
  Rly Stn, 43
NPS Bal, Brigadier, 262

Om Mehta, 190
  State Minister for Home, 206
Operation
  Blue Star (OBS) In Amritsar, 259, 261-264, 270, 272, 273, 277, 283, 285, 286, 287, 293, 295, 297, 299, 302, 317
  Of Robbery, 87
  Woodrose, (Operation of Search), 259, 278
Oxford University, As Model of AMU, 58

Paddy New Crop from Punjab, 228
Paharia, MOS, 170

Pakistan, 39, 44, 46, 47, 49, 58, 70, 94, 104, 107, 108, 126, 210, 274, 278
  Army, 49, 50
Pakistani
  Aggression on Kashmir, 55
  Armoured Force, 107
  Ranks, 108
  Spy, 126
Pal, BP, Ex Dir ICAR, 176
Palestine and Egypt Area, 31
Pande, BD,
  Appointed Governor on Retirement, 71
  Chief Secretary, 146
  Government of Punjab, 107
  Governor, 268
  ICS, 71
  Later Chief Secretary Govt. of India, 71
Pande, Ram Lochan, Bihar Astrologer, 198, 199
Pandey, DGP Bihar, 120
Pandit, Vijay Laxmi, Mrs. 174
Panipat Battle, 158
Panj Piaras, 288
Panja Saheb Gurdwara Pakistan, 209
Pannikar, KM, 70
Pannu, Daljit Singh, 308, 309
Pant, GB, Home Minister, 162
Pant, KC, 302, 347
  Central Minister, 288
Parja Mandal, 29
Parliamentary Elections, 216, 232
Partition of
  India, 44-52
  Punjab, 52
Pathak, Arun, New MD of Cooperatives, 201
Pathan Tribesmen, 25
Patiala, Princely State, 28
Patliputra, 196
Patna
  Gurudwara, 119
  High Court, 71, 115, 117
  Medical College Hospital, 252
  Medical College, 207
  Sikhs, 299
  University, 71
Patnaik, Biju, 110
  Strongman of Orissa, 110
Paton Tanks, 107
Patwant Singh, 299
Peer Bahlol Dastigir, 22
Peri Shastri, RVS, 343-352
Peshwas, 26
PGI Chandigarh, 231
Phula Singh, Akali Leader, 288
Pimputkar, MG, ICS, 152, 153-155
  Booked his Wife for Breaking Traffic Rules, 152
  Design Director of National Academy of Administration, 152
Pioneer Regiment of British Indian Army, 22
Pitroda, Sam, Rajiv Gandhi's Friend, 325
PL-480, 193, 194
Placements, 236
Police
  Intelligence, 268
  Manual, 165
Political
  Development, 35
  Leaders of India, 45, 47, 78, 85, 216
  Masters, 73
  Parties in India, 39
Polling Stations, 84
Poona Horse, 46, 47
  Allotted to India, 46

Pooni, AS, IAS, Home Secretary, 276
Postal Service, 154
Power and Fertilizers Industries, 92
Pran Prasad, 98, 148
Primary Health Centres, 203
Prime Minister of Czechoslovakia, 126
Prince of Wales and *Repulse* (Ships), 31
Prisoners of War, 31
Pritam Singh, 48
Private Espionage Network, 153
Probationers Handbook, 153, 154
Pro-Khalistan Sikhs, 264
Pro-Pakistan Dons, 58
Public
  Administration, 69
  Interest Petition, 297
  Order, 139
Punjab
  Agricultural University VC, 281
  Assembly Elections, 317
  Bhawan, 267,319
  Central and Eastern, 21
  Crisis, 284
  Farmers, 228
  IAS Cadre, 272, 284
  IAS Officer Close to Buta Singh, 288
    Baba Santa Singh, 288
    Buddha Dal Nihang Chief, 288
  Imbroglio, 267
  Leader in Agricultural Production, 272
  Problem, 266
  School of Administration, 268
  University, 36, 40
  University Examination, 52
Punjabi, 275
  Hindus, 286
  Refugees, 147

Quakers, 51
Quit India 1942, 30, 51
  Agitation in 1942, 39, 33
  Movement, 195
Qureshi, ICS, Secretary Cooperatives, 172

Raag
  Ramkali, 122
  Suhi Mohala Panjwan, 138
Radcliffe, Sir Cycil, 45
  Award on Boundary, 43
Radhakrishnan,
  Author's Whole Time Principal (during training), 71
  ICS, 71
Radhasoamis of Beas, 223
Radical Democratic Party, 37
Raghubar Dayal Commission of Enquiry, 106, 149
Ragi Prof. Darshan Singh, 306, 317
Rai Bareilly, 216, 217
Rai Kalha, 242
Railway Strike in 1949, 54
Raj Dev Singh, IPS, 232
Raj Narain, 214, 219, 321
Raja of Ramgarh in Bihar, 312
Raja, ST, 131
Rajendra Prasad, Dr. 96, 97, 198
  First Indian President, 97
Rajeshwar Lal, 133, 134, 144, 148
Rajiv Gandhi Longowal Accord, 315
Rakhi System, 21
Ram Bagh Garden, 38
Rama Devi, Law Secretary, 343
Ram Kesari, A Behari Veteran, 233
Rama Rao, NT, CM Andhra Pradesh, 246
Ramachandran, IAS, 158
  South Indian Brahmin, 158

Raman, CK, ICS, 71, 129, 130, 355
Ramanujam, K, Director, 262
Ramashinder Singh, West Bengal Cadre, 279
Ramayana and Mahabharata, 203
Rami Chhabra, Journalist, 323
Ramlingswamy, DG ICAR, 333
Ramnaumi Procession, 102, 103
Ranade, BT, 52
Ranchi, 101, 103, 105, 106, 110, 111-113, 118, 122, 127, 129-133, 137, 141-147, 197
  Bar Association, 146
  Communal Riots, 149
  Courts, 139
  Riots, 150
  Town, 126
  University, 135
Randhawa, MS, 228
Ranjit Singh, Maharaja, 38, 244
Rao Birendra Singh, 244, 245
  Ahir Politician of Haryana, 244
Rao Saheb Krishnaswamy, 263, 265, 266
Rao, MS, Chief Secretary, 130
Rao, Narasimha P, 67, 320, 324, 325, 327, 329, 331, 334-337, 353
Rao, NDJ, 201
Rao, PS,
  Adviser to Rajapramukh (Governor), 278
  ICS, 278, 279
Rao Tula Ram, 244
Rarewala, Gian Singh, 258
Ravana, 83
RAW (Research and Analysis Wing), 182, 226, 283, 308
Ray, Sidharth Shankar, 352
Razmak, 25, 27
Records of Rights, 79
Recovery System, 151
Reddy, Brahmanand, 190
  Cabinet Minister for Home Affairs, 190
Reddy, Chenna, 246
Reddy, Karl, IAS Mess President, 154, 155
Referral Hospitals, 203
Regimental Centre
  HQs, 42
  Of Bihar Regiment, 106, 108
Regional Dy. Director of Health Services, 208
  Kingpin of Fraud, 208
  Related to Bindeshwary Dubey, 208
Relationships of Civil Servants and Politicians, 73
Reservation
  In All Recruitments, 251
  In Medical Colleges—On Merit, 319
  Regulations, 250
Reservations, 320
  For Admission to Medical Colleges, 319
Review Committee (Min of Industrial Development), 172, 341
Reward Money, 204
Rights to Ownership of Land to Land Tillers, 79
Riots, 41, 42
  In Noakhali, 39
  In Punjab, 45
Risalpur, 44, 46, 47, 49
  In NWFP, 210
  Now Peshawar, 41, 42, 43
River
  Baghmati, 77
  Beas, 107
  Gandak, 77
  Ganga, 74, 86, 196, 197, 230
  Kamla Balan, 77
  Karamnasa, 86

Kosi, 77
Punpun, 196
Son, 196
Rivers, Euphrates, and Tigris, 181
RML Hospital, 219
Rode, Harcharan Singh, Bhindranwale Brother, 287
Rohtas Hill, 88
Roper Thermal Power Station, 293
Rosy, Author's Elder Daughter, 220, 229, 239, 301
Royal Salute Scotch Whishky, 192
Rules of Execution of Business, 269
Ruling Princes and Zamindars, UP, 162
Rural Dispensaries, 205
Rushdie, Salman, 266

Sadam Hussain, 180
Sadasiv Rao Bhau, Commander of Maratha Army, 158
Safdarjung Airfield, 170
Sahay, KB, 93, 95, 95-98, 121, 122, 133, 135, 142-145, 148, 201
CM, 100, 102, 105, 108, 110, 111, 111, 112
Parliamentary Secretary, 71, 73
Sahay, Tribeni, 148, 149
Most Notorious Lawyer of Ranchi, 148
Saheb Singh, Author of Grammar of Granth Sahib, 37
Saint Edwards High School, 63
Salman Rushdie, Author, 266
Salunica in Greece, 22
Sam Manekshaw, Gen., 192
Samant, AD, Maharashtra Cadre IAS, 243
Sandhu, Harcharan Singh, 304
Sandhurst Great Britain, 41
Sant
Fateh Singh, 123
Harchand Longowal, 303, 304
Nirankari Mandal, 220
Nischal Singh of Jagadhri, 94
Singh, Author's Father, 21
In Bombay Sappers and Miners, 22
Santhal
Parganas, 86
Uprising, 1856-57, 84
Santhals, 82
Santokh Singh, Delhi Sikh Leader, 261
Sarao, BS,
Chief Commissioner of Chandigarh, 237
IAS-1952 Batch-Assam, 235
Sarbat Khalsa, 264, 277, 298, 299, 306
Sardar Baldev Singh, 108, 109
First Defence Minister, 108
Sardar Buta Singh, 264, 277, 287, 289, 298, 299, 306, 307, 323, 324, 328, 343-346
Declared Tankhahia, 306
Home Minister, 341, 342
Sardar Darbara Singh, 268
Later Chief Minister, 268
Sardar Datar Singh, 213
Sardar Gurnam Singh, Ex-Akali CM, 308
Sardar Kartar Singh, 64
Sardar Mohan Singh, 308
Sardar Mohinder Singh Zaildar, 64
Sardar Patel, 109, 274, 339, 354
Sardar Rawail Singh, 289
Sardar Saran Singh, Chief Secretary, 196
Sardar Tarlochan Singh, 289
Sarma, AU,
Author's Friend, 252, 253
Commissioner, 197
CS of Bihar, 341, 342

Sarna, S Paramjit Singh, Akali Leader, 303
Sasaram, 180
Famous for Rohtas Fort, 180
Tomb of Sher Shah Suri, 180
Satanic Theory of Hostages, 43
Satarawala, 268, 294
Appointed Governor, 268, 289
Parsi-Ex Army Officer, 268
Sathe, Dinkar D, 158-162, 168, 176, 187
Satya Narain Rai, 182
Savita Behan, 171, 183
In Managing Committee of Super Bazar, 177
Sawhney, Dy Commissioner Punjab, 297, 298
SEBI, 353
Secundarabad Club, 240
Seigell, SV, 342, 343, 345, 347, 351, 352
Sen, LP, Ex-Brigade Commander of 161 Brigade, 54
Seshan, TN, Cabinet Secretary, 345, 353
Shah Commission, 215, 218, 224, 233, 255
Shahabad, 86
Shamsher Singh of Kakron Village, 37
Shankranand, Health Minister, 300
Sharma, OP, 238
Author's Friend and Senior Counsel, 188, 232, 340
Sharma, SN, 198, 199, 200, 201
IAS, 193
Managing Director BFCS Corp., 198
Sharma, Vinod, Congress MLA, 311
Shastri, Bhola, Minister for Works and Housing, 185
Shastri, Lal Bahadur PM, 107, 108, 122
Came to Ranchi after Ceasefire, 108
In Tashkent, 109
Sheikh Abdullah, 345
Shiromani Gurdwara Prabhandak Committee (SGPC), 23, 122, 221, 222, 264, 289, 292, 296
Amritsar, 209
Granthis, 264
Shiromani Akali Dal (SAD), 23, 116, 221, 261, 262
Shorie, Arun, 353
Shukla, JM, 152, 153
Ex-Superindent Police Ranchi, 153
Shukla, VC, 216
Siddhu, SS, Adviser to Governor, 293
Sikh
Agricultural Experts, 227
Army Officers, 45
Chief of Army, 273
Citizens of Bihar, 121
Code of Conduct, 116
Community (ies), 40, 119, 120, 121, 123, 244, 258, 259, 273, 299, 304, 316, 347
Of Coal Mines, 94
Demonstrations-(Against Nirankari), 222
Extremist Leaders, 58
Extremists, 278, 286, 296
In Border Districts-Gurdaspur and Amritsar, 278
Granthis, 220
Gurdwara Management, 22
Gurus, 223, 339
High Priests, 288-290, 305
IAS Officers, 272
Intelligentia, 123
Jatha, 48

Leaders, 109
Leadership, 339
Marriage Sanctity, 66
Organizations, 121
Organizations in Bihar, 258
SGPC and SAD, 258
Panth, 289
Pilgrims, 209
Politicians, 274
Prime Minister, 273
Psyche, 270
Refugees, 46
Regiment, 42
Regiment Centre Ramgarh, 262
Religion, 94, 164
Sabha, 271
Security Guards, 299, 300
Separate Nation, 241
Soldiers, 23, 28
Students Federation, 316
Tenets, 123, 241
Tenets and Traditions, 22
Traders, 299
Traditions, 119, 121
Troops, 22, 221, 262
Volunteers, 46
Sikh-Hindu Ratio, 275
Sikhism, 273
Sikhs
In India—Second Class Citizens, 257
Of Dhanbad, 94
Sikhs—Martial Race, 199
Singh
Sabha, 27, 35, 230
Sangats, 120
Singh, Chandra Shekher, 253, 254
Singh, CPN of Bihar, 112, 245
Ambassador to Nepal, 112
Governor of UP in Indira Gandhi's Time, 245
Singh, DP, 166
Vice Chancellor Agricultural University, 165
Singh, Dr. HN, 201, 202, 205, 206
Voluntary Retirement, 206
Singh, JP, 86
Singh, KK, 211
Singh, LP, 177
ICS, Chief Secretary of Bihar, 71, 109
Singh, MP, 201
Director Family Planning, 206
Singh, NK, 174, 188, 189, 192, 193, 215, 216, 233
Singh, Prem Shankar, 256
Singh, Ramashray Prasad, 193, 205
Singh, Satyendra N, CM Bihar, 206, 342, 342
Leader of Rajputs, 206
Singh, SP,
Court of Enquiry Judge, 148, 149
Singh, TP, 134
Chief Secretary, 133
Sr. Bihar Officer and Agricultural Secretary, 170
Singh, VP, 251, 347
Finance Minister, 328
Sinha, BP, 92, 93, 100, 101
Sinha, Dr. Anugraha Narain, 96
Sinha, Dr. Ram Sharma, Hd Dept. of Surgery, 252
Sinha, Dr. SK, 91
Sinha, Mahamaya Prasad, 140, 141, 146
Sinha, RAP, Chief, Bihar Police Intelligence, 111
Sinha, RK, JS Min of Industrial Development, 341
Sinha, Shashi Shekher, 197
Sinha, SK, 96, 112, 133, 193
CM Bihar, 152, 195
First Chief Minister of Bihar, 96

Sinha, SK,
General, 254
State Industrial Guest House, House of-, 195
Sinha, Yashwant, 147, 347
Sirhind, 47, 48
Sivaraman, B, 164, 165
Slum Development, 217
Smith, Leslie, British Colonel, 22
Snipers, 46
Social
Justice, 218
Structure and Customs, 79
Sodhi, Khatri, 38
Married Bibi Bhani, 38
Sohi, Sardar Pritam Singh, 258
Nominee of SGPC on Gurdwara Committee, 258
Sohoni, Chief Secretary, 147
Author's First Commissioner, 130
Son Canal, 86
Soni, RK, 167, 190, 215
Industrial Tycoon, 167
Manufacturer of Ammunition and Defence Supplies, 215
Of Ludhiana, 186
Soviet
Russia, 59
Union, 108
Sparrow, Rajender Singh, Retired Army General, 314
President of Punjab Pradesh Congress, 314
Spirited Pursuits, 32
Spiritual Tradition, 122
Sports, 36
Sri Chand Hinduja, 335
Srinagar-Baramula Road, 50
Srinivas Ramanujam, South Indian IAS Officer, 114
Srivastava, KK, 187, 243, 263
CS Bihar, 253, 254
Srivastava, Surat Das, Author's Friend and Batchmate, 263
Stalin, Joseph, Soviet Dictator, 37, 59
State
Administration, 28
Civil Services of Jammu and Kashmir, 190
Trading Corporation, (STC), 178, 179
Transport Corporation, 251
Sterilization of Males and Females, 203
Student
Leaders, 137
Politics, 58
Students Disturbances, 149
Disturbances in Ranchi, 152
Instigated by Political Parties, 152
Study Circle of Leftists, 37
Subramaniam, C, Agriculture Minister, 227, 292, 204, 312
Subramaniam, Gopal, 352
Subramaniam, RV, 263, 307
Senior Adviser, 269
Subramaniam, Sr. Advocate, 290, 292
Sukhadia, (Mohan Lal), CM of Rajasthan, 154
Sukhdev Kaur (Hence Referred only Sukhdev By Author). 62-64, 77, 85, 103-105, 132, 138, 157, 159, 163, 172, 173, 183, 184, 199, 208, 220, 229, 239, 240, 241, 246, 247, 253, 267, 285, 295, 298, 319, 335
Sukhdev and Sathe, 170
Sukhdev's Father Sardar Kartar Singh, 62
Sukhdev Singh, Dr., 36, 228
Sukhmani Path, 229

Sun Set Law, 78
Sundarji, General, 286
  Chief Western Command, 262
Super Bazar, 169-188
  A Cooperative Store, Delhi, 169
  Initiate Export of Consumer Goods, 178
Supreme Court
  Bar Association, 340
  Of India, 320, 330, 340
  Of India Orders, 319
Suresh Kumar, Author's Friend, 192
  Consul General in Indian Embassy Germany, 192
Surinder Nath, IPS, 269, 278
Surjit, Author's Sister, 26, 41
Survey and Settlement Operation, 81, 86
Swaminathan, MS, 225, 227, 233, 234 235, 238
  DG ICAR, 227
  Paper-From Begging Bowl to Bread Basket, 227
  Scientist and Administrator, 225
Swaran Singh, 215
Swindale, 242
  Dr. LD, Director General, 238, 240
  Scientist for National Laboratory, 238
Syed Ahmed Khan, Sir, 57, 58
System of
  Accountability, 257
  Communication, 48
System of Rate Control, 204

TADA, 282
Takhat
  Harmandir Saheb, 120
  Patna Sahib, 260, 298, 299
  Sahib Gurdwara, 258, 260
Talha, 182, 183
Tana Bhagat, Tribal, 124
  Joined Non Cooperation Movement against British Rule, 124
Tandon, Bishan, JS, 171, 186, 190
Tandon, JS to Prime Minister, 185, 186
Tandon, PL, 178
Tankhahia, 289, 306
Tara Singh Master, 40, 244
Tara Singh's Leadership, 40
Taruna Dal, 288
Tashkent Peace Accord, 108
Tatt Khalsa, 261, 364
Tea Plantation, 215
Teargas, 138
Technical Education Institutions, 92
Technology Mission, 324
Teja Singh Samundari Hall, 221
  Office of SGPC, 221
Teresa, Goanese Christian Girl, 184
Tewari, ND, 351
  Congress Chief Minister, 351
Thakur, Karpuri, 192, 218, 219
  CM Bihar, 217
  Socialist Leader, 192
Tiwana, Sardar Kartar Singh, 241
Todar Mal, Revenue Minister of Akbar, 78
Tohra, Gurcharan Singh, 316
Tolstoy, 51
Topographical Maps of India, 249
Trade
  Fair in Pragati Maidan, 340
  Fairs Zambia, 178
  Unions, 92, 93
Traditional Hindu Religion, 98
Transfer of Power, 36, 45
  To Indians, 39
Tribal
  Areas, 50
  Customs, 125

Justice, 125
Mobs, 101
Population, 124, 125
Birhors, 134
In Deoghar, 82
Mundas, 124
Oraons, 124
Santhals, 124
Women Declared Witch, 125
Tripathi, VS, IAS MP Cadre, 254
Trivedi, RK, 345
Trivedi, Sir Chandu Lal, ICS, 89
Tubectomy, 203
Turkey, 28

Udasi Sadhus, 83
Uma Shankar, IAS Add. Secretary, 328
Umrangal, Jiwan Singh, 221
Uncontrolled Irrigation, 181
Under Trial Prisoners, 255
UNESCO, 320
Union
Elections, 59
Public Service Commission (UPSC), 59
Unionist Party, 33
United
Nations Organization (UNO), 60
States, 108
Universal Program of Immunization, 324
Untrained Midwives, 323
Uppal, KK, Author's Batchmate, 243, 244
Chairman, Bombay Port Trust, 243
Urban
Centres, 44
Development, 256
Urdu,
Cultural Language of Muslims, 147
Status of Second Language, 147
USAID, 337
USSR, 37

V Shankar, Mrs. ICS, 197
Vaccines to Immunization Program, 206
Vagaiwalla, Parsi, ICS, 69
Vice-Chancellor, 81
Vaidya, General, Army Chief, 262
Vaidyanathan, CR, 321
Union Secretary for Health and Family Planning, 302, 303
Vaishnav, PH, 312
Finance Commissioner, 283, 284
Punjab Cadre IAS, 284
Valikandhari, Muslim Pir, 209
Vasectomy, 203, 321
Vasudev,
Chief Secretary Punjab, 268
CS, Ousted by Author, 284
Vedas, 274
Venkataraman, Finance Secretary, 331
Verghese, BG, Editor, 175
Verma, BP, JS, 331
SDM, 249
Sub-Divisional Officer, 142
Verma, RK, 285
Vijay Ranjan, 141, 147
Village
Chinarthal, 36
Council, 85
Dhamot in Ludhiana District, 24, 25
Gharuan, 21, 26, 27, 32, 33, 37, 133
Jagannathpur, 126

Malikpur Near Khanna, 48
Violation of Inter State Agreements, 294
Vishwakarma,
Director General, 331
Orthopaedic Surgeon, 327, 328, 329
Vizag Docks, 133
Vohra, Moti Lal, 337, 338
Vohra, NN, 298
Home Secretary, 285
Vora, BB, IAS, Secretary Ministry of Petroleum, 223
Vyas, MP, Chairman Managing Committee, 169, 170, 171

Wali, MKK, Home Secretary, 261
Walia, Dr.BNS, 338, 339
Wana, 25
War of 1965 Against Pakistan, 314
Waterlogging, 78
Wathen, (Principal), 35
Wats, Dr., 329
Welfare Activities, 160
Wellington Hospital, 229
West
Bengal Cadre, 177
Punjab, 41
Western Command
C-in-C, 276
Simla, 293
Westminister Cabinet Model, 236
Wildlife, 242
Witch Hunting, 129
Women of Thoa Khalsa, 41
World
AIDS Awareness, 334
Health Assembly, 334
Health Organization, 327, 328, 334
Sikh Conference, 277
War I, 21, 23, 27, 28, 51
War II, 25, 40, 51

Yadvindra Singh, Maharaja of Patiala, 109
YOL Camp, 56
Yudhistra, 294

Zail Singh, 214
CM Punjab, 214
Giani, 29, 177, 232, 233, 237, 268, 289, 306
Giani, President, 300
Zakir Hussain, 58
As Vice Chancellor Aligarh Mus. University, 58
Nationalist Muslim Educationalist, 58
Zambian Trade Minister, 179
Zamindari System, 78
Zamindars, 78, 79
Zeitgeist, 139, 148
Zia-ul-Haque, 241
Pakistan Dictator, 241